Dietrich Bonhoeffer and Arnold Köster

Dietrich Bonhoeffer and Arnold Köster

Two Distinct Voices
in the midst of Germany's Third Reich Turmoil

Paul Spanring

Foreword by
Keith W. Clements

◦PICKWICK *Publications* • Eugene, Oregon

DIETRICH BONHOEFFER AND ARNOLD KÖSTER
Two Distinct Voices in the midst of Germany's Third Reich Turmoil

Copyright © 2013 Paul Spanring. All rights reserved. Except for brief quotations in critical publications or reviews, no part of this book may be reproduced in any manner without prior written permission from the publisher. Write: Permissions, Wipf and Stock Publishers, 199 W. 8th Ave., Suite 3, Eugene, OR 97401.

"New Revised Standard Version Bible: Anglicized Edition, copyright 1989, 1995, Division of Christian Education of the National Council of the Churches of Christ in the United States of America. Used by permission. All rights reserved."

Scripture quotations marked (NIV) are taken from the Holy Bible, New International Version®, NIV®. Copyright © 1973, 1978, 1984, 2011 by Biblica, Inc.™ Used by permission of Zondervan. All rights reserved worldwide. www.zondervan.com The "NIV" and "New International Version" are trademarks registered in the United States Patent and Trademark Office by Biblica, Inc.™

Pickwick Publications
An Imprint of Wipf and Stock Publishers
199 W. 8th Ave., Suite 3
Eugene, OR 97401

www.wipfandstock.com

ISBN 13: 978-1-62032-226-0

Cataloguing-in-Publication data:

Spanring, Paul.

Dietrich Bonhoeffer and Arnold Köster : two distinct voices in the midst of Germany's third reich turmoil / Paul Spanring ; foreword by Keith W. Clements.

xiv + 276 pp. ; 23 cm. Includes bibliographical references.

ISBN 13: 978-1-62032-226-0

1. Church and state—Germany—History—1933-1945. 2. Christianity and politics—Protestant churches—History of doctrines—20th century. 3. Bonhoeffer, Dietrich, 1906–1945. 4. Köster, Arnold, 1896–1960. I. Clements, Keith W. II. Title.

BR856 .S63 2013

Manufactured in the U.S.A.

I dedicate this book to my wife Susie
and to our children, Andreas, Robert, and Anna.

Contents

Foreword by Keith W. Clements | ix
Preface | xiii

1. Following Jesus | 1
2. Dietrich Bonhoeffer | 14
3. Arnold Köster | 32
4. The World | 53
5. Engaging with the World | 97
6. The Church | 137
7. Salvation | 181
8. Conclusion | 212

Appendices
1. *A Fictional Encounter* | 229
2. *Interviews* | 237
3. *Arnold Köster Source Material* | 259

Bibliography | 269

Foreword

THIS BOOK IS A highly significant study on the concept of Christian discipleship as it was forged in response to the Nazi tyranny. There is no shortage of studies on the stances of the German churches under the Third Reich, a scenario which continues to excite debate and controversy today. Paul Spanring's contribution however is unusual and indeed quite original, for from that traumatic period he brings into mutual relation German Lutheranism's most famous figure of resistance and martyrdom and an almost unknown Baptist pastor who in his own and rather different way also rejected the idolatry of blood, race and soil.

Dietrich Bonhoeffer (1906–1945), executed at Flossenbürg barely a month before the Second World War ended, by now hardly needs any introduction. His record of brilliant theological acumen began to be written even during his student days, followed by his role as theological teacher and seminary director in the Confessing Church, that section of the historic Reformation churches of Germany which resisted the nazification of the gospel and Christianity. Bonhoeffer, however, went much further than most Lutheran pastors in actual political resistance, becoming in a small but decisive and fateful way a participant in the plot to overthrow Hitler.

By contrast, the name of Arnold Köster (1896–1960) will be new to almost all readers. A German Baptist pastor with (in comparison with Bonhoeffer) relatively little formal theological education but of deeply studious mind and a voracious reader, in 1929 he went to serve as pastor in Vienna, remaining there after the *Anschluss* of 1938, then throughout the war and its aftermath until his death. His ministry was largely confined to his own modest congregation, centered on his Sunday preaching and weeknight Bible studies and lectures. He sought no overtly active political role but in his preaching and teaching persistently warned against the seductive appeal of the prevailing ideology. It is well said that in a totalitarian state there is no apolitical existence. Köster, the evangelical preacher who welcomed Jews at

Foreword

his services, said and did enough to make him familiar to the Gestapo yet remarkably survived.

Bonhoeffer and Köster, though both were German and wore the "Protestant" label, were in important respects very different people not least in their ecclesial backgrounds. Bonhoeffer the Lutheran belonged to a historic national church entrenched in German culture and tradition and up until 1918 secure in the tie of "throne and altar." Köster the Baptist belonged to one of the free churches, very much a minority movement in Germany and Austria, dating there only from the first half of the nineteenth century, rejecting any ties with the state, decidedly pietistic and other-worldly in ethos, and widely regarded in Germany as an alien missionary import from Britain and America. There was little love lost between the main historic churches and these newer arrivals who in Lutheran and Reformed eyes resembled the dangerous "enthusiasts" of the radical Reformation four centuries earlier.

Yet both Bonhoeffer and Köster markedly stood out from their respective traditions. Bonhoeffer came to reject what Lutheranism had made of Martin Luther's own distinction between the *zwei Reiche*, the spiritual and the secular realms, church and world, gospel and law, the inward and the outward. That had led in Bonhoeffer's time to a dangerous abnegation of responsibility by the majority of Christians who were content to let Hitler get on with it in the world without challenge in the name of the gospel. Bonhoeffer in his *Ethics* sharply attacked this "thinking in two realms": in Christ, God and the world are united and that determines the responsibility of faith. For his part, Köster was much more prepared than his typical fellow-Baptists to criticize theologically what was happening on the political and cultural scene, and to examine contemporary developments in the light of the Biblical witness. Like Bonhoeffer, he had read his Karl Barth! And for both Bonhoeffer and Köster, discipleship, *Nachfolge*, following Jesus, was the central term for Christian identity. How they came to work this out in practice, and what this meant for their respective understandings of the church, constitutes a major theme of Paul Spanring's study. It has great relevance to contemporary dialogue between the "free church" and "national" or "people's church" (*Volkskirche*) traditions, not to mention the renewed interest in the Anabaptist movement of the radical Reformation.

It will be apparent to readers versed in the story of the churches under Hitler how significant a feature of this study is the highlighting of Arnold Köster himself as an exceptional German Baptist of his time. By and large the German free churches, Baptists and Methodists included, acquiesced in the Nazi revolution and the impositions of the Third Reich. There was no Free Church equivalent of the Confessing Church. The shame and guilt of that acquiescence has been fully owned and confessed by the German

Foreword

Baptists and others since. The darkness of the record is incontrovertible. But that makes it important to note and to study seriously any exception. Köster himself would not have wanted to be hailed as a hero; but he was a Baptist exception and deserves to be recognized and honored as such. It is entirely appropriate therefore that Paul Spanring includes in this volume an imaginary conversation between the famous Bonhoeffer and the inconspicuous Köster. Theology is inherently conversational, and it is important that in our own time when "radical discipleship" is in the air and "the real place of the church" in the world is being debated as vigorously as ever, we should ourselves continue to converse with those who pursued these questions, sometimes at greatest cost to themselves, in their contexts. This might also prove to be a lesson in humility.

Finally, it should be said that no one is better qualified that Paul Spanring to conduct this study. His own Austrian background and personal acquaintance with both the Lutheran and Baptist traditions give him a special perspective enabling him to empathize, though never uncritically in either case, with both Bonhoeffer and Köster. The result is a fine contribution both to church history and to contemporary exploration on what it means to be Christian and church in the world, which deserves to be read and reflected upon as widely as possible in all traditions and in all places.

Keith W. Clements

Preface

WHEN I FIRST BEGAN to follow Jesus as a teenager, I soon heard stories, songs, and snippets about the life and witness of Dietrich Bonhoffer. His writings continued to challenge and influence my faith and discipleship as I progressed on my journey with Jesus. Many years later I began to wonder how Baptist Christians coped with the Nazi regime. I soon discovered a disturbing lack of stories of courage and faithful witness. That was until 2004 when I came across a book containing excerpts of sermons and lectures of a Baptist pastor called Arnold Köster.

The credit for the rediscovery of Arnold Köster belongs to Dr. Franz Graf-Stuhlhofer. As a member of the Baptist Church Vienna-Mollardgasse 35, he heard stories and in due course discovered that many of Köster's sermons had been noted down, copied, and distributed. Since then most of them had been forgotten but gradually these papers—stored in the attics, cellars and boxes of older members of the Baptist church in Vienna—began to reappear. Rather than recycle the lot, he and Köster's son-in-law Richard Matschinger laboriously sorted through these documents and collected hundreds of pages.

Franz Graf-Stuhlhofer opened the doors of his home and the archive at the Baptist Church Vienna-Mollardgasse 35 to me. After every visit I returned weighed down with a rich hoard of unique historical material. These documents and the accounts of people, who still remembered Köster, opened a window into the past of this critical war period. I began to hear and sense the passion and struggles of a Baptist theologian who, like his contemporary Bonhoeffer, simply sought to follow Jesus.

Reading Bonhoeffer and Köster together gave me a deeper appreciation of each. I was able to develop a sense of perspective regarding the most central issue of the Christian faith: following Jesus in a complex world. It is my prayer and hope that readers of this book will be similarly enriched. All of the Köster material is my own translation, as are quotes from other German works. Introducing Köster to the English world for the first time made it seem appropriate to make extensive use of footnotes containing substantial parts of the German original.

1

Following Jesus

Introduction

A DISTINCT FEATURE OF the New Testament gospels is the calling, forming and commissioning of disciples by Jesus Christ. Like every other message, the Good News needs messengers. The historical context, in which followers of Christ live and work, shapes and affects the nature and demands of their discipleship. During times of crisis and hostility, the distinctive identity of a disciple becomes much more apparent than at times of ease, tolerance, general acceptance, or even positive aspiration.[1] Following the period of persecution of the early church, the rise of Christendom altered the nature of discipleship. What had been a costly and radical call became a respected and desirable aspiration. The needs and demands for an ordered human society became interwoven with Christian convictions. Thus, to be a good citizen was often equated with being a good Christian. More recently this union has been challenged by the rise of a secular worldview which has brought about the relegation of faith matters into a separate private sphere which remains unconnected to the public sphere of life. Our present post-Christendom world is undergoing prolonged divorce proceedings occasionally interrupted by mediation sessions. What does Jesus' command "come and follow me" mean today?

Throughout church history, various groups and monastic communities, often forced to exist on the margin of the church, sought to preserve significant features of what they perceived to be authentic Christian

---

1. Dulles, *Models*, 204: "The close connection between Church and discipleship remained as long as Christians were a persecuted minority in a predominantly pagan society. But a new crisis for the Church arose after the conversion of Constantine, when Christianity became the established religion of the empire."

discipleship. The effect of these prophetic communities has frequently revitalized the Church and challenged parts of Christendom to rediscover some of its distinct "following" identity.

Two Stories, Two Distinct Voices

This dissertation attempts to listen and learn from two distinct prophetic voices who sought to articulate the call of Christ to follow him, in the midst of the tumultuous period of Nazi Germany. They were German and contemporaries, but each faced a very different context. Dietrich Bonhoeffer was a Lutheran pastor and theologian who profited from a privileged and extensive education followed by numerous international encounters and experiences. Arnold Köster was a Baptist pastor in Vienna and deeply affected by a Bible-based, conservative pietism. He was nurtured and rooted in a tradition that had as its central concern radical following. Bonhoeffer was part of the numerically dominant church-of-the-people (*Volkskirche*). Köster was a member of what most German citizens perceived as a Christian fringe movement, the Baptist denomination (*Freiwilligkeitskirche*, Free Church).

At a time when church was generally viewed as a necessary and integral part of society, the respective members of *Volkskirche* and *Freiwilligkeitskirche* tended to define the nature of church quite differently. At its best, the central concern of the *Volkskirche* model of church is to be "salt." Salt seasons and preserves food, thus the primary function of the church is to influence and shape the whole of society with gospel truths. It is the soluble nature of salt which allows it to penetrate and season the whole. This apparent strength makes it difficult to identify the individual kernel. Similarly membership to the *Volkskirche* can be simply assumed by virtue of cultural and traditional association. At its best, the *Freiwilligkeitskirche* model of church, emphasizing the gathered church, perceives its primary role to be "light." Unlike salt, light does not mingle or mix with darkness. By its very nature, it constitutes the opposite. Thus the distinction between who is in or out is defined much more rigorously. The gathered nature of the community is based on the voluntary choice—usually expressed in believer's baptism—of its members.

Intertwined with divergent theological emphases, are social and cultural factors which also influence every believing community as it seeks to express its identity or ecclesiology. Minority movements characteristically distinguish themselves more radically from the rest, simply because they are a minority. The following statement by the American theologian Robert Friedmann is an interesting example of this: "Ever since the days of the apostolic church, Anabaptism is the only example in church history of an 'existential Christianity' where there existed no basic split between faith and life, even though the struggle for realization or actualization of this faith into practice remained a perennial task."[2]

For anyone outside the separatist tradition this is a bold and provocative claim. The "only example" effectively excludes other attempts of undivided following. Does history support such a claim? Friedmann provides a caveat by admitting that the Anabaptist experiment is locked into a "struggle for realization." Is this an admission of the fact that mere participation in a struggle does not in itself guarantee a positive outcome? After all, the outcome of every struggle can either be success or failure and, more frequently, is a confusing mixture of both.

The historical documents and the life stories of Dietrich Bonhoeffer and Arnold Köster bear witness to the fact that both sought to actualize their faith into practice. They were comrades in the same struggle, yet each remained within their own separate church tradition and each sought to embody following Jesus in their own unique personal contexts, opportunities, and challenges. There are no records of any personal encounters between them and it seems unlikely that either of them read or studied articles or publications by the other. Their spheres of influence were quite apart, yet each sought to be, and challenged others to become, faithful followers of Christ. This study attempts to listen to both of these voices and to glean from them some of the crucial and abiding issues every follower of Christ inevitably faces.

Why Listen to Them?

A critic may interject: "Why listen to them? How can the past help us understand what following Jesus means now? Surely, today's disciples are faced with a different world and new challenges." Clearly the struggles of the past don't always provide comprehensive up-to-date solutions. And yet, knowing that what worked yesterday does not necessarily work today does not negate the fact that a Christian community suffering from collective amnesia becomes rootless and confused.

More important than a courteous bow towards the past is to appreciate that the German experience of 1932–45 was a period of extreme crisis. The German people had been shaped for centuries by its Christendom heritage and culture. Yet, within a few years, government, laws, the arts, religion, morality, in short everything that had provided order and an inner cohesion

2. Friedmann, *Theology of Anabaptism*, 27.

to society fell apart. What does following Jesus mean in a world that is totally out of kilter? No longer protected by the safe confines of their churches, Christians were directly exposed to the pervasive influences of the world and a secular and twisted regime. Clear boundary lines between right and wrong, loyalty and betrayal, duty and decadence became blurred and often indistinguishable. Within that context, followers of Jesus were pushed to the edges of their faith as they sought to embody the truths of the gospel.

In his *Theologische Ethik*, the German theologian Helmut Thielicke frequently draws on the notion of borderline situations (*Grenzsituationen*).[3] He argues that it is not sufficient to have an understanding of God's word and commandments that is only applicable within a normal and ordered situation.[4] Ethical principles which work only in a Christendom paradigm but collapse under the strain of extreme borderline situations are of little or no value. The philosopher Karl Jaspers, who first conceived the term *Grenzsituation*, claimed that "to exist and experience the borderline situation is the same."[5] For him, being was defined by the extreme experience of limits. The borderlines of pain, death, and guilt challenge and question the mundane. At these points, ultimate questions have to be faced, and it is the borderline perspective that leads to a deeper and more meaningful understanding of life. Thielicke, building on Jaspers' existential analysis argues that the borderline was also an important characteristic of the biblical worldview. The Scriptures' understanding of humanity and the world is profoundly influenced by a view from the extreme boundaries of beginning and end.

Jürgen Moltmann argued in his *Theology of Hope* that it is the end-view, the *eschaton*, that judges, interprets, and challenges the present. "Peace with God means conflict with the world, for the goad of the promised future stabs inexorably into the flesh of every unfulfilled present."[6] In this meditation on hope, Moltmann links peace with God to resurrection hope. However, this peace also acts as a trigger for conflict ("un-peace," in the German original) with the world. This is because the world is now viewed from the extremes

---

3. Thielicke, *Ethik* 2/1, 214–30. See also Tillich, *On the Boundary*, 13: "The boundary is the best place for acquiring knowledge."

4. Ibid., 214: "Wer eine Lehre von den Geboten Gottes hat, die nur innerhalb eines *corpus christianum* oder einer regulär funktionierenden Demokratie gilt, die aber hilflos gegenüber einer Zeit steht, die 'aus den Fugen' ist, hat im Grunde überhaupt keine derartige Lehre besessen, sondern vermutlich nur eine religiös-ideologische Überhöhung jener 'ordentlichen' Situation."

5. Ibid., 217–20, quoting Karl Jaspers, *Philosophie*, vol. 2, *Existenzerhellung* (Berlin: Springer, 1932) 204: "Grenzsituationen erfahren und existieren ist dasselbe."

6. Moltmann, *Theology of Hope*, 21.

of (a) beginning: what God initially intended, and (b) end: the outer limits of total, human, sinful distortion and God's judgment and renewal.

Followers of Jesus are not always pushed to the extreme limits of their faith. Nevertheless, a robust Christian faith ought to be informed and shaped by the borderline situation. It is not a bizarre love for the extreme that motivates the focus on borderline situations, but the hope that it will reveal insights, expose weaknesses and teach healthy principles for the believing community. To remain within the realm of ordered normality risks blunting the church's response in the face of crisis. Furthermore, it makes the church lose sight of what was always a vital part of following Jesus, the element of crisis.

Why listen to Bonhoeffer and Köster? Simply because their historical context constituted an extreme borderline situation. Their generation of Christians was faced with agonizing dilemmas. The German politician Gebhard Müller said then: "A Christian cannot fold his hands in prayer and watch how the evil forces of his country destroy people that have been entrusted into his care and desecrate every value he considers sacred."[7]

They, like every other Christian, had to respond in some way or another. Responses were varied and had to fit particular contexts and personalities. Whatever the circumstances, choices had to be made. The aim of this study is not to choose between either of them, but to listen and learn from two distinct witnesses, who sought to integrate faith and life in their own personal life stories.

Dietrich Bonhoeffer requires little introduction. He has become *the* dominant Christian voice and witness of the Third Reich period. A recent biographer described him as "Martyr, Thinker, Man of Resistance"[8] and according to the German theologian Dorethee Soelle, "Dietrich Bonhoeffer is the one German theologian who will lead us into the third millennium."[9] Clearly, Bonhoeffer casts an extensive shadow.

Pastor Arnold Köster, although still remembered at the Baptist Church Vienna-Mollardgasse 35, is unknown and unresearched in English. The only published book containing a selection of his sermons has been out of print for many years.[10] In the German language, the Baptist church historian Franz Graf-Stuhlhofer has published selected excerpts of Köster's sermons

---

7. Thielicke, *Ethik* 2/1, 222, quoting Gebhard Müller 1900–90, Badisch-Württembergischer Minsterpräsident: "Er kann nicht mit gefalteten Händen zusehen, wie die Mächte des Abgrundes sein Land, die ihm anvertrauten Menschen und alle Werte, die ihm heilig sind, verwüsten und vernichten."

8. Schlingensiepen, *Dietrich Bonhoeffer, 1906–1945*.

9. From the dustcover of Bonhoeffer, *Sanctorum Communio*.

10. Köster, *Lampenlicht*.

for the purpose of demonstrating that Arnold Köster was a rare outspoken public critic of National Socialism.[11] This is in itself an extraordinary claim, especially since Andrea Strübind, deploring the silence and introspectiveness of Baptists during the Third Reich, referred to the Baptist "free church as a bound and muzzled church."[12] Although Arnold Köster's voice is beginning to gain a little recognition in German, no comparison between the well-known Lutheran Bonhoeffer and the obscure Baptist Köster has been undertaken either in German or in English. Köster's unpublished source material is stored in the archive of the Baptist Church Vienna-Mollardgasse 35. Köster's sermons and lectures are unavailable in English. All translations of selected texts are mine and it seemed appropriate to footnote Köster's quotes extensively.

Following Jesus or Discipleship

The most frequent term used for those who became associated with Jesus was *mathetes*, "disciple." *Mathetes* is the substantive of the verb "to learn." The learner or pupil is thus defined in contrast to the teacher or rabbi. This usage suggests that gaining insight is the primary focus of discipleship. This concurs with the first century practice of rabbis teaching disciples the Torah. These students in turn aspired to become teachers themselves.[13] However, a distinctive feature of Jesus' disciples was that their role was primarily defined by following rather than knowing. Ernest Best states in his study on Mark's gospel that "throughout the Gospel the word 'follow' is used almost exclusively of the disciples of Jesus."[14] Furthermore, the evangelists portray the disciples as role models for every successive Christian: "Jesus' teaching as Mark views it was not primarily intended for the few, Peter, James, Andrew and John who were sitting or standing around Jesus, but was intended for all who would be his followers; the role of the disciples in the gospel is then to be examples to the community."[15]

11. Graf-Stuhlhofer, *Öffentliche Kritik*.

12. Strübind, *Die unfreie Freikirche*, 323.

13. Bornkamm, *Tradition and Interpretation*, 40: "Discipleship of Jesus does not arise on the basis of a free attachment to a teacher, but on the basis of a call to follow him which issues from Jesus. Jesus does not exercise authority over his disciples on account of his knowledge of the Torah, nor is he a means to the end of gaining a similar wisdom in the law. Further, the position of a *mathetes* is not a preliminary stage, with the intention that the disciple himself shall become a *didaskalos* (23.8 ff.), but signifies a lasting relationship to Jesus."

14. Best, *Disciples*, 5.

15. Ibid., 130.

Theologians from the Anabaptist tradition have argued that discipleship is the "essence of Christianity."[16] For the radical reformers of the Anabaptist[17] communities, the key word was not "faith," as it was with the magisterial reformers, but "following."[18] Such an emphasis begs for further clarification. Who is a disciple? What distinguishes a believer from a disciple? Indeed is there a distinction at all? The Mennonite historian Harold S. Bender speaks of being transformed and fashioned after Christ. These terms suggest an inner change and outward patterns of distinct Christ-like living. What remains obscure and difficult to define is the point of transition. When has a believer become a disciple? What are the basic characteristics and disciplines of a disciple?

A disciple's most basic task is to be a follower, to participate in a journey. Probably the earliest self-description which followers of Christ applied to themselves was "those of the Way."[19] The gospel's emphasis on motion rather than ontological change through imitation is in agreement with how faith is frequently expressed in the Old Testament. The patriarch Abraham was challenged to leave his native home and to discover God on the move. When Moses desired to know God's name at the burning bush he was told that it is, YHWH, I am who I am. McClendon translates it as "I will always be ahead of you. Find Me as you follow the journey."[20] Moses is then sent to lead the people out of Egypt. For the people of Israel, the exodus journey becomes and remains the identity defining experience. John Goldingay states in his Old Testament Theology: "It is of the essence of Israel to be a people with a story."[21] The life and work of Jesus is both continuation and culmina-

---

16. Bender, *Anabaptist Vision*, 26: "First and fundamental in the Anabaptist vision was the conception of the essence of Christianity as discipleship. It was a concept which meant the transformation of the entire way of life of the individual believer and of society so that it should be fashioned after the teachings and example of Christ."

17. Cahill, *Love Your Enemies*, 157–58: "Anabaptists . . . first emerging as a real movement in Zurich in 1524 under the leadership of Conrad Grebel and Felix Manz, the Anabaptists were to repudiate not only Roman Catholicism, but also the Lutheran ('evangelical') and Calvinist ('Reformed') movements. They were in search of a more radical return to biblical discipleship. The radical reformers wanted a full restitution of the New Testament life and saw persecution and suffering as marks of the true church. Although they preferred the name 'Christian Brethren,' their opponents called them Anabaptists ('rebaptizers') because they accepted only adult baptism as reflective of early Christian practice. The concrete and practical aspects of discipleship were of utmost importance to them, especially the formation of voluntary and disciplined communities, the integral relations of faith and works, and the rejection of participation in government."

18. McClendon, *Ethics*, 29.

19. Acts 9:2; 19:9, 23; 22:4; 24:14, 22.

20. McClendon, *Doctrine*, 285.

21. Goldingay, *Old Testament Theology*, 30.

tion of this story. The dynamic challenge of YHWH became a personal encounter and challenge for those who heeded Christ's call. Responding to the dilemma that not everyone within the old community was willing to follow, Jesus formed a new community[22] of followers. It was in the act of following that men and women discovered that Christ was always ahead and that they found God as they followed the journey.

The value of the term *following* is that it focuses on a simple act. Those that follow may be unaware or uncertain concerning their final destination. Their following may at times be a steady purposeful gait, at other times it may be a weary stumble. Yet, each constitutes an act of following. A basic answer to the question, "What do disciples do?" is, "They follow." In contrast, the term *discipleship* covers a much broader spectrum of meaning such as believing in Christ, imitation, being in Christ, ethical purity, and behavior. As one engages in the act of following, these themes are invariably encountered, yet the humble admission of merely following, indicates that much is yet to be discovered and worked out. Being on the way demands an openness and a willingness to engage with whatever, whenever. "In this sense we may say that the journey is open-ended. It would be a dead-end if it ended at the cross; it is open-ended because the leader on the Way is alive."[23]

The sermons, writings and reflections of Bonhoeffer and Köster do not yield a detailed manual for discipleship. Their historical context of extreme crisis prohibited them from drawing up a catalogue of discipleship features. Nevertheless, their own tentative and at times confused walk with the Lord, is best described as *following*.[24] The meaning of following is also expressed in the German word *nachfolgen* from which the noun *Nachfolge*[25] is derived—the original German title of Dietrich Bonhoeffer's book *The Cost of Discipleship*.

Story, Crisis, and Conflict

The concept of journeying, concretely expressed in the unfolding of life stories, is a key characteristic of biblical faith. Faith is expressed in and through

22. Ibid., 839.

23. Best, *Disciples*, 15.

24. Longenecker et al., *Patterns*, 2: "The verb 'to follow' (*akolouthein*) and the adjectival participle 'those who follow' (*hoi akolouthountes*) appear regularly in the Gospels to identify the crowds who thronged around Jesus. But they are also used in the Gospels to identify the 'disciples' as those committed to Jesus."

25. Bonhoeffer, *Nachfolge*.

the lives of those who are on a journey of following. The nature of the lived Christian faith is tested by crisis and the borderline situation. Experiences that are gained at these extreme limits provide important criteria for the practical and ethical challenges of following.

A substantial part of this thesis is based upon two distinct biographical stories. Each protagonist was not just faced with difficult personal choices, but also sought to offer leadership to their respective church communities. They operated within different ecclesiological premises and came occasionally to different conclusions.

This investigation of their stories has a similar purpose to that mentioned by the Baptist theologian James McClendon in his examination of the Radical Reformers. In his *Ethics* he writes: "For if we can penetrate their times, seeing that which was central to them but noxious to the religious and political authorities, picking out the hinges on which their story turned, we may be able to see the ways in which our story is like or unlike theirs, and the ways in which a theology in light of the baptist vision must have a distinctive (dangerous?) shape and scope."[26]

The metaphor of "picking out the hinges on which their story turned" provides an appropriate image for the task of this study. The distinct feature of the Bonhoeffer-Köster context is that unlike the Radical Reformers, both men shared an oppressive historical context even though Bonhoeffer's original allegiance was to the established church. Yet he soon realized that the threat of the Nazi regime was equally dangerous to members of the established church and to the separatist churches.

These hinges are attached to a double door, the writings of Bonhoeffer and Köster. Bonhoeffer's books are widely available and they have left their mark on subsequent Lutheran theologians and many others. Much lesser known are the writings and sermons of Arnold Köster. The bulk of the Köster source material consists of articles written for Baptist periodicals and typed manuscripts of sermons and lectures delivered from 1939 onwards. These notes were written down by a member of the congregation called Gertrud Hoffmann. She had shorthand and typing skills and has, unbeknown to her, bequeathed to successive generations unique and historically useful documents of this critical period. Relevant extracts from Köster's documents will be quoted extensively and worked into the main text because the source material is unavailable in English.

"Picking out the hinges" requires the application of a certain methodology. This study seeks to explore three interlocking themes and their relevance to the topic of following Jesus. Each of these themes incorporates

---

26. McClendon, *Ethics*, 20.

elements of story, crisis and conflict. Attempting to impose a hierarchical order either by sequence or importance would be misleading. After all, a door that is only fixed to the doorframe by a single hinge is positively dangerous. In the same way, following Jesus involves not one, but at least three interdependent theme-clusters, namely salvation, church and world.

Salvation, Church, and World

A disciple's encounter with the savior is the foundational starting point of the journey. The gospels report that the nature of these encounters were varied and of different intensity. Common to all was that "they are called by Him [Jesus] into discipleship."[27] A positive response to the command "come and follow," inevitably involved a redirection of the whole life, but also the possibility of failure. The challenge of following is to hear and retain the double message of: "You must persevere, and by God's grace, you will."[28] Set within the challenges of borderline situations this leads to the inner conflict of having to integrate the reality of sin into the follower's life-story without tolerating it. Examining the hinge of salvation in the stories and the theological reflections of Bonhoeffer and Köster provides an opportunity "to see the ways in which our story is like or unlike theirs."

Beyond the initial encounter with the savior, the disciple finds companions on the Way.[29] The story of self is grafted into the counter-story of the Christ community. The horticultural image of grafting suggests the cutting off and insertion of a branch into a different plant or tree. In a similar way, to be grafted implies that the self is cut and placed into a larger body. Ernest Best conveys the radical difference between discipleship and a self-focused lifestyle so common to sinful nature. What does it mean to follow Jesus? It means to drop in behind him, to be ready to go to the cross as he did, to write oneself off in terms of importance, privilege or right, and to spend one's time only in the service of the needs of others.[30]

The central importance of the body of Christ is a recurring New Testament theme. The inner cohesion, life and vitality of a church community are tested in the context of borderline situations. How is a follower of Jesus to respond when the church has become seduced by the lure of power or the desire for a peaceful existence? Is it ever right to jeopardize, for the sake

---

27. Rengsdorf, "Mathetes," 444: "A fundamental mark of the *mathetai* of Jesus in the tradition is that they are called by Him to discipleship."
28. McClendon, *Doctrine*, 142.
29. Acts 9:2.
30. Best, *Disciples*,13.

of justice, the livelihood and viability of the church? How is the follower of Jesus to respond when the community which has hitherto defined and sustained the believer becomes unfaithful to its calling?

Both Bonhoeffer and Köster were involved in the struggle for the true church. Their responses and reflections on church constitute the second hinge of this study. Again the task is "to see the ways in which our story is like or unlike theirs."

To follow Christ is to work with Jesus and to participate in his mission. "As He Himself does not turn inward into Himself, but girds Himself for service, so He directs the gaze and powers of His disciples to His task, which by their association with Him is theirs."[31]

As followers of Christ its people are *ekklesia*, a called out community. In the words of the evangelist John, "They do not belong to the world" (John 17:14, 16). At the same time their task is to engage with the world, for Christ's word and prayer is, "I have sent them into the world" (John 17:18). The New Testament insists that the church and the world are not the same.[32] There is a clear divide and yet the church's task is to bridge that division with the gospel message.

The borderline situation of Nazi Germany increased and sharpened these dilemmas even further. How can the church maintain its identity when the world attempts to highjack church and use the gospel for its own ends? How are followers of Jesus meant to protect themselves from a world they inhabit and are inextricably a part of? Is it always right and legitimate to "be subject to the governing authorities?"[33] What comfort can the church draw from the apocalyptical accounts of Scripture during times of extreme crisis? Given the church's "mandate to go,"[34] when, if ever, is it legitimate to opt for prudent self-preservation and let the world go its own course?

Goal and Method

The goal of this book is to explore the marks of faithful following. In this case it is an ecumenical exercise, in that two separate voices, a Lutheran and a Baptist, are represented. An important strength of this approach is its bifocal perspective. Two distinct Christians and pastors, in spite of their

---

31. Rengstorf, "Mathetes," 452.

32. McClendon, *Ethics*, 17: "The struggle begins with the humble fact that the church is not the world. This means that Christians face an interior struggle, inasmuch as the line between church and world passes right through each Christian heart."

33. Rom 13:1–7.

34. Matt 28:19.

different church traditions and life settings, shared the same struggle: to be faithful followers of Jesus.

More than half a century after the Third Reich of Nazi Germany, much has changed. Yet, even though the church is now facing a different world, the basic challenge still remains—to be followers of Jesus. Is it not reasonable to expect that the shadows of the past could become important guides for our future?

The method of the argument is both biographical and theological. Chapter two explores the life and writing of Dietrich Bonhoeffer. A major focus of this chapter is Bonhoeffer's controversial involvement in the plot to assassinate Adolf Hitler. This clearly sets his struggle into the realm of the borderline situation. Arnold Köster's life and ministry are explored in chapter three. While one might feel that Bonhoeffer has gone beyond the limit, Köster himself described his struggle as going to the limit. Each biographical chapter will attempt to briefly draw on their reflections on salvation, the church and the world.

In chapter four the historical and theological developments of the term 'world' are explored. The purpose of chapter five is to discover how the Lutheran Bonhoeffer and the Baptist Köster sought to respond to the claims of a totalitarian regime and its worldview. Chapter six explores their understanding of church, rooted for each of them in distinct ecclesiologies. The last topic, chapter seven, is that of salvation. The reason for reversing the order salvation, church and world is that during the Nazi period, *Weltreich*, or the realm of the world, sought to claim every aspect of life. The totalitarian state's aim was to claim the space of the church for its own ideological purposes, thus forcing the church either to submit or to resist. The conclusions drawn from this study are presented in chapter eight.

2

Dietrich Bonhoeffer

Introduction

BONHOEFFER'S LIFE AND WRITINGS have been extensively interpreted. He has been portrayed as a champion of the liberal cause, posing the question, "How do we speak . . . in a 'worldly' way about 'God'?"[1] His critique of "cheap grace"[2] and his call for radical discipleship has earned him a place amongst radical reformers and pietistic groups. Jeffrey Pugh sums up the dilemma by asking, "When everyone from abortion clinic bombers to radical secularists lay claim to his legacy how do we read him in our day without projecting onto him our agendas?"[3] The wide spectrum of interpreters and interpretations are partly the result of the nature of his later work. Evocative and visionary thoughts were preserved in an unfinished fashion. Thus, "what he sowed grew up in a variety of ways, depending on the kind of soil where his legacy bore fruit."[4] However, this *sowing* and *growing* of his thoughts, life and death are not only linked to Bonhoeffer's own unique historical context but also to those of his subsequent interpreters.

The focus of this chapter is not to give a detailed account of Bonhoeffer's life but to explore the ethical tension between resistance and Christian submission. The German title of his *Letters and Papers from Prison* (*Widerstand und Ergebung*),[5] aptly described the borderline dilemma Bonhoeffer faced and lived. For him the choice was not *either* resistance *or* submission

---

1. Bonhoeffer, *Letters and Papers*, 364.

2. Bonhoeffer, *Discipleship*, 53: "Like ravens we have gathered around the carcass of cheap grace. From it we have imbibed the poison which has killed the following of Jesus among us."

3. Pugh, *Religionless*, 5.

4. Dumas, *Dietrich Bonhoeffer*, 237.

5. Bonhoeffer, *Letters and Papers*, 5: "Resistance and Submission."

but the willingness, expressed in the "*and*," to cling to both in spite of their irreconcilable contradiction.⁶ Was this choice doomed to tragic failure or was it costly discipleship?

The Biographical Narrative

Eberhard Bethge, a close friend and author of the definitive Bonhoeffer biography, detected a definite change in the life of the then twenty-five year old Dietrich Bonhoeffer. At that time he had finished his academic theological training, completed his doctoral theses *Sanctorum Communio*, and his second book, *Act and Being*. As a minister in training he had gained experience as an assistant Pastor in Barcelona and had begun to work as an assistant lecturer in Berlin. Bonhoeffer disliked the term "conversion,"⁷ however his choice of words, written to a personal friend Elizabeth Zinn in 1936, bear witness to a clear turning point in his life. "I plunged into my work in a very unchristian way, quite lacking in humility. I was terribly ambitious. . . . Then something happened which has tossed about and changed my life to this day. . . . I know that what I was doing then was using the cause of Jesus Christ for my own advantage, and being terribly vain about it. . . . Also I had never prayed, or only very little. . . . Then the Bible freed me from that, in particular the Sermon on the Mount."⁸

Bethge aptly entitles the relevant section of his biography, "The Theologian Becomes a Christian."⁹ The same title is also used by McClendon, who then proceeds to explore the "deep springs of his action"¹⁰ which, according to his viewpoint, eventually ended tragically. Bonhoeffer explicitly mentioned the Bible, a book which he now began to read in a different way, discovering it as a personal message from God.¹¹ His reference to the Sermon on the Mount revealed what, at a later date, was to become the central theme of *Cost of Discipleship*. On a practical level, the changed life expressed itself in personal Bible meditation, commitment to communal life and reflections on Christian engagement with the world. Bonhoeffer's

---

6. Bonhoeffer, *Letters and Papers*, 304: "Both must be seized resolutely."

7. Bethge, *Dietrich Bonhoeffer*, 156: "Bonhoeffer always greatly disliked stories of conversion told by pietists for purposes of edification."

8. Schlingensiepen, *Dietrich Bonhoeffer*, 95.

9. Bethge, *Dietrich Bonhoeffer*, 153.

10. McClendon, *Ethics*, 199.

11. Bethge, *Dietrich Bonhoeffer*, 154. A student remembers a conversation: "We should not forget that every word of Holy Scripture was a quite personal message of God's love for us, and he asked us whether we loved Jesus."

comment of, "turning from the phraseological to the real"[12] points in two further directions. First, to the turning away from the theological phrases and concepts so prominent in German academia, to a turning towards the reality of God. Second, it indicates engagement with the burning political issues he and the church began to face. In response to the political success of Hitler and rising nationalism, with its associated ideology, he wrote to his brother Karl-Friedrich in 1935: "I think I am right in saying that I would only achieve true inner clarity and honesty by really starting to take the Sermon on the Mount seriously. Here alone lies the force that can blow all this hocus-pocus sky-high—like fireworks, leaving only a few burnt-out shells behind."[13]

This blowing up in the context of the Sermon of the Mount takes Jesus' commandment "love your enemy" utterly seriously. Commenting on Matthew 5:38–42 Bonhoeffer wrote: "Suffering passes when it is borne. The evil comes to an end when we permit it to pass over us, without defense. . . . Assault is condemned by not being met with violence."[14]

Whatever phrase is used in order to describe the inner transformation Bonhoeffer experienced, it was not limited to a private and personal pious experience of "Jesus is *my* Lord."[15] The vertical element of this change also involved a radical horizontal engagement with God's world.[16] Jesus was *the* Lord and this claim included Christian brothers and sisters, the Christian church and the political and national context. Both *Cost of Discipleship* and *Life Together* were a prophetic call to the Christian church to embody the reality of God in the world.

The world around him grew increasingly hostile to the Confessing Church, of which Bonhoeffer had become a leading theologian. This conflict eventually led to the state enforced closure of the Finkenwalde seminary of the Confessing Church in November 1937.[17] Bonhoeffer was forced to give up his teaching post, but continued by stealth to teach and train pastors of the Confessing Church. In 1940 the state police informed Bonhoeffer that he was forbidden to publish any further articles or works and to make any public speeches.[18] Consequently, Bonhoeffer's ability to participate in and

12. Bonhoeffer, *Letters and Papers*, 358.
13. Bonhoeffer, *London*, 285. Bethge, *Dietrich Bonhoeffer*, 155.
14. Bonhoeffer, *Discipleship*, 133.
15. Clements, "Freedom of the Church," 165: "There is every reason to believe that the authorities were content to allow a continued proclamation which centered on '*Jesus ist mein Herr*' rather than '*Jesus ist der Herr*.'"
16. Bonhoeffer, *Discipleship*, 262.
17. Bethge, *Dietrich Bonhoeffer*, 483–91.
18. Ibid., 602.

to influence the Confessing Church diminished and he was subsequently drawn into the secretive world of the resisters. McClendon acknowledges that Bonhoeffer did not abandon "the centrality of Christ and church during these spy years."[19] Yet, McClendon argued, what he affirmed theologically was muddied by his involvement in a resistance movement.

At this point in time Bonhoeffer was leading a double life. Employed by the *Abwehr*, a government organization whose purpose was to elicit useful information concerning enemy activity and policies, he was able to stay in Germany without getting drafted into military service. At the same time this position brought him close to other conspirators, who were operating within the *Abwehr*. Was this life style, demanding subterfuge and deception, a desperate expression of Christian resistance? It can either be interpreted as an attempt to "seize the wheel"[20] or as "a remarkable, sinful failure in his life."[21]

James Wm. McClendon interweaves into his *Ethics* three biographical narratives in order to exemplify particular key aspects of his arguments. Bonhoeffer's narrative illustrates positively the "embodied witness" strand of McClendon's thesis, but fails on the second strand entitled "community of care." The sobering aspect of this failure was that the early Bonhoeffer gave equal weight to radical discipleship and its corresponding communal expression. However, McClendon argues, the final years of his life were marked by tragic failure. His decision to participate in a conspiracy that adopted violence and murder[22] led him outside the bounds of Christian teaching and practice. "The pathos of Bonhoeffer's own story lay in bringing together the needs of the soul and the needs of society in a single life, and the instrument he so unerringly grasped in response, and so tragically lost, was the political life of church and congregation."[23]

"Tragic" is the preferred description of this particular interpretation. However, McClendon is unwilling to simply make him a "tragic victim of tragic times."[24] The scope of this tragedy was larger than the personal

---

19. McClendon, *Ethics*, 209.

20. Bonhoeffer, *Berlin*, 365. Zimmermann and Smith, *I Knew Dietrich Bonhoeffer*, 82.

21. McClendon, *Ethics*, 211.

22. Ibid., 209: "Even while his contemporary writing affirmed the superiority of Christ over all life, he served a plot whose prime goal was only the replacement of Hitler's with another government, and a conservative, even elitist, government, at that. Moreover, one means adopted was assassination. . . . That the means of resistance chosen was not only inconsistent with Bonhoeffer's long-formed Christian convictions, but was ineffectual as well, seems only to heighten the irony that shadows the entire story."

23. Ibid., 214.

24. Ibid., 210.

struggle of an individual Christian. "My thesis, then, is that Bonhoeffer's grisly death was part and parcel of the tragic dimension of his life, and that in turn but an element in the greater tragedy of the Christian community of Germany."[25]

For McClendon the locus of failure has to be sought in a weak Christian church—a Christian community that failed to uphold structures and practices, that engaged in political life and was capable of nonviolent resistance.

Key Theological Themes

Seeking to discern some of the inner motifs of this narrative, one has to remember that Bonhoeffer was a Lutheran pastor and theologian. He frequently criticized his own traditions but remained nevertheless a Lutheran Christian. What were the distinctly Lutheran concepts that contributed and steered Bonhoeffer towards following a path of violent resistance? Corresponding to the general structure of this study the material is grouped into three themes: salvation, church and the world.

Salvation is Costly Grace

The first chapter of *Discipleship* sets the tone of the rest of the book. It is a passionate critique of cheap grace and urges the church to rediscover the wealth of costly grace. From the outset Bonhoeffer argued against a fatal misunderstanding of Luther.[26] Fellow Lutherans, eager to proclaim a *sola gratia* gospel, had turned it into a proclamation of free and unconditional forgiveness of sin that left the sinner unchallenged. Bonhoeffer insisted that what had been fatefully cut asunder, justification from sanctification, were *two* sides of *one* coin. "Justification is the new creation of the new human being. Sanctification is their preservation and safekeeping unto the day of Jesus Christ."[27]

Responding to possible objections that costly grace implied salvation by good works, a life under the law rather than grace, Bonhoeffer affirmed two equally true propositions: "*Only the believers obey*, and *only the obedient*

---

25. McClendon, *Ethics*, 211: "Put in the briefest terms, the thesis is that they had no effective communal moral structure in the church that was adequate to the crucial need of church and German people (to say nothing of the need of Jewish people; to say nothing of the world's people). No structures, no practices, no skills of political life existed that were capable of resisting, Christianly resisting, the totalitarianism of the times."

26. Bonhoeffer, *Discipleship*, 49.

27. Ibid., 260.

believe."[28] Faith and obedience, two realities separated in an attempt to guard the reformation's *sola fide*, were knitted together. Faith included good works, but, it was not the obedient life or merit that defined the Christian's position (*den Christenstand*). All was dependent on the believer's "alien righteousness" which was encountered *extra nos* through God's call, claim and justification.[29] In a typical Lutheran fashion Bonhoeffer thought in and applied opposite truths. He was "a paradoxical thinker."[30] The challenge of thinking in paradoxes is to bear the weight of two opposing theories and to endure the tension this creates. Within this tension faith and obedience are redefined.

The Church Is the Present Christ Himself[31]

The struggle between the Nationalistic Church and the Confessing Church invariably led to questions concerning the nature and boundaries of the *true* church. The Barmen declaration introduced a schism in the church. Bonhoeffer refused to view the church struggle as a political battle for ecclesiastical power. To him the key question was not whether the Confessing Church was an effective opposition[32] but whether it *was* and *remained* God's true church.[33] Attempting to define the boundaries of the church,[34] he argued that the marks of the true church were proper administration of the sacraments and faithful proclamation of God's Word. With regard to sacraments he critically reflected on the practice of infant baptism. "We gave away preaching and sacraments cheaply; we performed baptism and confirmations; we absolved an entire people, unquestioned and unconditional; out of human love we handed over what was holy to the scornful and unbelievers."[35]

This was an open-eyed recognition that infant baptism had an inbuilt tendency towards cheap grace. However, this insight did not lead him to repudiate it but led him to insist that where there is firm faith within the

28. Ibid., 63.
29. Bonhoeffer, *Life Together*, 31.
30. Dumas, *Dietrich Bonhoeffer*, 293.
31. Bonhoeffer, *Discipleship*, 218.
32. Bethge, *Dietrich Bonhoeffer*, 296.
33. Ibid., 434–35: "Either the Barmen Declaration was a true confession to the Lord Jesus effected through the Holy Spirit, in which case its character is one that shapes and divides the Church, or it was an expression of opinions, without binding force, of a few theologians, in which case the Confessing Church has been treading a wrong and fateful path ever since."
34. Bonhoeffer, *Way to Freedom*, 75: "The Reformation, and particularly the Lutheran concept, first says what the church is and leaves the question of its boundaries open."
35. Bonhoeffer, *Discipleship*, 53.

context of "a living church-community," infant baptism has its validity.[36] To a Baptist this was contradictory, yet for Bonhoeffer it was a paradox he was happy to embrace. Similarly, the church as the body of Christ was both a visible community[37] and hidden because its true nature was linked to the real presence of Christ. The visibility of God's presence can be observed, Bonhoeffer argued, in the preaching of the word, sacraments and in the daily lives of its followers. As a concrete visible body, it required a physical living space (*Lebensraum*)[38] and boundaries. However in spite of its concrete visible reality as the incarnated body of Christ, the church had a hidden quality. Bonhoeffer illustrated this by comparing the church's nature with that of the incarnated Christ; his physical body was visible to all, but his divine sonship was only visible to the eye of faith.[39]

Yet again, Bonhoeffer explored the tension of two opposites. God's church was concretely and visibly expressed through Word, sacrament and Christian fellowship. Occasionally the visible community was forced to define boundaries, principally for the purpose of inviting those that were outside, rather than to condemn them as lost. Nevertheless, statements like "The government of the National Church has cut itself off from the Christian church. The Confessing Church is the true Church of Jesus Christ in Germany,"[40] revealed that Bonhoeffer was also willing to define church in restrictive terms. However, God's church was created by God's gracious presence rather than institutional boundaries. Church was the real presence of Christ and as such, its reality was being formed (*gestaltet*) by the living Christ.[41]

Volkskirche and *Freiwilligkeitskirche*

Both themes, salvation and church, focus on what God does in and through the reality of Christ. Andre Dumas detected in Bonhoeffer a "constant emphasis on the concrete."[42] In relation to Bonhoeffer's biographical journey Dumas wrote that, as a young man, he first discovered this reality (*Wirklichkeit*) in the state church which refused, "for conservative reasons,

---

36. Bonhoeffer, *Discipleship*, 205–12. The issue reemerged in 1942. See Bonhoeffer, *Conspiracy*, 551–73; Bethge, *Dietrich Bonhoeffer*, 611–12.

37. Bonhoeffer, *Discipleship*, 213–52; chapter 10, "The Body of Christ"; chapter 11, "The Visible Church-Community."

38. Ibid., 232.

39. Ibid., 225.

40. Bonhoeffer, *Way to Freedom*, 87.

41. Dumas, *Dietrich Bonhoeffer*, 226.

42. Ibid., 231.

Dietrich Bonhoeffer

to succumb to the temptations of perfectionist separatism."[43] Influenced by his classical and liberal upbringing, Bonhoeffer, at an early stage of his life, defended Christendom and valued terms like "culture" and "tradition." During the church struggle Bonhoeffer became convinced that God-reality was embodied in the Confessing Church. Taking into account his conservative instincts, this made him, in certain respects, a separatist.

Bearing in mind the historical and ecclesiastical situation of the time, what does the term separatist mean? Bonhoeffer toyed with a fully fledged separatist church model yet ultimately he resisted rejecting the historical model of the church-of-the-people (*Volkskirche*). What he opposed was that the National Church had become a nationalistic church. The emergence of the Confessing Church was a direct result of the degeneration of the church-of-the-people. During the early stages of the church struggle, the possibility of establishing a free church was seriously considered[44] by some of the Confessing Church leaders.[45] This option was eventually abandoned in favor of taking the high ground, at least theologically, by claiming that the Confessing Church was the true church-of-the-people, even though the now nationalistic National Church was officially recognized by the state as the only legitimate church-of-the-people.[46] The ideological exploitation of the nationalistic concept of *Volk* made the term *Volkskirche* highly misleading. Bonhoeffer opted for the term Evangelical Church in Germany (*Evangelische Kirche Deutschlands*), for which he claimed the existing structures of the church-of-the-people paradigm. In doing this he was fully aware of the

---

43. Ibid., 231.

44. Bethge, *Dietrich Bonhoeffer*, 250: "Bonhoeffer and Hildebrandt now began [in 1933] to reconsider the question of the need for a free church."

45. Scharf, *Widerstehen*, 125–26:"Bei späteren Treffen haben wir gegeneinander diskutiert, Bonhoeffer und sein Freund Franz Hildebrandt auf der einen, Martin Niemöller, Heinrich Vogel and andere, auch ich, auf der anderen Seite. Im Sommer 1933 haben wir gegeneinander diskutiert darüber, ob wir in der Volkskirche bleiben dürfen. Bonhoeffer trat dafür ein, aus dieser Kirche, die nicht mehr Kirche Jesu Christi sei, auszutreten und eine Freikirche zu bilden. Wir hielten es für nötig, um die Kirche der Väter 'innerhalb des Hauses' zu kämpfen, die Rechtsform, die sie im Laufe ihrer Geschichte als Großkirche gefunden habe, von uns aus—als der allein legitimen Kirchenleitung—in Anspruch zu nehmen und diese Rechtsform einzusetzen im Kampf um ihre Befreiung aus dem staatlichen Zwang, im Kampf für ihren Auftrag, allem Volk Gottes Wahrheit zu bezeugen."

46. De Gruchy, "Freedom," 179. Writing from London in 1934, Bonhoeffer sought to correct the assumption, held by Henriod of the World Alliance, that the Confessing Church was now a separate church: "I think you are misrepresenting the legal construction of the Confessional Church in this point. There is not the claim or even the wish to be a Free Church besides the Reichskirche, but there is the claim to be the only theologically and legally legitimate Evangelical Church in Germany."

Dietrich Bonhoeffer and Arnold Köster

fact that the church of God had "a relative exterior boundary, which is given in baptism, and at the same time an inner boundary which embraces only a part of those who have been baptized."[47] Indeed, the essence of the church was the gathered members, who, in their active expression of discipleship, were the central core of the church. *Volkskirche*, the outer boundary, cannot exist without those who, willingly and voluntarily respond to the Gospel's call (*Freiwilligkeitskirche*), and in so doing represent the inner boundary. Bonhoeffer resisted choosing between either of the two models by maintaining that the dialectic between *Volkskirche* and *Freiwilligkeitskirche* was necessary and mutually sustaining. "This means the *sanctorum communio*, which by its nature presents itself as a church-of-the-people [*Volkskirche*], also calls for the voluntary church [*Freiwilligkeitskirche*] and continually establishes itself as such; that is, the *sanctorum communio* bears the others, so to speak, who have the latent potential to become 'real' members of the church by virtue of the word that is both the author of the church and of the message it preaches."[48]

McClendon, as a separatist, located the crux of Bonhoeffer's tragic failure within a failing Christian church. This perceived weakness of the church conforms to his analysis of church history which was highly critical of the post-Constantine Christendom development. To McClendon it was indicative of the time when the old New Testament concept that the church was the community of saints "watching over one another with care,"[49] sharing and witnessing the good news, was replaced with "an institution from which proceeds the communion of saints."[50]

It is tempting to speculate whether a more radical separatist stance of the Confessing Church, following a Free Church ecclesiology latent in Bonhoeffer's book *Discipleship*, would have made a different impact on the German nation and whether it would have altered the moral and ethical choices Bonhoeffer made. What is apparent is that Bonhoeffer clearly perceived discrepancies between nominal and effective membership, national and true church and, by extension, in the world of politics. Bonhoeffer had to live between opposites in the realm of difficult ethical choices. An integral part of his Lutheran heritage was to acknowledge and creatively embrace juxtapositions.

---

47. Bonhoeffer, *Way to Freedom*, 80.
48. Bonhoeffer, *Sanctorum*, 220.
49. McClendon, *Ethics*, 58–59.
50. Ibid., 58, quoting Adolf Harnack.

World-Reality Invaded by God-Reality[51]

For Bonhoeffer the central task of the church was to bring God's Word into the world. As a community it had to "claim a specific space for itself within the world, thus drawing a clear dividing line between itself and the world."[52] This space had to be guarded, for it was a holy and sanctified space. However, Bonhoeffer was also quick to admit that something of the world still lived in the church and that the one who was real in the church, Jesus Christ, was also real in the world.[53] The pre-1940 Bonhoeffer sought to guard the church's sacred space. In his later work he was forced to focus on the messy edges and overlaps where God's reality was also present. At a time when his personal involvement with the *Abwehr* forced him to adopt a double life of deception he sought to reflect theologically and discern a responsible engagement with a world out of kilter. At the time when Bonhoeffer worked on his *Ethics* (1940–42), the Confessing Church, to which he had tied his fate, had become divided and weak. The success[54] of the German divisions had muzzled all critical voices and allowed Hitler to extend his political grip over the German people. The unfinished pages of the *Ethics* represent a rich collection of borderline theological engagement with the world, but they do not yield an explicit moral justification for a Christian's participation in a revolutionary plot. Nevertheless, some of the concepts Bonhoeffer developed during these difficult months provide some relevant clues with regard to his own motives and moral choices.

Readers of *Ethics* are invariably struck by the frequent use of the term reality (*Wirklichkeit*). Bonhoeffer's concern was to discern the link between the transcendent and immanent God-reality. Reality, Bonhoeffer argued cannot be divided; neither is it possible to distinguish apart from Christ between good and evil. Bonhoeffer insisted that the only true reality was the Christ-reality. Christ was the abiding link, the prism, the center through which both God and world-reality had to be viewed and understood. Only through Christ could real ethical engagement take place. God's Word and concrete reality were neither limited to the salvation of the soul, nor to the salvation of the saints. Rather God-reality was also present in "the

---

51. Bonhoeffer, *Ethics*, 54: "In Jesus Christ the reality of God entered into the reality of this world."

52. Bonhoeffer, *Discipleship*, 261.

53. Bonhoeffer, *Ethics*, 74: "But the will of God is nothing other than the realization of the Christ-reality among us in our world."

54. Ibid., 89: "When the figure of a successful person becomes especially prominent, the majority falls into idolizing success. They become blind to right and wrong, truth and lie, decency and malice."

ambiguous and contorted everyday world where good and evil exist side by side."[55] Although, ultimately, the individual Christian and the community of saints were justified—declared perfect and sinless—penultimately, they were still entangled in the world.

The Ultimate and the Penultimate

This search for God-reality in the context of an ambiguous world could, Bonhoeffer realized, either lead to despair or to an inner retreat. Despair could manifest itself either as radicalism, the desire to overthrow godless structures, or compromise, a pragmatic and resigned outlook which becomes content with the lesser evil. To Bonhoeffer this inner retreat usually manifested itself in the pietistic concern for salvation and the sanctification of the soul. The dead-end extremes of radicalism and compromise had to be overcome, Bonhoeffer argued, through a proper understanding of what he called the ultimate and the penultimate. Similar to the eschatological tension of the "already" and the "not yet" biblical scholarship rediscovered following the lead of Oscar Cullmann,[56] Bonhoeffer applied ultimate and penultimate to the ethical tensions a Christian had to face, living the Christ-reality in the midst of the world-reality.

Bonhoeffer began by exploring the ultimate Word, the justification of the sinner by grace alone.[57] True to his Lutheran background he set the issue into the paradoxical reality of salvation. For in salvation what was irreconcilable was reconciled not through human effort, but through God's word and love. This was utter grace simply based on faith in the life, death and resurrection of Christ. "Everything is given to me in the event of justification, but only faith justifies. All that Christ is and has is made mine in the encounter with Christ, but my life is justified only by that which belongs to Christ and never by what became mine."[58]

The central issue was not *what* was received but *who* was encountered. The "what is made mine" question led to cheap grace, a calculating faith that misguidedly sought to claim what Christ gave, detaching the gift from the giver. The "who do I encounter" question led directly to the giver and consequently to a Christian life which was always "life-in-Christ."[59]

---

55. Dumas, *Dietrich Bonhoeffer*, 156.
56. Oscar Cullmann's *Christus und die Zeit* was first published in 1946.
57. Bonhoeffer, *Ethics*, 146.
58. Ibid., 148.
59. Ibid., 149.

God's ultimate word was also his last word in a twofold way. First, in a qualitative sense, it was the final word for "there is nothing greater than a life that is justified before God."[60] All that preceded it was judged by it, and all that sprung from it was not gained by striving but in being in Christ. Second, it was God's final word in a chronological sense. God's last word comes at the end. The end is preceded by what comes before it. The ultimate is preceded by the penultimate or to use a similar concept from the world of sports: first comes the semifinal, then the final. The Christian, although already qualified by God's final word, was still engaging in semifinal activities, efforts, hopes, trials and tribulations. Every person's existential journey through time means that the ultimate cannot be claimed without walking the way of the penultimate. "The penultimate remains in existence, even though it is completely superseded by the ultimate and is no longer in force."[61]

The penultimate was the present context in which the Christian life had to be lived. The crucial ethical question, Bonhoeffer argued, was the Christian's attitude towards it. Should it be endured, suffered, embraced or treated with contempt? According to Bonhoeffer the overemphasis of the ultimate—in itself a form of Christian radicalism—led to a hatred of God's creation. Equally an overemphasis of the penultimate—a form of Christian compromise—led to a bland form of secularism. To Bonhoeffer, the solution was Christological. In the incarnated Christ, God revealed himself as one who utterly immersed himself into the creation reality. Thus God himself accepted and honored the penultimate. In the crucified Christ, God's ultimate word of judgment was pronounced over everything penultimate. Yet at the same time it was also a word of grace, for "the ultimate holds open a certain space for the penultimate."[62] In the risen Christ, what is ultimate has begun to take root in the midst of the penultimate, yet in such a way that it does not yet cancel out the penultimate.

The Preparing of the Way

Having explained these two related concepts, Bonhoeffer proceeded to draw out their practical ethical implications. Just as Christ walked the way from the ultimate into the penultimate, thus taking whatever is *now* seriously, so the Christian and the Christian church, during their journey from the penultimate towards the ultimate need to engage in the task of "preparing

60. Ibid., 149.
61. Ibid., 151.
62. Ibid., 159.

the way."[63] This preparation endeavors to create an environment that would not hinder the approach of God's ultimate word. For example, the hungry need to be fed before they are able to hear the gospel. Conversely, systems of injustice and exploitation that prevent the proclamation of God's final gospel word needed to be opposed. Bonhoeffer insisted that this Christian responsibility was not a method whereby what was done penultimately (i.e., giving bread to the hungry) would impose the arrival of the ultimate (i.e., acceptance of the gospel). Rather, the Christian responsibility of preparing the way was merely the humble participation of Christ's own encounter with the world. For Bonhoeffer, the task of preparing the way was not limited to the Christian community, but was also expressed in the structures or mandates that God graciously ordained for the preservation of a fallen world.[64] Being human (*Menschsein*) and being good (*Gutsein*) were categories of the penultimate, yet the upholding of human dignity, worth and respect were a vital aspect of preparing the way for the ultimate. "We as *human beings* can and should live a 'good' life in given order. But where human beings become things, commodities, or machines—where the orders are arbitrarily destroyed and the distinction is no longer made between 'good' and 'evil'—a special hindrance is placed in the way of receiving Christ that goes beyond the world's general sinfulness and forlornness. There the world destroys itself; it is in serious danger of becoming demonic."[65]

Bonhoeffer did not argue that the ultimate was affected by human neglect or rebellion, yet as the world journeyed towards the ultimate, Christians, the church and government had been entrusted with the God-given task and responsibility of preparing the way.[66]

Theology, Ethics, and Embodied Choices

After this brief survey of Bonhoeffer's life and thoughts are we anywhere nearer to answering the original question? Can the active participation in an assassination plot ever be seen as a legitimate expression of following Jesus? Bonhoeffer was a highly gifted man, a radical, thorough and original thinker who dared to walk a borderline path. Bonhoeffer learned and applied theology shaped and guided by the Lutheran tradition. With respect to

---

63. Ibid., 161.
64. Ibid., 388–408.
65. Ibid., 165–66.
66. Ibid., 167–68: "Only Christ brings us the ultimate, the justification of our lives before God; still, or rather therefore, we are not deprived of, or spared, living in the penultimate."

salvation, Bonhoeffer rejected a false dichotomy between justification and sanctification. He balanced his radical call to discipleship and obedience with grace and faith. The identity of a follower of Christ *coram Deo* (before God), did not depend on performance but on what was declared and received *extra nos* (from outside). In the words of Martin Luther, a disciple was always both justified and sinner, *similus iustius et peccator*.

With respect to the church, Bonhoeffer argued that the essence of the church was the gathered community of disciples. However, next to this inner boundary he was willing to include into the church an outer one: the potential community of saints. Bonhoeffer's thinking was characterized by restlessness and tension. Since God's church was ultimately defined by the presence of his living word, all human attempts to clearly define the boundaries of God's church were inadequate.

With respect to the world, Bonhoeffer's Christological focus prevented him from drawing a sharp distinction between world and church. God had, in Christ, embraced, judged and reconciled the world. Every form of reality was therefore tied and woven together in Christ. To be human and to do good could only be achieved by participating in the Christ-reality (*Christuswirklichkeit*). All true reality was God reality and available to the believer in and through Christ. At this point Bonhoeffer's argument could be seen as too simple and unified. However, by introducing the concepts of the penultimate and the ultimate, paradox and tension were reintroduced.

Throughout his life, Bonhoeffer explored tensions and opposites. He rejected what he perceived to be false dichotomies and creatively explored those he judged true. His response to the increasing resentments the German people felt against other nations was a keen interest in pacifism and nonviolent resistance. In his *Discipleship* he wrote, "The more terrible the evil, the more willing the disciple should be to suffer. Evil persons must be delivered to the hands of Jesus."[67] Four to five years later Bonhoeffer had to witness how established orders were arbitrarily destroyed, and the distinction between good and evil was lost. As early as 1933 he argued that the churches' task might be "not just to bind up the wounds of the victims beneath the wheel but to seize the wheel itself."[68] Could it be right for the author of *Discipleship* to take it upon himself to put a spoke in the works?

---

67. Bonhoeffer, *Discipleship*,134.

68. Bethge, *Dietrich Bonhoeffer*, 208; Bonhoeffer, *Berlin*, 365; Schlingensiepen, *Dietrich Bonhoeffer*, 126.

Dietrich Bonhoeffer and Arnold Köster

The Melting Pot

Bonhoeffer's 1933 "seize the wheel" comment was directed towards the church rather than towards an individual. At this stage in Bonhoeffer's life, it seems that he would have agreed with his modern day critic McClendon. McClendon argued that, "It is in such radical gatherings (so goes my thesis) that directives for the pilgrimage of each and a shared witness to the outside world appear."[69] Thus, resistance was to be shaped by the community of disciples rather than by the courage of individuals. Bonhoeffer had engaged in legitimate communal resistance from as early as 1933.[70] Six years later, upon his return from America, any resistance had been made illegal by the ruthless totalitarian regime. Hitler had skillfully abused the democratic system of the Weimar Republic and transformed it into a dictatorship. His program of race, blood and earth led to the pogroms against the Jews and the establishment of concentration camps. Policies of eugenics led to the mass murder of the weak and the sick. Worst of all, the *Wehrmacht* was at that time victorious and seemingly unstoppable.

For McClendon the place of directives for the pilgrimage of each Christian was firmly set within the context of the radical gatherings, i.e., the church community. As an avowed pacifist, the only form of legitimate Christian resistance for McClendon is nonviolent or passive resistance. The pre-1939 Bonhoeffer had frequently expressed similar concerns.[71] He demonstrated his commitment to the inner processes of radical gatherings in his allegiance to the Confessing Church. He had argued as early as 1933 for a kind of interdict, which effectively would have been an act of communal nonviolent resistance. Yet Bonhoeffer's proposal that all clergy should refuse to take part in any funeral services was rejected.[72] The effectiveness of such a daring policy was later demonstrated in Norway in 1941.[73] What was possible in Norway in 1941 was not possible anymore in the Germany of 1941. By that time the Confessing Church had become weakened and divided and a large part of its leadership had either fallen or were scattered on the front.

In his discussion on pacifism McClendon perceptively comments: "Indeed, the more popular non-violence becomes here [in America], the more dangerous a way it will be. The worldly conformity of most Christians has

69. McClendon, *Ethics*, 214.
70. Bethge, *Dietrich Bonhoeffer*, 194.
71. Ibid., 255. See also 313: "Christians may not use weapons against one another because they know that in so doing they are aiming those weapons at Christ himself."
72. Ibid., 224.
73. Ibid., 656.

for a long time sheltered the nonconformity of the inconsequential few: if the few were to become many, the shelter would likely vanish."[74]

Arguably, the shelter equally vanishes when a state system abandons basic human rights, destroys established orders and when the distinction between good and evil is lost. Can the Christian church, when faced with chaos and rampant evil, respond by sanctioning the status quo or should it engage in violent resistance? The answer must be, it cannot do either. The step of violent resistance can only be taken "outside" the confines of the church.[75] The crucial question is then, whether it is possible that certain extreme discipleship decisions are forced upon followers of Christ, outside the sheltered confines of the community of saints?

It is vital to note that set within the historical context of the Third Reich, the conspirators acted with utmost restraint. Bonhoeffer and his fellow conspirators extensively debated and desperately sought other options. Both their sense of honor and their Christian consciences were repelled by the thought of murder. Every other option proved useless, principally because each soldier of the *Wehrmacht* had given his oath of allegiance to the *Führer* and not to the constitution or *Vaterland*. In effect Hitler had stamped his version of Germany on everyone and bound them by oath. Only a dead Hitler could break that bond.[76] When they did choose to act, the conspirators never claimed that their plans and intentions were either right or justified. They understood their role as shouldering a burden of guilt, leaving them as Christians only one hope, the justification of the sinner.

Conclusion

Bonhoeffer's ethical pilgrimage was extraordinary. Whatever the precise inner workings of his decisions were will remain obscure. However, as a Christian theologian he thought in paradoxes and as a follower of Christ he bore the tensions of conflicting truths. His search for the reality of Christ prevented him from withdrawing into safer regions. God had incarnated

---

74. McClendon, *Ethics*, 321.

75. Thielicke, *Ethik* 2/2, 439. Thielicke records that a delegate of the plotters was sent to bishop Wurm in order to secure the blessing of the church for the planned assassination attempt. The delegate tempered the request by adding that, in spite of his own support, he felt that the final consequences of such an act had to be borne by the conscience of the individual Christians not by the community of saints: "Er selbst, der Sendbote, bejahe zwar das Attentat. Doch das habe er *coram Deo* mit seinem Gewissen auszumachen, und zwar in seiner Eigenschaft als Einzelner Christ, nicht aber als Träger des geistlichen Amtes und damit als 'Arm der Kirche.'"

76. Ibid., 439.

his son into the world of Judaism and as a German and a Christian, Bonhoeffer was embedded within Germany. As a Lutheran, he passionately criticized extremes and humbly sought to hold opposite truths together in Christ. Committed to the church of God, circumstances eventually led him to his personal and lonely Gethsemane.[77] There he found and joined others, now less well-known men. With them he engaged, struggled and no doubt, prayed. There is an element of tragedy in all of this, but in a strange way, that band of conspirators was united by one aim—to make peace—and in that sense they sought to become peacemakers.[78]

Painting the scene of 9 April 1945, McClendon writes: "The prisoners are conspirators—apprehended, convicted, sentenced to death by a desperate regime. Canaris, Oster, Sack, others, . . . Dietrich Bonhoeffer. . . . What is Dietrich Bonhoeffer doing among those doomed 'public enemies'? Why is he there?"[79] It is reasonable to assume that he was there because he was a follower of Christ. As a disciple of Jesus he was unwilling to cheapen the gospel and determined to face perplexing and ultimately unsolvable paradoxes with courage, embracing the costly dictum of Martin Luther, sin boldly, but believe and rejoice in Christ more boldly still.[80]

---

77. Bonheffer, *Temptation*, 31: "In the concrete temptation of Christ there is also, therefore, to be distinguished the hand of the devil and the hand of God, there is the question of resistance and of submission in the right place; that is, resistance to the devil is only possible in the fullest submission to the hand of God."

78. McClendon, *Ethics*, 320: "To be sure the root meaning of pacifist is peacemaker."

79. Ibid., 193.

80. Bonhoeffer, *Discipleship*, 51. *Pecca fortiter, sed fortius fide et gaude in Christo.*

3

Arnold Köster

Introduction

IN 1934 A RELATIVELY small group of local churches celebrated "100 years of German-speaking Baptist churches."[1] These churches were, at the national level, loosely joined together by a union called the *Baptistenbund*. Pastor Arnold Köster, then thirty-eight years old, wrote about the distinct characteristics of the first German Baptist men and women in an article published by the Baptist journal, *Wahrheitszeuge*. (The journal's title links the two English words: Truth and Witness.) "Thus, at the beginning of German Baptists stands a small group of Christ-believing men and women, 'laypeople' who had in their hands the greatest gift, the Word of God. This Word they held and began to apply with the aid of Christ's Spirit and church, becoming grace-endowed 'practical theologians of discipleship.'"[2]

For Köster the important features of these first German Baptists were, believing in Christ and the application of God's word in the context of the church and the guidance of the Spirit. Especially important to him was the practical nature of this faith, resulting in the formation of what he termed grace-endowed theologians *praktischer Jesusnachfolge*. During the course of that century (1834–1934) the convictions of the German Baptists were tested in the fire of public scorn and in a prolonged struggle for legal recognition

---

1. The first German Baptist church was established in Hamburg on 23 April 1834.

2. Graf-Stuhlhofer, *Öffentliche Kritik*, 170. Köster wrote this article commenting on the historical dimension of the German Baptists (*Hundert Jahre Baptisten-Gemeinden deutscher Zunge*, 1834–19, 4): "So steht am Anfang des Weges des deutschen Baptismus eine kleine Schar christusgläubiger Männer und Frauen, die in ihren 'Laienhänden' Gottes Wort als die beste Gabe haben und handhaben und durch den Christusgeist der Christusgemeinde zu begnadeten 'Theologen praktischer Jesusnachfolge' werden."

and the right to exist as a separate group of independent and free churches. Public recognition of the Baptist movement as an authentic expression of the Christian faith had been either non-existent or very precarious.[3] The coming to power of the National Socialist Party in January 1933 filled some Baptists with hope for a better and more secure political position; others kept a critical distance to the new regime,[4] amongst them, Arnold Köster. During the next years his pastoral ministry became dominated by an urgent sense to offer a prophetic interpretation of God's Word and a critical evaluation of the ideological influences and trends of that complex and difficult period. What lessons can be learned today? How did becoming "a practical theologian of discipleship" manifest itself in the teaching and life of a Baptist pastor in the context of these critical years? Attempting to answer this question makes it necessary to discern not only *what* was preached at that time but also *who* said it.

Biographical Narrative

Arnold Köster and his twin brother were born 2 March 1896 in a small provincial village called Wiedenest, east of Cologne.[5] His parents were devout Christians and committed to a faith expressed in and through the Baptist tradition.[6] His father trained for the ministry at the Bible school in Wiedenest and then served, together with his wife,[7] as Baptist minister at five different churches. Arnold was baptized by his father in 1910 and had a clear

---

3. Strübind, *Die unfreie Freikirche*, 38: "To sum it up, Baptists were originally viewed as a defamed sect and were persecuted by the state. They were forced to adopt a dissenting position and chose to disobey the state authorities when the laws regulated against their faith and practices. During the time of the revolution Baptist were viewed as an apolitical group living at the margins of societal and ecclesiological life. Gradually the Baptists gained the status of a legally recognized and tolerated religious group. In turn the Baptists adopted a patriotical and loyal attitude to the governing authorities (embodied in the German Kaiser) and served the state with absolute obedience."

4. Strübind, *Die unfreie Freikirche*, 82: "Enthusiastic excitement and critical distancing stood side by side in the same edition of the WZ (Truth Witness). This is a clear indication that sentiments concerning the new government were extremely varied within the Baptist movement."

5. His twin brother died in 1922.

6. Father, Ludwig Heinrich Köster (1865–1950); Mother, Emilie Köster (1867–1937).

7. Köster, 1946, Revelation, 145: "I am deeply indebted to my mother. She taught me how to read when I was six years old so that I could read my Bible. A few years ago I travelled home in an express train, after one of our services to see my dying mother. Standing beside her bedside I express my gratitude to her. The last words she said to me were: 'Soon, all will be overcome by the blood of the lamb, which works great wonder in our darkest hours!' That was the theology of this very critical woman."

sense of calling into the ministry during his late teens.[8] He was drafted into the German army during the First World War and spent a lot of his time reading the Bible.[9] After the war he enrolled as a student at the theological seminary in Hamburg-Horn and completed the four year course (1919–1923) designed to prepare him for the Baptist ministry. His first two pastorates were in Germany,[10] but in 1929 he accepted the calling of a pastorate in the capital of Austria. He remained the pastor of Vienna-Mollardgasse 35 until his death in 1960.[11]

The congregation of Vienna-Mollardgasse 35 called a minister who was thirty-three years old, had six years of pastoral experience, was rooted in the pietistic revivalist tradition, and was equipped with a critical intellect[12] and a rhetorical gift. Arnold Köster deeply believed in the transforming power of God's Word when preached "undivided and undistorted."[13] Looking back at his first years of ministry in Vienna, Köster commented in 1938: "The life of the church was strongly influenced by world views rooted in Anthroposophy and Marxism. The influence of liberal theology brought decay . . . there was no orientation on God's word. . . . The talk was of 'modern Baptist persuasions' . . . and there were many who sought to use the church as a platform to proclaim their particular world views and confusing prophecies."[14]

8. Graf-Stuhlhofer, *Öffentliche Kritik*, 20: "In 1914 he preached for the first time in a small fellowship, after he had felt called to the ministry in the previous year."

9. Graf-Stuhlhofer, *Öffentliche Kritik*, 20n5: "Ostermann wrote in his obituary: During the war years Köster had a decisive encounter with the Bible, which he read again and again being the only available book during his service as a soldier."

10. Wilhelmsburg, about 100 members (from 4 July 1923); and Friedenskapelle, in Köln, about 250 members (from 1924 until 1929).

11. Köster arrived in Vienna 3 February 1929; died 28 October 1960.

12. Graf-Stuhlhofer, *Öffentliche Kritik*, 88–92. Graf-Stuhlhofer attempts to reconstruct the theological emphasis of the theological seminary in Hamburg-Horn during the years of 1919–23: "The education program of the seminar in Hamburg had three distinctive focal points. Theology: the study of German evangelical theological works which were mostly of a conservative nature. General knowledge: study and critical reflection of generally known literary, philosophical and musical works. Piety: Exposure to the modern revivalist movements."

13. Graf-Stuhlhofer, *Öffentliche Kritik*, 49, quoting Köster: "Die Machtwirkungen des ungeteilten und nicht umgebogenen Wortes Gottes."

14. Ibid.: "Das gesamte Gemeindeleben stand stark unter dem Einfluss anthroposophischer und marxistischer Weltanschauung. Die Orientierung am Bibelwort war durch Zersetzungsarbeit liberaler Theologie kaum gegeben. . . . Man sprach in der Gemeinde von einem 'modernen Baptismus' und versuchte in den ersten Monaten meiner Arbeit, mich auf diese Gleise zu schieben. Vorstandssitzungen und Gemeindestunden waren unter diesen Umständen meist der Tummelplatz aller möglichen und unmöglichen Auseinandersetzungen, und immer wieder strebten die einzelnen weltanschaulichen Führer

This comment shows that the members and visitors of the Baptist congregation did not remain unaffected by the intellectual and philosophical climate typical of that era. But it also reveals that their new pastor was both critical of these ideas, and determined to refocus the attention of the church on biblical teaching. Thus, the battle for the minds of those committed into his care began at an early stage. Köster established *Studienkreise*: groups that met to study and debate, employing a strategy that involved (a) expounding what was true and (b) exposing what was false. In due course this became also the strategy he was forced to adopt when addressing the political events of Nazi-Germany, although due to the repressive measures of the totalitarian system, exposing what was false became a more delicate and dangerous endeavor.

Köster himself dated the beginning of his growing suspicion of Nazi ideology as early as 1920.[15] He recalled expressing his sentiments publicly in 1923 in the context of the German Baptist Union.[16] In his article, *Hackenkreuz und Sowjetstern*[17] (Swastika and Soviet star) he interpreted both of these symbols, and the ideology they represented, as the sign of the Antichrist. The article was published in 1932 in the Baptist publication called *Täufer-Bote* (Baptist Messenger). At the time, the overwhelming response of the readership was negative. "Only one elderly man responded positively, the other reactions I received consisted of oily [i.e., dirty] pamphlets."[18] It is interesting to note that Köster's article was published in spite of the fact that leading Baptist figures began to adopt a strictly apolitical strategy. The absence of a hierarchical structure combined with the autonomy of the local churches made it impossible to enforce this policy, but nevertheless it was strongly argued and pursued at many different levels. Köster himself recalls in 1946 how he was put under considerable pressure from leading members of the Baptist Union.

---

nach der Macht in der Gemeinde, um sie zur Plattform ihrer oft so sehr verworrenen Prophetie zu machen."

15. Köster, 1946, Revelation, 80–81: "My first encounter with the national socialist movement was in 1920 through our brother Fiehler from Munich—he was an intimate friend of Hitler and subsequently committed suicide. My own biblical position made me wary and I knew that one had to stay away from it."

16. Ibid., 81: "It was in 1923 in the context of the German Bund when I drew attention to the fact that a terrible illusion is spreading all over Germany threatening to gag the hearts and minds of everyone."

17. Köster, *Lampenlicht*, 143–48.

18. Köster, 1946, Revelation, 102: "Ich habe nur von einem alten Mann eine zustimmende Antwort bekommen, alles andere, was kam, waren schmierige Pamphlete."

> I was sitting together with leading members of the German Baptist Union at a decisive moment in 1933. They thoroughly grilled me for several hours; "What is your argument with National Socialism? Why don't you keep your mouth shut? After all, you endanger the whole Baptist movement...." When I drew their attention to the prophetic word, pointing out that this rising power is but a "fading power," and that the aim of this political movement is the spread of antichristian thinking—the men of the German Baptist movement laughed at me![19]

This comment reflects and confirms what became the official policy of the German *Baptisten Bund*. A policy of accommodation was adopted in order to secure the continued existence of the Baptist churches. The argument was that it was the duty of every Christian to submit to those who are in authority[20] (Romans 13) and that the appropriate Christian focus was the life and growth of the church and its mission. These tasks, it was argued, could be pursued quite apart from Nazi ideology and politics.[21] The small number of Baptist ministers who openly criticized this pragmatic stance and voiced political views were a cause of great concern for the leadership, which was repeatedly forced to patch things up with government officials.[22]

In due course publications of the Baptist Union such as the *Wahrheitszeuge* and *Täufer-Bote* were stopped[23] due to economic pressures. This meant that Köster's primary public forums were the Sunday services and the Thursday evening sessions held at Vienna-Mollardgasse 35. The historian Franz Graf-Stuhlhofer estimates that the congregation consisted of about 300 people and that a sermon usually lasted for one hour.[24] Arnold Köster

---

19. Ibid., 55: "Ich saß in einer entscheidenden Stunde mit den führenden Männern des deutschen Bundes (Baptisten-) zusammen im Jahr 1933. Sie haben mich tüchtig geschruppt durch Stunden hindurch, was ich denn eigentlich mit dem Nationalsozialismus vor hätte, ich möchte doch gefälligst den Mund halten, da ich ja den ganzen Baptismus gefährde. Als ich aufmerksam machte vom prophetischen Wort her, dass es bei dieser Machtergreifung um nichts anderes gehe als eine 'vergehende Macht,' und dass mit dieser politischen Machtergreifung es gehe um die Ausbreitung antichristlichen Denkens—da haben mich die Männer des deutschen Baptismus ausgelacht!"

20. Strübind, *Die unfreie Freikirche*, 41, quoting a statement of Paul Schmidt (General Secretary) given in 1946: "The position of the Bund in relation to the totalitarian state was based on the sense of duty which the apostle Paul placed on the church in Romans 13. The clear word of Romans 13 could not be twisted or reduced to extraordinary conditions—it had to be obeyed."

21. Ibid., 320.

22. Ibid., 289.

23. Graf-Stuhlhofer, *Öffentliche Kritik*, 185. (1941 Wahrheitszeuge, 1942 Täuferboten).

24. Ibid., 113. From 1939 onwards, Köster's sermons were meticulously copied down in shorthand and subsequently typed by Gertrud Hoffmann (d. 1983). Most of

remained critical and distant to the Nazi regime and felt called to speak God's word into the contemporary situation. Preaching a sermon on 2 January 1944 he said: "I was always conscious of a mysterious divine command to preach God's word openly. God desires to be heeded and understood! I endeavored to go to the limits."[25] This going to the limits (*die Grenze des Möglichen*) expressed itself in arguing against pervasive propaganda and in proclaiming a biblical worldview as a radical alternative. He was too public a figure to remain unnoticed and was repeatedly interrogated by the Gestapo. He recalls, in 1946, how a Gestapo official urged him in 1942 to embrace the Nazi worldview. His response was: "Dear Sir, if I were to accept your world view, I would have to confirm publicly that this kind of world view will accomplish victory. That I cannot do. You cannot expect that from me, since it is my view that this world view will end in a terrible catastrophe!"[26]

The very fact that Arnold Köster was able to maintain his opposition whilst remaining a free man shows that his *going to the limits* was an extraordinary high-wire act.[27] As a Christian he drew his inspiration from God's word, struggled to maintain his integrity and sought to remain a faithful follower of Christ throughout these difficult years.

The focus of this thesis is not how Arnold Köster conducted himself as a critic of the Nazi regime but how he discerned and applied guiding principles and passed them on to the members of his congregation in order for them to become practical theologians of discipleship. In keeping with the structure of this study, this will be explored by the key theological themes of: salvation, church and world.

---

these texts (originals or carbon copies) have been preserved and stored in the archive of the Baptist Church Vienna-Mollardgasse 35.

25. Ibid., 206.

26. Köster, 1946, Revelation, 101: "Lieber Herr, wenn ich diese Weltanschauung annehmen würde, müsste ich in aller Öffentlichkeit bestätigen, was ich nicht kann, dass dieser Weltanschauung der Sieg gehört. Das können Sie nicht von mir erwarten, denn meine Anschauung ist, dass diese Weltanschauung zu einer furchtbaren Katastrophe führt!"

27. Graf-Stuhlhofer, "Grenzen des Möglichen," 13–35. In his final paragraph (p. 35) Graf-Stuhlhofer concludes: "The fact that Köster remained alone in his 'going to the limits' was not that others didn't have the insights or the courage; rather there were others who were equally courageous but did not have the good fortune (or divine protection) of escaping the grip of the Gestapo."

Salvation—"What is Righteousness? Belonging to Jesus."[28]

A central concern of the Baptist movement in Germany was proclaiming the gospel of Jesus Christ. Arnold Köster realized that evangelism from the pulpit of the Mollardgasse 35 would not be effective in reaching either the Catholic or the secular and religiously suspicious part of the population. He endeavored to find a way to meet people where they were, in the pubs, cafes, parks and in their homes. Gradually a number of home groups formed,[29] usually consisting of about ten but occasionally as many as sixty participants. His method proved to be very effective and increased the membership of the church considerably.[30]

A personal, trusting relationship with Jesus was for Köster central to the message of the gospel.[31] He saw salvation as utterly dependent on God's "unconditional offer."[32] For humans, the first step is simply receiving that offer and becoming a child of God. Then, and only then, follow the instructions of the Christian life.[33] Luther's insights and the central concerns of the nineteenth century neo-pietistic movement were embraced by Köster who was, in this respect, true to his own tradition. The founder of the first Baptist Church in Germany, Johann Georg Oncken, rejected the "rationalistic atmosphere of the reformed church"[34] and came to a living faith while in England. The so-called movement of neo-pietism in Germany had a profound influence on the German Baptist churches. It was a reaction against rationalism and at the same time embraced insights gained by the American and English revivalist movement. Strübind notes that this expressed itself

---

28. Köster, 1943–44, *Bergpredigt*, 33.

29. Graf-Stuhlhofer, *Öffentliche Kritik*, 49–51. Köster called these groups "house churches" (*Hausgemeinden*).

30. Ibid., 48. Due to the fact that smaller fellowship were included in the membership list of the Mollardgasse it is difficult to estimate exact numbers. What can be said is that "during the first decade of Köster's ministry . . . Baptist membership in Austria increased 260 percent."

31. Graf-Stuhlhofer, *Öffentliche Kritik*, 65–66. For Köster the five central characteristics of the Christian faith were: "(1) An exclusive emphasis on the person of Jesus, (2) The cross of Jesus as the work of God, (3) Resurrection and ascension of Jesus as his enthronement, (4) The return of Jesus, (5) Paul's teaching on grace."

32. Köster, 1943–44, *Bergpredigt*, 34.

33. Ibid.: "There is a great difference between message and teaching. The first is concerned with the offer of unconditional salvation. Once a person has received salvation, he becomes a child of God. The teaching [Ethic] only follows on from there, never the other way round. It is *never* the case that one has to come first to the teaching. This organic sequence is taught by Jesus at the beginning of the Sermon of the Mount . . . from the soil of the gospel grows the life and conduct of the church."

34. Köster, *Lampenlicht*, 59.

in an emphasis on (a) a personal experience of faith and conversion, (b) a deepening sense of a mystical piety, and (c) an active expression of the Christian faith.[35]

Köster frequently contrasts true New Testament faith with false forms of a culturally acquired or learned Christendom or piety. He was critical of the liberal agenda that reduced Christ into a great moral teacher[36] and groups that sought to recapture the notion of Christian commitment like the Moral Re-Armament Movement.[37] Equally inadequate for him was the notion of a political Jesus. Köster deliberately prefaced his expositions of the Sermon on the Mount with a critical evaluation of Tolstoy's argument,[38] who sought to turn the Sermon on the Mount into a political program for all people and nations. Köster's concern was that anyone embracing the ethics of the Sermon of the Mount as gospel was in danger of erecting a wall against the ethic of grace, freely given in Christ Jesus.[39]

A central concern for Köster was to remind his listeners that there was an important gap between the message of salvation and ethical teaching. He felt that the proper concern of ethics was to establish and maintain a righteous life. God's righteousness, in the biblical sense, was indeed the only order capable of bringing health and healing to all creation. Commenting on Matthew 5:6, Köster affirmed that true righteousness was total conformity of every aspect of life to God's laws. However, the fundamental problem was humanity's inability to achieve such conformity. He saw God's law ultimately as an ineffective guide to righteousness, its purpose being rather to expose the ugly fact of human sin and failure. The disciple's hunger and thirst for righteousness could only be satisfied by God through an act of grace.[40]

Köster sought to expose the dangerous distortion of sin and sinners as they attempted to build their own righteousness, whether in the manner

---

35. Strübind, *Die unfreie Freikirche*, 27: "Als Gegenbewegung zur Aufklärung und zum Rationalismus zielte die sog. Erweckung in ihrer ersten Phase vor allem auf die persönliche Glaubenserfahrung und Bekehrung sowie auf die vertiefte Frömmigkeit des einzelnen und die aktive Betätigung des Glaubens."

36. Köster, 1946, Revelation, 16. He referred to theologians that had embraced the teaching of Harnack.

37. Ibid., 15.

38. Köster, *Lampenlicht*, 20: "I once met the former secretary of the Russian poet and author Tolstoy. I asked him where the difference lies between Tolstoy's Christianity and Paul's. He answered: delete everything by Paul that teaches the substitutionary love of Jesus Christ, what will remain is Jesus the teacher, the example."

39. Köster, 1943–44, *Berpredigt*, 1–5: "Dass der, der bei der Bergpredigt Jesu, bei der Ethik der Bergpredigt stehen bleibt sich den Weg verbaut zur Ethik der Gnade, die uns in Christus Jesus gegeben ist."

40. Ibid., 1–20.

of the Pharisees or the Zealots, which Köster paralleled with the National Socialists of his day (Nov. 1943). This daring analogy is especially poignant to a biblically-trained mind. One only needs to remember that the Zealots' attempts to establish a Jewish state ended in a catastrophic military defeat. Beyond the individual and personal dimension, sin also worked its way into the whole of society and various political movements. Köster pointed to history where nations and states frequently sought to impose their version of righteousness on the battle fields yet, "it is impossible to establish with unrighteous hands and works of injustice a new world of righteousness and justice . . . this new world cannot be established by human hands . . . but only by Jesus who proclaimed, 'behold I make all things new.'"[41]

Köster insisted that the believers of the New Testament church first and foremost encountered Christ as crucified, risen and ascended Lord and only from that viewpoint sought to understand and live the teaching of the Sermon on the Mount.[42] He was emphatic in stressing grace, God's forgiveness made concrete through Christ's death on the cross, and in calling his listeners to embrace in faith God's offer of forgiveness, cleansing and healing.[43]

In summary, Köster was vocal in warning against false messiahs, prophets and ideologists. However, he was at the same time reluctant to give clear ethical direction. He was convinced that belonging to Jesus would in due course trigger a transformation process of the whole person. Bearing in mind what Bonhoeffer sought to show with the term "costly grace versus cheap grace" one has to ask the question whether Köster's determined stress on forgiveness as a free gift was a dangerous overemphasis? Yet, an important difference between the two was that respective ecclesiological context. Bonhoeffer's intended audience was the wider German population which was part of the established church-of-the-people (*Volkskirche*). Almost everyone had been baptized, confirmed and paid their church taxes. In contrast, the Baptist's concept of church made a radical distinction between conscious followers of Christ and people who considered themselves set within Christendom's heritage and culture.

---

41. Ibid., 20: "Es ist unmöglich mit ungerechten Händen, mit unreinen Händen, mit Werken voller Ungerechtigkeit eine neue Welt der Gerechtigkeit aufbauen zu wollen! Wenn eine neue Welt der Gerechtigkeit kommt, nach der wir alle hungern und dürsten, dann durch keines Menschen Hand! Es ist in keines Menschen gelegt, diese Welt zu begnaden mit dieser Gerechtigkeit. 'Ich mache alles neu!' sagt Jesus."

42. Köster, 1946, Revelation, 16.

43. Köster, 1943–44, *Bergpredigt*, 35: "God cleanses man through the forgiveness of sins."

The Church of Christ[44]

For Köster the ability to confess one's own personal faith in Jesus Christ was the basic precondition for baptism[45] and subsequently, membership of a local Baptist church. In the context of the Catholic and Lutheran practice of infant baptism, the insistence on believers' baptism was not just to argue for a particular mode of the rite, but reflected the view that church was the gathered community of disciples.[46] This view of church was radically different to what was widely understood within the parameters of the established churches (*Volkskirchen*). It demanded a voluntary choice, with the usual consequence of being considered by the wider public and frequently one's own family, as decidedly odd and suspicious.

In his preaching Köster emphasized the quality of having to work out one's own convictions and of living a countercultural life. In this, Köster became increasingly isolated within his own Baptist denomination. The leadership of the German Baptist Union (*Baptistenbund*) had chosen to adopt their apolitical stance in order to conform and fit in. This was essentially a pragmatic choice designed to ensure the legal survival of its associated local churches. Subsequently a theological attempt was made to justify the strict distinction between matters of faith and politics. However, the practical outcome was that the Baptist Union invariably leaned towards accommodation and the gradual absorption of the nationalistic Nazi agenda.

Köster reminded his congregation, five days before the outbreak of the war,[47] that it would be wrong of the church to go out and bless weapons—a historical reference to First World War events. Rather, the church is called to a sense of holy responsibility and to intercede in a priestly manner for people and nation, praying, "Lord, forgive us our sins."[48] These sober words indicate a determined desire not to be swept away by nationalistic senti-

---

44. Köster, 27 August 1939, *Gott spricht*. See also Graf-Stuhlhofer, "Nationalsozialismus," 160: "The church of Jesus Christ is a group of people that want to hear God speak, they want to take seriously what God communicates in a matter-of-fact manner and they want to stand by him."

45. Köster, *Lampenlicht*, 62: "Precondition for Baptism is a personally confessed faith in Jesus Christ."

46. Ibid.: "We recognize that the Holy Spirit is at work in the established churches, but we also take seriously Kierkegaard's word of instilling in people a false or forged faith. It is in this sense, that some of the traditions of the historical churches are a great hindrance to continuing existence of the church."

47. Köster, 27 August 1939, *4 Gebetszüge*. War was declared on 1 September 1939.

48. Köster, 27 August 1939, *4 Gebetszüge*: "Die Gemeinde Jesu Christi ist gesetzt zu heiligem Priesterdienst für ihr Volk, sie kann nur in heiligem Verantwortungsbewußtsein für ihr Volk vor das Angesicht Gottes treten, wie ein Daniel mit der Schuld des eigenen Volkes und der Völker, und in tiefer Beugung flehen: 'und vergib uns unsere Schuld.'"

ments while at the same time remaining consciously aware of one's own national identity. The lives of the men and women he addressed were, after all, tied to their own context and time. Yet, Köster argued, beyond all national considerations, the ultimate task for the Christian disciple was to remain true to God's word—a word that demands an abiding attitude of repentance. "Repentance means a changed mind. Repentance does not mean that you stop doing evil things but that you think how God orders it in his Word. The whole of preaching is the Spirit's eternal struggle over and against the thinking of the world."[49]

Thus, the church was clearly set in opposition to the world. Köster granted that the world may have a vague notion of God; the church's task was therefore to point to clarity and certainty—"to lead the world from darkness into the light."[50] In his view the world was trapped in a process of decay that could neither be stopped nor hindered by human endeavor. The only remedy was what Jesus had provided. He placed a band of disciples into a decaying world and through them God was mysteriously at work. Encounters with the followers of Christ bring healing and cleansing to anyone who embraces the gospel of forgiveness.[51]

Arnold Köster's emphasis was the role and responsibility of the church. He saw the community of disciples as the salt of the earth in order to offer the message of forgiveness. The church was the light of the world in order to bring light to a world that was lost in the darkness of human efforts, schemes and false hopes. The church's being and calling sprang forth from a proper understanding of God's word. A listening community would always be transformed into an acting body of believers; "being saved bestows a saving mind."[52] However, the motivation for service and acts of practical love was not duty but gratitude towards God.

For Köster the primary struggle of the church was the proper wrestling with God's word and its application.[53] Thus, the rallying around God's word

---

49. Köster, 1946, Revelation, 77: "Buße heißt Sinneswende, Buße heißt nicht, dass du das böse Werk lässt sondern dass du denkst, wie Gott es vorschreibt in seinem Wort. Die ganze Wortverkündigung ist ein ewiger Geisteskampf mit dem Denken dieser Welt fertig zu werden."

50. Köster, 1943–44, *Bergpredigt*, 37 "Die Gemeinde Jesu Christi hat die Aufgabe, die Welt heraus zu führen aus aller Finsternis."

51. Köster, 1943–44, *Bergpredigt*, 35: "Christ places the disciples into the world as a great mystery. The mystery is that everyone can become clean through an encounter with the followers of Jesus."

52. Ibid., 38. Köster, quoting Bodelschwingh.

53. Köster, 21 February 1943, *Kein Unglück fürchten*: "The central characteristic of the church is the proclamation of God's Word." (Das Wesentliche in der Gemeinde ist die Verkündigung des Wortes Gottes.)

became the distinct and central feature of the worship services. A typical service structure was, (a) a hymn sung by the congregation, (b) prayer, (c) Bible reading, (d) one hymn sung by the choir followed by (e) the sermon.[54] Members of the congregation were for the most part engaged in listening to prayers, reading and a Bible exposition of considerable length. This Scriptural emphasis naturally demanded that the leader of the church be a gifted preacher and teacher. Without a doubt this was how Köster himself understood his own role and calling. The biblical model he felt mostly drawn to were the ministries of some Old Testament prophets. He was reluctant to claim for himself that his preaching was in any way comparable with a Jeremiah, yet he clearly empathized with Jeremiah's lot and task and drew comfort and strength from the prophet's example for his own ministry. His task, he felt, was to expound God's Word so that the members of the congregation would be equipped in their faith and in their life choices.

In a strange way this style of leadership, with its emphasis on authority—although in this case it was the authority of God's word, rightly interpreted—mirrored to some extent what was encountered in the political arena of the world. After all, Hitler was *der Führer*. As the ultimate leader, he had abolished the inefficient and ineffective democratic system, had united the people and had brought what seemed a simple clarity to confused minds. The task of the church was to battle against this worldview and fill hearts and thoughts with the alternative biblical worldview. In this sense, the church community through its gathering for the ministry of the Word, delivered "sword blows" against, what Köster called in 1946, the "satanic worldview."[55] Prophetic proclamation was the church's task. However, almost all of the proclaiming was done by the minister; what was the duty and calling of the average member? Köster's response was: "You ask, what is your part in this [prophetic] task? Not everyone is called to be a preacher. Maybe your part in the task is your participation in the gathering and by virtue of being part of the meetings you proclaim your yes. The world takes notice—and maybe it is that, which God expects from you at this time."[56]

---

54. Köster, *Lampenlicht*, 63. Köster made these comments in 1959 in a lecture to theology students of the university. In spite of the fact that these comments were made fourteen years after the war it is reasonable to assume that during the war years worship services were conducted in a similar manner.

55. Köster, 1946, Revelation, 37: "Every sermon is a sword-blow.... The fight we fought, every Sunday and Thursday against the satanic worldview, which desired to dominate our minds and hearts."

56. Köster, 20 October 1940: *Prophetische Situation*. "Das ist die prophetische Situation in der Gemeinde, dass wir reden müssen und nicht schweigen dürfen.... Welchen Anteil Du an dieser Aufgabe hast? Nicht jeder ist berufen, Prediger zu sein. Vielleicht ist dein Anteil an der Aufgabe der, dass du in die Versammlungen kommst und dadurch

Dietrich Bonhoeffer and Arnold Köster

The World Viewed from the Perspective of Eternity[57]

The eschatological perspective was the defining theme in Köster's thinking and preaching. To him it functioned as the guiding principle that made it possible to make sense of God's word and the world. "The whole gospel is apocalyptical and concerned with the coming end."[58] Köster was convinced that whenever the church lost this end-time perspective, Christianity degenerated into mere moral effort.[59] Human effort or the desire to build lasting security, i.e., salvation apart from God, was what distinguished the world from the Christian church. Leaders of the world called their subjects into action; build, fight, work for a better life, a better future. In contrast, the church's characteristic was to wait for the coming Christ.[60] Nevertheless, the struggle of every Christian was to be in the world yet not of it.[61] The everyday challenge was to follow Christ and listen to his word in the midst of a noisy world and confusing dilemmas. As a practical theologian Köster sought to enable the church community in this task by frequently exploring three interlocked themes or strategies in his preaching.

Deconstruction of Existing Worldviews

In Köster's analysis, all "natural thinking"[62] was focused on the elevation of humanity. It was the "idea from below,"[63] the ancient lie of the tempter, "you will be like God" (Gen 3:5). This basic idea wove itself into countless ideologies typically aimed at achieving human salvation through human strength,

---

dein Ja bekundest. Die Welt sieht das—und vielleicht ist es das, was Gott von dir gerade erwartet."

57. Köster, 19 May 1940, *Könige der Erde*: "Wir aber haben die Schau in die Dinge der Welt vom Standort der Ewigkeit her."

58. Köster, 1943–44, *Bergpredigt*, 5: "All of Jesus' teaching is eschatologically orientated i.e. focused towards the end . . . the whole gospel is apocalyptical and is concerned with the coming end."

59. Ibid.: "The church fathers radically diverted their expectations of the returning Christ and subsequently Christianity was reduced to moral effort."

60. Köster, 1946, Revelation, 9: "Jesus has called us into the faith and expects that we await his return. Anyone who believes in Christ can wait."

61. Ibid., 115: "There is a great difference between being in this world and to be of this world, i.e. to embrace this world with a greedy heart and to love it! That is the great difference. What Paul wrote applies here also . . .—'to use the world without being in need of it'—that is the holy skill and discipline of the believers, the glorious freedom of the children of God."

62. Ibid., 117.

63. Ibid., 113.

a common human spirit (*Geist*) and collective human effort. Köster repentantly deconstructed human aspirations, human systems and methods. It was his conviction that only God provides salvation. Therefore, betterment was only accessible through faith and a deeper understanding and openness to God—not human achievement.

In his exposition on the Sermon on the Mount, Köster was especially careful to deconstruct Tolstoy's[64] attempt to make Jesus' sermon into a program of human moral effort. Köster insisted that Jesus was not a new demanding master but a giving Lord.[65] In his view even Kierkegaard, to whom he granted some understanding of grace, failed to understand fully this insight. "I would like to point out that Sören Kierkegaard, by placing demands on every Christian, misunderstood the Sermon of the Mount. . . . Kierkegaard knew of the grace of God, but he never preached it in the manner of Paul."[66]

Similarly, Köster interpreted pharisaic legalism[67] as human effort seeking to achieve a righteous status before God. These efforts may have been sincere, noble and proper, yet ultimately they achieved the opposite—condemnation and failure. In his rigorous deconstruction, Köster also critically noted tendencies within his own Baptist tradition and forms of piety,[68] where a living personal faith in Christ had shifted to an acquired cultural moral piety.

A more combative form of deconstruction was his analysis of political systems, powers and ideologies which equally appeared to promise human salvation through human effort. On 1 January 1943 Köster preached: "The main concern of demons is not dark occult meetings of the Poltergeist but wonderful worldviews that glorify humanity."[69] In other words, he linked

---

64. Köster, 1943–44, *Bergpredigt*, 1, 51, 54, 64.

65. Ibid., 15: "It is not demands but God's gift that Jesus seeks to bring. We are made into a new humanity through God's gift."

66. Ibid., 64: "Ich möchte darauf hinweisen, dass Sören Kierkegaard in seiner Forderung an die Christen heute von einem falschen Verständnis der Bergpredigt herkam, darum ist sein Christentum überspitzt. Obwohl Kierkegaard die Gnade Gottes kennt, kommt sie nicht zur Darstellung, wie Paulus sie gepredigt hat." See also Köster, 1946, *Revelation*, 25, 46, esp. 140: "Kierkegaard despaired over this task and his only answer was: 'To be a Christian means becoming a follower of Jesus.' Yet the concept of discipleship is of no help in these dark and serious days unless our orientation is the New Testament! Being a Christian means knowing that Jesus promised: 'Behold, I am coming soon!'"

67. Köster, 1943–44, *Bergpredigt*, 27, 30, 33, 36, 38, 40, 42, 44, 46, 48, 49, 52, 55, 57.

68. Köster, 1943–44, *Bergpredigt*, 33.

69. Köster, 1 January 1943, *Tisch des Herrn*: "Das Hauptanliegen der Dämonen ist nicht das Anliegen der Poltergeister spiritistischer Sitzungen, sondern eine wunderbare,

the worldview of his day, National Socialism, to a demonic origin. Three years later, after the defeat of Nazi Germany, he could express his sentiments more openly. "Hitler was, in my view, an open and empty conduit through whom the mighty ideologies of the demonic world swept in order to fill every part where there was,—please notice the word—where there was an empty space."[70]

Köster's concern was here not just to explain the phenomenon Adolf Hitler, but to draw attention to the fact that everyone's thinking was equally endangered if not filled by the mystery of the cross, God's offer of reconciliation and promise to bring salvation to the world through the coming of his son. He was emphatic that salvation could not be offered by the world but by God alone. Where world rulers would always fail, *the* world ruler, Christ, would not. During the years of Nazi Germany, Köster steered a determined course of deconstructing the dominant political worldview, reminding his congregation of the biblical worldview.[71] He was convinced that only an eschatological perspective could protect the church from ideological seduction. "I just want to remind you that there were and still are many National Socialists amongst the rank of Baptist churches—and the only reason for this is that the church has ignored the teaching of the book of Revelation. Those who reject that word will not be protected from the powers of the seducers (Rev. 3:10)."[72]

This sentiment remained true for Köster, even in the post-war situation. Ideologies like democratic socialism, bolshevism and Americanism were equally deconstructed in his 1946 exposition of the book of Revelation.[73]

---

den Menschen verherrlichende Weltanschauung!"

70. Köster, 1946, Revelation, 80: "Ich sage von Hitler, er ist der offene leere Kanal gewesen, durch den die gewaltigen Ideologien der dämonischen Welt hindurchgerast, hindurchgetost sind und die überall da Fuß gefasst haben und Fuß fassen konnten und mussten,—bitte beachtet das Wort,—wo eben leerer Raum war."

71. Ibid., 37: "Only one thing can save the church from danger and that is, to think radically differently. The worldview from yesterday needs to be totally rejected and the biblical worldview needs to be embraced."

72. Ibid., 7: "Ich erinnere nur daran, dass es in den Reihen der Baptistischen Gemeinden des Reichs viele Nationalsozialisten gab und noch gibt,—und das liegt nur daran, dass man das Wort der Offenbarung beiseite ließ. Wer das Wort nicht will, der kann auch keine 'Bewahrung' vor den Mächten der Verführung haben (Offb. 3:10)."

73. Ibid., 126: "We have to reject all attempts, and view peace conferences, socialism, Bolshevism, Americanism as something preliminary, failing attempts to answer unsolved questions of mankind's history. Only the parusia, only the return of Jesus, only the personal presence of Jesus . . . is eternal, lasting."

Authority, a God-Given Mandate

Rigorous deconstruction begs the question as to how the Christian and the church can respect and live under these unmasked powers. The answer, for Köster was yet again the eschatological viewpoint. It was clear to him that the spirit of this world was dominated by the prince of darkness. However, as children of the faith this could be overcome. Living through this dark time was everybody's lot and burden but the believers must also know that they had been infused with eternity. Thus a follower of Christ was released from the total absorption and constraints of time. "Eternity... [has entered] time... this is a paradox that can only be borne by faith... it means to be a citizen of a different world, but to conform to the laws of this world and time, knowing that this world will pass away."[74]

Conformity to the laws of the time was a necessary part of the disciple's waiting existence. One characteristic of this existence was submission to governing authorities (*Obrigkeit*). Köster qualified submission by pointing out that it could never mean idolatrous worship.[75] He argued that, honoring governing authority was based on the fact that it was God's gift. Authority was therefore dependent on the giver rather than on those to whom it had been entrusted. "We are able to submit, not because the one who has power is glorious, fascinating, smart, handsome or praiseworthy, not because of his 'successes'; we are not taken in by his personality but we submit because his authority has been given to him by God—authority for the purpose of establishing order. Everyone who has been created by God bears the very image of God—in spite of the fact that it is a distorted image."[76]

---

74. Köster, March 1939, *Christ und Zeit*: "Wir müssen wissen, daß dieser 'Weltgeist' vom Fürsten der Finsternis inspiriert ist. Wir müssen diese Zeit gewissermaßen im Glauben überwinden, weil wir Teilhaber ewigen Lebens geworden sind. Ewigkeit in der Zeit, keine Vermischung! Ich habe es noch nicht ergriffen—das ist das Paradoxe, das nur der Glaube zu ertragen vermag, denn Glaube ist, daß ich Ewigkeit in diese Zeit hineingewonnen habe! 'Schicket euch in die Zeit' (Diesen Satz enthielten Luther-Übersetzungen in Römer 12,11 (anstelle von 'Dient dem Herrn'). Ein Teil der handschriftlichen Überlieferung enthält hier anstelle von 'dem Herrn' (kurio) 'der Zeit' (kairo) heißt nicht 'gleichschalten', es heißt, Bürger einer anderen Welt sein, sich aber den Gesetzen dieser Weltzeit fügen, wissend, daß diese Welt vergeht."

75. Köster, 1943–44, *Bergpredigt*, 13–14.

76. Graf-Stuhlhofer, "Nationalsozialismus," 150. Köster, 1938–39, 1 Peter: "Wir sind fähig zur Unterordnung, nicht weil der, welcher die Gewalt ausübt, herrlich, faszinierend, klug, schön, mächtig und prächtig ist, weil das 'Glück' ihm hold ist und ihm alles gelingt, wir berauschen uns nicht an seiner Person, sondern wir unterordnen uns unter die Gewalt, weil Gott Gewalt eingesetzt hat, um die Ordnung unter den Menschen zu erhalten, und [weil] jeder, dem die Ausübung der Gewalt anvertraut ist, ein von Gott geschaffener Mensch ist, ein 'Ebenbild Gottes,' auch wenn es verzerrt ist."

Dietrich Bonhoeffer and Arnold Köster

Köster addressed and criticized the then popular glorification of Hitler but attempted, at the same time, to be faithful to Romans 13[77] and 1 Peter 2:13: "Submit yourselves for the Lord's sake to every authority instituted among men." Leaders entrusted with governing authority were mere tools God intended to use for his purposes. In a sermon preached on the Sunday when Hitler's birthday was celebrated throughout the *Reich*, Köster made the distinction that "being God's tool is not the same as having a deeper understanding of God."[78] Köster applied the biblical parallel of the Babylonian king Nebuchadnezzar, who was used by God as a tool, but remained at the same time under God's judgment. In his view, the challenge for the leader of the German people was to use the "free rein" entrusted to him "to serve the world as a tool of God and to accomplish what God intends."[79]

In 1939 some members of the congregation might still have hoped that the Nazi rule would somehow yield to God's purposes. However, that prospect was quickly eradicated by subsequent events. Increasingly, the burning question for many was how to submit to a governing authority that was blatantly anti-God? At this point, Köster expressed full confidence in the fact that any misuse of a God-given position of authority would eventually be sorted out by God himself. "When a state trespasses God-given limits, God himself will take action. Many nations are no more, because of that. We don't need to stage a revolution—God will take matters into his hands. When a state misbehaves it will suffer the consequences."[80]

The obvious practical consequence of this view was that the notion of resistance got located in the believer's mind and heart rather than in active participation of subversive acts. A critical internal mental distance was created between worldly propaganda and the biblical eschatological viewpoint. The heart's allegiance was focused on the coming king rather than on the misbehaving pseudo leaders.

---

77. Köster, 17 January 1943, *Gottes Führung*.

78. Köster, 23 April 1939, Isaiah: "Es ist nicht das gleiche, Werkzeug zu sein—und Gottes Erkenntnis zu besitzen. Es ist nicht das gleiche, Gottes 'Beruf' auszuführen—und Gemeinschaft mit Ihm zu haben. Ein Nebukadnezar übte auch den 'Beruf' Gottes aus, aber da war keine Gemeinschaft mit Gott! Über seinem Leben stand auch das 'Mene tekel' Gottes!"

79. Köster, 23 April 1939, Isaiah: "Freie Bahn ist ihm geschenkt, um in der Weltgeschichte als Werkzeug Gottes zu dienen, [um] das auszuführen, was Gott will."

80. Köster, 25 February 1943, *Gottes Geduld*: "Wenn ein Staat die ihm von Gott gesetzten Grenzen überschreitet, erlaubt sich Gott, ihn beim Wickel zu nehmen. Viele Staaten sind deshalb nicht mehr, weil sie das taten. Wir brauchen keine Revolution machen—Gott selbst wird da schon zugreifen, wenn der Staat sich Gott gegenüber benimmt wie ein Lümmel."

Arnold Köster

What Is God Doing?

For Köster God's rule was a certain future reality. Followers of Christ could take some comfort in this truth, but at the same time had to face present tensions; pain, injustice, senseless loss and suffering. Commenting on the beatitude: "Blessed are those who mourn[81] for they will be comforted," (Matt 5:4) Köster addressed some painful pastoral issues. In his view, to bear the burden of pain and loss was to recognize and to stand willingly under the consequences of sin. "Suffering is not borne because of its ennobling effect but because it is a burden of God's judgment placed upon the shoulders of all humanity."[82] This note of realism took into account that God's people were not immune to the struggles of the present. Suffering was at one level caused by human sin and pride but was also the yoke God had put on his people. This burden was, however, coupled with Jesus' promise that in the end the law of suffering would be dissolved.[83]

Theologically, Köster advocated the sovereignty of God but stated at the same time that "the war is not the work of God, it is merely permitted. The work of destruction is always Satan's."[84] Within the realm of the permissive will of God, powers and principalities raged against God's holy will, but he would ultimately triumph over all.

> If everything happens according to God's will . . . what is the result of the years between 1938 and 1946? . . . The dark deeds, the catastrophes are not just the playground of demons. Yes, the demonic is active and stirring, but we also know that over and above the demonic, rules God's holy will. We know that the demon who attempts to enslave the whole earth will one day be struck by God's hand and will be vanquished. That is the comfort of the Church, at rest in God's salvation, but at the same time on a journey through times of trials and judgments.[85]

81. In German, "mourn" is *Leid tragen*—"to bear pain or suffering."

82. Köster, 1943–44, *Bergpredigt*, 11: "Man trägt das Leid, weil man es als das Geschick des Sündigens erkannt hat. Man trägt es nicht als etwas, was einfach mitläuft im Leben, oder weil man 'geadelt wird' durch das Leid. Man trägt das Leid, weil es eine, von Gottes Gerichtsernst in die Menschheit hineingelegte Last ist."

83. Ibid., 13: "Man trägt es, weil man es als Joch Gottes weiß. Umso größer steht die Verheißung Jesu vor uns von der völligen Aufhebung des Gesetztes des Leidens, das ist hier das Entscheidende!"

84. Köster, 25 February 1943: *Gottes Geduld*. See also Graf-Stuhlhofer, Öffentliche Kritik, 202–3, 212. "Der Krieg ist Gottes Zulassung, aber nicht Gottes Werk! Das Werk der Zerstörung ist immer Satans Werk."

85. Köster, 1946, Revelation, 108: "[Was ist der Ertrag der Jahre 1938–1946?] Die dunklen Dinge, alle die Katastrophen sind nicht der Tummelplatz der Dämonen, wenn

Köster felt that through God's word, the Christian church was given an inside view. Its task was to interpret God's judgments to a world numbed by a fear of senseless terror. The gospel function of judgment was to expose the fallacy of human securities and the need to trust Christ. Using the image of the trumpet calls from the book of Revelation, Köster challenged the church to interpret the message of these calls to the world.[86] The church had to speak of the gospel in the context of God's judgment—for in judgment, God was deconstructing the lies of a false security. Thus, trying to make sense of the German catastrophe in 1946, Köster argued that the judgment over Germany had a substitutionary nature. It revealed that even the best got corrupted when truth was rejected. Germany's terrible fate was therefore a wake-up call to all nations. "America, Russia, etc. look at Germany; this is the final destiny of your ways [if] you persist against God and his Christ! Germany suffers a substitutionary judgment so that you see, what God desires and accomplishes. If you choose not to love the truth you will be condemned to love the lie. Germany was the land of the gospel and for that reason it was first in God's final judgment."[87]

Conclusion

The underlying motif of Arnold Köster's preaching was eschatology. The Christian disciple was primarily awaiting the return of the Lord. This perspective allowed temporary issues to be placed into the bigger apocalyptic picture. The world was ravaged by human sin and little could humanly be done to save this world. The practical manifestations of sin were human attempts to create systems of security separate from God. Part of God's dealing with the world was to undercut and destroy all such attempts—this would eventually lead to the recognition that he alone was the only possible rescue. Salvation was trust in God and utter dependency on God's son who

---

auch das ganze Dämonische aufgewühlt ist und zutage tritt, wir wissen, es waltet auch über dem Spiel der Dämonen der heilige Wille Gottes. Wir wissen, dass dem Dämon, der die ganze Erde versucht, in seine Gewalt zu bekommen, eines Tages das Genick zerquetscht wird von den Händen Gottes. Das ist die Tröstung für die Gemeinde, das ist die Ruhe der Erlösten Gottes, die als Kinder ihrer Zeit hinein müssen in die Katastrophengerichte."

86. Ibid., 78–79.

87. Ibid., 84: "Amerika, Russland, usw. seht Deutschland an, das ist das Ende auch euerer Tage gegen Gott und seinen Christus! Deutschland leidet stellvertretend im Gericht damit ihr seht, was Gott will und was Gott tut! Wenn ihr die Liebe zur Wahrheit nicht wollt, werdet ihr die Liebe zur Lüge wollen müssen! Deutschland war das Land des Evangeliums, darum das erste in dem Endgericht des lebendigen Gottes."

Arnold Köster

by virtue of his death, resurrection and ascension offered the possibility of a personal relationship with him and the call to follow him. God continued to offer salvation to the world through the community of disciples; they were salt and light in the midst of corruption and darkness.

In what Köster perceived to be a battle between conflicting worldviews, the use of eschatological images enabled him to voice criticism against the regime in such a way that it was clear to biblically trained insiders, but often remained obscure to possible spies and informers. He countered the charge, "you are a terrible pessimist"[88] with the claim of being a prophetic realist. Painting dark prospects of God's judgment subversively deflated Nazi attempts to claim the dawn of a new age lasting a thousand years. It represented the very opposite of German propaganda efforts.

It seems reasonable to conjecture that Köster's grim determination to stand his ground, even against large sections of the Baptist denomination, was in part inspired by his view of the imminent return of Christ. In contrast to the leadership of the *Baptistenbund* and their policy of apolitical accommodation, Köster was unyielding and willing to suffer the consequences.[89] At a practical level the denominational leadership feared for the survival of a fragile community of churches which the regime could have easily declared illegal and dispossessed. Taking the view of the imminent return of the Lord, such political decisions and arguments had little weight. Why cling to buildings, when martyrdom may well be the next challenge for Christ's followers?

The church community at Vienna-Mollardgasse 35 was, like most people during these troubled years, faced with a world that was falling apart. The possibility of instigating significant change in the unfolding world events was for them, as a small band of believers, practically nonexistent. They were facing the real possibility of Oswald Spengler's *The Decline of the West*,[90] a book much read at the time and frequently referred to by Köster. Given this sense of helpless despair, the eschatological perspective offered a sense of order in the midst of a chaotic world. In the words of Psalm 2, "Nations conspire . . . people plot . . . kings and rulers gather to take their stand," but the one seated on the throne, God almighty, is still in control and he will prevail.

> One can only understand my hope in the returning Christ, if one knows that I have studied all human endeavors searching for the possibility of human redemption, until I finally realized:

---

88. Ibid., 120: "Man hält mich manchmal für einen furchtbaren Pessimisten."
89. Graf-Stuhlhofer, *Öffentliche Kritik*, 252–58.
90. Spengler, *Decline of the West*.

there is only one solution for this world crisis, and that is the returning Lord! That is why this is the ground motif of my preaching, I cannot see any other resolution from this chaos apart from Christ stepping in and making everything new.[91]

Arnold Köster managed to remain the pastor of this local church, while at the same time "resisting to the limit" as a preacher of God's word. He had marked out a course of countercultural resistance and remained true to it by rejecting an ideology he criticized and unmasked for his listeners as anti-Christian. Within the constraints of his time, gifts and abilities he walked the path of a practical theologian of discipleship.

---

91. Köster, 31 January 1943, Psalm 46. See also Graf-Stuhlhofer, *Öffentliche Kritik*, 177: "Man kann mich in meiner Hoffnung auf den wiederkommenden Christus auch nur verstehen, wenn man weiß, wie ich in allen menschlichen Unternehmungen nach der Erlösung der Menschheit geforscht und gesucht habe, bis ich mir gesagt habe: Es gibt nur eine Lösung der Weltkrisis, und das ist der wiederkommende Herr! Darum ist das dauernd der Ton, der durch meine Verkündigung durchschwingt, weil ich keinen anderen Ausweg aus dem Chaos sehe, als bis der Christus zugreift und alles neu macht!"

4

The World

Introduction

Bonhoeffer and Köster shared the sense of being in the center of a world crisis. As German citizens this had a political relevance and as Christians it sharpened and shaped their theological thinking. The demands of the world were of a magnitude which made it impossible to contemplate both the nature of the church and salvation in isolation. The world and its demands set the agenda and context in which Christians of that time had to act and discern ways of remaining faithful followers of Christ. How Bonhoeffer and Köster responded to this challenge in their separate contexts requires careful unpicking.

The historical context of Bonhoeffer's and Köster's world was Germany's Third Reich period. It represented an environment where the intrusion of the state into every aspect of life was coupled with an attempt to demand total allegiance of every citizen. The Nazi state ideology sought to claim total commitment and conformity, thus effectively negating the claim God places on those he calls to follow. This total claim, indicative of totalitarian systems, is contrary to the Christian view of being in but not of the world. The totalitarian claim of the Third Reich came as a gradual process and was only expressed bluntly at a late stage. At first, the focus was on the half-truth that every Christian was part of the world and had therefore an obligation towards it. The Nazi's method was to equate being German with being part of the German people *(Volk)*. At one level German identity *(Volkstum)* corresponded with a culture that had been informed and shaped by strong Christian traditions. However, at another more basic level, it simply referred to a racial identity. The struggle of a disciple inhabiting such a context was to remain faithful to God's story, a story always engaged in the transformation of the world. Part of the gospel's transforming power was finding new and apt expressions of making the reality of Christ appropriate to every culture and time. However, therein lay also a danger, especially when the world began to use and twist the gospel story for its own purposes. In these instances a disciple had to remain faithful and discerning. An important safeguard and reference point in this task was to manage the double claims on the life of the disciple correctly. First there was God's claim and secondly there was the disciples' commission into the world. In drawing a distinction between the two, freedom and inner space are created that resist any attempts of the world to claim the whole person.

Yet, when a follower of Jesus faces a political system of the world demanding total conformity *(Gleichschaltung)* a conflict becomes inevitable. Helmut Moltke, one of the conspirators arrested after the failed assassination attempt against Hitler, exasperated the Nazi Judge Roland Freisler by his Christian stance. During the trial Freisler shouted, "We and Christianity are the same in one thing only: We demand the entire person!"[1] In a letter to his wife Moltke wrote: "I stood before Freisler not as a landowner, not as a nobleman, not as a Prussian, not even indeed as a German—no, I stood before him as a Christian and as nothing else."[2]

During this late stage[3] of the Third Reich the clash between the two opposing worldviews was in the open. Yet, both prior to and after these desperate last gasps of the Third Reich, every Christian had and still needs to ponder how to apply the words of Jesus, "Give to Caesar what is Caesar's, and to God what is God's."[4]

Individuals Shaped by Their Context

Bonhoeffer and Köster were equally exposed to a totalitarian ideology by the simple fact of being German citizens. Both had serious misgivings from as early as 1932 and both had the courage to voice these publicly and maintain a critical opposition towards their own state.[5] They inhabited the same world. However, their life stories were set in different and unique sets of

---

1. Barnett, *For the Soul*, 203.
2. Ibid., 203.
3. The assassination attempt was made 20 July 1944.
4. Matt 22:21.
5. Schlingensiepen, *Dietrich Bonhoeffer*, 90. Graf-Stuhlhofer, *Öffentliche Kritik*, 140–152.

circumstances. Their political outlooks were shaped by family backgrounds and circumstances as were their respective tasks and realms of influence. Access to sensitive information and hard facts about the dark side of the regime were available to Bonhoeffer through his family connections while Köster was far removed from these. The context in which each had to make responsible ethical choices was quite different and distinct.

In spite of the unique set of circumstances surrounding each of these individuals, both, by virtue of their opposition to their world (the political realities of the Third Reich), were forced to reflect theologically on the Christian's role and duty towards the world. What were the key concepts that guided them in this struggle and are these still useful today? Rather than researching the historical context both prior to and during the Third Reich this thesis' focus is to explore how men like Bonhoeffer and Köster were able to see beyond the immediate historical context, discerning dangers where others merely saw opportunities. Part of the answer to this question is that both knew and critically evaluated concepts, ideas and words that were used at the time, either unthinkingly, inappropriately or simply with the intent to mould people in order to support a particular viewpoint that favored the worldview of the time.

Language provides the framework for thought. Concepts and meanings are transported by language and our worldview is primarily built by the words we use in order to describe it. Words and concepts are however rooted in history; they come to the present from the past. However, the meaning of words is not locked in the past, for every living language continues to develop and change. Nevertheless, clear thinking demands an awareness of how critical ideas and concepts have evolved and developed. The language of the Third Reich used concepts that had deep German historical roots but frequently used these to support their nationalistic slant—a slant not only heard and believed by the general public, but also by Christians who were members of Germany's varied churches. Being a follower of Jesus in the world always demanded a certain political response to the world. What then was the political language available to Dietrich Bonhoeffer and Arnold Köster?

Exploring Available (Theological) Language

Clearly, the reference point for Bonhoeffer and Köster was the Bible. Yet, this is where the problem begins. Can one find a uniform message in the Scriptures concerning a disciple's life in the world? How can one coherently interpret key passages like the Sermon on the Mount (Matthew 5–7), the apostles' instructions concerning "governing authorities"[6] and the message of Revelation with its veiled but unmistakable warnings concerning destructive political power?

The theological language available to Bonhoeffer and Köster was Luther's *Zwei Reiche Lehre*, his teaching on the two realms. Luther's thoughts were a theological attempt to wrestle with the issue of Christian political responsibility, freedom and duty to Jesus. This Lutheran political theory had become deeply embedded in German history, culture and outlook. In varying degrees all German political structures since Luther were partly shaped and informed by his treatise on *Temporal Authority: To What Extent It Should Be Obeyed*.[7] Luther's original target audience was the German nobility, who had sought his advice as they felt torn between their obligation to rule (i.e., punish criminals, defend their subjects) and their desire to follow the ethical precepts of the Sermon on the Mount. Subsequently, German nobility considered it their basic Christian duty to support and further Christian values in their realms. The abdication of the German Kaiser in 1918 brought an end to the monarchy and the introduction of democracy. The turbulent period of the Weimar Republic (1919–33) made it a necessity to rethink and reconstitute the state, its political structures and the role of the "governing authority" (*Obrigkeit*). For the first time the right of religious freedom and freedom of expression became part of the new democratic state constitution. This brought legitimacy to Free Church organizational structures; nevertheless, many of its members still expressed unease concerning the state's new neutral position in matters of faith.[8]

Luther's political theory provided the language and resource for every thoughtful protestant Christian attempting to evaluate and respond to these changes. Paradoxically, it was also the language used by Christians who were either ardent supporters of the Nazi regime like the German Christians or Christians who preferred to remain politically neutral and disengaged. Some scholars claim that "the failure of the German church to oppose Hitler in the 1930s is widely seen as reflecting the inadequacies of Luther's political thought."[9] What are these "inadequacies"? Are they found in Luther's teaching itself or in its subsequent interpretation? What were these interpretations and what did each one seek to address? How did these views impact Bonhoeffer and Köster and how did they respond?

---

6. Rom 13:1–7; 2 Pet 2:13 NRSV.
7. Luther, *Christian in Society*.
8. Zimmermann, *Zwischen Selbsterhaltung und Anpassung*, 12.
9. McGrath, *Reformation Thought*, 207–8.

Luther's Teaching

A cornerstone of the reformation was Luther's rediscovery of the gospel, primarily expressed by the phrase "justification by faith alone." At a practical level the growing community of those who shared this insight had to find ways of living this faith in the historical circumstances and context of the sixteenth century. Faith was not—and never is—just a matter of doctrine. Convictions translate themselves into practice and thus need to respond to the world a believer indwells and encounters. Part of the context of Luther's ethical and political considerations was his polemic against the Catholic view that Christians were called into different levels of perfection. According to that view perfect obedience was only possible to those who had committed themselves to a monastic life. Christians who chose to remain in the world had to adhere to a less strict regime. "In order not to make heathens of the princes, they [the sophists] taught that Christ did not command these things but merely offered them as advice or counsel to those who would be perfect. . . . Their poisonous error has spread thus through the whole world until everyone regards these teachings of Christ not as precepts binding to all Christians alike but as mere counsels for the perfect."[10]

However, Luther's teaching was also a polemic against radical claims of emerging groups whose intention was either to withdraw from the world, or reimagine society in a totally different way. In either case the nub of the question was; what are the responsibilities and duties of a disciple of Christ whose life is intricately tied to a world with its own unique structures and orders? Luther began to address these questions in the year 1522. The basic outline of his political theory was given in a series of six sermons which he delivered before the princes at Weimar. The treatise, *Temporal Authority: To What Extent It Should Be Obeyed*, was completed in the same year and published in 1523.[11]

The unique contribution of Luther's teaching on the two realms lies in the fact that he sought to differentiate clearly between matters of individual faith and freedom versus life in the world and duty. He then attempted to unite these key areas of life into a coherent whole. By defining these distinctive roles and responsibilities of the church and the world he gave the Christian community a theological model which subsequently shaped the political world of Germany.[12]

---

10. Luther, *Christian in Society*, 82.
11. Ibid., 79–80.
12. Holl, *Gesammelte Aufsätze*, 326–50.

Dietrich Bonhoeffer and Arnold Köster

Historical Context and Necessities

Luther's theological rediscovery of the Christian gospel and his attempt to reform the church triggered political consequences of great magnitude. When the church authorities rejected the reform attempts made by this insignificant German monk, he and those who had accepted the new teaching were forced to make tough decisions.[13] The radical break with the all-pervasive presence of the Roman Catholic Church made it necessary to adapt and change the political situation on the ground. The Christendom worldview of the sixteenth century western world was all-encompassing. There was no clear distinction between secular and sacred, both were tied together into an intricate web. A political leader had to fulfill and maintain various obligations that were part of the political feudal system of the day, including the charge to protect the lives of his subjects and to support the church in its task of preserving the faith in the realm. A member of the clergy had pastoral responsibilities in his parish and frequently gave counsel and advice to the ruler. Political rulers had little desire to interfere with the pastoral and spiritual duties of their priests, but were nevertheless obliged to use their executive powers to combat heresy. Luther's political ruler, Duke Frederick the Wise, had to deal with this rebellious monk if he believed him to be a heretic. Luther's life and the survival of the reformation were politically dependent on the protection and support of the German princes. Sixteenth century Germany was a conglomeration of fiercely independent states (*Länder*) each ruled by a prince (*Landesfürst*) who had pledged an oath of allegiance to the Spanish Catholic Habsburger emperor Karl V. The emperor's ability to interfere in internal affairs of the various states was however limited.

The break of some of Germany's *Länder* with the unified Western church, marked a paradigmatic shift which in turn produced political uncertainty, friction and stress. An important part of this general upheaval was also the Anabaptist movement. It consisted of groups of Christians who rediscovered the Scriptures and sought to think outside the Christendom paradigm. Werner Packull made a distinction between what he called Communal and Princely Reformation. "Communal Reformation was implicitly or explicitly premised on the notion that the local congregation constituted the hermeneutic community, qualified to discern the meaning of Scripture."[14]

---

13. Oberman, *Luther*, 197–206.
14. Packull, *Hutterite Beginnings*, 9.

These radical grass-root community experiments needed a political environment that gave them legitimacy and support denied to them by Lutheran and Catholic rulers. These new political experiments were most successful in distant and forgotten corners of the empire or in independent regions like Zurich where powerful and autonomous city authorities were persuaded and won over by these new ideas.

Once it became clear that the Catholic Church resisted the reform efforts[15] Germany's princes of the various states had to decide either to remain Catholic, which was the explicit order of the emperor Karl, or to seek some kind of new religious independence. Some of these princes also were concerned about possible peasant uprisings and attempts from the bottom end of the hierarchical structured society to construct a different and more just and egalitarian society.[16] The political leaders were faced with difficult choices. Should they stick to the tried and tested path of maintaining a close cooperation with ecclesial authorities? After all, part of the role of religion was to provide cohesion to a very diverse and otherwise fragmented empire. Or should they listen to and be persuaded by these new ideas? At a political level the question was whether these new ideas could be practically applied. Who would give moral leadership? What was the role and responsibility of each ruler and would it not be political suicide to break one's oath of allegiance?

The purpose of this all too brief historical summary is firstly to draw attention to the political context that prompted and shaped Luther's political theory of the *Zwei-Reiche-Lehre*. Second, it also reveals that every model of political thought demands frequent reapplication especially during times of significant political change.

Two Kingdoms

Cargill Thompson argues in his book *The Political Thought of Martin Luther* that Luther's political theory was informed by St. Augustine's *City of God*.[17] However, Luther was too creative as a theologian to simply copy Augustine's thoughts. He developed and sharpened these ideas and applied these to speak into the context he himself faced.

Luther developed a genuine political theory in a way that Augustine, whose ideas always remained in the realm of the nebulous and abstract, never did. Whereas Augustine's ideas were so vague as to be capable in subsequent

---

15. The pope excommunicated Luther in January 1521.

16. Bender, *Anabaptist Vision*. Packull, *Hutterite Beginnings*. Snyder, "Birth and Evolution."

17. Schaff, *Nicene and Post-Nicene Fathers*.

centuries of being interpreted in a wide variety of different ways, Luther's were relatively clear, concrete, and unmistakable in their meaning.[18]

Paradoxically, what is said clearly and unmistakably is never above subsequent distortion and misleading simplifications. Theologians have continued to debate and argue about a proper interpretation of Luther's teaching and have over the centuries come to different conclusions. The eminent German Lutheran scholar Paul Althaus wrote in 1957 a defense entitled, "Luther's Teaching on the Two Kingdoms in the Line of Fire."[19] The title alone makes it clear that unmistakable meaning has proved to be elusive. The task at hand is thus fraught with difficulties and needs to be focused in its intention. The aim is to gain an insight into the basic ideas of Luther's teaching and to explore how the various developing interpretations of the so called *Zwei-Reiche-Lehre* impacted Christians like Bonhoeffer and Köster facing the Third Reich ideology.

A distinct feature of Luther was his extensive use of dichotomies.[20] This was also true for Luther's teaching on the two realms (*Zwei-Reiche-Lehre*). His political insights were often directly related to other dichotomies he had employed in order to describe the reality of the Christian faith.

According to Luther every human being was utterly corrupted by sin and therefore unable to attain, even through the most rigorous efforts, a right standing before a holy God. Salvation must therefore be in its entirety an act of God and freely granted to the sinner. Justification remained impossible for humans but was made possible through the saving grace which was granted in and through Jesus Christ. A sinner's trust (faith alone) in the crucified and risen Christ altered his standing before God. Yet, even though this resulted in a passive righteousness of the believer, the person was still rooted into this life and world and therefore remained a sinner.[21] "Justification does not remove sin or make the Christian perfect; it simply means

---

18. Thompson, *Political Thought*, 3.

19. Althaus, *Um die Wahrheit des Evangeliums*, 263–92. The chapter title is: "Luthers Lehre von den beiden Reichen im Feuer der Kritik." Althaus addressed these issues as early as 1935. He gave a lecture in Hannover which was subsequently published under the title *Church and State according to Lutheran Doctrine* (*Kirche und Staat nach lutherischen Lehre*).

20. Some of Luther's key concepts are: Law and Gospel; Flesh and Spirit; Old and New Man; *simul justus, simul peccator*.

21. Luther, *Commentary on Romans*, 83. Commenting on Rom 4:7: "Believers inwardly are always sinners; therefore justified from without. . . . By 'inwardly' I mean, as we appear in our own judgment and opinion, by from 'without' I mean, as we appear before God and His judgment. We are righteous 'outside ourselves' when our righteousness does not flow from our works; but is ours alone by divine imputation."

that his sins are no longer counted against him."[22] Nevertheless, becoming a new creation had direct ethical consequences, for the savior was also Lord. A Christian was now part of two separate kingdoms. His allegiance to the world (temporal authority) remained simply by virtue of being born into a particular societal structure. However, by virtue of the new birth into the kingdom of God, the Christian was now also part of the spiritual realm. "He [the Christian] is obligated to the emperor and to Christ at the same time; to the emperor for his outward life, to Christ inwardly with his conscience and in faith."[23]

What God offered, salvation, was furthermore informed by the dichotomy of law and gospel. In both God's will was revealed. The law revealed God's will and acted as a "relentless accuser."[24] It brought to light the tragic effects of sin in every human being. Nevertheless, the harsh and condemning labor of the law awakened, scared and prompted the human soul to search for God's mercy and to find it in the gospel. The merciful *yes* of the gospel went beyond and overcame the wrathful *no* of the law. Thus although the law was superseded by the gospel there remained a continuing secular or political role for the law. "We are not freed from the Law by the Gospel and are still subject to it, the Christian also needs the Law in this world. For since he remains a sinner, he remains in need of the Law to curb his sinful nature. Thus the Law is still binding not only on unbelievers but also on Christians in this life. It provides the basis of natural law and of human laws which are ultimately an emanation of divine law."[25]

Luther's teaching on the two realms built on previous faith-related dogmatic insights and incorporated these into his political theory, the *Zwei-Reiche-Lehre*. The foremost concern for Luther was to draw a clear line between what was to be seen as the spiritual and what was to be seen as the temporal realm. In his view, mixing these two distinct realms with each other was a recipe for disaster.[26] A unique strength of this teaching was distinguishing between "what is specifically Christian and what is generically human,"[27] thus providing a realistic account of the tension a Christian experiences regarding life in the world. The fine art of drawing a distinction may

---

22. Thompson, *Political Thought*, 21.

23. Althaus, *Ethics*, 62.

24. *Bekenntnisschriften*, 194: "Denn das Gesetz klagt uns ohne Unterlaß an, dieweil wir es nicht vollkömmlich halten können."

25. Thompson, *Political Thought*, 27.

26. Nygren, "Luther's Doctrine," 301.

27. Braaten, "Doctrine of the Two Kingdoms," 500.

be summarized by pointing out three distinct but complementary levels or layers[28] in Luther's *Zwei-Reiche-Lehre*.

A useful analogy might be a painting. Looking at a finished painting one would initially see all of it. For instance, background, groups or clusters and the details of a single character set in the foreground. Further reflection might lead one to contemplate how the artist moved from one level to the next. Did the painter start with the individual face, filling in the background at a later stage, or vice versa? Luther's *Zwei-Reiche-Lehre* can be likened to a complex and intricate painting that seeks to discern order and symmetry in how God provided structure for the world and how he personally and mercifully engaged in the gospel story with the world.

God versus Devil

Luther's distinction between God's kingdom *(regnum dei)* and the devil's kingdom, also referred to as the kingdom of the world *(regnum diaboli, regnum mundi)*, provides the background for the other features. In this, Luther's thoughts were very close to Augustine.[29] The reality of a conflict raging within God's creation, ever since Genesis chapter 3, determined and influenced how God's will and rule were worked out. At this background level the duality of the two kingdoms represent a total antithesis. The Scriptures reveal the ultimate and final victor, yet, until the eschatological finale, all of life, and in particular the use and exercise of political power, was shaped by this struggle between God's versus the devil's rule. The dynamics of human history and life were dramatically shaped by this antithetical background setting. It was this larger conflict that made the other layers of the painting necessary.[30] They became the tools or "weapons God uses in order to restrain and counter the '*regnum diaboli*.' The character and method of the other layers is therefore largely determined by the needs of that struggle."[31]

---

28. Thompson, *Political Thought*, 36–61. Thompson refers to them as three elements.

29. Schaff, *Nicene and Post-Nicene Fathers*, 286–88.

30. Althaus, *Ethics*, 50. Paul Althaus was of the opinion that Luther largely abandoned this focus at a later stage of his life. He wrote: "If this observation is correct . . . Luther no longer bases his doctrine on the opposition between the kingdom of God and the kingdom of Satan which originally characterized his doctrine."

31. Thompson, *Political Thought*, 39. Nessan, "Reappropriating," 306: "Luther's two kingdoms teaching is not about two separate and unrelated realms, but rather about two different types of divine activity. . . . In God's contest with the kingdom of Satan, God employs two distinct strategies to thwart Satan's influence and bring forth the kingdom of God."

The World

Two God-Ordained Orders

To continue with the painting analogy, set within the larger background, people cluster and populate the painting. According to Luther, God provided a twofold order for humanity. On the one hand there was a worldly order (*weltliches Regiment*) and on the other there was a spiritual order (*geistliches Regiment*).[32] The key insight was that *both* are God-ordained orders and were therefore not in conflict with each other. Although God remained largely hidden in the worldly order he nevertheless provided life sustaining structures for all of humanity through it. For Luther the realm of this worldly order included not only political authority and governments but also other life preserving structures. His list included marriage, family and households, property, business and the various stations and vocations God had instituted. The principle function and task of *weltliches Regiment* was to establish external peace and to restrain chaos. Its primary task was the ordering of the external world, which included the use of the sword in order to punish and protect the people from "all manner of rascality."[33] These external structures, upheld by the rule of law, customs and norms of a human society, were framing and maintaining a context in which life could flourish.

Of equal importance was the *geistliches Regiment*, the spiritual kingdom which had been established by Christ. Luther insisted that "neither one is sufficient in the world without the other."[34] This spiritual rule addressed the inner person for it was the work of the Holy Spirit that transformed hearts and established righteousness before God. The offer of salvation was extended through the gospel not through the works of law. The church's task was to proclaim the message of forgiveness and reconciliation. Temporal government on the other hand needed to preserve order by justly punishing evildoers. Although Luther addresses a society structured around the Christendom paradigm he nevertheless was somewhat weary of it. "Christ's government does not extend over all men, rather, Christians are always a minority in the midst of non-Christians."[35]

Luther argued that God employed a twofold strategy when dealing with the world. On the one hand, often referred to as his left hand, God maintained order via secular or temporal governments.[36] However, with his

32. Thompson, *Political Thought*, 38.
33. Luther, *Christian in Society*, 92.
34. Ibid.
35. Ibid.
36. Nessan, "Reappropriating," 306: "God uses two hands in the battle against Satan: 1) a right hand strategy that involves the proclamation of the gospel of Jesus Christ and the administration of the Holy Sacraments of baptism and the Lord's

right hand, God reached into the world through the message and life of his son Jesus Christ. The realm to the left was dominated by law, government (*Obrigkeit*) and justice. The realm to the right was concerned with the gospel, church, salvation and forgiveness. Christians, amongst themselves were not given the task of preserving order; after all they are instructed to suffer injustice willingly. However, the neighbor's well being was best served by these orders of preservation until the gospel message could be heard and received. Thus temporal structures, in as much as they are good ("*gut Regiment*"[37]) served the gospel by establishing peace and justice. Therefore God's eternal purposes, made known by the proclamation of the gospel (right hand), needed the temporal context of an ordered world (left hand). According to Luther, each was tied to the other in as much as no good reign could be sustained without the revelation and instruction of God's word and conversely godly preaching and teaching required order and protection.

The Individual Christian Is "Christ & Weltmensch"

Having surveyed the painting's background and the two dominant clusters or groups, the eyes are now drawn to the individual person positioned in the foreground. Luther's focus was the life of the individual Christian which manifested itself in a duality of existence.[38] First there was the external and natural order, the realm of the flesh. For Luther the term flesh referred to basic physical needs and necessities but spoke also of the sinful cravings of the flesh. Human existence in this realm was always set in the context of complex interconnections with other people. These human interactions were ideally fair, orderly and conducted in a loving and responsible manner. Luther contrasted the corporal existence with the Christian life lived solely in relation to God, by virtue of a personal faith. Luther insisted that faith can only be discovered freely and embraced individually. Such a faith issued into a new life in the Spirit. Essentially, Spirit-life expressed itself concretely in obedience to the double command, to love God and to love one's neighbor.

Supper and 2) a left hand strategy that involves the establishment of just order in society through the institutions of the state, economy, law, education, family and church. Always these two strategies complement one another. Never are they in competition with each other. God is ambidextrous and very coordinated in the use of both hands to save and preserve the world."

37. Althaus, *Um die Wahrheit*, 267: "Es kann kein Reich oder Polizei ohne das Priestertum und Lehre oder Erkenntnis der Wahrheit glückselig und ruhig bestehen; herwiederum auch kein Priestertum oder heilsame Lehre der Wahrheit recht gehalten und geführt werden ohne zeitlich Regiment guter Polizei."

38. Thompson, *Political Thought*, 58.

The Sermon on the Mount was a detailed description of this new Spirit-life available to all those who, knowing of their own poverty of the Spirit, were now equipped by the presence of the Spirit.

This two-fold tension, belonging both to God's new kingdom and the world, was an existential experience for every Christian. Being part of the structures of the world inevitably demanded active involvement and the humble acceptance of world-related roles and responsibilities. In the temporal or secular role (*Amt*) a Christian might be placed in a position of authority or service. Within that realm it was the role of the external law to guide and assist. However, a believer's inner rule, guide and hope was the gospel. Set within the complexities of life, a ruler's or magistrate's role was to judge fairly, which potentially demanded (especially in Luther's lifetime) the pronouncement of a death sentence. Fulfilling one's duty in this worldly realm did not exclude the inner struggle a Christian magistrate would face as he would at the same time sincerely pray for the offending person and offer the gospel message of forgiveness to the accused. Luther was keen to stress the distinction between the two realms but also recognized that at an existential and ethical level these two areas overlapped and were united in a kind of creative and painful tension within the Christian person. What he envisaged was not a settled and harmonious union but one which willingly endured and lived the tension of law and gospel, flesh and spirit, obligation and freedom.[39]

Luther's political theory was forged by the pressures and constraints of sixteenth century Germany. Subsequent generations had to apply and adjust Luther's teaching to new political developments. A critical test of the *Zwei-Reiche-Lehre* came with the Third Reich and the corresponding use and abuse of Luther's teaching. At that time political talk within the wider Christian Church was significantly shaped by the language employed by nineteenth century theologians and political theorists.

---

39. Nestingen, "Two Kingdoms," 270: "Making the distinction is as critical as it is problematic. Left undistinguished, the law overpowers the gospel, asserting obedience to itself as a condition of salvation. Or the gospel undermines the law, reducing the specific promise, 'Your sin is forgiven for Jesus' sake,' to a generic endorsement, 'That's okay, don't let it bother you.' Confused, law and gospel destroy one another. At the same time, the gospel is an alien word that comes from outside human experience; the law is one of the ineluctable powers of everyday life that constantly subverts the gospel for its own functions. Truly distinguishing law and gospel is not the stereotypical separation of imperatives from indicatives, the former to the thrown away, but, as Luther described it, like writing in the water."

Dietrich Bonhoeffer and Arnold Köster

Nineteenth-Century Developments of Luther's *Zwei-Reiche-Lehre*

Lutheran Perspectives

From a historical perspective the interpretation and application of Luther's political theory shaped the political development of Germany but was equally shaped by it. In the nineteenth century Germany still had nobility. However, the governing and political powers were increasingly transferred to the institution state (*Rechtsstaat*).[40] The nineteenth century worldview was very different to Luther's sixteenth century world. Enlightenment thought had eroded much of traditional Christianity. God's direct role and involvement in life had been pushed to the mysterious edges of life by technical and scientific advances. The Zeitgeist of the time demanded a reconsideration of the church's role and place in this new secular and modern society. In response to these changes Luther's *Zwei-Reiche-Lehre* became gradually reinterpreted.[41] How theologians attempted to apply Luther's political theory to the contemporary context varied greatly. Nevertheless these concepts and ideas became part of the German church's available language as it faced the twentieth century challenge of the Third Reich.

The first significant development was an increasingly rigid separation of the two regiments. The realm of the world (*Weltreich*, a term coined by Luthardt)[42] became the exclusive responsibility of the state. Theologically, the state and its order were necessitated by sin[43] but it was also sanctioned and legitimated by the God-given law of nature (*Naturordnung*). In contrast, the kingdom of God (*Gottesreich*) was governed by the order of grace and salvation *(Heilsordnung)*. This dualism was based on Luther's distinction of the two realms, however in this version the fluid line of dividing both was exchanged with a solid wall. The realm of the world was theologically released into a kind of autonomy. God's will was still present in the worldly order in the provision of the law (*Rechtsordnung*), but the concerns of the world were now *worlds apart* from the kingdom of God. In 1867 Chr. Ernst Luthardt wrote a book with the title, "The Basic Premises of Luther's Ethics," in which he stated, "Characteristically the order of grace belongs to the kingdom of God, the order of law however belongs characteristically to the

---

40. Barnett, *For the Soul*, 11.
41. Duchrow, *Umdeutung*.
42. Ibid., 14.
43. Ibid., 16, quoting from Friedrich J. Stahl, *Rechts-und Staatslehre auf der Grundlage christlicher Weltanschauung* (Heidelberg: Mohr, 1837): "Durch die Sünde aber sind Recht und Staat nothwendig."

realm of the world. Thus, they are totally different categories and do not belong together, but belong to different worlds."[44]

This autonomy of the world and its law was not seen as being autonomous from God but from the gospel. The world, and the need to act and engage with the world were increasingly perceived as totally separate endeavors. For Luther, separating the two realms was a matter of 'writing in the water'[45]—a metaphor that indicated blurredness and fluidity. The modern trend was to dig trenches, pour foundations and build a wall. By the year 1918 a typical image explaining the complexity of the Christian existence was to liken the Christian to a person working in the city (the world) but having a home far away from the city walls, its factories and pollution. The home, which signified a person's Christian existence, is placed at the edge of a forest providing shade and "a beautiful blue lake, blooming roses, birds that are singing and it is endowed with a sense of heavenly peace. The inhabitants of this earthly paradise travel every day by train to the city. There is the factory; big chimneys constantly belch out smoke. There are huge machines, whirling, swirling, hauling."[46]

The imagery suggested that everyday life still needed to be lived in both realms; one was dominated by duty, responsibility and drudgery while the other was a foretaste of heaven. Since each realm was viewed as separate, ultimately two different sets of ethics were applied assisting the believer to travel from one realm to the other. The nature of these realms became dichotomous: one was blissful and beautiful the other was relentless and mechanized.

Not surprisingly this led Christians to retreat into an interior and private world. Again it was Luthardt who articulated this change. "Luther's position rests on his differentiation of God's kingdom (*Gottesreich*) and the world's kingdom (*Weltreich*), as he calls it, or in other words on the concept

---

44. Ibid., 30, quoting from C. E. Luthardt, *Die Ethik Luthers in ihren Grundzügen* (Leipzig: Dörffling & Franke, 1867): "Das Charakteristische für das Reich Christi ist die Gnadenordung, das Charakteristische für das Weltreich und das Weltleben ist die Rechtsordnung. Also sind sie ganz verschiedener Gattung und liegen nicht auf der gleichen Linie, sondern gehören verschiedenen Welten an."

45. Nestingen, "Two Kingdoms," 270.

46. Duchrow, *Umdeutung*, 72. The quote is from D. Vorwerk and Jakob Wallrabenstein, *Der Spiegel des Pastors*: "Der Christ wird zutreffend einem Bewohner der Weltstadt verglichen, dessen Wohnsitz sich weit außerhalb der Stadtmauern befindet. Sein Haus liegt am Rande eines schattigen Waldes. Ein schöner, blauer See gibt der Landschaft Leben. Rosen blühen dort, Tauben gurren himmlische Ruhe und Frieden liegen über allem. Der Bewohner dieses irdischen Paradieses reist jeden Tag mit der Bahn in die Großstadt. Dort ist die Fabrik. Die hohen Schornsteine stoßen den ganzen Tag über Rauch aus, die riesigen Maschinen sausen, brummen, poltern, klappern, tosen. Schmutziger Staub bedeckt die dunklen Fenster. Blasse unzufriedene Arbeiter gehen hin und her. Hier ist er verpflichtet zu arbeiten, hier hat er sein alltägliches Heim."

of the interiority of Christianity in contrast to the exteriority of a life in the world based on creation structures."[47]

The phrase "in other words" became the gateway for a reinterpretation of Luther. Luther's concept of the two regiments was based on two realms which were separate yet interrelated. Luthardt separated and divided the inner and the outer life and focused Christian piety on the inner and personal life. The life of the exterior world was structured by its 'own laws and reason, quite apart from the Holy Spirit'.[48] He claimed that Jesus Christ himself was unconcerned about matters of the world, leaving government and rulers to deal with them. Christ's kingdom was therefore primarily a matter of the heart (*Gesinnung*). The kingdom of the world was a matter for the head (reason) and demanded of its citizens obedience and duty (*Pflicht*).

Once these seeds were sown, subsequent interpreters of Luther's *Zwei-Reiche-Lehre* developed either a program of withdrawal from the world or a theological retrieval of this modern but secular world.

Reclaiming the World

A central aspect to the reclaiming agenda was the insistence that the realm and structures of the world were an intricate and inevitable part of nature. In 1904 W. Herrmann argued in his *Ethik*[49] that the struggle for survival was a natural necessity. Given that particular life setting, the internal structure of a state (which he defined as "a governed order through which a group of people, brought together by nature and history, seeks to defend and sustain their union")[50] was an integral part of God's creation. The task of

47. Duchrow, *Umdeutung*, 29, quoting Chr. Ernst Luthardt, 1867, *Die Ethik Luthers in ihren Grundzügen* (S. 76–80): "Seine Stellung nahm Luther in der Unterscheidung zwischen dem Gottesreich und dem Weltreich, wie er es nennt, oder mit anderen Worten in dem Satz von der Innerlichkeit des Christenthums im Unterschied von dem äußeren Leben in der Welt wie es auf der Schöpfung beruht."

48. Ibid., quoting Luthardt, *Ethik* (S. 76–80): "Daraus folgt, dass es nicht der Beruf Jesu Christi oder des Evangeliums ist, die Ordnungen des weltlichen Lebens zu ändern und neu aufzurichten. Vielmehr hat Christus mit diesem Gebiet nichts zu schaffen sondern lässt es gewähren. Er hat nicht etwa dem Kaiser Augustus zu lehren wie er die Regierung führen soll, auch 'bedarf man des Herrn Jesus nicht' zu Handel und Wandel, sondern das alles unterliegt seinen eigenen Gesetzen und der Vernunft: dazu man 'des heiligen Geistes nicht bedarf.'"

49. Wilhelm J. G. Herrmann, *Ethik* (Tübingen, Germany: Mohr, 1904).

50. Duchrow, *Umdeutung*, 45, quoting Herrmann, *Ethik*: "Der Staat ist die von einer Obrigkeit gehandhabte Ordnung, durch die sich eine durch Natur and Geschichte zusammengeführte Menschengruppe in ihrer Zusammengehörigkeit zu behaupten sucht. Die durch die Natur gegebene Grundlage des Staates ist das Volk und seine Heimat."

governance was therefore to maintain the unity of its people by developing their own and unique cultural identity and to defend the state's interest against other competing states and forces. At its most laudable, Herrmann's analysis sought to reclaim a world dominated by technological and scientific structures into the realm of the religious. God was not, he claimed, excluded from this secular and modern world, rather the world was part of God's creation order (*Naturordnung*). It was therefore one's Christian duty to embrace and support the state as it sought to preserve order and prevent chaos, even when the methods of state government were less than perfect. "Once a Christian understands the moral purpose of the state, he will see that obedience towards authority is a vital part of his calling in the state. For the continuation of the state, which relies on the authority of governance, is more important than the eradication of certain imperfections of the state."[51]

Herrmann stopped short of arguing for a blind Christian obedience and allowed for the possibility of a civil disobedience. However, in such extreme cases he advocated not the preaching of revolution but willing acceptance of punishment for acts of disobedience. Nevertheless, the effect of reclaiming the world as a separate God-given structure with little interconnection with God's realm (i.e., the church) provided a strong incentive for a Christian patriotism that viewed the state and its structures as God's indisputable gift.

Luther had urged those in authority to be mindful of their divine calling but was at the same time very blunt even calling them "thieves and scoundrels."[52] He judged the princes realistically as being easily corrupted. Theologians like Herrmann, living in a different Germany, sought to apply Luther's political theory to the institution of the state governed by the rule of law (*Rechtstaat*). With the benefit of hindsight, the price for reclaiming the realm of the state theologically was giving a political structure divine legitimacy. Theologians like Herrmann added the caveat that this legitimacy depended on a state's good governance in accordance with the law. Yet what was one to do when the state began to be corrupt and abused the law?

The call for a Christian obedience towards authority led to the inevitable tension of either having to act according to the ideals of Jesus' teaching

---

51. Duchrow *Umdeutung*, 45, quoting Herrmann, *Ethik*: "Hat der Christ die sittliche Bedeutung des Staates verstanden, so wird er als seinen Beruf im Staat vor allem den Gehorsam gegen die Obrigkeit ansehen. Denn der Bestand des Staates überhaupt, der auf der Autorität der Obrigkeit beruht, ist wichtiger als die Beseitigung einzelner Mängel im Staate."

52. Luther, *Christian in Society*, 109: "They [the temporal lords] behave worse than any thief or scoundrel, and their temporal rule has sunk quite as low as that of the spiritual tyrants."

or applying a reasonable and responsible realism. This choice was succinctly expressed in 1919 by the sociologist Max Weber (1864–1920). He used the terms, ethics of conviction (*Gesinnungsethik*) versus an ethics of responsibility (*Verantwortungsethik*).[53] Max Weber was no Lutheran theologian but a keen political thinker. He was well aware of the religious influence within society and politics. He argued in his essay "Vocation for Politics" that the two ethics were separated by an unbridgeable gap. For him the choice was either to act according to inner ethos and conviction (*gesinnungsethisch*— which he interpreted as doing the right thing no matter what the outcome might be) or acting in accordance with critical rational reckoning (*verantwortungsethisch*—which he interpreted as seeking to evaluate and predict every possible consequence). Whilst Weber claimed that both, in spite of their conflicting orientation, were necessary to guide those who followed their calling into politics,[54] the mere fact that the world was now governed by a separate rationale—empirically calculated causes and effects—revealed that the locus of ethics had shifted. The practical outcome of Weber's analysis was to recognize the importance of convictions, religious or otherwise, as a necessary factor in order to produce a "true human being." Once this was attained the act (*handeln*) became the responsibility of the individual.

The goal of Weber's ethical project aims at cultivating a character who can willfully bring together these conflicting formal virtues to create what he calls "total personality" (*Gesamtpersönlichkeit*).[55]

When Luther hammered out his *Zwei-Reiche-Lehre* in the sixteenth century he addressed political leaders who understood themselves to be part of a Christian community and obligated to uphold Christian values. Weber's audience of the early twentieth century was much more diverse. A multitude of convictions and values were in competition with one another and the Christian church had been pushed to the periphery of society. Indeed, following Weber the goal for true human beings was to emancipate themselves from religious interference.

In contrast to Max Weber and the inevitable slide towards a secular world was Albrecht Ritschl's (1822–89) earlier attempt to extend the kingdom of God beyond the Christian church into the world. Ritschl, an eminent liberal theologian, drew on Luther's teaching of the two realms

---

53. Duchrow, *Umdeutung*, 58–62. See Max Weber, "Politik als Beruf."

54. Duchrow, *Umdeutung*, 62: "The ethic of conviction and the ethic of responsibility are not absolute opposites. They are complementary to one another, and only in combination do they produce the true human being who is capable of having a 'vocation for politics.'"

55. See *Stanford Encyclopedia of Philosophy*, s.v. "Max Weber," section 6.3, online: http://plato.stanford.edu/entries/weber/#EthConRes.

and argued that the world (the state) was ordained by God and that the state's primary task was the establishment of peace. As the kingdom of the world committed itself to that task it was in effect creating the space for the moral and religious transformation of society. The logical consequence was therefore a fruitful cooperation between the kingdom of God and world. For Ritschl the kingdom of God manifested itself through a morality based on virtue and on the law of love. The mission of the church was thus defined as the transformation of the world. Ritschl argued for a grand reinterpretation of the Christendom paradigm,[56] and perceived Christianity as a reservoir of power sending powerful impulses of its virtues and love into society.[57] The Christian faith, based on Jesus Christ and his saving life, set believers free and provided them with the motivation to act in love. Ritschl sought to focus the ethical task of the church towards the moral organization of humanity and the establishment of God's kingdom which manifested itself by happiness and fellowship with God. The world and its structures became integrated into this grand scheme of God's kingdom. The role of the church was to occupy the space the world provided and to live proclaiming a message of change and transformation. The logic of this position was that worldly government deserved Christian support and obedience. "It follows that the rule of law for a society (*Rechtsgemeinschaft*) is the necessary means to secure moral freedom which in turn is the unavoidable precondition enabling Christians to pursue the tasks of the kingdom of God amongst moral society as a whole."[58]

Ritschl and his so-called school wielded considerable influence in nineteenth century Germany. His thoughts represented a daring revival of the Christendom paradigm. He argued for an active cooperation between the church and the state for the purpose of achieving a Christian transformation of a society by shaping people's culture and moral formation. The basic premise of this culture-shaping version of the protestant faith (*Kulturprotestantismus*) was the willing and benevolent support of the state. Yet, what would happen if the state were to develop its own anti-Christian

---

56. Duchrow, *Umdeutung*, 34, quoting Albrecht Ritschl (1874): "Das Christenthum aber ist in erster Linie auf den Endzweck des Reiches Gottes gegründet. . . . Im Vergleich mit dieser Bedeutung des Christenthums muß die Herrschaft des Rechtes über die Menschen als positive Voraussetzung anerkannt werden."

57. Thielicke, *Modern Faith*, 334.

58. Duchrow, *Umdeutung*, 37, quoting Albrecht Ritschl (1881): "Denn die Rechtsgemeinschaft ist als nothwendiges Mittel zur Sicherung der sittlichen Freiheit auch die unumgängliche Bedingung dafür, dass die Christen die Aufgaben des Reiches Gottes in allen Gebieten der sittlichen Gemeinschaft lösen können."

agenda? How could a church that had affirmed a positive entanglement with the state disentangle itself again?

Withdrawal from the World

In contrast to Ritschl's and others' attempts at reclaiming the world, withdrawal from it became a characteristic feature of the pietistic movement. Pietism (*Pietismus*) was a reform movement of seventeenth century Lutheranism. The so-called father of pietism, Jacob Spener (1635–1705) was troubled by the dry cerebral orthodoxy of his time and the corrupt condition of the church. To counter these he suggested a number of Christian disciplines in order to facilitate "a reformation of life."[59] Abiding emphasis of the movement are personal piety, a devout union with Christ, concern for godliness and a desire for a holy life. Early forms of pietism made little distinction between a holy life and the whole of life. Their concern was not simply winning a soul but "service of the body."[60] Nevertheless during the eighteenth century subtle distinctions were made between the civic and the religious sphere. These changes "marked the beginning of the shift from early to later Pietism, with its proclivity toward escapism and its construction of an absolute dualism between the sacred and the profane."[61]

The concentration on an inner holy and disciplined life could lead to a purposeful existence and a profound commitment to neighborly love and mission. But it could also lead into an introspective view of life disengaged from worldly affairs. World structures were then viewed as necessary but ultimately left to their own devices.

Baptist Perspectives

Johann G. Oncken, founder of the contemporary German Baptist movement was baptized with six other people in the river Elbe in 1834. This new German Baptist community was primarily influenced by nineteenth century pietism and the revival movements of England and America. Typical key concerns for Baptists were personal faith and conversion, piety and the active participation of each believer in the life of the fellowship. Their understanding of church and world was influenced by the American model of a strict division between church and state. Andrea Strübind, a German

---

59. Spener, *Pia Desideria*, 10: "Erneuerung des Christlichen Lebens."
60. Bosch, *Transforming Mission*, 252–55.
61. Ibid., 255.

Baptist historian, notes that a frequently stated opinion was that the state was political but the church spiritual and the two were further apart from each other than heaven and earth.[62]

Strübind's historical analysis was focused on the early twentieth century. In her book she does not mention other, older voices and influences that must have also been heard and known by nineteenth and twentieth century Baptists. Arnold Köster's ministry was located in Vienna, the very place where the Anabaptist Balthasar Hubmaier was burned at the stake in 1528. Köster made frequent references to Hubmaier, Jacob Hutter and Thomas Münzer[63] thus giving a strong indication that he and many other Baptists were acquainted with the much earlier Anabaptist history—a history that was directly linked to Luther's original *Zwei-Reiche-Lehre*. Luther's political theory had also been, at least in part, a polemic against dangerous Anabaptist views of society. From a historical perspective it is difficult to disentangle the complex interactions between religiously and socially motivated attempts at reform. Were all the leaders of the numerous peasant revolts inspired by this new Anabaptist teaching? What seems to be certain is that many people viewed the Reformation (Luther's and otherwise) not just as religious but expected that it would also lead to social reforms and a more egalitarian society. The historian Arnold Snyder states that the peasants' "revolt was not primarily a religious event. It was a search for social, economic and political redress which found ideological legitimization in Reformation concepts."[64] The turmoil and upheaval of the sixteenth century became the context of a rich spectrum of various convictions. Some of these were pursued by violent means that went tragically wrong (i.e., Münster).[65] Other more peaceful attempts at building new communities were brutally oppressed by the authorities. Intense persecution and being cast in the role of rebels, heretics or enthusiasts (*Schwärmer*)[66] by those whose writings ultimately became the primary source material for the present day view of the sixteenth century, makes it difficult to hear the Anabaptist contribution to the political question.

Nevertheless, two distinct Anabaptist voices wrestled with the question of how an intentional Christian church can live in the world. One was

---

62. Strübind, *Die unfreie Freikirche*, 43.
63. Graf-Stuhlhofer, *Öffentliche Kritik*, 119f, 121,133, 166, 179.
64. Snyder, *Anabaptist*, 32.
65. Horsch, "Rise and Fall." See also Horsch, "Menno Simons"; Wolkan, *Die Hutterer*.
66. Holl, *Gesammelte Aufsätze*, 420–67.

the pacifist position, labeled at the time as the *Stäbler*⁶⁷ (People of the Staff). The other group was referred to as the *Schwertler* (People of the Sword).⁶⁸

One leading proponent of the *Schwertler* was Balthasar Hubmaier. In the early 1520s he became the priest of Waldshut, a little town on the Rhine. Very soon he experienced an inner transformation and became a convinced Anabaptist, instigating a reform movement that spread throughout the town. In 1525 Waldshut gave military assistance to the peasants' army that had surrounded the city. Apparently Hubmaier believed that the peasant's struggle was justified resistance against tyranny. Thus, the Christian Anabaptist men of Waldshut took it upon themselves to bear the sword.⁶⁹ An even more radical stance was taken by the Anabaptist Müntzer who urged the princes to wield the sword for the destruction of the godless, and that if they did not do this, the sword would have to be taken from them. In contrast to this, Hubmaier strongly advocated due respect for temporal authority *(Obrigkeit)*. He referred to it as a "'handmaid of God' the task of which was to protect the righteous with the sword and to punish and root out the wicked."⁷⁰ For Hubmaier the office of a ruler was fraught with difficulties and temptations. In his view, unbelieving rulers were prone to abuse their powers while Christians ought to view it as a service to God. Furthermore, subjects were bound to obey their respective rulers. However, "If authorities should prove to be immature or foolish or quite incapable of governing, it is right and proper to replace them with others in peace and without any kind of rebellion."⁷¹

The pacifist (*Stäbler*) position was drawn up under the leadership of Michael Sattler at a gathering of brethren in 1527. The outcome of this gathering was "The Schleitheim Anabaptist Confession of Faith," which consisted of seven articles. Article four (on separation) and six (the sword) directly address the political issue. Article four concludes, "Therefore there will also unquestionably fall from us the unchristian, devilish weapons of force—such as sword, armour and the like, and all their use (either) for friends or against one's enemies—by virtue of the Word of Christ. Resist not (him that is) evil."⁷²

---

67. Wolkan, *Hutterer*, 4–5.
68. Liechty, "Andreas Fischer," 130–32.
69. Bergsten, *Balthasar Hubmaier*, 210–25.
70. Ibid., 223.
71. Ibid.
72. Akin, "Expositional Analysis," 359. See also "Schleitheim Confession," n.p., online: http://www.anabaptists.org/history/schleith.html.

In article six the brethren affirmed their intention not to get involved in public offices and be mindful of their citizenship of heaven which demanded a spiritual engagement with the world rather than one with steel and iron. Thus, the vision and intention of this community was based on a separation from the world. In contrast with the magisterial reformation model it refused to address the issue of how society as a whole ought to be ruled and governed. Its own unique contribution lay in the intention of living and modeling an alternative and countercultural vision of church and society.

In the succeeding years the *Stäbler*-type pacifist position survived as an underground movement and became in turn *the* political ethic of contemporary Anabaptists.[73] Ultimately, "Hubmaier could not find a practical solution to the problem of the relationship of church and state."[74] Nevertheless, the able theologian Hubmaier wrestled with these issues at a deeper and more thorough level than the Swiss Anabaptist authors of the Schleitheim Confession. The confession was content to quote Scripture adding little comment. Hubmaier engaged theologically with difficult Scripture passages regarding the sword and the issues of temporal authority.[75] Hubmaier acknowledged that there were separate realms and sought to discern ways to live in both of them. The Schleitheim confession on the other hand was an unflinching declaration of living separate from the world with the full knowledge that this meant embracing "suffering" in the world.

Both Köster and Bonhoeffer were informed in their response to the Third Reich by these political models and reactions of the Christian church. Having surveyed the theological and historical background the next section focuses on the Third Reich period and how Bonhoeffer and Köster sought to remain faithful to the call of following Christ in a confusing and hostile world.

The Crisis of Modernity

The German experience of the world in the 1920s and 1930s was inextricably linked to the upheavals of World War I and the chaotic post-war period. The terrible years of war, loss of life, consequent defeat, national humiliation, severe economical hardship and the collapse of the political system led to a prolonged and intense crisis. For the ordinary man and woman it was an existential crisis which meant scarcity of food, hyper-inflation and unemployment. Politically, the demise of the monarchy and the tentative introduction of a democratic system increased the acute sense of instability

---

73. Yoder, *Politics of Jesus*.
74. Bergsten *Balthasar Hubmaier*, 364.
75. Chatfield, "Balthasar Hubmaier," 273–85.

amongst the German people. The overriding perception was a loss of values and coherence. The sense of crisis was not only felt by the individual but also had a collective dimension, prompting many to question whether the German people and nation would survive.[76]

During the turbulent years of the Weimar Republic the political spectrum included a great variety of parties, none of which commanded a significant majority in the polls. Some advocated a return to a monarchy; others championed communism, liberalism, socialism or nationalism. Which party would be able to restore order and hope to the people? The initial pro-democratic enthusiasm soon waned when the ineffective process of government proved to be unable to solve the national crisis. Very soon the political tide turned either towards left-wing communism or right-wing nationalist movements.

The traditional churches of Germany—Catholic, Lutheran and Reformed—had throughout history maintained close ties to the respective governments of the counties *(Länder)*. Aristocratic landowners considered it their duty to provide places of worship and pastoral leaders for their population. The church tax was integrated in the national tax regime and paid for the salaries and pensions of ministers and theological educators of the church. The legal status of a protestant church employee was that of a civil servant *(Beamter)* which gave them security, status and certain privileges.

Theologically, a large section of the Lutheran Church of the early twentieth century had gravitated towards a liberal Cultural Protestantism *(Kulturprotestantismus)*. The influence of Enlightenment Thought with its emphasis on reason and the autonomous individual had a significant impact on the church. Theologians of the late nineteenth and early twentieth century committed themselves to scientific research, such as the historical-critical-method. It was an attempt to secure reliable scientific basis for faith at a time when relativism and intellectual doubt had become common currency. The church understood itself as an integral part of the people (*Volk*) and the state, and taught an ethic that welded together Luther's two kingdoms into one. The role of the church in Christendom *(Christliches Abendland)* was to educate the people and to provide pastoral care. The church, both loyal

---

76. Reimer, *Emanuel Hirsch and Paul Tillich Debate*, 139, quoting S. W. Halperin, *Germany Tried Democracy* (New York: Norton, 1965), 103: "On November 11, 1918, after an unsuccessful attempt to have the harsh terms set by the victorious Allies modified, Germany—under compulsion—signed the armistice. While military operations ended, starvation continued. In fact, the Allies continued the blockade of food shipments for Germans while thousands died daily of malnutrition. 'The memory of this horrible experience," says S. William Halperin in his 1946 classic, "lived on in the minds of Germans of every class. It bred bitterness which the years assuaged but which could all too easily be resuscitated upon the first recurrence of adversity."

to and dependent on the state, effectively became the religious face of the state. This ordered and cultured world reached a political zenith in 1914. The Great War and the post-war crisis severely damaged this worldview. The German theologian Gogarten wrote, "The God about whom people were asking in traditional theology was the highest thought or the highest good—that which brought human life to a rounded conclusion."[77] In the new revolutionary and liberal climate a new form of government emerged that intended to separate the religious from the secular. The new political context, desperate social needs and divisions and the intellectual crisis of modernity, demanded fresh theological responses.

Next to liberal theology other theological options were explored. This new theology perceived itself, in Gogarten's terminology, as standing "between the times"[78] and sought to discover God in the midst of uncertainty and turmoil. "The God about whom we were asking in the new theological approach was an uncanny reality, the question, the rift, the contradiction of which, running through all human life and through all that is in human life, was kept open to an intolerable degree."[79]

Crisis Theology

During these years of crisis, three significant theological proposals emerged. Each one was to some extent a reaction against Confessional Theology,[80] which sought to preserve the purity and distinctive nature of the Lutheran faith, and liberal Protestantism of which Adolf von Harnack was a leading representative. The new theological alternatives were shaped by the acute sense of crisis ubiquitously present in the academic disciplines and in the economical and national life. Some theologians endeavored to construct a political theology. They were "Religious Socialism as represented by Paul Tillich; National Lutheranism as represented by Emanuel Hirsch; and Dialectical Theology as represented by Karl Barth."[81]

Historically the legacy of National Lutheranism and Dialectical Theology are well attested.[82] The advantage of hindsight makes the former into a

---

77. Scholder, *Requiem*, 43, quoting F. Gogarten, *Der Zerfall des Humanismus und die Gottesfrage* (Stuttgart: Kohlhammer, 1937).

78. Title of the theological journal, *Zwischen den Zeiten*.

79. Scholder, *Requiem*, 43, quoting Gogarten.

80. Green, *Lutherans*, 49.

81. Reimer, *Emanuel Hirsch and Paul Tillich Debate*, 202.

82. Reimer, *Emanuel Hirsch and Paul Tillich Debate*. Ericksen, *Theologians under Hitler*. Green, *Lutherans*. Scholder, *Requiem*.

villain and the latter into a hero. Yet, within the confines of their own time and in the face of crisis, none of these theologians was able to foresee the unfolding of events. These various schools shared the same intellectual and historical soil and their main representatives maintained cordial relationships with each other. Karl Barth was sympathetic to socialist ideas[83] and Emanuel Hirsch and Paul Tillich were close friends during their student days and continued to read and evaluate each other's literary work. Their friendship finally ruptured in 1934 when both engaged in a painful public dispute, bitterly criticizing each other's point of view and political choices. Nevertheless, as James A. Reimer has shown in his study, the two theologians employed, in spite of their different political choices, similar theological methods and frequently reached similar conclusions.[84] The theologies of Hirsch and Tillich share a common political concern as the mutual use of the word socialism clearly indicates. One type of socialism positioned itself on the left, the other on the right. Barth shared some socialist aspirations but pursued a different theological methodology.

The following section seeks to engage briefly with each of these schools, which were attempts to respond theologically to a human and national crisis and in turn shaped the language theologians and pastors like Bonhoeffer and Köster used. The chronological emergence of these schools provides a useful clue of how these ideas developed and affected each other. The democratic period gave rise to Religious Socialism in the 1920s. This was followed by the rapid emergence of National Lutheranism in the 1930s. Confessional Lutheranism sought to respond to the nationalistic German Christians as did Karl Barth.

Religious Socialism (Paul Tillich)

Religious Socialism critically engaged with the socialist movement which was a powerful political force during the years of revolution and the early years of the Weimar Republic.[85] In 1914 the young theologian Paul Tillich enthusiastically joined the war effort and served on the front as an army chaplain until 1918. The war years profoundly challenged Tillich's idyllic and intellectual prewar existence. Reflecting on these years he wrote:

---

83. Ericksen, *Theologians under Hitler*, 178: "[Barth's] political views were liberal, democratic and socialist in orientation."

84. Reimer, *Emanuel Hirsch and Paul Tillich Debate*.

85. Ibid., 179–95.

The First World War was the end of my period of preparation. Together with my whole generation, I was grasped by the overwhelming experience of a nation-wide community—of the end of a merely individualistic and predominantly theoretical existence. . . . The first weeks had not passed before one's original enthusiasm disappeared, after a few months I became convinced that the war would last indefinitely and ruin all of Europe. Above all, I saw that the unity of the first weeks was an illusion, that the nation was split into classes, and that the industrial masses considered the Church as an unquestioned ally of the ruling groups. The situation became more and more manifest towards the end of the war. It produced the revolution, in which imperial Germany collapsed.[86]

After the war Tillich worked in Berlin and became a co-founder of the Religious Socialists,[87] also called the Kairos Circle. The group began to analyze the interrelation of capitalism and imperialism, the class struggle and possible solutions. Tillich wanted to respond theologically to the political reality of post-war Germany. He was not interested in party-political involvement but hoped to provide a prophetic voice to the effort of joining Christianity and Socialism. He did not join a political party until 1929 when he became a member of the Social Democratic Party. Central to his thinking were firstly the hope and aspiration of the new eschatological kingdom, secondly the critical evaluation of communist ideas such as the class struggle and thirdly the ideal of a universal classless society. Tillich employed Marxist conceptual tools in order to analyze history and society, but also sought to go "behind Marx and Hegel to the prophetic attitude of Biblical tradition and placed the socialist dialectic within the context of transcendence, transcendence paradoxically present in history."[88]

Discerning God's presence and will within the historical realities and processes had been an important concern since the nineteenth century. Karl Holl, whose teaching and writing had a profound influence on many of the young emerging theologians, argued that an increased historical focus of German theological thinking was a dominant feature of the nineteenth century. He even suggested that it was possible to date this new paradigmatic change of thinking. According to Holl it was brought about by another collective experience of war, the German War of Liberation (1812–1815). Historically, it marked the beginning of German Idealism and a new

---

86. Tillich, *Theology*, 12.

87. Marsden, "Paul Tillich."

88. Reimer, *Emanuel Hirsch and Paul Tillich Debate*, 194, quoting J. R. Stumme, *Socialism in Theological Perspective* (Missoula, MT: Scholars, 1978), 198.

God-image (*Gottesbild*) or perception of God. The God of the enlightenment was perceived as grand thinker, mathematician and artist. This God had established and maintained a perfect and constant creation order. The new view of God saw him active in history, bringing about sudden change, raising up and casting down nations and the mighty. His will was not predetermined, it was free and extraordinary. Faith therefore meant finding God in the complex tensions of life and in the taking of risky choices.[89]

Tillich's attempt to interpret history was shared by many theologians and thinkers of the time. What they also shared was strongly developed notion of choice. The historian Green referred to it as decisionism, apparent in the frequent references of "the German hour" and of having to "make the right decision."[90]

Another concept, important to Hirsch and Tillich, was the rediscovery of the people, *das Volk*. For Hirsch, *Volk* became the most important historical reality. Tillich's preferred term was either the mass or the proletariat. This focus on a collective people represented a deliberate reaction against a liberal Protestant's focus on the individual and, in ethical terms, on a virtuous and dutiful life. The center of the new ethical responsibility was community, solidarity, commitment and self-sacrifice. The young Bonhoeffer responding to these socialist concepts wrote in 1929: "Tillich's ideas about the 'holiness of the formless mass' have nothing to do with Christian theology."[91] Nevertheless, Bonhoeffer also used socialist concepts and language when he described the German church of his time as "bourgeois."[92] He argued that the proletariat had turned away from the church; the challenge was therefore "to take the church-community to the proletariat, and to transform the masses into the church-communities."[93] Clearly the social question (*die soziale Frage*) was a dominant issue for the German people and could not be ignored by the church.

Paul Tillich remained critical of the nationalistic movements and its growing popularity. In 1933 he witnessed the public burning of books, including his own book *The Socialist Decision*. The Nazis dismissed him from his teaching post at the University of Frankfurt and consequently he was forced to emigrate to America.

---

89. Holl, *Bedeutung*, 76.
90. Green, *Lutherans*, 98.
91. Bonhoeffer, *Sanctorum*, 239.
92. Ibid., 272.
93. Ibid., 273.

National Lutheranism (Emanuel Hirsch)

Tillich's close friend Emanuel Hirsch[94] interpreted the historical upsurge of nationalistic sentiments differently. Hirsch judged Hitler's rise to power as God's work. He wrote, "One can feel the work of the almighty Lord for whom we are simple instruments."[95] Hirsch became an ardent supporter of the Nazi cause and underpinned his convictions with rigorous intellectual engagement rather than emotional enthusiastic nationalistic sentiment. Even theologians who opposed his stance respected him nonetheless. For instance when Karl Barth critically engaged with Hirsch's publication, *Die gegenwärtige geistige Lage*, he said: "We can and must praise it too for the fact that its author, in contrast to many of his fellow believers, has, with what he declared today, remained in line with what he has always meant, intended and maintained. If anyone is genuine and has the right to speak in this affair, it is Emanuel Hirsch."[96]

Ericksen referred to Hirsch as a "Nazi Intellectual"[97] which was, in retrospect, not flattering. However, it acknowledges that Hirsch attempted to develop a political ethic which engaged with a real crisis and was intellectually and theologically consistent. Did Hirsch's political ethic challenge and affect the thinking of Christians like Bonhoeffer and Köster?

Both Tillich and Hirsch were Lutheran theologians but moved away from Luther's two kingdom teaching. Tillich exchanged it for an eschatological interpretation and Hirsch sought to reinterpret Luther's teaching. Both criticized the tendency of Liberal Cultural Protestantism to merge God's kingdom into the kingdom of bourgeois culture. In response, Religious Socialism viewed the kingdom of God as the coming kingdom which had to be realized now. God's kingdom was translated into a powerful aspiration. Every Christian's calling was to embrace the task of making the historic actualization of the attributes and characteristics of the future kingdom a present reality. Tolstoy's interpretation of the Sermon of the Mount was a typical example of this notion. Tolstoy's Jesus radically called into question the present circumstances and issued the challenge to live lives that embodied a totally different set of values, the values of God's kingdom.

---

94. Tillich, *On the Boundary*, 76.

95. Hirsch, *Die gegenwärtige geistige Lage*, 36: "Es bricht in ihm [Adolf Hitler], gerade wenn er auf das Geheimnis des Blutbundes und die Aufgabe seiner Bewahrung kommt, fast am lebendigsten das in ihm mächtige ursprüngliche religiöse Gefühl durch. Hier ist das Werk des allmächtigen Herrn zu spüren, dem wir lediglich Werkzeuge zu sein haben."

96. Barth, "German Church Conflict," 30.

97. Ericksen, *Theologians under Hitler*, 120.

Emanuel Hirsch rejected this interpretation and argued that Tolstoy's error was his inability to understand Jesus' distinction between the two kingdoms.[98] Interestingly, Köster was also critical of Tolstoy and feared that his interpretation of the Sermon on the Mount merely achieved setting up a new law rather than pointing to the enormity of God's grace.[99]

Hirsch was convinced that the ethical imperatives, expressed in the gospels, could only be realistically achieved by differentiating between the two kingdoms. Luther had referred to them as the eternal and the temporal kingdoms. Hirsch reinterpreted them as the "invisible community of conscience in God and the visible community of law, nation, and state."[100] His distinction was between two communities and not between the individual and a secular world. Hirsch's concern was to show that in spite of the fact that God's church was trans-temporal (eternal) and international, it still concretely expressed itself by the joining together of individuals, these in turn constituted themselves as an actual historic community with unique characteristics. The visible community (temporal) provided the order and the context which made human life possible. Thus law, nation and state, Hirsch argued, were not God's kingdom but were nevertheless the God-given context of life. Each realm was ordered by a different set of laws that could not be mixed and it was therefore futile attempting to transform the visible community of the state into the invisible kingdom of God-community. The two realms had to remain distinct but were at the same time linked by the fact that God was at work in both of them.

For Hirsch, human existence had a tragic aspect, for every human being was set within the constraints of a certain historical and cultural context, yet as a gospel-people God's presence, will and purpose could nevertheless be found within these constraining historical realities. The unique service and duty of the community of conscience to the worldly community was to bring to it, through the individual acts of decision-making, a spiritual insight and power which in turn was to organize and shape the world of the visible community of law, nation and state. The existential interface between these two realms was in the individual act of decision making set within the concrete historical context.

Hirsch applied a similar interpretive structure to history and gave it a double character. It had, he argued, a "metaphysical kernel and a concrete historical expression"[101] of that inner core. The inner hidden metaphysical

---

98. Reimer, *Emanuel Hirsch and Paul Tillich Debate*, 151.
99. Köster, *Lampenlicht*, 20.
100. Reimer, *Emanuel Hirsch and Paul Tillich Debate*, 151.
101. Ibid.

core gave substance to the outer historical circumstances. This inner kernel could never be known or encountered in its unadulterated form. Thus, all human decision-making was constrained by outer historical conditions and the complex interaction of nature and nurture.[102] Yet in spite of the accidental complexity of every historical context, it still had, at its core, a metaphysical kernel. The task for the members of the community of conscience was to discern God's will behind the historical boundaries and possibilities in order to obey faithfully. For "out of the certainty of its relation to an Eternal an individual soul unifies itself with the Eternal through an affirmation of a particular duty."[103] Hirsch carefully located certainty not in knowing what was God's will but in the individual's relation with the Eternal. This allowed for being in error or mistaken but it was not possible to remain undecided and free floating. To use a Kierkegaardian phrase, Christian ethics involved for Hirsch, who was also a renowned expert on Kierkegaard, a risky and existential leap of faith. "The existence of the state and society in each of their forms depend on the fact that in them people selflessly, committedly, and genuinely . . . oppose the power of particular egoism which destroys also the natural conditions of being and thus, according to the Sermon on the Mount, become the salt of the earth. The kingdom of God is the life-bestowing mystery over all visible changes of history."[104]

For Germany the 1933 events brought fundamental visible changes. Emanuel Hirsch judged these as a holy hour, a time where he could detect the metaphysical kernel glimmer through the seams of dramatic political events.[105] He distanced himself from German Christians who drew a direct link between the emerging nationalistic government and divine approval. Yet, in spite of certain tacit theological reservation, Hirsch did affirm and embrace the Nazi government. His understanding of Luther's doctrine of the two kingdoms led him to view the new regime as earthly order, ordained by God, to preserve and order human life through the law, by exercising coercion and authority. He felt obliged to make an ethical and Christian choice, believing it to be right, but also knowing that it was not necessarily sealed with divine approval.[106]

102. Ibid., 347. Hirsch refers to the limiting or restraining factors of all human-historical life as a boundary.

103. Ibid., 152, quoting from Hirsch, *Deutschlands Schicksal* (1925), 21.

104. Reimer, *Emanuel Hirsch and Paul Tillich Debate*, 153.

105. Ericksen, *Theologians under Hitler*, 148. Hirsch wrote in the early summer of 1933: "No other Volk in the world has a leading statesman such as ours, who takes Christianity so seriously. On 1 May when Adolf Hitler closed his great speech with a prayer, the whole world could sense the wonderful sincerity in that."

106. Reimer, *Emanuel Hirsch and Paul Tillich Debate*, 310. Hirsch wrote regarding

The uncertainty of the individual conscience required to make a daring decision could only be removed through subsequent unfolding historical events. Thus, success became the final arbiter of Hirsch's ethics. Bonhoeffer rejected such reasoning calling it "idolizing success. The form of the crucified disarms all thinking aimed at success, for it is a denial of judgment. . . . Jesus is certainly no advocate for the successful in history."[107] Another critic of Hirsch, Paul Tillich drew attention to the fact that Hirsch's sharp separation between an external-political and internal-spiritual kingdom robbed him of the conceptual tools he would have needed to critically evaluate the political realm. "Hirsch is removing the political sphere from the normativeness of the kingdom of God."[108]

To Hirsch, the link between the two kingdoms was the individual's conscience. In some way this was contradictory since the individual, according to Hirsch, was integrated in the invisible community of conscience. Ultimately, Hirsch did not opt for a communal ethic but an existential, individualistic one. The ethical choices that history thrusts upon every individual were daring "either/or" decisions that had to be made. Hirsch did not allow himself a neutral vantage point from which he could conduct a rigorous and critical evaluation of the historical context. He had to choose. Tillich's free-floating spirit and detached manner were for Hirsch highly undesirable.[109] He understood his own nationality and earthly situation as a God-given fate and felt compelled to respond faithfully and courageously to an ambiguous situation. Hirsch felt compelled to leap and take sides.

Hirsch's lofty theological ideas and concepts were exploited and practically applied by the German Christian movement. Its members welded together religious and political conviction and hoped to achieve on a practical

---

his pledge to earthly authorities: "I give and pledge them their earthly place, trusting in the God and being obedient to the God who bids me so to give and to pledge; and this latter trust and obedience carries me and hallows me in my total commitment to earthly bondage. If it pleases God to shatter my particular position as false, then out of a sense of crushing shame over such a judgment I have to find my way back to a new trust and obedience under Him and thus struggle for a new and binding position; and the new position will again be a completely genuine actualization of a life in earthly bondage" (Hirsch, *Christliche Freiheit und Politische Bindung, Ein Brief an den Herrn Dr. Stapel*, 1935, 34–35).

107. Bonhoeffer, *Ethics*, 89–90.

108. Reimer, *Emanuel Hirsch and Paul Tillich Debate*, 340.

109. Ibid., 306–7, quoting Hirsch: "Tillich ist irgendwie gelöst, wo ich gebunden bin. Er findet seinen Dienst am bewegten geschichtlichen Ganzen in prophetischer Haltung, wie er es ausdrückt, das heißt als ein frei schwebender Einzelner, der im Überschau über den ganzen strömenden Lebenszusammenhang der Welt sich seine Stellung und Aufgabe bestimmt in einer innerlich gerechtfertigten, aber nicht streng beweisbaren Intuition."

level what intellectuals like Hirsch wrote in academic journals. Hirsch's relationship with the German Christians was complex and confusing. He remained an independent thinker and theologian but supported at the same time the principle aims of the German Christians and the National Socialists. He distanced himself from fanatical or radical segments of the movement but eventually became an adviser to *Reichsbischof* Müller.

German Christians (Deutsche Christen)

The German Christians shared a common national concern and were profoundly influenced by writers like J. G. Fichte and Ernst Moritz Arndt. At a first glance the impression might be that the German Christians represented a united front during these turbulent years. A closer look reveals that the movement was quite fragmented and by no means monolithic in its nature. James Reimer,[110] informed by the work of J. A. Zabel, divides the various strands into three main groups; conservative, opportunistic and radical wings.[111]

CONSERVATIVE

Leading theologians of the conservative wing were Hirsch, Paul Althaus and Heinrich Bornkamm. The wider movement or party called itself the *Christliche-Deutsche Bewegung* (CDB) and was established in 1930 but only lasted until 1933. The membership was "made up largely of people from an 'upper class' background who politically supported 'a traditional and conservative Prussian-nationalism' and had affinities with the German National People's Party (DNVP) rather than the Social Democratic or Center Party."[112]

Members were keen to participate in what Hitler called the "preservation of our national culture. . . . [and in] the work for the national and moral renewal of our nation."[113] It was the only group which placed "Christian" before "German." This was in itself an indication that their desire was to

---

110. Ibid., 65–67.
111. See Zabel, *Nazism and the Pastors*.
112. Reimer, *Emanuel Hirsch and Paul Tillich Debate*, 66.
113. Matheson, *Third Reich*, 9. From a policy statement by Hitler, broadcasted on 23 March 1933. Hitler declared: "The national government will guarantee the Christian confessions their due influence in school and educational matters. It is concerned to foster a frank and harmonious relationship between church and state. The fight against a materialistic view of the world and for the creation of a genuine national community is as much in the interest of the German nation as of those of our Christian faith."

remain theologically close to Lutheran Orthodoxy which had embraced nationalistic sentiments while distancing itself from more radical nationalist groups. Members of this conservative wing brought a measure of moderation and restraint to the wider movement. Nevertheless during the critical years of the emerging Nazis, their voices lent the new regime respectability amongst the wider German Protestant Church.

Opportunistic

Zabel applied the label "opportunistic" because the overriding concern of this group, *Glaubensbewegung Deutscher Christen* (GDC), was to put Party principles first and Christian principles second. The group was established by the Nazi Party in June 1932 but collapsed after the Sport Palace fiasco in November 1933.[114] A favorite phrase of theirs was the ambiguous term "positive Christianity."[115] The slogan was part of the NSDAP platform of 1920 and its deliberate vagueness allowed anyone and any group to fill it with their own wishful thinking.

The GDC's aim was to bring together as many Christian nationalist groups as possible for the purpose of uniting these behind the Nazi party program and to help bring about the recovery of the German people and the German Protestant church. Its members sought to emulate the authoritarian leadership style of the Nazis, shared their anti-semitic sentiments and agreed with racial policies. Their explicit endorsement of Nazi policy was clearly and enthusiastically put in writing in the ten "Guiding Principles of the Faith Movement of the German Christians."[116] Principle number nine states: "We regard the mission to the Jews as a grave danger to our culture.

---

114. Scholder, *Requiem*, 102: "A speech by a radical German Christian [Dr. Krause] at a rally in the Berlin Sport Palace on 13 November 1933 calling for the abolition of the Old Testament, the liquidation of Paul's Jewish theology and allegiance to a heroic figure of Jesus led to a widespread dissolution of the German Christian organization and the almost complete loss of its foundations."

115. Reimer, *Emanuel Hirsch and Paul Tillich Debate*, 198. (*Nationalsozialistische Deutsche Arbeitspartei*, NSDAP). It adopted twenty five theses as its program. Number twenty four included the reference to the party's espousal of positive Christianity: "We demand the freedom of all religious confessions in the state, insofar as they do not endanger its existence or strike against the ethical and moral feeling of the Germanic peoples. The party as such represents the standpoint of a positive Christianity without binding itself to any particular confession. It fights the Jewish materialistic spirit within and without us and is convinced that a lasting recovery of our nation can succeed only from within outward on the basis of: Common good before personal good [*Gemeinnutz vor Eigennutz*]."

116. These principles were drafted on 6 June 1932.

Through its doors alien blood is imported into the body of our nation. It has no right to exist except as Overseas Mission. We oppose any mission to the Jews in Germany as long as the Jews have the right to citizenship and there is therefore a danger of bastardisation and an obscuring of racial differences. Holy Scripture also has something to say about righteous anger and the failure of love. In particular marriage between Germans and Jews must be prohibited."[117]

Radical

The most unorthodox and extreme group was led and established in Thuringia by two pietistic revivalist pastors with neo-Pentecostal leanings.[118] Siegfried Leffler and Julius Leutheuser firmly believed that a completely new interpretation of Christianity was needed. Their enthusiastic claim was that the *Führer* was "the redeemer in the history of the Germans. Hitler stood there like a rock in the wide desert . . . in the darkest night of our Christian church history, Hitler became for our time that marvellous transparency the window through which light fell on the history of Christianity."[119]

The movement of the *Kirchenbewegung Deutsche Christen* (KDC) began in 1927 and continued under various names until 1940. According to Zabel it attracted people who were deliberately anti-intellectual and anti-doctrinal, "people whose theology was emotional, fluid and enthusiastic."[120]

Clearly the movement of the German Christians consisted of distinct groups with varied concerns. For a brief moment these separate movements were united. However, after the Sport Palace fiasco in 1933 that unity rapidly disintegrated. The conservatives gave the nationalistic movement a certain intellectual credibility whilst radicals tapped into the emotional needs and hopes of the people. The opportunists employed astute and ruthless political pragmatism and orchestrated a massive administrative change in the Protestant church structures. Yet once the office of a *Reichsbischof* and the establishment of a centralized church administration had been achieved, their success was short-lived. A protest movement within the church prompted some territorial churches (*Landeskirchen*) to resist being drawn into the centralized *Deutsche Evangelische Kirche*. Others joined together and formed the Confessing Church in 1934. Increasing resistance within the Lutheran churches and a change in the political strategies of

117. Matheson, *Third Reich*, 6.
118. Green, *Lutherans*, 45.
119. Conway, *Nazi Persecution*, 11.
120. Reimer, *Emanuel Hirsch and Paul Tillich Debate*, 67, quoting Zabel.

Nazi government officials led to the collapse of the grand church-political schemes of the German Christians.

The vision of the German Christian Movement was to make a failing and increasingly irrelevant Lutheran church relevant and modern. Their aspiration was a united German church in tune with the political ideologies of its time, proclaiming a message that addressed the contemporary needs and concerns of the people. From the outset Bonhoeffer and Köster were opposed to this upsurge of nationalistic Christian enthusiasm. Choosing to resist this hugely popular tide they had to ground their arguments on firm theological foundations. Köster turned to Scripture and from it he developed a distinct and alternative biblical worldview. Bonhoeffer also turned to Scripture and to the Lutheran Confession.

Confessional Lutheranism

Confessional Lutheranism was not overly concerned with relevancy but was passionate about identity. Lutherans of this particular persuasion sought to retain the nature and characteristics of the historical Lutheran church. They argued that Luther had clearly separated the world and its political concerns from the church. Confessional Lutheranism had little patience with the political interference of the state in matters of the church and based their arguments on Lutheran Confessions which had been collected and published in 1580 as *The Book of Concord*. The Lutheran Church's practice, order and theology was based on these documents.

Historically, the German Lutheran Church had emerged and established itself as separate territorial churches. These twenty nine territorial churches (*Landeskirchen*) maintained an organizational independence but were theologically united through the Lutheran Confessions. The original purpose of these various confessional documents was to define and defend the tenants of the protestant faith before the rulers of the sixteenth century. Once these confessions had become accepted and the Lutheran church had gained religious toleration in the Holy Roman Empire of the sixteenth century, these documents acquired a legal status that defined how church and state were to relate to each other. Beyond the typical Lutheran theological themes of law and gospel, justification by faith and the two kingdoms, these documents also provided an important bulwark against the increasing interference of the state in church matters.

In 1918 the legal status of the territorial churches, who were then the established churches of the various territories (*Länder*), was abandoned by the Weimar government. Nevertheless, the various Lutheran territorial churches (*Landeskirchen*) maintained a loose union via the German Evangelical Church Federation (*Deutscher evangelischer Kirchen Bund*).[121] When Hitler came to power in 1933 he sought to make use of the church. His aim was to draw people together into a national unified church, rather than just a loose federation of churches, and he proposed to establish a united German Evangelical Church (*Deutsche evangelische Kirche, DEK*). Initially, this proposal was welcomed by many representatives of the various territorial churches. The widely respected Friedrich von Bodelschwingh was given the task of drawing up a constitution and was eventually elected to be the first Reich bishop of the new DEK on 27.05.1933. But Hitler, not approving of Bodelschwingh, favored the German Christian Ludwig Müller. A fierce campaign against Bodelschwingh was launched which prompted some church leaders to waver and to withdraw their support. On 24.06.1933 Bodelschwingh resigned. The German Christians, assisted by the Nazi party, had prevailed and subsequently managed to secure the position of the Reich Bishop for their candidate, Ludwig Müller.

Following this painful experience, Bodelschwingh directed his energies in preparing a new statement or confession to meet the challenges of the time. In August of 1933 he brought together some young theologians with the expressed aim of formulating a new Lutheran declaration. He wrote about the aims and intentions of this group to a Lutheran pastor. "The wish has repeatedly arisen to work out a position statement concerning current questions from the perspective of the Lutheran confession in order to establish a firm basis within these disputes that might also provide support for lonely warriors. . . . We agreed that first a small circle of theologians meet here to begin this work."[122]

The small group of theologians, of which Bonhoeffer was one, scripted in August 1933 the Bethel Confession.[123] Its first draft was distributed to a number of leading Reformed and Lutheran theologians. Unfortunately it was not possible to reach consensus. For Karl Barth it was "too Lutheran; [and] Schlatter considered it too Barthian."[124] Martin Niemöller was given the thankless task of writing a revised version that included some of the suggested alterations. This diluted version was in turn rejected by two of the original authors, Dietrich Bonhoeffer and Hermann Sasse. Historically, the Bethel Confession was a failure and died a quiet death. Yet, according to the confessional historian Lowell C. Green, theologically, "the August 1933

---

121. Green, *Lutherans*, 81.
122. Bonhoeffer, *Berlin*, 504.
123. Müller, *Bekenntnis*.
124. Green, *Lutherans*, 163.

Bethel Confession was probably the best of all the doctrinal statements written during the Third Reich."[125]

The Bethel confession was shaped by the spirit and documents of the Book of Concord and its key Lutheran theological tenets. Its authors sought to give the "lonely warriors" a new statement of the Lutheran Confessions and thus hoped that the Bethel confession would unite the faithful and expose the fallacies of German Christian theology. To a lesser degree the confession also revealed what was distinctive Lutheran rather than reformed theology.

In the first part of the confession the authors affirmed both the Old and the New Testament as sacred Scriptures. Rejecting the German Christian's contemptuous view of the Old Testament, the confession not only gave an equal regard to both testaments but also referred to them as, "the sole source and measure of the doctrine of the church."[126] This revelation was historical and led to the establishment of the church. Yet, rather than being a mere passive product of God's revelation, the abiding task of the church was to participate in God's ongoing revelation through the faithful exposition and proclamation of the Scriptures. Thus the place of God's continuing revelation, apart from the Scriptures, was in his church rather than other historical movements or happenings. Theologians like Hirsch and Althaus gave historical events a tentative revelatory quality. More enthusiastic supporters of the German Christians spoke with great certainty of God's mighty hand and revealed will.[127]

It is interesting to contrast this nuanced statement with Karl Barth's categorical refusal to all claims of divine revelation save through Jesus Christ and the Scriptures. Barth's approach was a determined "No!"[128] and outright rejection of natural theology. The Bethel Confession did not totally reject natural theology but qualified it by stating, "Faith and natural knowledge are therefore no longer one and the same because we live in a fallen world, that is, because the world is no longer visibly and unambiguously the Word

---

125. Ibid., 164.

126. Bonhoeffer, *Berlin*, 375: "The Holy Scriptures alone witness to the divine revelation. They reveal a one-time, unrepeatable, and self-contained history of salvation, beginning with the promises given to the fallen Adam and culminating in the founding of the church. The church proclaims this history as God's revelatory act, meant for us. In bearing witness to these acts of God, the Scriptures are God's word to us. The church can proclaim God's revelation only by interpreting this word, which bears witness to it."

127. Ibid., 386: "We reject the false doctrine that in a particular 'hour of history' God is speaking to us directly and is revealed in direct action in the created world, for it is enthusiasm [Schwärmerei] to think that one understands the will of God without the express words of the Holy Scriptures, to which God is bound."

128. Brunner and Barth, *Natural Theology*, 67–128.

of God."[129] Revelation was bound to God who remained hidden in nature (*Deus absconditus*) but revealed himself in Jesus Christ (*Deus revelatus*). Divine revelation was therefore tied to the Scriptures and in a secondary sense to the community who proclaimed these Scriptures. God's presence and work may still be discerned in historical events and in the structures of creation yet there remained a clear and qualitative difference. Living in a fallen world meant that God's will remained, within the realm of nature, obscure and ambiguous.[130] According to Luther's two kingdom teaching God actively ordered the natural realm and gave it a life-sustaining structure. Bonhoeffer called these orders in his ethics "mandates of creation."[131] These structures could either be seen as crutches, enabling fallen humanity to survive, or as a God-given privilege and gift. In his own writings Bonhoeffer increasingly preferred to speak of "orders of preservation,"[132] thus emphasizing humans' responsibility towards creation rather than their right to dominate. The Bethel confession listed the following orders: the sexes, marriage, the family, the *Volk*, property (employment and industry), and civil rule. It also insisted that civil rule and the church had to remain separate thus making the notion of a national church, in which the church became the soul of the state, an impossibility. "We reject any attempt to set up the visible rule of God on earth, through the church, as interference with the state's order of authority."[133]

Again, this statement clearly distanced itself from the German Christian vision but equally rejected the aspirations of Religious Socialism. The writers made clear that these listed orders "are not the orders of the original creation"[134] but were provisional structures provided by God to a fallen world until the end of all things.

Another important Lutheran theological feature was the dichotomy between law and gospel. For some German Christians, i.e., Wilhelm Stapel,[135] discerning what was God's law was a matter of proper interpretation. They embarked on this interpretive task by comparing favorably New Testament laws against Old Testament laws and ended by equating *Volk*-law

---

129. Bonhoeffer, *Berlin*, 384.

130. Ibid., 385: "Only in obedience to the word of God in the Scriptures can we know the Creator, and not through any interpretation of events in the world."

131. Bonhoeffer, *Ethics*, 390; *Berlin*, 387–92.

132. Bonhoeffer, *Creation*, 140.

133. Bonhoeffer, *Berlin*, 416.

134. Ibid., 387.

135. Reimer, *Emanuel Hirsch and Paul Tillich Debate*, 211: "For Stapel, the nation had its own God-ordained order, 'a law of life which, in conformity to its nature, defined its inner and outer form, its cult, its ethos, its system of government, its law.'"

with God's law. Emanuel Hirsch even spoke of a unique "German Nomos and Logos." Part of this interpretative process was the remolding of God's law into the ideological presuppositions of the person engaged in the act of interpretation. The Bethel Confession responded to this methodology by upholding Luther's law versus gospel distinction. A proper understanding of the law can only be gained through the revealed word of God and not through changeable opinions of individuals or mysteriously deep rooted notions of a particular *Volk* or *Völker*.

The theology of the Bethel Confession was faithful to the sixteenth century Lutheran Confessions but employed the language of its own time to forge a message which sought to address contemporary problems. It maintained the typical Lutheran distinction between the two governments, law and gospel, the hidden and the revealed God and sought to defend these tenets against false or distorted interpretations.

It was a significant achievement in the midst of these critical years. The Bethel Confession's clear and explicit rejection of anti-Semitic racism was remarkable. "We reject the false doctrine that would make the crucifixion of Christ the fault of the Jewish people alone, as though other people and races had not crucified him. All races and peoples, even the mightiest, share in the guilt for his death and become guilty of it every day anew, when they commit outrage against the Spirit of grace."[136]

The writers distanced themselves from the notion of a nationalistic German church whose membership consisted of Christians of the Aryan race. "The fellowship of those who belong to the church is determined not by blood nor, therefore, by race, but by the Holy Spirit and baptism."[137] What Barmen lacked, a clear renunciation of Anti-Semitism, was clearly stated in the first draft of the Bethel Confession where section VI.6 bore the title, "The Church and the Jews."[138]

In spite of its historical obscurity the Bethel Confession was a significant statement and an important attempt to respond to the political upheaval of the time. It also showed that the assessment of McGrath, who links the German church's failure to oppose the Nazis to the "inadequacies of Luther's political thought,"[139] is at best a tentative one, at its worst misleading.

---

136. Bonhoeffer, *Berlin*, 398.
137. Ibid., 419.
138. Ibid., 416–21.
139. McGrath, *Reformation Thought*, 207–8.

Confessing Church (Karl Barth)

The rise of the German Christian movement with its outright political agenda of integrating (*Gleichschaltung*) the church with the state prompted the formation of the Pastor's Emergency League under the leadership of Pastor Martin Niemöller. Members of this group (in January 1934 about 40 per cent of all Protestant pastors) were in opposition to the nazification of the church and stood by the Lutheran confessions. This loose and diverse group, supported at that time by two intact territorial churches[140] that had resisted being drafted into the German Evangelical Church met at Barmen in May 1934 and signed a declaration whose principal author was Karl Barth.

Karl Barth's message to a politically entangled church, torn between religious nationalism and religious socialism, was to reconsider its true calling. For Barth this meant the task of engaging with God's word rather than seeking "God elsewhere than in Jesus Christ and seek Christ elsewhere than in the Holy Scriptures."[141] The church's calling was not politics but theology. The German church historian Klaus Scholder wrote: "The historical significance of the Theological Declaration lay primarily in the fact that it did not make it necessary to raise the political questions which at that time were overpowering. Herein lay its liberating power, and also the mystery of its effect. And if I understand the Barmen message rightly in this respect, this is still an important point: that the church did not allow any political theme—whether appropriate or inappropriate—to be forced on it."[142]

Karl Barth was fully aware that a totally detached and neutral theology was not possible. Every theology had to engage with the world and was therefore always also political. What Barth resisted was making politics a priority. What, he asked, drove the reflective process? Was theology driven by political opportunities and constraints or was the church's political response motivated by a theological understanding? Barth sought to base the church on theological grounds rather than on political ones. Consequently, when the church needed to protest against political policies it had to be motivated by theological grounds rather than political approval or disapproval. The church's role was not just to consider policies in the light of humane pragmatism or cultured realism, but to ask the deeper questions such as whether policies were in conformity with God's word or were in fact, heretical.[143]

---

140. So-called intact churches were territorial churches that refused to be drawn into the *Deutsche Evangelische Kirche*.

141. Scholder, *Requiem*, 79.

142. Ibid., 80.

143. Reimer, *Emanuel Hirsch and Paul Tillich Debate*, 77. Hirsch wrote in 1934: "For German Christians all conversations with Karl Barth are impossible. He calls us 'wild heretics.'"

The Barmen declaration understood itself as a theological statement addressing a current issue rather than a confession. It consisted of six short theses. Each began with a Scripture reference followed by a brief affirmative statement and subsequent repudiation. Keith Clements provided a useful summery of the six theses. For the sake of clarity, it is worth noting more fully the "We repudiate . . ." section of the first two statements.

1. Jesus Christ alone is God's Word of revelation; *We repudiate the false teaching that the church can and must recognize yet other happenings and powers, images and truths as divine revelation . . .*

2. Christ's forgiveness and sanctifying grace cover all areas of life; *We repudiate the false teaching that there are areas of our life in which we belong not to Jesus Christ but another lord . . .*

3. the church is to conform to the law of Christ and is not to be subjected to ideological or political pressures in its order or teaching,

4. its ministry has to reflect the servant-pattern of Christ;

5. church and state are not interchangeable in their roles;

6. the Word and work of the Lord can never be conscripted into alien purposes.[144]

By affirming that Christ was the one and only revelation of God, Barmen rejected other "happenings and powers, images and truths as divine revelation alongside this one Word of God."[145]

Theses one and two are a clear rejection of any theology that attempted to construct its own view of God, based on other historical happenings and powers. Whenever this happened, Asmussen explained in his report to the church synod in 1934, "other lords than Jesus Christ, other commands than his command gain power over us. They offer themselves to us as redeemers, but they prove to be the torturers of an unredeemed world."[146] Neither Adolf Hitler nor the German Christians were directly named; nevertheless the intention of the declaration was crystal clear.

At Barmen the different groups were briefly united in their opposition. Out of Barmen emerged the Confessing Church which became one of the few places where it was possible to be critical of the Nazi regime. Neither Barmen nor Bethel was able to unite theologically the various and diverse groups of

---

144. Clements, *What Freedom?*, 73.
145. Scholder, *Requiem*, 90.
146. Ibid., 91.

the Lutheran and Reformed churches. Confessional theologians rejected the Barmen text, noting that it did not address the questions of natural theology, the order of creation, and the ethos of Christian action. In spite of the intended theological thrust Barmen and the Confessing Church became a synonym for political opposition against the Nazi regime. Helmut Gollwitzer, a member of the Confessing Church, recalls: "Reich bishop Müller once said, 'My goal is that there will be only National Socialists, above the pulpit and below the pulpit.' Our goal had to be that those above and below the pulpit would see clearly the contradiction between Nazism and Christianity."[147]

What Barmen and subsequently the Confessing Church made clear was that a line had to be drawn between truth and heresy. The efforts of the German Christians to reshape the gospel and to turn Jesus into a Nazi hero figure could no longer be viewed as another possible variant of the Christian church. Bonhoeffer wrote about the Barmen Declaration that, "there can only be a Yes or a No."[148] The significance of the Barmen Declaration was not only that it gave the church a brief euphoric moment of unity but in the historic watershed it represented. The implicit claim of Barmen was that the nature of the true church was not constituted by government decree but only through its faithful allegiance to Jesus Christ and the Scriptures.

The supporters of Barmen viewed the declaration as a timely and necessary expression of the *status confessionis*. Historically this term was used by sixteenth century theologians who sought to differentiate between neutral matters (*adiaphora*)—issues that did not endanger the gospel—from matters that did and therefore demanded a confessional stand (*Bekenntnisstand*). The *status confessionis* had a certain fluidity in that what might be considered a neutral matter during a certain period could become a confessional issue in a different historical situation. For Bonhoeffer the *status confessonis* had already been reached in 1933 with the Aryran paragraph, which stipulated that only Aryans—not Jews—could become civil servants.[149] Since Lutheran pastors were civil servants this new law had serious implications for the church.

The issues at Barmen were of a theological rather than a direct political nature. The church was trying to hold its own and resisted being dominated and dragged into the political process. Ultimately the theological statements had inevitable political implications, yet in the early 1930s Barth's principal

147. Barnett, *For the Soul*, 55.
148. Ibid., 496, quoting Bonhoeffer.
149. Bonhoeffer, *Berlin*, 165 (September 1933; letter to Karl Barth): "Several of us are now very drawn to the idea of a free church.... There can be no doubt that a *status confessionis* exists, but what is the most appropriate way today to express what the confession says?—that is not clear to us."

concern was theological. He, and the Confessing Church, saw their role to be theologians and teachers rather than politicians. Nevertheless, the Nazis detected the danger of this Barthian influence on the church and classified his theology as an attempt to create a religious zone into which people could withdraw and isolate themselves from the demands of the modern state.[150]

---

150. Pangritz, "Politischer Gottesdienst," 215–47. SS Lagebericht (1934): "Eine starke Stütze hat der Pfarrernotbund an den Reformierten, die sich um den Bonner Professor Barth scharen. Die Richtung Barths muß als wirkliche Gefahr bezeichnet werden. Er schafft in seiner Theologie Inseln, auf denen Menschen sich isolieren, um so den Forderungen des heutigen Staates unter religiöser Begründung ausweichen zu können."

5

Engaging with the World

The Apolitical "Solution"—Arnold Köster

Introduction

TILLICH AND HIRSCH WERE committed to opposing viewpoints but shared an intense concern for the political process. Between the extremes of left (socialism) and right (nationalism) there was a much larger group of Christians whose commitment to any particular political persuasion was much more tentative. During the Weimar years numerous political parties had occupied the space gapping between left and right. The Nazi propaganda and government pushed these parties to the fringes or silenced them altogether. The population of Germany hoped that strong leadership would bring about the necessary changes. However, the main concern of the average person was to find ways of coping with life and the difficult economical circumstances. This retreat into the private world, where political opinions had no immediate relevance, was primarily a survival strategy.[1] Even Jews or those who had a Jewish spouse sought to maintain a semblance of normality and hoped that it would be possible to get through the crisis and to sit it out.[2]

---

1. Barnett, *For the Soul*, 74.
2. Klepper, *Unter dem Schatten*, 1133. Jochen Klepper was married to a Jew. He, his wife, and their daughter committed suicide 10 December 1942. His final entry: "Nachmittags die Verhandlung auf dem Sicherheitsdienst. Wir sterben nun—ach, auch das steht by Gott—Wir gehen heute nacht gemeinsam in den Tod. Über uns steht in den letzten Stunden das Bild des Segnenden Christus, der um uns ringt. In dessen Anblick endet unser Leben."

Dietrich Bonhoeffer and Arnold Köster

Eminent Lutheran theologians like Paul Althaus distanced themselves from the wild claims of nationalist enthusiasts, yet also cautiously welcomed the Nazi government. In a 1935 publication, Althaus interpreted the recent events as God's healing hands upon an aching nation. However, he rejected the notion that these events could be represented as a direct divine intervention.[3] Emphasizing a clear separation between the role of the state and the church, Althaus sought the middle ground. The rationale of arguing for a politically neutral ground was the hope that it would allow the church to get on with church matters as long as it refrained from political interference.

Theologians opposed to the emerging political captivity of the church rallied around the confessions of Bethel and Barmen. As a confession, the initial draft of Bethel was more overtly political than Barmen. Each confession sought to resist the influences of ideological enthusiasts who had emerged from within the ranks of the church. Barmen's main thrust was to call the church back to its theological task and mission. However, this theological stance became political simply because it was expressed at a time when a totalitarian state insisted that everything was political. Consequently, Barth and those that followed his lead became increasingly political. To many Christians the platform of the Confessing Church soon became the only possible place to resist the Nazi ideology. Nevertheless, it became increasingly difficult for the leadership of the Confessing Church to remain united.

The Nonconformist "Free" Church

Resisting state interference in a church that was historically and organizationally intertwined with the state was a complex struggle. Salaries of church officials, pastors and educators were drawn from the state treasury, academic training and accreditation and issues of ownership had complicated and entrenched ties to state government. Compared to the cumbersome Lutheran church structure it would appear that the nonconformist *Freikirche* would be more independent and free. Payments of stipends were raised locally and the recognition of theological training or qualification was not dependent on a system of state accreditation. Nevertheless, the legal recognition and protection of these relatively small faith communities were dependent on the law of the land. Thus, in practice the freedom of the free churches was constricted by their desire to preserve their public recognition, status and protection. Being mindful of political necessities and maintaining an amicable relationship to the state fell to the leadership of the *Baptistenbund*. At

---

3. Althaus, "Kirche und Staat," 15.

Engaging with the World

the local level Baptists held a wide spectrum of opinions of which there are few surviving historical records. The next section seeks to provide a sketchy overview in order to indicate the diversity of Baptist responses as they faced the challenges of that period.

Snapshots of Baptist Life

The Influence of Paul Schmidt

Schmidt was born in 1888 and studied at the Baptist seminar at Hamburg Horn during the years 1911–14 and 1919. His first pastorates were in Breslau and Zurich during which he continued to study Theology and Philosophy. In 1928 he became the editor of the Baptist publishing house and was entrusted with various tasks and functions within the Baptist Union (*Baptistenbund*). He was politically active and, joining the CSVD[4], he became a member of parliament for Berlin in 1930 until 1932. In 1935 he became the General Secretary (*Bundesdirektor*) of the Baptist Union in Germany. Schmidt was a keen observer, an able negotiator and leader. He was recognized and respected amongst other separatist church leaders.[5] His word and opinion had considerable weight and influence. In 1932 he critically judged the emergence of the Nazi regime as rather dangerous. "To the left of the church a front of brutal godlessness is being formed, to her right the state is idolized and race and blood are glorified. The left wants the destruction of Christianity and the right wants to absorb and subdue it. Both fronts are life threatening to the church."[6]

Schmidt perceived both communism and nationalism as serious dangers. Yet, once the Nazi government had been established, his understanding of Romans 13 obliged him to embrace a course of obedience and accommodation. In his capacity as General Secretary he frequently sent congratulatory telegrams to Hitler that expressed Baptist loyalty and support to *Volk* and *Führer*.

The basic message of Paul Schmidt to the member churches constituting the *Baptistenbund* was to steer a neutral and apolitical course. It was hoped that this non-confrontational strategy would assure the church's legal

---

4. The CSVD was an amalgamation of two parties, the *Christlichen Volksdienst* and the *Christlich-Sozialen Reichsvereinigung*, and was established in December 1929. The ethos of the CSVD was to pursue and support Christian policies that are free from both royalist and nationalistic tendencies.

5. From 1929 onwards he supported the Union of Evangelical Free Churches. (VEF, *Vereinigung Evangelischer Freikirchen*).

6. Zimmermann, *Zwischen Selbsterhaltung und Anpassung*, 17.

Dietrich Bonhoeffer and Arnold Köster

legitimacy and gain the church the permission to evangelize throughout the country.[7] The pragmatism of this approach was obvious in as much as the organizational livelihood of a small religious organization depended on the benevolent toleration of the state authorities. Although the word 'free' was part of their collective self-description, in practice it was the state that either granted or withheld the freedom to meet, to own property and to have a recognized and protected status within the law. The Baptist historian Strübind observed that Schmidt hoped that a united German Free Church would create a strong and credible alternative to the German church-of-the-people. He pursued this vision with the tireless energy of a church diplomat. Theologically, he embraced a dualistic interpretation of the two kingdoms that diminished the political sphere and emphasized the more urgent need to build God's church in view of the imminent return of Christ.[8]

Observations made by Dr. L. G. Champion

In September 1931 Champion, who later became the principal of Bristol Baptist College, went to Germany to complete two years of post-graduate studies. He was a student of Martin Dibelius and studied at the universities of Heidelberg and Marburg. During his stay, Champion also made contact with various Baptist communities and recorded his impressions.[9] Champion was an outsider who happened to be living in Germany from autumn 1931 until February 1934 and established contacts with local Baptist churches. He wrote about visiting a Baptist church, which involved walking a considerable distance with a preacher's son called Herr Euler. He records how the minister's wife engaged them in a conversation after the service.

> The service was fair and the communion as usual. After that we drank coffee with the minister's wife and had an argument. First of all she pitched into the Nazis and as Herr Euler was a strong Nazi this made things interesting. Some of her information was quite new to me and on one point I violently disagreed though

---

7. Zimmermann, *Selbsterhaltung und Anpassung*, 45, quoting from Paul Schmidt, *Unser Weg als Bund Evangelisch-Freikirchlicher Gemeinden in den Jahren 1941–1946* (Stuttgart: Onken, 1946), 8: "Immer wieder wurde die Frage in das Licht von Römer 13 gerückt und immer wieder wurde von neuem erkannt, daß das große Nein der Gemeinde Jesu gegenüber dem Staat und seiner Führung erst dann zu sprechen sei, wenn die Verkündigung des Evangeliums verboten werden und die persönliche christliche Lebensführung desgleichen."

8. Strübind, *Die unfreie Freikirche*, 321.

9. Champion's collected diary entries and letters are stored at the Bristol Baptist College Library.

> I did not say so. I believe it is quite a common thing here for Baptists to refrain from voting at the elections. There are difficulties of course for probably many partially support Hitler and yet because of his religious standpoint—some say definitely anti-Christian, some say, desirous of reducing the church to a mere social organization—they hesitate to do so. And the other parties do not offer a very brilliant selection. So in this position a religious belief is found as support for not voting, namely that the fate of the nation is in the hands of God who will do as He wills irrespective of the activity of men and consequently whether one votes or not the result is the same. Also among many there seems to be the thought that the End is near and so it really doesn't matter.[10]

Clearly a variety of opinions were held amongst the local Baptist community at Hassenhausen. Champion regarded some as "strong" Nazis; others however he judged as highly critical. Some advocated a policy of abstaining and justified it as leaving it in the hands of a sovereign God.

Another contact of Champion was a Baptist community in the village of Mauer. During one of his visits he was invited by a Baptist family to dinner. After dinner, he reported that his host, a Herr Martens, basically agreed with popular Anti-Semitism and claimed that "according to the Bible the Jews are laid under a curse by God on account of the death of Christ." Since the arguments were based on the authority of the Bible, Champion found it difficult to argue for a different point of view. He also noted that in 1933, many held the opinion that the Jews only got what they deserved and that this was frighteningly widespread even amongst Christians of a stricter type.

Again, these observations indicate that the Baptist spectrum of opinions and interpretations were varied and diverse. Some, like Paul Schmidt, were highly intelligent and politically active; others would have considered themselves as ordinary people reading their Bibles. Everyone's reading of Scripture and current events was shaped by their past, personal experiences and dominant opinions of the time. The turbulent events of the 1930s had a profound impact on the German people. No doubt, many Baptists were swept along by the hope and enthusiasm that the Nazis managed to conjure up. Others, who bore the responsibility of leadership, sought to steer a course of relative safety. A few, for example Arnold Köster, attempted to stand firm and argued against the rising tide of nationalism.

---

10. Champion notes, Bristol Baptist College.

Dietrich Bonhoeffer and Arnold Köster

Influences and Motivation of Köster

During the critical years prior to the outbreak of the war, Christians of all denominations struggled to respond to a rapidly changing political climate. The period of 1932 until 1936 was the time when the Nazi government established itself. These early years of the Third Reich were marked by areas of uncertainty. The churches of Germany had to adjust to the new emerging political landscape and articulate appropriate responses. With the gradual introduction of totalitarian measures, room to maneuver was drastically reduced. For the purpose of this study it is important to look at a period when ethical choices and the freedom to express these were still possible.

The following section seeks to explore the response of one Baptist minister, Arnold Köster. What did he write and preach during these critical years and how did he interpret the political events of that period? Our analysis is based on two historical sources: *Allianz* protocols and a monthly publication, the *Täufer-Bote*. The protocols are minutes of the Evangelical Alliance of Vienna. These dated records span about thirty-five years (1926 to 1960) and are kept at the archive of the Baptist Church Vienna-Mollardgasse 35.[11] The Evangelical Alliance in Vienna was at that time a regional rather than national cooperation between individual Christian leaders for the purpose of pooling resources, organizing cooperative activities, mutual discussion, edification and prayer. Most of the support and commitment for the Evangelical Alliance in Vienna came from the Baptist and Methodist churches and from Christian organizations such as the Bible Society, Salvation Army, YMCA (*CVJM*) and the *Volksmission*. Leaders of these groups met to plan and discuss organizational matters and to theologically explore either a biblical passage or a relevant topic. Notes were taken and recorded by the acting secretary in a protocol book. The detail, quality and extensiveness of these recorded minutes vary greatly. Nevertheless, since Köster regularly supported and contributed to these meetings, the surviving protocols represent an important historical record. The second source is the publications of the *Täufer-Bote*. An almost entire record of this publication has been electronically preserved by Johannes Fleischer's grandson and entrusted to church historian Franz Graf-Stuhlhofer.[12]

---

11. An unpublished electronic version has been made available to me by Franz Graf-Stuhlhofer. References are formatted as: Allianz, date (of relevant entry).

12. References to the Täufer-Bote are formatted as; Täufer-Bote, year, number/month, page.

The Baptist Herald (Täufer-Bote)

The Readership

The December edition of 1931 contained a map[13] entitled the '*Donauländer*'. The drawing indicates the geographical area of its distribution. To the west the map contained a small part of Germany and the whole of Austria. To the east were the shores of the Black Sea and in between were the so called *Donauländer* (Danube countries). Little triangles mark the places of either a Baptist fellowship or mission station in the countries of Austria, Czechoslovakia, Hungary, Yugoslavia, Romania and Bulgaria.

Prior to the First World War large sections of these areas were part of the Austrian-Hungarian empire. In the distant past, Austrian and German rulers had actively encouraged emigration to these border lands from the German speaking heartland. Policies and laws that granted emigrants the rights to become landholders attracted pioneers who had no such prospects in their homelands. Other communities, including some Anabaptists, moved into these areas in the sixteenth century with the hope of finding tolerance and respite from persecution. Some Austrian Lutheran communities were forcefully moved into these areas by a number of Catholic rulers.

After the collapse of the Austrian-Hungarian Empire many of these eastern German-speaking settlements remained intact. These communities were eager to preserve the German language, culture and traditions. Central to the endeavor of preserving a German cultural identity was their protestant faith, their German Bibles, hymns and church life. In the aftermath of World War I the political existence of these settlements became more fragile, yet deep roots had been established and many chose to remain. No doubt many of these German-speaking communities longed for a less uncertain existence and welcomed for that reason the arrival of the German *Wehrmacht* in the 1940s.

The readership of the *Täufer-Bote* was a scattered people who shared a common language and Baptist outlook. It also included Christian workers and missionaries who worked amongst these communities and sought to bring the gospel to the other peoples of Eastern Europe. These missionaries did not restrict their work and ministry to the German speaking language group.

The demand for the paper was sufficiently high to ensure its continued publication during difficult years. In an article in 1934 Köster provides a little insight into some of the responses and comments the editors received from their readership. "Letters have been sent from distant places and

---

13. Täufer-Bote, 1931, No. 12, 13.

countries. Some urge us to keep going and not to grow weary but others offer harsh criticism."[14]

The Editors

The three prominent names are Arnold Köster, Johannes Fleischer and Karl Füllbrandt. The editors of the *Täufer-Bote* were located in Vienna (Köster and Füllbrandt) and in Bucharest (Fleischer). The monthly paper sought to gather from and bring news to the varied eastern locations, provide encouragement, biblical edification and comment theologically on current issues and developments considered to be of interest to the remote German speaking communities. Since Austria remained separate from Germany until April 1938 the editors were able to observe and critically comment on the political changes within Germany. The *Täufer-Bote* continued to be published until 1942. Until December 1934 Köster appeared to have acted as a chief editor, for the next seven years this task fell to Johannes Fleischer. During 1935 the publication, printing and distribution of the *Täufer-Bote* was gradually relocated from Vienna to Bucharest.

Köster's Political and Theological Analysis

Köster was convinced that the world was going through an intense crisis. In the 1931 November edition he wrote, "It is a fearful thing to live in a world that is shaken to the core by acts of God's wrath and judgments. We are afraid in a world that has been delivered up."[15] The term "delivered up" (*dahingegeben*) was a clear allusion to Romans 1:26.

Due to the widespread and distant readership of the *Täufer-Bote*, Köster's world and interests were not just reduced to a narrow German perspective. His scope included both the east and the west of Europe. The east was the place where German speaking communities had carved out their livelihoods but also maintained many international links and frequently received support from American Baptists. The very first edition of the *Täufer-Bote* contained a short article entitled "Greetings to the German Baptist Churches in North America."[16] Its content was an expression of gratitude for the help communities along the Danube had received, during the post-war years. Their support financed missionaries and en-

---

14. Täufer-Bote, 1934, No. 6–7, 3.
15. Täufer-Bote, 1931, No. 11, 1.
16. Täufer-Bote, 1930, No. 1, 4.

abled various fellowships to acquire and build houses for the purpose of meeting and worshipping together. In spite of this far flung network of people and communities, their common and uniting feature was the German language and culture.

Köster's Risky This-Is-That Application

A characteristic feature of Köster's political analysis was applying creative interpretive links between the world of the Bible and the world he inhabited. McClendon claimed that the "this-is-that" methodology was a shared feature of many separatist groups[17] and churches that had to carve out their existence outside magisterial church structures. A common concern of these communities was to become the true church by modeling their teaching, practice and lives on the early church as it was represented in the New Testament accounts. Thus, these radical groups stubbornly insisted that believers' baptism was not only biblical but had to be "this-is-that." Consequently *this* infant baptism can never be *that* baptism as it was recorded in the New Testament. Köster was deeply rooted in the Baptist way of life. Beyond the relatively brief history of the German Baptists, who traced their origins to 1834, he was also well acquainted with Anabaptist leaders and documents from the sixteenth century. These diverse groups often reached different conclusions, but were nevertheless united by their high regard for the Scriptures and their desire to make it the organizing principle for their communal lives and practice.[18]

Critics and opponents soon called these radical faith communities "enthusiasts" (*Schwärmer*). Theirs was the ardent desire "to finish what Luther had only begun."[19] They resisted being squeezed into the mould of the world and were consequently severely persecuted. Their courage and determination was largely motivated by a vision of an alternative world, which they had gained from reading their Bibles. To them this new biblical worldview challenged the assumptions of their contemporaries. Their separatism expressed itself in a counter cultural perspective that resisted compromise and constantly sought to relate every aspect of daily life to their reading of the Bible. The danger of this prophetic methodology was that a this-is-that interpretation has the tendency to assume the same weight and authority of an Old Testament prophecy that began with the formula, "This is what the Lord says."[20] How can a daring

---

17. McClendon, *Ethics*, 32–33.
18. Murray, *Biblical Interpretation*.
19. Holl, *Gesammelte Aufsätze*, 423.
20. Exod 4:22, etc.

this-is-that interpretation of a preacher be heard and weighed by others? A close look at one of Köster's articles shows how Köster himself understood his own calling and how he applied this hermeneutical method. The article was published in the 1930 March edition of the *Täufer-Bote* and at one point commented on the Bolshevik threat.[21] The dangers and suppressive measures of Russian communism under Stalin were at that time an international concern. Due to their geographical proximity the population of the *Donauländer* were especially affected and troubled.

The article's biblical reference and starting point was Isaiah 53:1, "Who has believed our report? And to whom has the arm of the LORD been revealed?" Köster began by building a link to the prophet's dilemma by claiming that Isaiah's problem had been shared by every faithful preacher ever since. First, because God's people were engaged in a risky faith. It was their belief that the spoken human word actually made the eternal living word audible. Thus, an insight and interpretation of God's mighty deeds on earth was provided. Yet, secondly, like Isaiah every faithful preacher also made the painful discovery that God's children, even though they heard the preached word, were often not attentive and were thus prevented from listening and understanding. This meant, Köster argued, that even though the people of God walked through the midst of complex events they neither saw nor experienced in the unfolding of events the mighty arm of God. Nevertheless, God's prophets had to speak God's word. They had to utter their daring proclamations and point both to and beyond the daily happenings in order to warn their people. They needed to continue to encounter the God who was at work in this world.

Köster felt a great affinity with the Old Testament prophets and understood his own sense of calling in a similar way. He saw himself as standing in the tradition of the old prophets and sought to speak God's word courageously. Important parts of the prophetic task, as he understood it, was to point at current events and interpret these as God being at work here on earth. Köster insisted that God was active in the most surprising and outrageous places. God often employed tools for his purposes which were, to God's people, shocking and deeply disturbing. Köster noted that God frequently challenged established assumptions. He then applied this argument by making an interpretive link into the real—and for many of his readers existentially frightening—world of politics.

> If God were to bring judgment on earth with his heavenly hosts, we would be impressed—yet when God uses the Russian Bolsheviks as a rod against a godless and Christ-less

---

21. Täufer-Bote, 1930, No. 3, 1–2.

Christianity—then everyone is in uproar. "This is a hard saying who can hear it!" We cannot understand that God can use an anti-god state, turning it into a servant for his purposes. We cannot comprehend that the persecutions of Christians in Russia are terrible indictments, the worst ever spoken on this earth: against Christianity. Why do we not hear what God says? Why do we not see his mighty arm? Because God speaks and acts in a spirit of lowliness.[22]

Köster's methodology led him to reach surprising conclusions that frequently challenged the public opinions of his day. In this case he resisted calling the Bolshevik regime either good or evil. He attempted to go beyond a mere moral assessment and challenged his readers to see in the political realities God's hand and call to rethink and above all to repent. Three months later, Köster responded to criticisms he had received concerning this particular this-is-that interpretation. Some readers did not agree with the notion that Bolshevism can be equated with God's judgment. Interestingly, his defense was that they (Johannes Fleischer and himself) were not the only ones who had offered such a reading, "others have also written about it."[23] He then moved on to point his critics to other biblical passages[24] that supported their argument. Finally, he sought to clarify that even though Bolshevism may be used as a tool of God this does not imply that everything the Bolsheviks do was of God. Neither does being used by God as a tool exempt one from being judged for one's own transgressions.

A reading of the *Allianz* protocols reveals that although Köster's contributions were appreciated by the group they also triggered debate, critical comments and questions. In a 1942 lecture the Methodist Bragmann challenged Köster's daring this-is-that interpretation and use of the Old Testament. In his lecture on the prophet Habakkuk Bragmann argued for a more careful and nuanced typological use of the Bible.[25]

Köster was not above criticism but felt nonetheless compelled to interpret the Bible prophetically to a readership and community that exercised the freedom to differ. Listeners heard what he had to say, yet ultimately, as was the case with the prophets of old, drew their own conclusions. Motivated by a sense of a prophetic watchman duty, Köster attempted to clarify and root his arguments further into the biblical texts and sought, wherever possible, to reach a shared consensus with others. As a Baptist Köster was

---

22. Täufer-Bote, 1930, No. 3, 2.
23. Täufer-Bote, 1930, No. 6, 5.
24. He mentions Darius (Isa 45:1) and Nebuchadnezzar (Jer 25:9; 43:10).
25. Graf-Stuhlhofer, *Öffentliche Kritik*, 100–101.

very much part of a community accustomed to embody biblical faith and a biblical worldview. Karl Barth's rediscovery of the Word of God as not just a mere document of ancient times, but a word that always addressed the present time, narrowed the gap between academic theology and a typical Baptist approach to the Bible. The *Allianz* protocols show that Köster and the other Christian leaders were acquainted with Barth's dialectical theology and influence. During a 1957 lecture, Köster referred to Barth's influence as "a wonderful time of spring that helped the prophetic word to blossom, followed by the onset of Nazi mildew."[26]

From as early as 1930 Köster sought to comment prophetically on the political and social upheavals of Germany. Convicted by his own sense of calling he felt compelled to offer daring and risky interpretations which at times may have appeared too simple or too exaggerated. As it happens, history has to a great extent justified his points of view which he consistently held throughout this turbulent period.

Two Historical Case Studies

The next section seeks to illustrate Köster's consistency and to show some of the key tenets that constituted Köster's basic message to the Christian church. The first example is an article published in the January 1932 edition of the *Täufer-Bote*, the second is a lecture Köster gave a decade later in December 1941 during an *Allianz* gathering in Vienna. Although separated by 10 years, both records share a number of similarities and illustrate what were the thematic features of Köster's core message. The aim of the next two sections is to show how Köster sought to forge and shape a Christian response to the political events and realities of the 1930s. The final section offers an analysis of four key political concepts frequently used by Köster in his writings and lectures.

1932, Dark and Mysterious

The January 1932 article bore the title "If You Had Known, Even You . . . !"[27] and was a prophetic exposition of Luke 19:41–44. Biblical exposition and political analysis of the German situation were woven together. In 1932 the Nazis were not yet in government but already had, as a political movement,

---

26. Ibid., 113. Köster said this 4 April 1957.
27. Täufer-Bote, 1932, No. 1, 1–3.

considerable influence and appeal to the wider German population. The other prominent movement within the Christian scene was the German Christians.

Köster began the article emphasizing the biblical role of the watchman (Ezekiel 33), whose difficult prophetic service, he claimed, was still urgently needed. He then contrasted the prophetic message, which was rooted in God's word, with the empty, self-serving propaganda of many churches and likened these to words that merely sought to fill an inner void. According to Köster there was much talk about God and his salvation (*Heil*) yet never was there a time when God's Word had become so rare. "It is terrifying to know that religious and pious talk does not always have to be God's word, but often is mere godless human chatter."[28] Köster admitted that it was impossible to claim that his own words were actually God's words—they too could easily be mere human talk. Nevertheless, he felt compelled to risk prophetic interpretation.

He then explored the first century context Jesus was addressing in Luke 19. At that time Jerusalem was dominated by a number of contentious issues that had created a state of tension (*Unfriede*). The first issue was religious discontent, which he exemplified by the fierce struggle between the Pharisee and the Sadducee parties and again by the massive divide that existed between the scribes and the common people. The second issue was social discontent between the rich and the poor, a topic Jesus himself often addressed. Third, there was political discontent: many Jews were outraged by the Roman presence and the party of the Zealots attracted many followers. Those that did not share their revolutionary vision and collaborated with the Roman system were hated and despised.

Building "this-is-that" links Köster asked: "Is that not the very face of our own time, especially the time of the German people?"[29] He then traced religious discontent to the many different religious churches, groups and sects, each claiming for themselves to represent the truth of the gospel. Social discontent was equally rife and it was disturbing to see that there were those who could afford to live without having to work while the vast majority of the population was unable to find work. Köster argued that this was terrible, yet what would be even more terrible was for the church of God to remain silent in the face of such injustice. Political discontent had reached massive proportions. Throughout the German *Vaterland* a storm raged against the slavery imposed on this and future generations by foreign powers. Köster's frank description expressed a sympathetic appreciation of their discontent. However, he urged his readers to maintain a critical distance

---

28. Täufer-Bote, 1932, No. 1, 1.
29. Täufer-Bote, 1932, No. 1, 2.

to these political groups promising liberation. The appeal of the German zealots was powerful and had led many to fill the ranks of the national socialists. Yet these present day zealots, like the first century ones, had little patience with those who refused to take part in this gathering storm. Their narrow vision reduced everything into simplistic either / or. Mere bystanders were branded as a modern equivalent of the ancient tax collectors and were considered to be traitors against the people (*Volk*). Köster finished the section with the words, "The path towards liberation is already soaked with the blood of brothers and in the coming days the shedding of blood will increase. Alas, there is no peace in the land!"[30]

He then continued his article with a plea for repentance. Köster reminded his readers that when Jesus spoke these words (Luke 19) he was overcome by sadness and wept over Jerusalem. Jesus was not just enraged by the blindness of the religious, social and political parties of his day, he was also deeply moved. Like Jeremiah in the Old Testament Jesus foresaw the national catastrophe and as in the days of Jeremiah words of warnings were not heeded. Opportunities for repentance were tragically missed. Köster proceeded to apply the this-is-that methodology: "We are under the distinct impression that neither our people nor the nations of our present time understand 'this your day.' . . . The time has come again for the people of God to weep. . . . The German people and all other nations don't understand 'this your day'. The catastrophe is unavoidable for this world and humanity."[31]

Köster's diagnosis was stark and final. He seemed to leave little room for hope. However, this pessimism appeared to be a deliberate use of Old Testament prophetic language. The prophets often pronounced seeming final condemnation in order to prompt the people to explore possibilities that could arise through the catharsis of repentance. To them, reversals of events were linked to and dependent on human responses to God's word. Köster continued his analysis of the contemporary situation by linking hope with the urgent need of a change of heart. He did this by pointing to Luke 19:44. Jerusalem did not know that it was their time of visitation yet would Germany? Would the world realize that this too was the time of its visitation? The word visitation in German (*Heimsuchung*) is a combination of two words; the noun "home" and the verb "to search." Köster extensively explored this semantic link by pointing out that visitation was a time of great distress but it was also a time when God actively searched for his people seeking to bring them home. Thus the most important question of this time was neither the

---

30. Täufer-Bote, 1932, No. 1, 2.
31. Täufer-Bote, 1932, No. 1, 2.

Engaging with the World

social nor the nationalist question but, what Köster called, the God question: the God who was both judging and searching for his people.

In the final part of the article Köster expressed his deep concern. Contrary to popular expressions of hope and enthusiasm he was filled with a sense that the people were blind and lacked understanding. He concluded that the central issue was ignored by German socialism which had become the hope of salvation for the people. The other group which had also ignored that core question was National Socialism. His verdict was severe:

> They stormed past with a defiant spirit and incredible impudence while the mass of the people, drunk and hypnotized, hoped that "this day would bring salvation. *Heil! Heil!*—and still there is no *Heil!*" Even the church—in still greater blindness—walks past the question of God while its representatives are dressed in holy and pious garb. The Catholic Church and the Protestant Church and the . . . ! He who has ears, let him hear! 1932! Dark and mysterious it lies before us, and into it we walk with trepidation. We have to. Despair is at our side. The alert church of God in her role as a prophet of God is burdened with the needs of this our time.[32]

In 1932 the future was dark and mysterious for Köster. This rather pessimistic assessment clashed with a growing nationalistic euphoria, but was also shared by others. What made Köster's stance interesting was its consistency and its practical and pastoral application.

1941, Obadiah and Typos

The title of the 1941 lecture was "The Message of Obadiah for the Church Today."[33] The attendance of the *Allianz* meeting consisted of eighteen named persons and "a few others." Miss Gertrud Hoffmann agreed at that meeting to serve as acting secretary and to take the minutes of the meeting. The records provide a short summary of the meeting and a detailed record of Köster's lecture.

He began the lecture by raising the more general question whether the Old Testament was in any way still relevant for the church today. He noted that many churches had begun to use Old Testament texts selectively, choosing to focus only on certain passages. At a time when some theologians, persuaded by the Nazi's anti-Semitism, disregarded the Jewish

---

32. Täufer-Bote, 1932, No. 1, 2–3.
33. Allianz, 8 December 1941.

Scriptures, Köster insisted that they were indeed God's word. He would rather stand with the apostles and Jesus than fanciful theologians. Since the apostles considered themselves connected to and united with the prophets and the whole of Jewish Scriptures, the church also needed to regard them as God's word. It was thus impossible to separate the New from the Old Testament simply because they were organically linked. Köster then drew attention to what he considered was a shared methodology to all those present at the meeting: the typological use and interpretation of Old and New Testament texts. He cited as examples Abraham's and Isaac's experience on Mount Moriah—which points to Golgotha—and Adam who was a type of the second Adam, Jesus Christ.

Köster then began to apply the typological or 'this-is-that' interpretation in his exposition of the minor prophet Obadiah. Edom, he argued, was not just a group of ancient historical people, the descendants of Esau. Edom was a typos or representative for the kingdom of the world, for the nation state (*des Staates schlechthin*). In the Old Testament these types had a fluid quality, Köster claimed, and were often used with great liberty by the prophets. A worldly state could be represented by mighty Babylon but also by a comparatively small nation like Edom. Yet, characteristically they were defined as: "vessels [structures or systems] that are inspired from below. At this point it is vital to be mindful of the dual nature of every nation state (*Weltstaat*). It has authority (*Obrigkeit*) because God wills it so. Woe to us, without the nation state and its ordering power, woe to us, when no authority stems and resists wanton human sin. . . . But [let us also remember that] the prince of this world is always eager to use this tool for his own wicked purposes which are exactly not God's will."[34]

The contrasting type in Obadiah was Jacob who represented the church of God. Köster argued that God's calling on Israel was a calling to be different. They were to become God's dwelling place on earth and were therefore a *typos* of the church of God, which is *ecclesia*—called out. Tragically Israel resisted that calling. They wanted to be like the other nations and to have, like them, their own king. Ultimately it was Israel's own failure that led to the destruction of their nation. Köster asked, "How much of modern Judaism is Israel?" He answered by drawing from Romans chapters 9–11 the insight that however misshaped the vessel might have become, however unsuitable to reflect God's glory, the people of Israel were still God's elect and he would not desert them. These were remarkable statements at a time when anti-Semitism and total obedience to the state had become the dominant propaganda message.

34. Ibid.

An important feature of Köster's typological interpretation was the reminder that Israel failed, because rather than being God's dwelling place on earth, it chose to focus on political ambition. This led him to elaborate on what he termed the overarching theme: the dichotomy between nation states of this world and the kingdom of God (*Weltstaat oder Gottesreich*). "Who should be in charge of the world?" Köster asked. "Should it be humans that take control in arrogant self glorification or should it be God?"[35] Obadiah's message was that God would judge Edom's arrogance. This led him to conclude that all self serving glorification of worldly nation states (*Weltstaat*) were under God's judgment. Therefore, the church must resist collaboration with the state. God's church, Köster insisted, was to remain distant. Clarity of sight was not gained by mixing in and by being absorbed in current political activities. God's people would only see clearly if they remained at a critical distance.

Part of the clarity gained through deliberate distancing, was the insight that a nation state's time of judgment had become imminent when it proudly asked, "Who can bring me down to the ground?"[36] Once such haughty claims were uttered, the church's task was to "stand before God as high priests." This priestly task was the task of the faithful watchman. Rather than stepping into the mist and fog of the time and becoming confused, it was better to be on the lookout and to bring vital words of warning. Faithfulness to that task was to bring God's people sleepless nights and fearful hearts. Yet, the arrogant claims of their leaders were bound to bring about inevitable consequences. As a watchman, Köster was painfully aware of the fact that "God will claim the blood of our people! We cannot help it if people refuse to repent and convert. But if we do not do our duty and service for our people we would act irresponsibly."[37] The sad role of the watchman prophet was to spoil the party. During times when people celebrated, the prophets brought messages of doom and gloom. Set in the context of 1941, when the German armies had gone from one success to another, Köster's comments were a message of doom at a time of apparent unstoppable success.

In Obadiah, God's judgment on Edom was caused "because of the violence against your brother Jacob."[38] This led Köster to conclude that judgment was triggered when God's people were being violated. Yet, even though God responded and acted on behalf of his people, God's people were not exempt from the terrible consequences of divine judgment. Köster argued that there

---

35. Ibid.
36. Obadiah 3.
37. Allianz, 8 December 1941.
38. Obadiah 10.

was no salvation from judgment but only a salvation through judgment. The church of God captivated by oppressive powers of the state *(Weltstaat)* ought to interpret its condition as an indication for the approaching judgment of God. Quoting Isaiah 10, Köster made the point that the sovereign God was free to use other nations or national states as tools for his acts of judgment. These states may become God's own rod of anger; nevertheless, these nations dare not go too far. Addressing the thorny issue of the Jews he said: "It can be said quite definitely, that the German nation, the German state with its hegemony has become God's rod against Israel and Christendom. But here is the danger: the German state trespasses the limits that God himself has set. The state has gone beyond what God permits."[39]

Köster both justified and condemned the actions of the national state against the Jews. He sought to strengthen his argument by drawing attention to the fate of six hundred thousand Germans who had lived in the Volga region of Russia.[40] According to the information available at the time, Köster concluded that the removal of the people and the cruel treatment that they had endured—the clubbing to death of women and children—was instigated by people who "ninety percent were Jews." Even though the factual accuracy of this statement is doubtful it is interesting that Köster argued firstly, not to yield to feelings of revenge and secondly, to be mindful of the limits God had set not just for his people but also for every national state.

Köster's final section took comfort in the fact that "the kingdom will be the Lord's."[41] God's kingdom outlasts the kingdoms of Edom and all its current manifestations. In spite of Jacob's weakness and Edom's strength, in the end God will rule. The people of God may rejoice in their role and privilege, yet this was no cause to gloat over the people of Israel. Now Israel may be covered with the veil of Moses but one day that veil will be removed and they will see.

---

39. Allianz, 8 December 1941.

40. Following the Russian Revolution, the Volga German Autonomous Soviet Socialist Republic (*Autonome Sozialistische Sowjet-Republik der Wolga*) was established in 1924, and it lasted until 1942. Its capital was Engels, known as "Pokrovsk" (*Kosakenstadt* in German) before 1931. When Hitler invaded the Soviet Union, Stalin worried that the Volga Germans might collaborate with them. On 28 August 1941, he dissolved the Volga-German ASSR and ordered the immediate relocation of ethnic Germans, both from the Volga and from a number of other traditional areas of settlement. These were stripped of their land and houses, and moved eastwards to Kazakhstan in Soviet Central Asia, Altai Krai in Siberia, and other remote areas. Similar deportations happened for other ethnic groups, including Poles, North Caucasian Muslim ethnic groups, Kalmyks, Balts and Crimean Tatars. In 1942 nearly all the able-bodied German population was conscripted to the labor army. About one third did not survive the labor camps.

41. Obadiah 21.

In the mean time we, as the New Testament people of God, can only think and feel of the people of Israel as the great apostle Paul has done in his letter to the Romans. "We can only think of them with the same trembling love he felt for them."[42]

Analysis: World & Politics

In 1932 the Nazis had not yet risen to power. By 1941 the efforts and the successes of the Third Reich were at their zenith. Köster's critical evaluation of the National Socialists remained consistent throughout. His later comments had to take account of the historical changes and were therefore slightly more guarded in their nature. The Nazi government had become the governing authority (*Obrigkeit*). Köster had to take this into account and used it to deliver a prophetic interpretation and challenge. God may use a national state as his tool but so could the prince of this world, the devil. In neither case was it possible for a state to abdicate responsibility. It, and its leaders and people, were obliged to act within specific God-given limits.

Köster argued for demythologizing the role and dignity of the national state. Its role was to maintain order and prevent chaos, yet entrusted with this task its humble role was to be a mere tool. At its best it was of use to God, at its worst it was exploited by the demonic. Köster viewed the world and human political endeavors as an arena where both the divine and the demonic forces were locked into an ongoing struggle. In a 1932 lecture he asked whether the demonic could ever be overcome.[43] To Köster the activities of the demonic, or Satan, were focused on finding suitable vessels that allowed the demonic to incarnate itself on earth. He was convinced that the demonic desired to become concrete reality on earth and argued that the temptation story of Jesus in the desert exemplified the characteristics of this strategy. The demonic manifested itself in the social, political and religious realms and in the vain hope that human effort can bring about appropriate solutions and ultimate worldly salvation *(Heil)*. The social issue, represented by turning stones into loaves of bread, was in itself a legitimate concern. Köster took issue with a church that remained silent in the face of social injustice, yet he tempered this by stating that "this issue is, until the end, under the curse of God and can therefore never be utterly solved. All attempts to gain an existence of material security are of a demonic kind."[44]

---

42. Allianz, 8 December 1941.

43. Allianz, 6 March 1932. The only available record is a 500 word summary of Köster's lecture contained in the minutes.

44. Ibid.

Government was a legitimate and necessary structure, yet when politics were used to bring about the kingdom of God by laws and policies, the *Weltstaat* became susceptible to the demonic forces from below. Attempts to bring about Gods' kingdom through religious piety based on human effort were represented by the third temptation.

To Köster, this world and its ideological movements were motivated by a sense of longing for God's kingdom. Frustrated by its absence, the kingdoms of the world attempted to bring about God's kingdom, yet by doing that they unwittingly became willing tools of Satan. In an article in 1933 Köster wrote: "Unable to tear the longing for God's kingdom out of the human breast, he [Satan] urges humans not to wait any longer—but to help themselves in their own sinful and pious power. Even Christianity is persuaded to use its power in order to heave a stuck-in-the-mud world out of it. The calls to rally behind the task are getting more urgent and strident every day."[45]

Rather than be swept along by strident calls to unite and support political movements and solutions, Köster urged his readers and listeners to maintain a critical distance. He was convinced that during this present epoch, prior to the return of Christ, the demonic would never be overcome. Thus, with respect to the world, "no immunity against the demonic can be gained. All there is, is God with us and the obligation to take the demonic seriously."[46]

Köster's analysis of the world and its political forces guarded him, and those who were persuaded by him, against political enthusiasm of any sort. It acted as a mental shield against wild claims of building a better world through human programs and structures. Within this construct a positive political system was one that embraced its own ambivalence and limited role. Addressing the systems and trends of his own time, Köster was highly critical of a popular enthusiasm, whose hope and firm belief was in a certain leader who had come to power through popular opinion and was elevated to the status of a "savior."[47] Such worship, he argued, was more akin to the Caesar cult of the Roman Empire, hinted at in the book of Revelation and referred to as "Satan's throne."[48] The subtle difference was that Christians of the first century were fully aware of the clash between God's claim and the claim of Caesar whilst in 1933 this form of idolatry expressed itself in "the

---

45. Täufer-Bote, 1933, No. 1, 2.
46. Allianz, 6 March 1932.
47. Täufer-Bote, 1932, No. 6–7, 3.
48. Rev 2:12–17.

Engaging with the World

cult of the people (*völkischen*), nation, patriotism with all its paraphernalia"[49] and was pursued with great vigor under the cover of Christendom.

Köster was careful to acknowledge that every state or *Obrigkeit* was, in his words, "double faced."[50] Worldly authority had the potential to be either a tool in God's hand or a tool of Satan. He appeared reluctant to explore this issue in detail and resisted getting tied into theological categories such as Luther's teaching on the two kingdoms. Nevertheless, his frank admission and repeated insistence that the demonic was active in worldly events actually took him very close to Luther's original thoughts. Luther's dichotomy was based on viewing the world as an arena of conflict. The kingdom of the devil (*regnum diaboli*) was in opposition to God's kingdom (*regnum dei*) and he expected the struggle to increase in intensity as the final day of the Lord drew closer.

It seems unlikely that Köster was unaware of the application of Luther's teaching on the two kingdoms amongst Baptist circles. His determined silence appears to be an indication that he considered this theological political construct to be unhelpful at this time of crisis. In contrast to Köster's restraint, his fellow editor of the *Täufer-Bote*, Johannes Fleischer, quoted in one of his articles the Baptist *Christenfibel's* reference to Romans 13:1. Fleischer, who was the author of these ethical guidelines, argued for a God-ordered structure of state and people but reminded his readers that, as children of God, their allegiance to this evil world was insubstantial since their names were already recorded in the book of the coming kingdom of God.[51] Köster was reluctant to explore the so called God-ordered structure of the state and preferred to speak of the ambivalent "double faced" dimension of the state or *Weltstaat*, a term that echoed Luther's *regnum mundi*.

Analysis: Word & Christendom

In 1932 Köster reported that he had recently visited some Baptist fellowships in Germany. During that visit he had noticed an absence of biblical teaching and a prominence of political enthusiasm. Describing the occasion to the readership of the *Täufer-Bote* he wrote: "One brother closed his talk on the Sunday previous to the election of the Reichspräsident with the following comment. 'Dear brothers and sisters! He who votes for Hindenburg, votes for Barabbas! He who votes for Hitler, votes for our Lord Jesus!' He who has ears . . . ! We are faced with an all encompassing

49. Täufer-Bote, 1933, No. 11–12, 2.
50. Allianz, 8 December 1941.
51. Strübind, *Die unfreie Freikirche*, 47.

national-socialist wave which has gripped our church life in Germany and the outcome is utter decay."⁵²

Köster lamented the fact that Germans, Baptists included, were eager to join noisy political rallies waving flags, but ignored the Holy Spirit, the spiritual discipline of quiet reflection before God and living a life of sincere witness before the world. The church, Köster diagnosed, was caught in a process of rot and decay. Official Baptist leaders, eager to demonstrate publicly political concern and timely involvement, neglected the desperately needed engagement with the eternal word of God. Köster was deeply troubled by this lack of biblical teaching⁵³ and sought to counter the church's fateful course into the world of politics by urging readers to engage prophetically with the Bible.⁵⁴ Interestingly, Köster's concern predates Karl Barth's June 1933 publication 'Theologische Existenz Heute' where Barth wrote,

> The mighty temptation of our age, is that we no longer appreciate the intensity and exclusiveness of the demand of the divine Word . . . so that in our anxiety in existing dangers we no longer put our whole trust in the authority of God's Word, but we think we ought to come to its aid with all sorts of contrivances, and we thus throw aside our confidence in the Word's power to triumph. . . . And this means that we seek for God elsewhere than in his Word, and seek his Word somewhere else than in Jesus Christ, and seek Jesus elsewhere than in the Holy Scriptures of the Old and New Testament.⁵⁵

---

52. Täufer-Bote, 1932, No. 4, 6.

53. Täufer-Bote, 1933, No. 3, 4: "Der Mangel aber an Schriftverständnis ist ungeheuer, so ungeheuer, dass heute ein nur einigermaßen richtiges Verhältnis für die Zentralwahrheit göttlicher Offenbarung, für das Reich Gottes, sehr selten ist."

54. Täufer-Bote, 1932, No. 1, 1: "Noch nie war Wort Gottes so rar." Täufer-Bote, 1932, No. 4, 6: "Die Kirche hat kein Lehramt." Täufer-Bote, 1933, No. 1, 3: "Aufgabe des Zeugendienstes. . . . der Welt das Wort von der Sündenvergebung zu sagen." Täufer-Bote, No. 10, 2, article on "Die prophetische Schau der Gemeinde." Täufer-Bote, 1934, No. 4, 2: "Ach die Not ist ins Ungeheuere gewachsen."

55. Barth, "Theologische Existenz Heute," 5–6: "[Die] Versuchung dieser Zeit: das wir über die Macht und Ansprüche die Intensität und Exklusivität des Anspruchs des göttlichen Wortes als solche nicht mehr und damit dieses Wort sofort überhaupt nicht mehr verstehen. Daß wir in der Ängstlichkeit vor allerhand Gefahren der Gewalt des Wortes Gottes nicht mehr so ganz trauen, sondern ihm mit allerhand Veranstaltungen zu Hilfe kommen zu müssen meinen und damit unser Vertrauen auf seinen Sieg ganz und gar wegwerfen . . . Daß wir unser Herz gar nicht beim Worte Gottes haben. Daß wir unter dem stürmischen Eindruck gewisser 'Mächte, Fürstentümer und Gewalten' Gott noch anderswo suchen als in seinem Wort und sein Wort noch anderswo als Jesus Christus und Jesus Christus noch anderswo als in der heiligen Schrift Alten und Neuen Testamentes und eben damit solche sind, die Gott gar nicht suchen." (English Translation, Vicencio, "Protestant Quest," 52–53)

Both Barth and Köster regarded the political enthusiasm of their respective churches as a grave danger and urged their readerships to understand that the Christian faith was rooted in God's word alone. To both men, placing trust and hope in anything else but God's word amounted to seeking God elsewhere. Both called for a radical reorientation and obedience to Jesus Christ. Although Barth and Köster were somewhat united by their concern, each spoke to a very different group of people. Barth, as a reformed theologian, addressed the Lutheran church-of-the-people which was tempted to tap into the popular appeal of the German Christians' message. In the February 1933 edition of the *Täufer-Bote*, Köster informed his readers concerning a recent visit of the Lutheran bishop (*Generalsuperintendent*) Dr. [Otto] Dibelius to Vienna. The lecture, Köster wrote, was dominated by a "proud and thoroughly carnal optimism" and concluded: "The Protestant Church of Germany believes that her hour of awakening has come, brought about by a popular upsurge of people (*völkische Erhebung*). And again the church will sell her inheritance rights for a bowl of stew, closing herself off from the possibility of repentance."[56]

This stark and uncompromising verdict was set within comments expressing concern for Baptist fellowships who also appeared to yield to that very same temptation. Köster was in no doubt that the issue was not just a Lutheran concern. He was troubled by the possibility that Baptist Christian fellowships could also opt for the path of least resistance and adopt strategies designed to impress and attract outsiders rather than remain faithful to Christ and God's word.

The great theologian Barth and the Baptist pastor Köster were, at this junction, united in their analysis and their call. The church of Christ needed to radically reorientate itself on God's word.[57] For Karl Barth this led to Barmen and its Christ-centered declaration. Köster's main focus, whilst also remaining Christ-centered, was the prophetic analysis of the present time and drawing attention to the dichotomy of God's kingdom over against the kingdom of the world. To Köster, the real danger lay in the church's inability to distinguish between these two realms and to remain blind to the canny tactics of Satan. Christians in Germany might have been on their guard facing an openly atheistic regime, as in Bolshevik Russia, but might be dangerously lulled into a false sense of security by a regime seemingly advocating a positive but vague Christendom.[58]

56. Täufer-Bote, 1933, No. 2, 3.

57. Scholder, *Requiem*. Karl Barth urges pastors to embrace a theological existence; by that he meant, "our attachment to God's word and plying our calling particularly to the ministry of the Word."

58. Täufer-Bote, 1932, No. 6–7, 3.

Dietrich Bonhoeffer and Arnold Köster

Again and again Köster did battle with the Christendom worldview of his days. The title of the main article in the April 1934 edition was, "The Christianization of the World—the great Temptation that is to come upon the whole Earth."[59] In it Köster argued that Satan eagerly used the concepts of Christ and Christendom for his own evil schemes. They were useful masks and guises that served him well in his battle against God. Köster urged his readers to look behind these masks and to uncover Satan's strategies. He argued that Jesus was able to withstand the tempter, because he had sought the quietness and the hardship of the desert. Therefore, Christians and the church needed to put a distance between the buzz and excitement of popular movements and to listen afresh to God's word. His call was not to heed words that inspired emotions, soul and blood but to heed God's word. He concluded his plea with the surprising statement to listen to "yes, the Jewish Torah!"[60] This conscious reference made it clear that Köster resisted the anti-Semitism that was prevalent at the time. For Köster the choice was either to be swept along by contemporary currents, movements and forces or to resist Satan. Taking a stand was hard and, Köster insisted, might even include a personal Golgotha for those who dared to speak and live a life of obedience to God the father.

To Köster the crisis of the western world was intimately tied to the fact that Christendom had become hollow and "Christ-less."[61] What was left were vague visions of reestablishing a moral and successful Christian society. Proponents of these visions tapped into powerful longings for God's kingdom, yet, to Köster, these efforts were a form of human hubris motivated by the snake's lie in Genesis: "You will be like God."[62] Köster feared that Christians who were being swept along by a Christendom Zeitgeist were in danger of losing their salvation. The urgent task was to test the spirits, to distinguish clearly between the living Christ and Christendom, between God's kingdom and the kingdom of the world *(Gottesreich versus Weltstaat)*. Central to this endeavor was Köster's pessimistic evaluation of the world which he himself contrasted with his optimistic hope in the coming kingdom. To him, part of the dangerous attraction and lure of this Christ-less Christendom was that the church in its very essence was an expectant community. "Since our hearts are filled with an attitude of expectant waiting, every gospel message concerning a glorious future represents a great danger. We therefore have to remember that there are also false messiahs. This means there are also false

---

59. Täufer-Bote, 1934, No. 4, 1.
60. Täufer-Bote, 1934, No. 4, 2.
61. Täufer-Bote, 1930 No. 3, 2.
62. Täufer-Bote, 1934, No. 4, 1.

leaders (*Führer*) whose future promises are merely a mirage in the desert, cruelly tempting the lost traveler. Let us remain sober and let us ask the Lord that he will give his church the gift of discernment."[63]

Christendom, he claimed was attractive because it was so close to the truth. Köster granted that it was deeply Christian to fight social injustice, to have policies and political leaders motivated by Christian convictions, to unite as a religious people. Yet, his concern was that the present attempts were motivated from below and not from above. The Christian culture of Christendom had become a power structure and was driven by human longing and distortion rather than by the Spirit of God.

Köster strongly advocated a policy of separation from the political movements of the time for the church. To him the only viable way for the church was the path into the desert, into hardship, isolation and loneliness. "Not into politics but out of it."[64] The church had to have no part in providing political solutions for the world. Theologically his point of view was informed by interpreting events and his historical context through apocalyptic lenses. This present day epoch was viewed as being under God's curse and shaped by Satan's reign. The future epoch was to arrive at the hour of the father's choosing. At this time, the church of Jesus had not been given the task of improving the world. "Christian" politicians and economists may have that task, but never the church of Jesus. Her task for this epoch in time until the end was to bear witness. The arena for this witness was not the political sphere or the economical marketplace offering some sort of "Christian" program. The task was to speak the message of forgiveness of sins.[65]

Köster's arguments against a political entanglement of the church were motivated by what he perceived to be false claims: the claims that this era, this government, this program was of God. Was this radical stance motivated by a narrow apocalyptic vision that roundly rejected any form of cooperation with the world? A simple reading of Köster's articles seems to indicate just that. Nevertheless, mindful of the historical context and setting of his thoughts in a highly politicized era his message was relevant. *Gleichschaltung*, total conformity to the political ideals of the Nazi government was the hallmark of these years. Everything was political; attempts to create islands of non-political existence were considered dangerous by the authorities and viewed as a threat to the common good. The Zeitgeist of the time had become a mighty current and to resist its pull demanded an equally mighty effort. Such strenuous concentration was demanded that it

63. Täufer-Bote, 1933, No. 5, 1.
64. Täufer-Bote, 1932, No. 6–7, 3.
65. Täufer-Bote, 1933, No. 1, 3.

gave little room, at least for Köster, to develop a nuanced political theology and led him to emphasize an apocalyptic reading of historical events.

Nevertheless, as shown in the last quotation, Köster's primary concern was to define and defend the task of the church. Almost all of his writings addressed the plural community of believers rather than the individual Christian. As a pastor his efforts were to "preserve the members of our fellowships."[66] He firmly believed that the church still had a duty and task to the world which he defined as the proclamation of the gospel and preaching the message of forgiveness. True salvation in this world was still possible and desirable but only through personal radical conversion and by being grafted into the community of God's church.

Conclusion

To Köster the realm of salvation on this earth was the church of Jesus. At a time when the national state (*Weltstaat*) demanded total submission, Köster's reading of the Bible led him to judge such totalitarian tendencies as demonic. The church was neither isolated from the world nor from God's judgment. Yet, in its role and service to the world it was to proclaim the gospel faithfully and offer its prophetic analysis of Satan's strategies. Köster was aware of Christian politicians and economists whose legitimate task was the improvement of the world. Yet in his writings he offered little help and ethical guidance to these individual Christians. His consistent message was urging the church to keep a critical distance. Köster did not argue for a total separation from the world but for a careful interaction with the world that tempered worldly enthusiasm with a dose of apocalyptic pessimism and the challenge to look beyond to the coming of God's kingdom. His persistent focus on the church as a community indicated that for him it was only possible to face the challenges of the time collectively. The frequent inclusion of Anabaptist material and references in the *Täufer-Bote* are also a strong indication that Köster was informed and shaped by these traditions: traditions that emphasized fellowship (*Gemeinschaft* and *Gemeinde*), the prophetic reading of the Bible and the willingness to suffer and die for one's faith.

66. Allianz, 3 May 1932.

The Integration of the World—Bonhoeffer

Bonhoeffer judged the world to be in a serious state of "disintegration."[67] As early as 1932 he expressed concerns regarding the inability of the church to proclaim a concrete ethical stance and felt that, "the problem is becoming increasingly and unbearably acute."[68] In his final and unfinished work *Ethics*, his aim was to reflect theologically on how God's will, as it was revealed in Jesus Christ, could take concrete shape in the reality of the world. He felt that this world, although complex and confusing, was nevertheless the context in which God's message and reality were at work. Bonhoeffer endeavored to hold both God-reality and world-reality in tension and resisted resolving this tension by way of conceptual divisions, compartmentalization and the creation of distinct realms. As the title of the theological journal *Zwischen den Zeiten* suggested, Bonhoeffer lived and worked at a time torn apart by opposing claims. Set within this particular context he sought to discern God's unified and undivided message to the "believing, knowing and acting human being."[69]

The focus of this section is to highlight some of the key arguments Bonhoeffer developed in his *Ethics*. He worked on the various manuscripts from 1940 until his arrest in 1943. A number of the topics were written as a direct response to issues that arose during these years. Bonhoeffer's hope and aim was that his *Ethics* would assist the church, Christians, conspirators and even good people whose values and convictions clashed with those of the Nazi regime. Although rooted in a historical context of crisis, Bonhoeffer also hoped to provide a constructive contribution for a time beyond war and destruction. Standing in between the times (*Zwischen den Zeiten*) he surveyed this contemporary context historically but also offered a model for a future society. He was determined to link thinking and acting consistently and deliberately to Christ, in whom freedom and responsible engagement with the world were made possible.

Decay and Disintegration

Bonhoeffer rooted his analysis of the world and his time in history. Alarmed by a world that was disintegrating, he sought to discern how the present upheavals and the crisis of humanity were embedded in events of the past.

---

67. Bonhoeffer, *Ethics*, 299. The title of chapter is "God's Love and the Disintegration of the World."
68. Ibid., 412. Letter to Erwin Sutz, 17 May 1932.
69. Ibid., 409, editor's afterword to the German edition.

Dietrich Bonhoeffer and Arnold Köster

Bonhoeffer took stock of the "Christian West"[70] in the manuscript "Heritage and Decay."[71] He used the term "the West [*Abendland*]"[72] to refer to a cultural heritage that had been profoundly shaped by the historical Jesus Christ. Geographically, this broadly included the people of Europe and North America. Christian values, movements and institutions had formed and influenced western history, but this, Bonhoeffer insisted, was not in itself a proof of God's approval. History contained both "God's Yes and God's No"[73] and remained somewhat ambivalent. It was wrong to assume that historical realities were always an expression of God's will and purpose. Thus a present day status quo was not in itself an expression of divine approval.[74]

Bonhoeffer surmised that in the coming of Jesus and through the spread of Christianity, God had shaped and established a common heritage amongst the various people of the West. However, this historic unity had become increasingly fractured and fragmented. Bonhoeffer judged that "driving out the Jew(s) from the West" had profound and disturbing implications, for it "must result in driving out Christ with them, for Jesus Christ was a Jew."[75] Christ, who had woven together the people of the West over centuries, was being discarded and rejected. This catastrophic occurrence was, for Bonhoeffer, symptomatic to the pattern of disintegration which had gripped the West. During the first millennium the unifying tendencies of the Roman heritage successfully established a far reaching empire. During the time of the Holy Roman Empire, efforts were made to establish and maintain a precarious unity of faith and political order. However, the tables turned with the age of the Renaissance, the Reformation and the Enlightenment when the antagonistic and divisive Greek heritage came to the fore. "The corpus christianum, the Western-Christian order, which was ruled and held together by emperor and pope as commissioned by Jesus Christ, was shattered by the Reformation. . . . Not that Luther wanted it so. He was completely devoted to the true unity of the church. But he recognized, through the power of the biblical word, that the unity of the church can consist only in the living Jesus Christ in word and sacrament, and not in political power."[76]

70. Ibid., 103.
71. Ibid., 103–33.
72. Ibid., 101.
73. Ibid., 104.
74. Ibid.: "Through the life and death of Jesus Christ, history becomes not the transient bearer of eternal values but, for the first time, thoroughly temporal. Precisely in its temporality, it is history affirmed by God."
75. Ibid., 105.
76. Ibid., 111.

The result was the separation of throne and altar, sword and word. In Germany the split between these two spheres was eventually theologically expressed in Luther's teaching on the two kingdoms. "There are two kingdoms, which, as long as the earth remains, must never be mixed together, yet never torn apart."[77] Bonhoeffer was well acquainted with Luther's teaching but in his view it was often misunderstood and distorted not only by the religious but also by the secular. Secularists tended to claim autonomy and in turn proceeded to explore, exploit and dissect a "desacralized world."[78] As reason began to reign, technological advances followed and set in motion the subjugation of nature on a hitherto unimaginable industrial scale. This began to shape western culture and in turn opened the gates for the rise of nationalism, unrestrained mass movements and the subsequent break-down of order.

The forces of decay and disintegration were powerfully and overwhelmingly at work. Faced with a shattered world, Bonhoeffer refused to yield either to deluded idealism or to resigned despair. His question was: what is God's message to the world he had come to save in Jesus Christ? How can his word be heard and proclaimed by the church? How can his will be lived and obeyed in the world?

Pathways toward Integration

Each of the *Ethics* manuscripts sought to engage theologically with the realities of the world—a world subjected to disintegration and decay, but also a world that was affirmed and loved by God. In Christ God had reclaimed the world, thus the reality of Christ was embedded in the reality of the world. Therefore the ethical must be radically rooted in Jesus Christ. Bonhoeffer made it his working premise that the world was claimed by God in Christ; thus every reality, issue, insight, choice and act had to be brought under the headship of Christ.

The aim of Bonhoeffer's *Ethics* was to provide the contemporary church with an exposition of what the apostle Paul had written to the Corinthians. "We demolish arguments and every pretension that sets itself up against the knowledge of God, and we take captive every thought to make it obedient to Christ."[79] Bonhoeffer wasn't openly able to name and demolish the pretensions of the Nazi regime, but nevertheless attempted to reflect theologically about the underlying causes of decay. Making every thought captive and obe-

77. Ibid., 112.
78. Ibid., 114.
79. 2 Cor 10:5 NIV.

dient to Christ became the cornerstone of his analysis and of his constructive reflections. Against a background of disunity and disintegration, Bonhoeffer chose to make Christ the unifying and integrating person and theme. In this respect his *Ethics* represents a departure from the then dominating theological language of separate realms and kingdoms. His consistent claim was that there was no reality outside Christ, and any attempt to distinguish, split or separate the reality of the world into spheres inevitably distorted the concern of Christ into a "partial, provincial affair within the whole of reality."[80] He charged "enthusiasts . . . [and] pseudo-Lutheranism"[81] of having committed this error. "As long as Christ and the world are conceived as two realms [*Räume*] bumping against and repelling each other, we are left with only the following options. Giving up on reality as a whole, either we place ourselves in one of the two realms, wanting Christ without the world or the world without Christ—and in both cases we deceive ourselves. Or we try to stand in the two realms at the same time, thereby becoming people in eternal conflict."[82]

Bonhoeffer objected against a distortion of Luther's doctrine of the two kingdoms. He stopped short of abandoning it altogether but argued for a right use of it.[83] Interestingly, the proper use of it was polemic rather than a means of holding together two different experiences. Thus, a church isolated from the world must be challenged by the world and equally, a world seeking to become autonomous needed to be challenged by God's word. Where Luther's doctrine became the means for the church or the world to withdraw into a separate existence independent from the other, the doctrine of the two kingdoms needed to be proclaimed polemically. With regard to a Christian view of the world, Bonhoeffer's constructive contribution was not a further refinement of the two kingdom teaching, but a fresh way of looking theologically at the organizing structures of human life and society and their relationship with each other.

Rather than speaking of orders or realms, his preferred term was mandates. Bonhoeffer defined these divine mandates as "divine commission . . . laying claim to, commandeering of, and formation of a certain earthly domain by the divine command."[84]

80. Bonhoeffer, *Ethics*, 57.
81. Ibid., 56.
82. Ibid., 57–58.
83. Ibid., 60. Bonhoeffer argued for a polemical use and pointed to Luther who, "in the name of a better Christianity . . . used the worldly to protest against a type of Christianity that was making itself independent by separating itself from the reality of Christ. Similarly, Christianity must be used polemically today against the worldly in the name of a better worldliness."
84. Ibid., 389.

Divine Mandates (*die vier Mandate*)[85]

Bonhoeffer argued that a biblical ordering of human life and society consists of four divine mandates: work (and culture), marriage (and family), government and the church. Each of these was set "from above as organizing structures"[86] for the proper ordering of life and the world. Each was a part of the whole reality which was the reality of Christ through whom "God's love for world and for human beings"[87] was revealed. Bonhoeffer's use of these four mandates introduced a different perspective upon how the reality of the world is perceived. It was a departure from a dualistically divided world of church versus worldly powers introducing a more complex, interdependent and integrated vision of reality. To Bonhoeffer, the term mandate emphasized that each was a divine commission and was therefore continually dependent on God's authorization. This was a deliberate departure from the German Christians' claim that "natural orders" such as "family, people [*Volk*] and race,"[88] had—intrinsic to themselves—God's approval quite independently from the gospel. Since these natural orders were beyond human reproach, the church had ceased to speak God's message into these orders of life. It had ceased to hold government accountable. Bonhoeffer's use of the mandates was also a protest against the totalitarian strategy of the regime, which claimed total control in every area of life. The role of government was important, but it was only of a subsidiary nature. Therefore wherever policies went beyond the God-given boundaries, God's will and purpose for the world were distorted.

The four mandates were a constructive contribution towards a Christian view of the world. Clearly the historical context of the Third Reich had a formative influence on how Bonhoeffer developed the theme, but the four mandates were also intended to provide a positive vision for the rebuilding und restructuring of society beyond the war. Bonhoeffer was unable to finish the manuscript "The Concrete Commandment and the Divine Mandates."[89] Nevertheless, the basic theological structure of the mandates are sufficiently developed and are therefore a useful comparison to the views and teaching embraced by the Baptist Köster.

---

85. Bonhoeffer, *Ethik*, 70.
86. Bonhoeffer, *Ethics*, 390.
87. Ibid., 390.
88. Ibid., 417.
89. Ibid., 388–408. Bonhoeffer's arrest on 5 April 1943 interrupted his work on the manuscript.

The term "mandates of God"[90] had been in use since the Middle Ages. Bonhoeffer also considered the use of the terms, estate, offices and vocation. However, wanting to emphasize that these structures were continually dependent on God's commissioning, he finally settled on the use of the word mandates "for the time being."[91] Bonhoeffer was somewhat ambivalent regarding his choice of this term—properly understood, he would have been content to use the term "order," except that in his contemporary theological context it had acquired a dubious meaning. However, what was clear to him was that these commissions were rooted in God's word and command.[92]

Work / Culture

The mandate of work, a feature of the creation account (Gen 2:15), was God's gift and invitation to participate in and continue God's own creative work. Set within the whole witness of Scripture, Bonhoeffer interpreted work as a unique possibility and commission for humanity. Humans were entrusted with shaping and preparing the world for a better understanding of Christ. "Through the divine mandate of work, a world should emerge that—knowing or unknowingly—expects Christ, is directed toward Christ, is open for Christ, and serves and glorifies Christ."[93]

Next to work, Bonhoeffer also included culture within this mandate, thus indicating a wider and more comprehensive scope. Work and culture were therefore not just a curse—the endless struggle against the forces of nature, against thorns and thistles—but a creative participatory opportunity of endless possibilities. Since it was a divine mandate, it was endowed with Christ-reality which gave it center and purpose. To some, Christ remained hidden and yet, in spite of their unknowing participation, the overall aim and direction of work and culture, Bonhoeffer insisted, was Christ. Bonhoeffer did not develop the mandate of work. Thus, detailed questions such as issues of unemployment, the old or infirm were not addressed at this point.[94] As with the other mandates, Bonhoeffer was merely able to depict them as a basic God-ordained structure of human life. This combination of work and culture made up the first of the four pillars of a flourishing humanity living in accordance with God's reality.

90. Ibid., 68n75.
91. Ibid., 390.
92. Ibid., 68; order and description are slightly changed on p. 392.
93. Ibid., 71.
94. Ibid., 185–96. See "Right to Bodily Life."

Marriage / Family

Next to work, marriage—also rooted in the creation story—constituted the second divine mandate. Bonhoeffer linked the becoming one of husband and wife before God, with Christ becoming one with the church. For Bonhoeffer the mandate of marriage, ordinary as it might seem, was infused with a mystery and wonder.[95] For as man and woman participate "in creating [*mitschaffend*] human beings [they] enter into the will of the Creator."[96] The individual choice of two people, prompted by love resulted in their resolve to get married. Yet once married, it was marriage that undergirded and protected their love for each other. Beyond personal happiness their role was to become representatives of God entrusted with the responsibility of educating children into obedience to Jesus Christ.[97]

As with work and culture, marriage and family represent the second pillar of human society and life. Issues relating to this mandate can be found in other sections of Bonhoeffer's Ethics. A number of related themes such as freedom, responsibility and obedience were discussed by him in "History and Good [2]."[98] However, he was unable to develop the topic systematically.

Government

Bonhoeffer defined the primary function of government as the support and protection of the divine mandates of work and marriage. In contrast to these, government had no creative function but, maintained "what is created in the order that was given to the creation by God's commission."[99] For Bonhoeffer, the struggle with a repressive government was existential and it was also a concern that shaped his *Ethics*. Nevertheless, good government was mandated by God and was crucial for the ordering of human life and upholding of justice. However, when—contrary to God's commandment—government pursued policies of domination and destruction, it could no longer claim divine authorization.

---

95. Bonhoeffer, *Letters and Papers*, 86: "Our earthly conditions are imbued with a divine radiance . . . and honor."

96. Bonhoeffer, *Ethics*, 71.

97. Bonhoeffer, *Letters and Papers*, 83: "In your love you see only each other in the world; in marriage you are a link in the chain of generations that God, for the sake of God's glory, allows to rise and fade away, and calls into God's kingdom."

98. Bonhoeffer, *Ethics*, 283–98. The manuscript ends with the title "Love and Responsibility."

99. Ibid., 72.

Dietrich Bonhoeffer and Arnold Köster

Church

The final and fourth mandate was the church. Through the ministry of the church the reality of Christ was to become real in "proclamation, church order, and the Christian life."[100] Distinctive to the church was that, as a community of believers, it was subject to Christ's will. However, the calling of the church embraced all of life, for as the body of Christ it was sent to a world which was Christ's. Bonhoeffer argued that "the reality of Christ embraces the reality of the world . . . the world has no reality independent of God's revelation in Christ."[101] Since the church was concerned with the salvation of the world, it was charged to speak and live Christ's presence into every aspect of human existence and life. "This is the witness the church has to give to the world, that all the other mandates are not there to divide people and tear them apart but to deal with them as whole people before God the Creator, Reconciler, and Redeemer—the reality in all its manifold aspects is ultimately one in God who became human, Jesus Christ."[102]

Their Nature and Connectedness

What was gained by this fourfold division of mandates as opposed to the twofold distinction of the kingdoms of God and world? Bonhoeffer was only able to provide a fragmentary conception of the four mandates and their relatedness towards each other. His thoughts can be likened to an architect's first sketchy drawing. Just as an experienced architect would be able to see beyond the chaos of a demolition site, Bonhoeffer also fashioned an imaginary structure. The architect's sketch would chart rough outlines and the potential form, order and beauty of a building yet to be constructed. The sketch would be lacking in detail, precise calculations and measurements, yet in spite of its shortcomings it would communicate potential design possibilities. Set within the historical context of the Third Reich, when order and justice had collapsed, Bonhoeffer sought to see beyond demolition and destruction and to recapture a biblical vision for life and reality. Central to his vision was the need to transcend the dichotomous division of reality, which had been adopted by church and secular society.

Bonhoeffer's construct regarding how God willed and ordered human society needs to be evaluated against the historical context of the Third Reich. The totalitarian state's aim was to bring every aspect of life

---

100. Ibid., 73.
101. Ibid., 58.
102. Ibid., 73.

under its domain and control. This was achieved through diverse and complex methods, ranging from propaganda and seductive persuasion to forceful coercion and execution. Bonhoeffer's use of the four divine mandates allowed no room for a totalitarian agenda. Government's role was subsidiary to the mandates of work and family and its task was not domination and control but support and justice. Bonhoeffer's vision of a society ordered and commandeered by the divine mandates was biblical and characteristic of western civilization. The social structures of work and family and the institutions of government were commonly recognizable features of society. The familiarity with this fourfold construct provided therefore an opportunity to debate this vision for the ordering of society with people outside the church. In the manuscript "Church and World I,"[103] Bonhoeffer takes note of the good people [*die Guten*]. These were people who abhorred "the persecution of justice, truth, humanity and freedom"[104] and who, although originally outside the church, had become drawn to Christ. The four mandates were therefore a Christian contribution to the task of rebuilding society and the ordering of human life in the world. In spite of its accessibility it was also profoundly and unashamedly Christian. Each of the four mandates originated in and expressed God's loving concern for the world. Each had an Christological focus, for their fulfillment and purpose was the reality of Christ.

Bonhoeffer merged Christ-centered doctrine with applied ethics. His vision of Christ was total—and since nothing was outside Christ, it was impossible for the church to withdraw into a separate, sacred place, leaving the world to its own divinely designated role and purpose. Divine authorization of the mandates was provisional and utterly dependent on each mandate cooperating, serving and challenging the other. Bonhoeffer stressed that "none of the mandates exists self-sufficiently, nor can one of them claim to replace all the others."[105] Only in their being with-one-another, for-one-another and against-one-another were they God's mandates. They were like four pillars of a grand construction providing a protective and stable structure for building and maintaining human life and society. Such a building could only remain upright as long as the weight of the structure was shared between them, as each supported the other and none sought to take the other's place. Each one had to relate and engage with the others in a cooperative, subsidiary and polemical manner. Whenever they ceased to do that, they ceased to be God's mandates.

---

103. Ibid., 339–51.
104. Ibid., 345.
105. Ibid., 393.

Dietrich Bonhoeffer and Arnold Köster

An Enthusiast's Critique

Bonhoeffer's vision of society was profoundly rooted and connected to a Christendom view of the West. For him the witness of the church, through the proclamation of the word and Christian lives, was of central importance. The church had a duty to speak polemically and prophetically into the structures of work, family and government. Deeply suspicious of dividing reality into separate realms, Bonhoeffer criticized the pseudo-Lutheran but also the Enthusiast[106] for whom the world was no longer a place where Christ was found but an arena reduced to building God's holy kingdom, separate from worldly corruption.[107]

Sadly, Bonhoeffer's critique was not theoretical but exposed the failure of many Christian churches. His words were relevant then and are relevant today. Attitudes that relinquish and taint a world that was loved, judged and redeemed by Christ, are contrary to the biblical message such as Colossians 1:15–20. Bonhoeffer's refusal to allow the reality of Christ to become theologically segregated and reduced was a timely correction to an increasingly provincial Christian outlook. Against this, Bonhoeffer, following the apostle Paul, claimed that Christ is all. All meant all—every sphere and reality was under Christ, even the devil[108] himself was subservient to Christ.

Set within an increasingly secular world, Bonhoeffer's determined effort of relating every thought and concept to Christ was remarkable and outrageous.[109] Such thinking represented a stark contrast to a pragmatic worldview dominated by what was heard and seen. This message was also outrageous to the church of Colossae who, compared to the might and vastness of the pagan Roman Empire, was but an insignificant small group of Christians. Nevertheless, Paul insisted that all things were held together in Christ and not by another authority or power (Col 1:17). What must

---

106. Ibid., 56, 263–64. Next to the typical Anabaptist enthusiast Bonhoeffer also refers to the modern enthusiasm of the American social gospel: "Optimism, the ideology of progress, does not take seriously the command of God (Luke 17:10). It is modern enthusiasm [*Schwärmertum*]. It fails to recognize human limits; it disregards the fundamental difference between the kingdom of the world and the kingdom of God" (Bonhoeffer, *Berlin*, 241).

107. Bonhoeffer, *Ethics*, 57. See footnote 38. Letter to Gerhard Leibholz: "The enthusiasts wanted to build the world on love and on the Sermon on the Mount. Luther saw therein a confusion of the kingdom of God with the earthly kingdom that could only have the most dangerous and chaotic consequences."

108. Ibid., 65: "The world is not divided between Christ and the devil; it is completely the world of Christ, whether it recognizes it or not."

109. Ibid., 134: "Since God became a human being in Christ, all thinking about human beings without Christ is unfruitful abstractions"; ibid., 262: "Trying to understand reality without the Real One means living in abstraction."

Engaging with the World

have been beyond the imagination of the New Testament churches was that the government's role could ever be viewed in a manner as described by Bonhoeffer's mandates. Clearly, Bonhoeffer's construct of the four divine mandates was both based on and woven into the Christendom paradigm. However, in April 1944 Bonhoeffer began to question the Christendom assumptions which were an integral part of the West's heritage and culture. Writing to Eberhard Bethge, he observed that "we are approaching a completely religionless age."[110] He came to the conclusion that "our entire nineteen hundred years of Christian preaching and theology are built on the 'religious a priori' in human beings."[111] At this point in time Bonhoeffer began to contemplate another crisis, the demise of Christendom.

Bonhoeffer's exposition of the four mandates was built on the "religious a priori" which, in 1944, he feared might no longer be a viable assumption. What became a distinct possibility to Bonhoeffer, had already been a reality to some enthusiasts, especially to those who had become practicing pacifists. They had found themselves outside the Christendom paradigm and had rejected it. In the Christian West their communities did not occupy a secure place opposite and in cooperation with government. Their experience was persecution inflicted upon them by government and the magisterial churches. Within the Christendom paradigm these groups were normally judged as simple, odd or dangerous.

Bonhoeffer's fourfold structure of society lacks coherence in a "religionless age." The removal of one pillar, the church, triggers the collapse of the interrelated balance and dependency of the four divine mandates. The realities of work, family and government would remain in some form. However, bereft of Christ being proclaimed, would they lack divine authorization? How would a church, ignored and marginalized by the world, proclaim the reality of Christ to a religionless society? Enthusiasts, like the Anabaptists, had to wrestle with these questions as early as the sixteenth century. Unable to offer grand social designs to society, their response was to form and live in communities that were shaped by discipleship values. Following Christ became a central concern and shared focus to these Christian communities. Clearly, such groups often gravitate towards a separatist point of view which makes, as Bonhoeffer charged, "the concern of Christ . . . a partial, provincial affair within the whole of reality."[112] They adopted what the American theologian Stanley Hauerwas called a "peasant view of Christianity." The peasant's humble concern was "to know who's ruling me and

---

110. Bonhoeffer, *Letters and Papers*, 362.
111. Ibid., 362.
112. Bonhoeffer, *Ethics*, 57.

how I can survive them. In the process, I hope to make a contribution to those who rule."¹¹³ Importantly, the possibility and the desire to "make a contribution" indicate that such a view does not necessarily commit adherents to a dualistic view of reality which isolates the church-community from the world. New Testament letters like Paul's Epistle to the Colossians demonstrate that even at the margins of a religionless society, the vision of the lordship of Christ can be sustained and the salvation of the world can remain the motivating task of the church. In the pre-Christendom context, the church was only able to offer a contribution from below rather than from above or as the fourth divine mandate. The post-Christendom era presents a similar challenge and opportunity.

Formation in the Image of Christ

A basic presupposition of Bonhoeffer's divine mandates was their hierarchical ordering. They were "clearly determined by above and below."¹¹⁴ For Bonhoeffer this was primarily a theological concept rather than a class division. He argued that abuse was equally possible from above as from below.¹¹⁵ However, irrespective of being either below or above, what united people was their shared willing submission to God's order. Bonhoeffer argued that the benefits of a hierarchically ordered world are persuasive to all as long as they are not abused and human interaction is governed by the proper application of God's mandates. Yet, how was one to act responsibly in a world that was falling apart? This was the challenge which Bonhoeffer, Köster and every Christian were facing.

Bonhoeffer's reflection on freedom and responsibility were meant to address some of these concerns. His thoughts also had a direct relevance to the ethical dilemmas with which conspirators struggled. In contrast to the ordered view of the divine mandates, engagement with the world became in this instance a matter from below. Institutions had ceased to provide structures of responsibility from above. Interaction with the world had to

---

113. Stanley Hauerwas, *BBC Radio 4, Start the Week*, 18 October 2010, 9:00–9:45 a.m: "I represent a form of Christianity which is non-Constantinian. Most of Christianity in recent times—well, since Constantine—thought it needed to rule. I represent what I like to call the peasant view of Christianity. I just want to know who's ruling me and how I can survive them. In the process, I hope to make a contribution [addressed] to those who rule."

114. Bonhoeffer, *Ethics*, 391.

115. Ibid., 391: "Abuse of being below is equal to and just as frequent as the above of being above that inflicts injury on the person below."

be rooted in the choices of individual people and in the personal structures of a responsible life.

Strands of a Responsible Life

Bonhoeffer rejected the notion that it was possible for an individual to "choose continually and exclusively between a clearly recognized good and a clearly recognized evil."[116] He claimed that the search for absolute standards reduced ethical interaction with the world into a simplistic formula. Such absolutes may offer a shallow guarantee by providing an individual with a numbed sense of personal goodness. However, the tragic outcome of such a scheme would be the prevention of a person's responsible action in concrete situations. Following mere norms or absolutes detaches a person from what is quintessential to humanity—acting and living "in encounter with other human people."[117] For Bonhoeffer, "the action's norm is not a universal principle, but the concrete neighbor, as given to me by God."[118] His emphasis was the other person encountered in genuine circumstances in which responsible action had to be risked. In absence of clear ethical categories, the responsible individual had to abandon certainty and must risk acting, "in the twilight that the historical situation casts over good and evil."[119]

Conclusion

It would be simplistic to suggest that Bonhoeffer merely replaced universal ethical principles with the historical situation. His intention was rather to expose and surmount the human tendency of using principles, duty, and even conscience for the purpose of self-justification, rather than a real concern for the other person's wellbeing. For Bonhoeffer, every concrete historical situation was intimately tied to the reality of Jesus Christ. Upon a follower of Christ, that reality manifests itself in judgment and gracious acceptance. Bound to Jesus, a Christian recognizes the other as a sinner, like himself and as loved by Christ, like himself. Thus, every human encounter becomes shaped by the pattern Christ had adopted and risked. If Jesus risked selfless responsible action rather than claiming ethical perfection, so must

---

116. Ibid., 219.

117. Ibid., 220.

118. Ibid., 221. See also 247: "It happens in the midst of our living bonds to people, things, institutions, and powers, that is, in the midst of our historical existence."

119. Ibid., 222.

his followers, for their lives are claimed by Christ. To follow Christ must therefore mean to risk, as Christ did, "vicarious representative action."[120] The Christ-like life carries the risk of sacrifice but it also carries the promise of a life of freedom: the freedom of leaving the ultimate judgment between right and wrong, good and evil in the hands of Christ; the freedom to risk, in accordance with Christ, a vicarious representative life pattern; the freedom to see "the 'world' . . . [as] the domain of concrete responsibility that is given to us in and through Jesus Christ."[121]

---

120. Ibid., 257.
121. Ibid., 267.

6

The Church

Background and Context of Köster's Ecclesiology

KÖSTER'S CALLING AND MINISTRY was that of a local pastor. His understanding of church was rooted in his work and life. This was also true for Bonhoeffer. Köster, however did not produce a systematic work of his ecclesiology. His thoughts are preserved in sermons and lectures addressing specific historical situations and were thus often influenced by the specific historical demands. Köster experienced church as a pastoral minister and in this role he responded to the issues and dangers he and his congregation were facing.

The focus of his ministry was the Baptist Church Vienna-Mollardgasse 35. Beyond his local ministry Köster also maintained contact with the Baptist Union of Germany and various other small Baptist congregations in Austria. His involvement and contributions to the monthly edition of the *Täufer-Bote* shows that he had a missionary concern for the countries east of Vienna. His own ministry as pastor of the Mollardgasse placed him at the most westerly part of the so called *Donaulandmission*, which was supported and funded by American Baptist churches. The population of the various Donauländer had either a strong Catholic, Lutheran or Orthodox Church tradition and was often quite suspicious of other church traditions. Austria was predominately Catholic with a few scattered Lutheran churches. Baptists and other separatist groups like the Methodists, Pentecostals and *Volksmission* were an even smaller minority. Leaders of these small minority churches organized joint activities and mutual support as members of the Evangelical Alliance.

Most of the churches pursued a policy of accommodation with the Third Reich government. Köster's consistent criticism of the Nazi state government was a significant exception. His stance was contrary to the German Baptist Union's attempts at protecting the survival of their local Baptist congregations by sending frequent messages of support to the Nazi government. Köster's outspoken criticism was not well received by the wider German Baptist family. Some of these glaring discrepancies are well documented in some of the articles and comments Köster contributed to the various editions of the *Täufer-Bote*.

During the early years of the Nazi regime some Baptists had placed a certain amount of hope in the new government. However, Baptists and other free churches feared that they could be forced to integrate themselves into the proposed new and united German *Reichskirche*. This fear triggered a crisis of identity and made the leadership focus on internal issues. Eager to assist the government, both Methodist and the Baptist leaders used their international links to counter the so called bad press (*Greuelpropaganda*) the Nazi regime had in Britain and America. The hope was that expressions of loyalty and accommodation towards the regime would help to secure their precarious existence. It was their pragmatic desire to secure some kind of political existence for their local congregations with the aim of securing the freedom to evangelize the population. This strategy effectively led to the captivity of the Free Church. Rainer Ebeling comments: "Most free churches perceived mission as their central task and calling. Therefore they measured their own freedom by how free they were to pursue their evangelizing activities. Such an understanding pushed ecclesiological concerns into the background. After all, it was argued, was not the central biblical concern a personal salvation experience and a living relationship with Christ? Next to such a viewpoint other Christian concerns were seen as secondary. They were matters for which one should not risk getting imprisoned."[1]

The freedom to evangelize provided a state-permitted focus to Baptist missionaries within the German Reich. This kind of freedom, the argument ran, was not granted to eastern countries where communism aggressively pursued a repressive atheistic policy. In and around Vienna there were a number of Baptist preacher-evangelists who had links to the Mollardgasse and received support in their efforts to establish new home churches (*Hausgemeinden*). One of Köster's sons-in-law, Herbert Fuchs was the son of such a *Hausgemeinden* missionary. He distinctly remembers that his father and the small group of Baptists in Ternitz rigorously separated matters of faith from politics. Their stated concern was to win souls for eternity.[2] They preached the gospel, urged people to repent and come to a living faith

---

1. Ebeling, *Dietrich Bonhoeffers Ringen*, 190.
2. Interviews with Herbert Fuchs, 3 August 2009.

in Jesus Christ. Such faith was however, neither related to nor affected by the world of politics and the ideologies of the day.

Köster's local church context was marked by at least two kinds of tension. The first was an inner tension in as much as it consisted of an internal Baptist issue. The extreme poles of this were on the one hand the leadership of the Union and on the other hand deeply ingrained assumptions of many members of the Baptist Church Mollardgasse. The Baptist leadership of Germany pursued a deliberate apolitical course when it came to matters of politics and state. Their policy was driven by a will for survival and fear. The Nazi government had to be placated and respected, rather than criticized. To ordinary local members of the congregation, the call to mission provided a theological rationale and purpose in that time of crisis. Matters of politics and the world were split into two separate and unrelated realms. Any energy left after the daily struggle for food and shelter, was directed towards outreach activities. Neither the official leadership nor the ordinary members of the local congregation were eager to have their minister express repeatedly and persistently his critical assessment of the state and its ideology. Yet this is what Köster did.

The other tension was brought into the congregation simply because in reality matters of faith and world could not be separated. Another of Köster's sons-in-law clearly remembers Sunday gatherings when two distinct groups were part of the same worshipping congregation. One group consisted of a number of people who were forced by government legislation to wear the yellow Star of David; the other group had come wearing the Nazi party emblem. He even recollects that at one point one man attended a service wearing his SS uniform. These two distinct groups represented two extremes that had the potential to split the congregation asunder. Some had become the victims of the political system while others had placed their hope and allegiance into the very same Nazi system. Possibly the majority of the congregation were somewhere between these two extreme reference points. Köster's ministry was to be the pastor of a local church, a community of ordinary people who held a great range of diverse convictions and opinions.

Other Theological Voices

Köster's own critical stance against the state would make it natural that he both sympathized and supported the struggles of the Confessing Church in Germany. It is interesting that apart from the rare passing remark little can be found in the Köster material which directly relates to the Confessing Church. One possible reason was that there was little local contact between the *Evangelische Kirche AB* (Lutheran Church) of Austria and separatist church leaders at that time. Another geographical reason could have been that Vienna was far removed from the areas where the Confessing Church was most active.

Köster was however, an ardent reader of a number of different theological journals that had become the mouthpiece of theologians who were leading figures in the German church struggle. Köster's son-in-law Herbert Fuchs has inherited a significant part of Köster's library which contains among others publications more than forty editions of *Zwischen den Zeiten* and fifteen editions of *Theologische Existenz Heute*. Some of the articles are extensively marked with Köster's distinct handwriting or are underlined with pencil or color crayons.

One can easily group the various articles into marked and unmarked. However it would be too simplistic to assume that Köster only studied the marked articles. The marked articles do indicate that he was a keen reader of Karl Barth, Eduard Thurneysen, Helmut Gollwitzer, Friedrich Gogarten, Herman Diem and Kurt Frör. At the very least it can be safely assumed that Köster kept himself well informed with the theological developments that had shaped the church struggle in Germany. A number of Karl Barth's contributions are prefaced with explanatory comments regarding certain historical events of church politics and the efforts of the German Christian movement.[3]

Köster also had a copy of the 1936 journal *Evangelische Theologie* in which Bonhoeffer's article *Zur Frage nach der Kirchengemeinschaft* was published. However this particular article does not have any original Köster markings.

The wealth of this material is a clear indicator that Köster critically engaged with the trends of dialectical theology. Köster used and transposed these insights into the pastoral situations and needs of his Baptist local church context.

An Incidental Ecclesiology

A reader of Köster's sermons is only able to piece together a patchwork of his ecclesiology. Most of his sermons are rooted in the crisis of the Third Reich period. Köster's arguments often had a certain combativeness about them. He perceived the political movements of his time as a direct threat to the church community. However, while speaking of powers of darkness and chaos he clung to the promises of God—the God who saves and the God who rules in spite of all the turbulent chaos raging in the world.

3. Barth, "Die Kirche Jesu Christi." See 3–10.

The Church

At a most basic level, Christ's church is where two or three are gathered in his name. Another definition adopted by post-reformation churches was that the church of God is found where God's word is preached and where the sacraments are administered. Seen together, the first statement makes clear what the church is—the coming together of believers—the second describes what the church does—listen to the Scripture, baptize and celebrate communion. As a discipleship community gathers it is shaped by God's word and will express its common life and faith through the sacraments of Baptism and the Lord's Table.

The Boundary of the Church: Baptism

To the Baptist Köster, believer's baptism marked the entry point into God's salvation community. He traced the praxis of believer's baptism to the "original church of Christ"[4] and sought to build the present day church according to the New Testament apostolic patterns. Unsurprisingly, this represented a clear rejection of the Christendom infant baptism model.

Quoting Kierkegaard he argued that: "it is the most tragic of crimes to rob a human of the most sacred choice, the decision for God. All children that are born into Christendom and are thus considered to be Christian by virtue of their nationality are robbed of the most holy good, their own clear and hearty voluntary decision."[5]

To Köster baptism was a multilayered decision. It was firstly, an individual person's decision for God but it was also secondly a decision for the gospel. The gospel was not just a set of words or a story but was first and foremost a genuine encounter with the living God. Third, at such a meeting a person would realize that their own decision was wrapped up in God's own decision. Thus, the human decision for God was never solely based on an individual's initiative but was always also rooted in God's own gracious calling. This insight equally emphasized the need for a genuine human decision motivated by repentance and the overarching divine activity of the Father, Son and Holy Spirit.

---

4. Köster, 1 December 1940, *Ansprache*, 1: "Stehen wir aber wirklich im Glauben an den Jesus von Nazareth, dann wollen wir es auch wagen, uns auf dem Boden seines Wortes zu stellen, dann wollen wir leben aus dem ursprünglichen Worte und wollen dort zu Hause sein, wo die ursprüngliche Christusgemeinde zu Hause war."

5. Köster, 2 May 1943, *Biblischer Sinn*: "Es ist tragisch zu nennen, es ist ein Verbrechen an den Menschen, sie um das Heiligste zu betrügen: für die Entscheidung für Gott! Alle Kinder, die in die Christenheit hineingeboren werden, und die dann von Staat wegen Christen sind, sind dadurch um das Letzte und Allerheiligste betrogen, sie können zu einer klaren Entscheidung ihres Herzens und ihres Willens nicht kommen!"

Dietrich Bonhoeffer and Arnold Köster

In another sermon Köster likens Cornelius (Acts 10–11) to a citizen of his own Christendom dominated time and culture. Both share a genuine religious and pious longing to find peace with God. This longing however, remains unfulfilled within the realm and scope of good charitable religion.[6] Just as Cornelius had to hear and receive God's answer to his own pressing questions so must also the most honorable religious person of Christendom. In baptism the inner emptiness is filled and sealed with the Holy Spirit. The inner reality of a new birth is given a public witness in the act of baptism.

From a Baptist point of view the tragic flaw of the *Volkskirche* model of church was that it weakened the Christian faith by effectively separating "being a Christian from obedience to Christ."[7] A Lutheran defense of infant baptism locates faith either in the wider church community or speaks of the potentiality of faith. In terms of discipleship the practice of infant baptism suspends the hard choices of following Jesus either indefinitely or to a later point in time. In contrast Köster advocated with believer's baptism that being a Christian and being obedient to Christ are one and the same.

The focus of a believer's baptism is the voluntary decision of a believer. Yet, in spite of this human focus Köster did not forget to emphasize that faith is based on divine initiative rather than human choice. In baptism God firstly claimed the individual person and secondly the individual yielded to God's gracious calling. The most momentous and holy human choice was only possible because of God's own prior and sovereign choosing. Nevertheless, the act of following Jesus began in baptism. Köster likened the risky decision of following Jesus to a leap of faith. Quoting Kierkegaard he said: "Faith is a leap into the dark! You have nothing to hold on to, there are only the words and promises of God's grace. It is impossible to experiment. Therefore baptism is always an amazing adventure."[8]

Since this typically Baptist understanding of baptism focused on the believer's voluntary act of obedience prompted by God's grace, Bonhoeffer's distinction between cheap and costly grace did not apply. Nevertheless, much time and energy of Köster's ministry was invested in reminding, challenging and drawing baptized followers of Christ again and again back into the realities of grace and obedience. To the Free Church theologian Köster, the boundary of the church was clearly defined. To the pastoral preacher,

---

6. Köster, 1 December 1940: "Viel Christentum unserer Tage ist nichts anderes als das Offenbargeworden-sein letzter Unruhe des menschlichen Herzens."

7. Täufer-Bote, 1932, No. 5, 4.

8. Köster, 2 May 1943: "Glaube ist der Sprung in das Dunkle, in die Finsternis! Du hast nichts in den Händen, es ist dir nur alles gesagt worden von Gottes Gnade. Experimentieren kannst du nicht! Darum ist Taufe das wunderbare Wagnis."

the constant need of actualizing the truths and reality to which baptism bore witness remained a perpetual task.

The Center: The Lord's Table

For Köster baptism was the entry point into the fellowship of followers of Jesus. In itself it was an expression of a human voluntary decision and a divine choice. While believer's baptism marked the boundary of the church community, the Lord's Table marked the center. During a communion service in which Köster's Bible text was Psalm 23 he stated, "This [the Lord's Table] is central to our faith existence."[9]

To Köster the fellowship round the Lord's Table was a celebration of faith—a faith strengthened by a sense of certainty (*Heilsgewißheit*) and based on the promised presence of the crucified and risen Lord. It was not an occasion to instill an emotionally charged mood for the purpose of inducing feelings of repentance among those that had gathered. Wrestling with guilt and sin, important as that might be, was for Köster not the focus of the feast. The table was prepared for sinners who had experienced God's forgiveness, who knew of redemption and who had found rest in God's presence.[10] The disciples gathered round the table because it had been prepared for them. It had been made possible by Jesus; he was the one who broke the bread for them. "With this the Lord made clear if you desire to be saved someone else has to do it. In this 'sacrament', as it is called by the church, we are shown through the word and the elements that only God can make it possible: you prepared for me!"[11]

For Köster the Lord's Table was the disciple's only safe place. This was where rest was found from the tireless accusations of one's own conscience. It was the place that truly satisfied. It was the place of forgiveness and fellowship. But it was also the place where the chasm between church and world was most apparent. In a sermon entitled, "You cannot partake of the Lord's Table and of the table of demons"[12] Köster reminded his congregation that stark opposites existed.

9. Köster, 7 December 1941, *Du bereitest*.

10. Ibid.: "Wir brauchen keine Stimmung der Buß erzwingen wollen um die rechte Bereitschaft zu kommen zum Tisch des Herrn, sondern es geht darum, die heilsgewiße Freude der Jünger Jesu Christ zu haben."

11. Ibid.: "Beim Abendmahl steht der Herr auf und bricht den Jüngern das Brot. Damit dokumentiert er, daß es ein anderer tun muß, willst du selig, errettet werden. In dem 'Sakrament,' wie die Kirche es nennt, wird mit Wort und Bild vor die Augen gestellt, es geht nur auf die göttliche Weise: Du bereitest mir!"

12. Köster, 1 January 1943, *Sitzen am Tisch*.

To gather round the table was to confess that the salvation *(Heil)* of the world was only to be found in the crucified Lord. This Lord was the *Kyrios*, the Lord of the world. The only appropriate symbol of salvation was the shameful cross and not the flaming wheel of the sun *(Flammensonnenrad)* which Köster understood to be the pagan origin of the Nazi swastika.[13]

To gather round the table was to reject any fellowship with demons. Köster was aware that in a thoroughly secular age most people had little time for ghost stories and demons, yet he located the demonic in what he called "a worldview that glorifies humanity."[14] To Köster these opposites were as far apart as the Lord's Table was from the table of demons. To eat at both of these tables was impossible for a disciple of Christ. Köster urged his congregation to remain at the Lord's Table.

The fellowship and unity experienced at the Lord's Table was with the crucified and living Lord. This Lord had willingly borne a shameful death that was contrary to ideologies of conquest and victory offering a false gospel of human salvation that sought to bypass the humiliation of the cross.

The Lord's Table created a unity that was entirely God's gracious gift. It was undeserved but was a reality wherever two or three had gathered in his name. In the coming together of ordinary disciples who gathered in faith around the Lord's Table they were reminded that they were Christ's visible body on earth. As such they were made aware of the highest gift for they had been claimed by love. Love was therefore the highest good on this earth. At the Lord's Table the disciples embodied new vision for humanity. This new humanity, shaped by love not enmity, was constituted by a common faith not by blood or race.

Nature and Calling of the Church

In his book *Discipleship* Bonhoeffer argued for a radical community of disciples emerging out of the existing church-of-the-people. Followers of Jesus would in turn revitalize and reshape God's church. The reality of the church-of-the-people model of church was that it consisted of potential and actual

---

13. Graf-Stuhlhofer, *Öffentliche Kritik*, 147: "Das Hackenkreuz ist das Zeichen des Sonnenrades..., das schon sehr früh ein heidnisch-religiöses Symbol war und... Selbsterlösung, Höherentwicklung aus eigner Kraft, Selbstvollendung zum Ausdruck bringt. Das Hackenkreuz, oder besser: das Sonnenrad in seiner ewigen Bewegung ist der sprechende Ausdruck für den Glauben des Menschen an sich selbst, an seine eigene Güte und Kraft."

14. Köster, 1 January 1943, *Sitzen am Tisch*: "Das Hauptanliegen der Dämonen ist nicht das Anliegen der Poltergeister spiritistischer Sitzungen, sondern eine wunderbare, den Menschen verherrlichende Weltanschauung!"

The Church

followers of Christ. Bonhoeffer was therefore forced to define church much more laboriously. In his thesis *Sanctorum Communio* Bonhoeffer's solution was to divide the church into three separate concentric circles.

Köster's Free Church model simply defined church as an intentional discipleship community. His was a more straightforward and radical ecclesiology, yet it would be simplistic to assume that the actual practice of following Jesus was consequently easier and less arduous. How a discipleship community constitutes itself was only one part of how faith and obedience towards Jesus were expressed. The other and ever current test was how a community expressed its faith and loyalty to God's word and will in its daily encounter with the world into which it had been called and was rooted. How did Köster define the nature of the church and how was the call to follow Jesus lived and expressed?

Nature of the Church

Köster developed this topic in one of his sermons in August 1943. The title was: "What the church of Jesus Christ is in this present period and what she should do."[15] He based his thoughts on 1 Timothy 3:13–16.[16] The text supplied him with three key metaphors which he then used to draw parallels to the church of the 1940s. The historical context of August 1943 was that it was six months after the German *Wehrmacht's* devastating defeat at Stalingrad.

He began this sermon by reminding his listeners that being Christ's church meant living in the paradox of being in the world but not of the world. Köster then used the image of a lighthouse in order to explain how the church was both in but also separate from the world. The church as a lighthouse of eternity was placed in the midst of a dark, turbulent and noisy world populated by the nations (*Völkerwelt*). The duty of the person who had been entrusted with managing a lighthouse was simply to keep lamps clean and burning. A lighthouse keeper need not be concerned whether the sea was calm or turbulent neither was it important whether anyone took notice or not. Köster's lighthouse image set the church apart

---

15. Köster, 1 August 1943, 1: "Was die Gemeinde Jesu Christ in dieser gegenwärtigen Weltzeit ist, und was sie tun soll."

16. The German Luther Bible translates it as: "Solches schreibe ich dir und hoffe, bald zu dir zu kommen; 15 so ich aber verzöge, daß du wissest, wie du wandeln sollst in dem Hause Gottes, welches ist die Gemeinde des lebendigen Gottes, ein Pfeiler und eine Grundfeste der Wahrheit. 16 Und kündlich groß ist das gottselige Geheimnis: Gott ist offenbart im Fleisch, gerechtfertigt im Geist, erschienen den Engeln, gepredigt den Heiden, geglaubt von der Welt, aufgenommen in die Herrlichkeit."

from the surrounding darkness but insisted at the same time that the role and purpose of God's church had an immediate relevance to the world into which it was placed.

The main section of Köster's sermon is structured around the apostle Paul's imagery in 1 Tim 3:15 where the church is likened to the house of God, then seen as the church of the living God and thirdly as the pillar and foundation of truth.

According to Köster the church as the house of God was for the world the only place in which a person could encounter God. Nature might communicate a sense of awe and wonder but it could not reveal a personal God. To Köster, personal knowledge of God came through his revealed word. The church was by its very nature shaped by that word and had thus become the space, or house in which the world could meet the one who had become word incarnate and continued to speak through the witness of his church. Köster was quite emphatic in his claim that the church was the only place where a human could personally encounter the living God.

As the church of the living God, the church was continually molded and affected by God's power. "The church of Jesus is in the world the object of God's special power. God acts on her and through her and thus affects the world. That is a noble thought.... We do not only gather so that we might be comforted, but as we are comforted, God works on us so that we can work in the world."[17]

A lighthouse was built of bricks and stone, the church was built by believers who had gathered. Köster expected that God worked in and through the coming together of believers which in turn provided the church community with the gift of light. This light was to bring comfort to those who had come together; however, through them light was also offered to the world. This made the church a pillar that upheld truth for everyone to behold. That truth although held up by the church, was not her's to own; it was merely entrusted to her.[18]

For Köster, truth was preserved in the Scriptures of the Old and New Testament, but it also occurred or happened in the very event of the believers coming together. To Köster, the church was built and sustained by

---

17. Köster, 1 August 1943, 2: "Die Gemeinde Jesu ist in der Welt der Gegenstand besonderer Wirkung Gottes. An ihr, und durch sie wirkt Gott an der Welt. Das ist der erhabene Gedanke. Das ist das Große, die Sache, das wir nicht nur zusammenkommen, um uns trösten zu lassen, sondern indem wir uns trösten lassen, wirkt Gott an uns, so dass wir wirken können an der Welt."

18. Ibid., 2: "Die Gemeinde ist nicht selbst die Wahrheit,—sie trägt die Wahrheit! Wie groß ist unsere Aufgabe, die Wahrheit hoch zu heben in einer Welt, die tyrannisiert ist von der Lüge."

God's word—its very existence was word based. It had received that word, it was shaped by that word and it was called to speak and proclaim that word prophetically. The life of the church was defined and sustained as it lived in the word.

In a 1940 sermon Köster spoke of "the prophetic situation of the church."[19] The sermon was based on Isaiah 6. The church, like the prophet Isaiah, was experiencing turbulent times. Thus the church constantly needed to follow the lead of the prophets, seeking new light from God's revelations. The church might not always be able to fully understand what God was revealing but it had to maintain a willing openness to learn new truths and insights.[20] Thus, Köster admitted that there was a tension between having God's word and understanding it. Neither was it easy to interpret the turbulent world events always correctly, yet it remained the church's calling to translate to the best of its ability God's word to the world. Revelation was not merely given for the edification of the gathered community. It was also addressing every living human being. The existence of the church was of a prophetic nature—prophetic in the sense that the church had the duty of interpreting the present context and events in the light of divine revelation. Like the ancient prophets, its role was to both translate and share with humanity the experience of sin and divine judgment. Yet beyond this cathartic recognition it had also a message revealing a merciful God. "Only a church that seeks insight from God and lives in the reality of God's merciful dealings can bring comfort to this world. Living in a merciless world we know a God of mercy."[21]

The Calling of the Church

Köster defined the nature of the church as a word-shaped and focused existence. The calling of the church was the natural extension of its central nature. To be God's church in the world required it to firstly remain in God's

---

19. Köster, 20 October 1940: "Die prophetische Situation der Gemeinde ist das Stehn im Erkenntiswort des Alten und Neuen Testamentes, das Leben im Bibelwort."

20. Ibid.: "Wenn die Zeitgeschehnisse uns umbranden wie die Propheten, so zwingen sie uns, so nötigen sie uns wie die Propheten immer wieder uns neues Licht zu holen von Gott her. Sie zu verstehen, das ist etwas viel verlangt, aber daß wir immer wieder offen sind für die gewaltigen Offenbarungen Gottes, um das geht es."

21. Ibid.: "Eine Gemeinde, die wirklich in der Erkenntnis vor dem Angesicht Gottes steht, die von den Erbarmungen Gottes lebt, die allein ist imstande die Welt zu trösten mit der Barmherzigkeit Gottes. Wir wissen in einer Welt der Unbarmherzigkeit von der Barmherzigkeit Gottes."

word and secondly to confess that word to the world of which the church community was an integral part.

Remaining in God's word

The duty of living in God's word, although shared by every believer, was the utmost concern of the preacher. Such a word-focused life was sustained by a godly piety but was also committed to a prophetic service (*Prophetendienst*). Köster frequently likened the church to the ministry of Old Testament prophets. Their lives and concern for their own people were but a *typos* for the present believing community.[22] Köster argued that the church needed a prophetic viewpoint,[23] that the church found itself in a prophetic situation and that there remained an abiding need for a prophetic word.[24] Karl Barth's call to the pastors and theologians of the German protestant church was to live a "theological existence."[25] Köster heeded that call but transposed the term theological into prophetic.

Barth and Köster warned against a political enthusiasm and the vain hope for a new national relevance of the church for the German people. Both argued against attempts of their respective church leaderships to associate themselves with the political revolution and the new Nazi government.[26] Both insisted that being a minister and teacher of God's word demanded undivided[27] attention to Scripture even when the result was public isolation and rejection.[28]

---

22. Köster, 29 June 1941, *Elia:* "Wir haben in der Geschichte dieser Prophetengestalt [Elia] einen prophetischen Typus. Aus dieser Geschichte kann uns das Licht hineinleuchten in unser Fragen . . . Weg und Schicksal Elias beispielhaft für uns . . . für alle Kirchen und kleine persönliche Glaubensgemeinschaften."

23. Täufer-Bote, 1933, No 10, 2: "Die prophetische Schau der Gemeinde."

24. Täufer-Bote, 1941, No 10, 1: "Warum immer wieder das prophetische Wort?"

25. Barth, "Theologische Existenz Heute."

26. Köster, 29 June 1941: "Wie haben die Kirchen und Gemeinden immer danach getrachtet, Öffentlichkeitscharkter zu bekommen in dieser Welt. Und haben es nicht verstanden, daß es göttlicher Wille war, daß sie Verborgenheitscharakter haben!"

27. Barth, "Theologische Existenz Heute," 5: "Und dies ists, was ich unsere theologische Existenz nenne: daß uns inmitten unsere sonstigen Existenz . . . das Wort Gottes das sein, was es nun einmal ist und was nur es uns sein kann und insbesondere unsere Berufung als Prediger und Lehrer uns so in Anspruch nehme, wie nur sie uns in Anspruch nehmen kann und darf." (Passage marked by Köster).

28. Ibid., 39: "Und dieser Auftrag will durchgeführt sein, gleichviel ob das Volk selbst es wünscht oder nicht wünscht, versteht oder nicht versteht, gutheißt oder nicht gutheißt. Wir dürfen weder Dank noch Ehre erwarten." (Passage marked by Köster).

For Köster the event of hearing God's word was located within the community of gathered believers. A preacher would spend time studying God's word in the lonely confines of a study, but the message only became God's prophetic word when it was delivered to a gathered church community. Every preacher remained mute, Köster claimed, unless there was a corresponding sounding board *(Resonanzboden)*. Utilizing the metaphor of a stringed instrument he likened the preacher to the string and the listening congregation to the resonating body. "A preacher, who is but a mere string, will never be able to deliver his message to the children of this world unless there is a sound board, too. Therefore, our coming together as a listening community is of vital importance. Only then can God's word be spoken into the hearts of people out there."[29]

The combined act of preaching and listening allowed God's word to resonate not just to those who were presently engaged in the actual event, but through them, it was also reaching out to those who were beyond the immediate circle of the believing community. Köster implicitly likened his own sense of calling to prophets like Jeremiah, yet also insisted that a prophet never served in isolation. Prophets were an integral part of a faith community. Thus, the gathered church was not likened to a passive receptacle into which God's word was poured through the ministry of a preacher. Rather, the communicative dynamic of God's word happened and reverberated through the lives of the gathered believers into an unbelieving world.

The church was defined as a community of believers who were shaped by God's word. In order to remain in God's word the act of coming together was crucial. No doubt many of those that had gathered in the Mollardgasse struggled with doubts and guilt, were fearful of the authorities, felt confused and unable to prophetically challenge the world. To those, Köster's pastoral message was: "Not everyone is called to be a preacher. Yet, your part could be to simply come as we gather and in your coming you give an affirmative witness. The world will notice it and maybe it is what God expects of you just now.... Where there is a resonating body in the church for the word of God, there the church is a city on a hill and a light to the world."[30]

---

29. Köster, 2 September 1943: "Ein Prediger der nur Seite ist aber keinen Resonanzboden hat, wird seine Botschaft nie anbringen können bei den Kindern dieser Welt. Darum ist es so nötig, dass wir besammen sind als hörende Gemeinde, damit Gott sein Wort hineinrufen und hineinsagen kann in die Herzen der Menschen da draußen!"

30. Köster, 20 October 1940: "Nicht jeder ist berufen Prediger zu sein. Vielleicht ist dein Anteil an der Aufgabe der, daß du in die Versammlung kommst und dadurch dein Ja bekundest. Die Welt sieht das und vielleicht ist es das, was Gott von dir gerade erwartet.... Wenn ein Resonanzboden da ist in der Gemeinde für das Wort Gottes, da wird diese Gemeinde eine Stadt auf dem Berge sein, ein Licht auf einem Leuchter!"

Dietrich Bonhoeffer and Arnold Köster

Confessing God's Word

The church was the house or location where encounters with the living God were possible. The church was also a pillar for the truth. The light it received was not just for those who had gathered in secrecy or relative security but was meant to shine forth like the lamps of a lighthouse. The prophetic word addressed and challenged the world and its assumptions through a confessing community. For Köster it was clear "we must not cease to speak."[31] The term "confessing church" to Köster was not a reference to a particular written confession but to the reception of and the witness to Jesus Christ.

Without a clear confession the church would neither be able to serve the world nor would it be able to withstand the threats it had to face. Köster insisted that the church was threatened by Satan whose aim always was to destroy the faith. The church community was threatened by false teachers who proclaimed myths rather than the truths of the apostle's teaching. These myths were but bubbles that had emerged from the murky ponds of the subconscious but were nevertheless dangerous distortions of God's word.[32] To confess truth implied the rejection of lies. Satan, the father of all lies, was busy engaging false prophets who offered their destructive and blinding versions of ideas, ideologies, and worldviews.[33] Köster did not argue for a quiet withdrawal of Christians or for an other-worldly eschatological hope that was designed to make present trials tolerable. He urged his congregation to confess and to live holy lives[34] in the midst of turmoil and upheaval.

In a 1941 sermon Köster described the nature, demands and dangers of a confessing community by paralleling it to the story of Elijah.[35] Like the prophet, the church needed to become painfully aware of the all too rampant godlessness and, in response, issue a critical challenge. The choice was between seeking God's kingdom or the things of this world. To the discipleship community this was not just a matter of issuing to the world a quick take it or leave it message, followed by a quick retreat into the safety of the church community. The challenge for the church was to internalize and carry in a priestly fashion the godlessness of the people. This agonizing process of connecting to the world stimulated in turn the witness of the church. It motivated it to preach a gospel that offered hope to the lost sin-

---

31. Köster, 20 October 1940, *Prophetische Situation*.

32. Köster, 1 August 1943, *Gemeinde*.

33. Köster, 7 March 1943: "Wenn ein Mensch einmal von einer Idee, einer Weltanschauung besessen ist, ist er radikal blind für das Evangelium."

34. Köster, 1 August 1943: "Wenn sie bekennende Gemeinde ist, und wenn sie fromme Gemeinde ist."

35. Köster, 29 June 1941: "Vom Weg und Schicksal der Kirchen in der Weltzeit."

ner rather than seeking to further vain attempts of propping up a general Christian culture.

For Köster, carrying the world's godlessness within its own heart represented the glory of the church. This was its call and painful duty. When the church addressed and exposed the emptiness of the world, conflict with the world was inevitable. To Köster the price of such a prophetic ministry was a sense of utter weariness. The demands were simply beyond human strength and it was therefore no surprise that the wider church, the heirs of the Reformation churches and the heirs of the Anabaptist churches, had become tired and exhausted. Köster asked, referencing this experience to Elijah's story, whether the present crisis spelled the end of God's church? Yet, in drawing parallels to the story of Elijah, Köster was able to interpret the experienced fears and depression as a possibility for a new vision given by God—a vision that was not confined to previous concepts and thought constructs, but was to bring new and surprising insights. The prophet could only meet God in this new way within the context of despair and loneliness. Köster urged the church to embrace the despair that was acutely felt in the 1940s with expectant hope. The new vision might even include the dissolution of the church as it was known, yet God's ways had not come to an end even then. "Even when the church of our days as we know it, in a conflict with the world state, is dissolved—God has already set a new epoch in motion! Let us not worry about the loss of public respectability. Let us not believe that God's work has come to an end. The vessel can break, so that the world can see what will remain for ever."[36]

The calling of God's church was to remain in and to confess God's word. Conflict with the forces that sought to oppose God's truth and God's people was part of the inevitable and unavoidable nature of the prophetic ministry envisaged by Köster. The church was therefore called to do battle against untruth, mostly represented in the false claims and ideologies of the world.

It has to be remembered that this battle lacked a clear dividing line between God's church and the world. The world with its structures, demands and propaganda was for ever present. Members of the church and their sons were called up into military service and were sent to the front. Supply of food and basic needs was sparse and distribution of it was the responsibility of state officials. The local church community simply was part of the people and equally affected by the constraints and demands of its historical context.

In the sermon he preached after the defeat at Stalingrad, Köster emphasized the priestly calling of the church and reminded his congregation that "we are placed in the midst of our German people—our calling is a priestly

---

36. Köster, 29 June 1941, *Elia*.

service."[37] His text was Jeremiah 8. Like the prophet Jeremiah, the church was called to stand against and with the people. Faced with an overwhelming disaster the prophet diagnosed the root cause as the godlessness of the people. Standing with the people meant for Köster the painful admission that the church had failed to speak the truth while at the same time it had willingly provided its blessing for untruth. What needed to be heard was that the people's only hope was God. Yet God's help could not be demanded or claimed, for it was only given when God becomes our home.[38] The term "home" was doubtless a play on the hyped-up Nazi version of *Heimat* or fatherland.

God's people shared the godlessness of their time, but they were also called to priestly ministry. Their task was to offer prayer and intercession and to ask on behalf of the people for a new outpouring of God's reviving grace.

An Eschatological Ecclesiology

In February 1945 Köster preached: "For almost thirty years I have been a preacher and it has been a strange experience that through the faithful reading of the Old and New Testament I have been powerfully led and steered by the eschatological word of the Bible. . . . Many of my colleagues became enticed by the spirit of the Antichrist, yet I was able to remain free from it because I maintained an eschatological perspective."[39]

To Köster the eschatological attitude or perspective was of utmost importance. His stubborn insistence of making the return of Jesus Christ a frequent topic in his preaching ministry made him a laughing stock to some, yet he persisted. For him the suffering world's only comfort was the message of the returning Christ.

This eschatological focus began as a student. Köster delivered a lecture at the graduation ceremony at the seminar Hamburg-Horn on the theme of the Antichrist.[40] This focus was then further developed and

37. Köster, 7 February 1943, *Mein Volk*.
38. Köster, 7 February 1943: "Wenn Gott uns wieder Heimat wird."
39. Köster, 8 February 1945: "Ich schaue heute auf eine lange Predigerzeit zurück, bald 30 Jahre. Und das Eigenartige ist gewesen, daß ich innerlich beim treuen Lesen des Alten und Neuen Testamentes mit einer ungeheuren Konsequenz und Gewalt zu dem sogenannten eschatologischen Wort der Bibel geführt worden bin. . . . Wenn viele meiner Kollegen dem antichristlichen Geist verfallen sind und nachher gewesen sind wie Fliegen auf dem Fliegenleim, habe ich die selige Freiheit behalten diesem antichristlichen Geist gegenüber um der eschatologischen Haltung meines Geistes willen. Man hat manchmal darüber gelacht, daß ich immer von der Wiederkunft Christi redete."
40. Graf-Stuhlhofer, *Öffentliche Kritik*, 21. Köster was one of three graduates who were asked to present a lecture during the graduation ceremony of 1923. The total

The Church

refined in his long ministry. How did this perspective shape his understanding of church? Did it lead him to propose a strict dichotomy between a world bereft of God's presence and a future heavenly hope of God's reign and glory? How did this waiting for the returning Jesus Christ impact the responses followers of Jesus had to make facing the challenges and struggles of the Third Reich period?

Köster, like many of his contemporaries, was acutely aware of a deepening crisis. As a young man he was drafted into military service during the Great War and in the aftermath observed the numerous competing ideologies of the Weimar Republic. Unlike many of his Baptist colleagues, he judged the emerging Nazi ideology atheistic and demonic. To him all human-made solutions were mere deceptive illusions. In the midst of all chaos the only viable hope was the return of the Lord. He claimed in February 1943 that he had reached this conclusion only after researching and surveying all human endeavors aimed at achieving the redemption of humanity but found them wanting. "My hope is based on the returning Christ . . . this is the constant theme of my preaching ministry. I cannot see any other solution out of this chaos but the returning and renewing Christ."[41]

Clearly this eschatological perspective was a central key to his theology. A more literal translation of the above quote is "a constant tone, which works its way through all my preaching." The term "*durchschwingender Ton*" indicates that eschatology was not only there explicitly but also implicitly giving shape and structure to his thinking as he interpreted and expounded biblical texts. This next section will attempt to discern how the theme of Köster's eschatological perspective shaped his ecclesiology. The main focus of this investigation is on a lengthy exposition of Paul's Second Letter to the Corinthians Köster preached during the first half of 1943.[42]

---

number of graduates was thirteen.

41. Köster, 31 January1943: "Man kann mich, in meiner Hoffnung auf den wiederkommenden Christus auch nur verstehen, wenn man weiß, wie ich geforscht und gesucht habe in allen menschlichen Unternehmungen nach der Erlösung der Menschheit, bis ich mir gesagt habe, es gibt nur eine Lösung der Weltkrisis, und das ist der wiederkommende Herr. Darum ist das dauernd der Ton, der durchschwingt durch meine Verkündigung, weil ich keinen anderen Ausweg sehe aus dem Chaos, als bis der Christus zugreift und alles neu macht!"

42. Köster started the 2 Corinthians series 17 January and finished it 6 July 1943. The document consists of 120 pages.

Dietrich Bonhoeffer and Arnold Köster

The Present Exposed by the End

The shrill tone of Köster's persistent deconstruction of all political solutions had become somewhat muted in 1943. During the 1930s he attempted to shield the members of his congregations and the readers of the *Täufer-Bote* from vain and empty political hopes.[43] In 1943 the pastoral demands had changed. People struggled with an increasing sense of despair and found themselves hopelessly caught in threatening world events. Yet to Köster, these events were part of the outworking of God's judgment. They exposed the extent of human hubris and, in spite of devastating consequences; these events still had the potential of becoming avenues of grace if people were to turn to the merciful God.

For Köster, the church of God, which could never be a mysterious "invisible church"[44] but was always a tangible and visible fellowship of believers, was called to be the body of Christ in the midst of this conflict and crisis. According to Köster's eschatological perspective, the church's place, purpose and role were therefore shaped by a cosmic struggle. The two opposing sides were on the one hand the spirit of Satan and on the other hand the spirit of Christ. However, the battle line between the two was not simply drawn between a godless world and the church. To be part of God's church was neither an automatic guarantee of purity, nor was the church a safe haven. The spiritual battle did not just rage outside the church but was also a constant challenge within. "There are always two possibilities . . . either the church of Jesus Christ receives her inspiration from the Christ or from Satan."[45] The medium and tools of Satan's power were ideas and persuasive speech designed to entice and capture the thinking of a human being. Contrary to popular, crude, medieval depictions of a horned and hoofed being, Köster saw Satan as being intelligent and clever—the master creator of worldviews that ensnared people through the use of reason and intelligence. Making it impossible for those trapped into these thought patterns to perceive truth

---

43. Köster, 16 April 1939: "Die Verkündigung von Jesus dem Christus ist der totale Angriff auf alle Sicherungen dieser Erde, auf ihre Macht und Größe. Die glaubende Gemeinde predigt den Christus als den Wiederkommenden, der das Ende für alle irdische Macht bedeutet."

44. Köster, 17 January 1943, 2 Cor, 4: "Man möchte doch ein wenig vorsichtiger sein mit dem Wort: unsichtbare Gemeinde! Eine Gemeinde Jesu Christi kann man greifen, man kann sie sehen, weil sie zusammenkommt. Eine 'unsichtbare Gemeinde,' die nicht zusammenkommt ist keine Gemeinde."

45. Ibid., 28: "Es gibt in der Gemeinde immer zwei Möglichkeiten . . . Entweder die Gemeinde Jesu Christi empfängt von dem Christus her ihre Inspiration, oder sie wird vom satanischen Geist her bewegt."

The Church

outside the narrow confines of their thinking.[46] But this, Köster insisted, was not only a real danger for the world but also an ever present danger for the church. Yet believers could embrace the elasticity and freedom of thought which was the unique gift of the Holy Spirit to the church. He urged his congregation, "we must leave the prisons of our thinking, only then can we learn to judge everything without being judged ourselves."[47]

He saw the church set within the world as a community of believers who needed the constant guidance of God's word and Spirit and a life that was shaped by a living relationship with Jesus Christ. The church's role was not to provide a sanctuary from the struggles that rage in the world. The ministry of the word was not to provide mere edifying and soothing comfort-talk but the clear and daring confrontation with Satan's deceptions. The church could not avoid battle and had to wield "the Spirit's sword"[48] or face defeat. To Köster, the church's call was to engage with the world through an offensive and daring strategy. He rejected notions of retreat or a pious "let's-keep-a-low-profile" policy. The church could not avoid being in the world, yet was to offer at the same time God's powerful gospel to a lost world. "It is necessary to preach the clear gospel in our city. Not a gospel, that calms the believing heart, making it still, drugging it into a cozy slumber, but the gospel which in combative energy does battle with today's worldview that is spreading darkness and lostness in this world. We know that we cannot achieve that by our own strength, but we can believe that God will use his word with creative power."[49]

---

46. Ibid., 47: "Wie arbeitet nun Satan . . . Er macht das so, daß er ihre Gedankenwelt mit einer festen Gedankenmeinung dämonisiert, so daß dann dieser Mensch diese Gedanken für wahr hält. 'Man kann doch gar nicht anders denken,' sagt dann solch ein in seiner Weltanschauung festgefahrener Mensch, 'wie kann man denn dieses christliche Denken, das über das Abendland solchen Unfug und Unsinn gebracht hat, noch weiter denken?'"

47. Ibid., 45: "Wir müssen heraus aus allen Gefängnissen unseres Denkens, damit wir alles beurteilen können, aber nicht verurteilt werden können, weil wir in der Freiheit eines Christusmenschen stehen. Wenn ein Mensch nicht willens ist, gedanklich zu kapitulieren, kann er nicht zur Erkenntnis der Wahrheit in Jesu Christi kommen. Wenn meine Gedankenwelt für mich heilig ist, tabu, dann lasse alle Hoffnung fahren!"

48. Ibid., 89: "In unseren Tagen können wir nicht mehr fertig werden mit diesem leichten Kämpfen, das so gar nicht verwundet durch die 'erbauliche' Predigt. In diesen Geisteskampf, in dem wir stehen, gehören die schweren Fechtinstrumente, das 'Schwert des Geistes,' soll der Kampf siegreich sein!"

49. Ibid., 48: "Laßt uns doch das eine heute wieder empfunden haben, wie nötig es ist, daß in unserer Stadt ein klares Evangelium ist. Nicht das Evangelium, das die gläubigen Herzen ein wenig stille macht und ein-lullt, ein-schlummert und narkotisiert, sondern ein Evangelium, das in streitbarer Energie sich auseinander zu setzen weiß mit der Weltanschauung, die heute die Welt umdüstert und sie verloren macht. Wir wissen, daß wir das nicht aus eigener Kraft haben, aber wir dürfen glauben, daß Gott sein Wort

Dietrich Bonhoeffer and Arnold Köster

Köster insisted the certain hope of Christ's return was the sustaining vision that the church needed in order to remain faithful to its calling and arduous task. Cross, resurrection and the reception of the Holy Spirit were monumental milestones in God's sovereign plan yet "the greatest and most beautiful"[50] was still to come with Christ's return.

Suffering Transformed by Future Hope

Combating the deceptive schemes of the world inevitably results in conflict and suffering. Köster was suspicious of any careful strategies designed to avoid suffering and lamented that the Christianity of his day was in acute danger of betraying Christ himself. He judged these policies as an outright "sell out" and a "willing cooperation with the spirit of this world"[51] in order to avoid suffering, humiliation and prison. Commenting on 2 Corinthians 1:3–11, Köster held up the example of the apostle Paul and urged the church not only to experience God's mercy, but also to accept the call to embrace the suffering of this time and this world.[52] However, he felt a distinction must be made between a general suffering that is simply a part of the curse-characteristic of this world and a specific suffering that is endured on account of following Jesus Christ.[53] Köster fully expected that one day the world's antagonism against the gospel would lead the church increasingly into a suffering for the sake of Christ.

Köster made clear that Christians were not immune from general suffering, but had to undergo the trials and tribulations of this world just like unbelievers. Yet, as believers they could bear witness to the comfort they had in their hope in Christ's return. Thus, in the shared experience of general suffering the church took on a priestly function and role. Following the example of its Lord the church was called to embrace suffering and through it,

---

in seiner schöpferischen Kraft gebrauchen wird."

50. Ibid., 22: "Daß er wiederkommt, daß ist wirklich das Größte und das Schönste! Alles andere ist nur ein Vorspiel von dem, was Gott noch tun will am Ende der Tage."

51. Ibid., 7: "Das ganze vorsichtige Getue der Christenheit unserer Tage, diese Vorsichtigkeit, die bis an den Verrat an der Sache des Christus grenzt ist in gewissem Sinne Leidensscheu! Man ist bereit, alles zu verkaufen. Wir stehen da vor der Tatsache, daß die Christenheit bereit ist, mit der Geisteshaltung dieser Welt mitzulaufen, damit sie nur ja nicht leiden müsse, daß sie nicht in Schmach und Gefängnis hinein muß!"

52. Ibid., 10: "Die Gemeinde Jesu Christi hat Anteil an der Kreuzesnachfolge. Die Gemeinde Jesu Christi ist nicht nur gerufen, die Barmherzigkeit Gottes zu erleben, sondern sie ist gerufen, in das Leid dieser Weltzeit einzutreten."

53. Ibid., 48: "Man muß einen Unterschied machen zwischen den Leiden, die ein Apostel hat um dem Namens Jesu Willen und den Leiden, in denen wir drinnenstehen, die uns erwachsen aus dem 'Fluch-charakter' dieser Welt."

meet, experience and be comforted by God. Köster stated, "In suffering we experience God, and through it we are enabled to proclaim God's comfort to a suffering humanity."[54] The church, guided by God's word, may reject the godless assumptions and schemes of the world but would nevertheless have to endure the dire consequences of the world's hubris. For Köster the nature of the clash was eschatological yet while this earthly conflict lasted the church shared in the general suffering and had to, when called upon, also embrace the specific suffering the faithful proclamation of the gospel of Jesus Christ might cause. As early as 1939 Köster preached, "one cannot overcome the evil of this world through evil, one can only overcome it by suffering through it."[55]

The fellowship of believers was thus set within the realities of the world but was also given an eschatological vantage point that provided and sustained it with hope and purpose. On the personal level God's transforming purposes were attained through the path of suffering and a dying to self. For Köster, suffering did not indicate a God-forsakenness, but the promise that God continued to work out his purposes not only for the individual believer's sanctification but in and through it God's blessings were offered to the world. In the suffering of God's people, the dying of Christ continued to be revealed and provided therefore a powerful and positive witness.[56]

An ever present fact and fear for many of Köster's congregation was the reality of death. The death of loved ones drafted into the *Wehrmacht* or a death within the relative safety of one's home. What happens to a believer at the point of death? "What happens to our dying brothers on the battlefields?"[57] Köster sought to address these existential and pastoral questions in his exposition on 2 Corinthians 5:1–10. Interestingly, as Köster explored the issues of death, his focus was the fate of the believer, leaving the wider question regarding everyone's death unanswered. In his exposition of the passage he likened dying to the final deconstruction of the earthly tent followed by the subsequent transformation of the inner person (*inwendige Mensch*) into the heavenly home.[58] The focus of his ex-

54. Ibid., 10: "Wir müssen leiden um Gott zu erfahren, damit wir Gott den leidenden Menschen als den Gott aller Tröstung verkündigen zu können."

55. Köster, 1938–39, 1 Peter: "Man kann das Böse in der Welt nicht durch Böses überwinden, man kann es nur besiegen, indem man daran leidet!"

56. Köster, 7 January 1943, 2 Cor, 52: "Aber hier ist noch ein letztes Ziel, das Gott mit dem Leid seiner Gläubigen verfolgt. Es soll fortwährend das Sterben Jesu offenbar werden . . . Das Leid ist nicht etwas Passives, sondern das Positivste in unserem Leben, weil da die ewigen Kräfte freigelegt werden zum Segen für andere."

57. Ibid., 56.

58. Ibid., 57: "Also, der inwendige Mensch, der gläubige Mensch, der Mensch Gottes

position was transformation rather than the immortality of the soul and the view that the body was a mere prison of the soul. God promised a resurrection body that would share some of the earthly body's characteristics but would be at the same time a new level of eternal existence. The inner person's first home was the earthly tent which would suffer final deconstruction at the point of death. Death might either occur while the believer was peacefully asleep or it might come violently on the battlefield. Yet, God promised to the believer—whatever the circumstances—the transforming gift of a new resurrection body, a new heavenly home.

The pastor Köster reminded his church that God has overcome death in Jesus Christ. On the one hand this took away an unnecessary fear of death. For the believer, death was a sudden moment of transition in which the inner person was welcomed into the heavenly home. Is it then legitimate for a Christian to long for a good death, to be released from the present struggles? Interestingly, while Köster affirmed the certainty of Christian hope, he also insisted at the same time that dying remained a serious matter. He remembered the intense inner struggles his own mother had at her death and consequently resisted making little of the grim reality of dying and death. For that reason alone, to be transformed in an instant, at Christ's return was, he felt, preferable to dying. Following Paul's argument (2 Cor 5:4) he insisted that the true longing of a follower of Christ is not for a good death but for the return of Christ, when the earthly body will be exchanged for the heavenly body, thus bypassing death.

A believer had therefore two exit strategies, each providing great comfort. He likened the two possible entry points into God's glorious *eschaton* to two doors. The first door—personal death—was small and required an uncomfortable squeeze, the second—Christ's return—was a massive glorious gateway that led straight into God's future.[59] The church could not know either time or place but it could be certain of that final exit.[60]

Conclusion

Köster's own claim that his ministry was built around eschatology *(durchschwingender Ton)* was correct. It is the eschatological perspective that

---

geht im Augenblick des Sterbens heraus aus der diesseitigen irdischen Wohnung in den ewigen himmlischen Bau, der im Himmel ist."

59. Ibid., 61.

60. Ibid., 51: "Auch bei meiner Lösung von meiner Leibesexistenz weiß ich, der Christus kommt, und macht alles neu! Und wenn es keinen anderen Ausweg gibt, und wenn es 10 Jahre, 100 Jahre, 1000 Jahre dauert, das ist der Ausweg!"

The Church

provides a sense of theological consistency to what first appears a fragmented ecclesiology. It is from this big eschatological vision that all lines are sketched into the daily concerns of the church and the individual believer's existence and discipleship. God's church, redeemed by the cross, called to follow its Lord, and sustained by the Holy Spirit was firmly rooted in the world. This world was not a wholesome world (*heile Welt*) but a world under God's curse, marred by suffering and subject to the sinful consequences of human choices. But as the church of God it was offered a unique vantage point, enabling it to see beyond the confines of this world into the heavenly realities that God has in store for his people and his world. Köster consistently affirmed both of these truths and used the inherent conflict and frustration the two produce as a creative tension, which in turn shaped his thinking and ministry as he followed Jesus.

Bonhoeffer and Church

The first half of this chapter sought to describe Köster's incidental ecclesiology. In contrast Bonhoeffer's ecclesiology was far from incidental; it was the subject of his doctoral thesis. In *Sanctorum Communio* he blended together sociological, theological and biblical exposition. He continued to develop his understanding of the church in his subsequent books, especially in *Discipleship* and in the *Ethics*. Even during the final part of his life, Bonhoeffer continued to reflect on the nature of the church, as the *Letters and Papers from Prison* clearly show.

The limited aim of the following section is to explore key themes of Bonhoeffer's understanding of church and to relate these to Köster's ecclesiology.

Bonhoeffer's Ecclesiology:
A Theological Study of the Sociology of the Church

A unique feature of Bonhoeffer's *Sanctorum Communio* was its attempt to combine insights of sociology and theology in order to achieve a better understanding of the church. The summary statement, "Christ existing as church-community,"[61] was not only arrived at via a theological process based on revelation, but was also deduced from the field of human sociology. The combination of theological and sociological arguments made Bonhoeffer's approach to ecclesiology interesting. However, his approach was not without

61. Bonhoeffer, *Sanctorum*, 121, 199, etc.

its critics. The sociologist Peter Berger argued that Bonhoeffer adopted an eclectic approach regarding his use of sociology. Ultimately, he remained a theologian who used sociology as a stepping stone for the purpose of constructing a theological argument.[62] His cousin Hans-Christoph von Hase commented: "there will not be many who really understand it, the Barthians won't because of sociology, and the sociologists won't because of Barth."[63]

As the title *Sanctorum Communio* suggests, Bonhoeffer's chosen description of the church was community. In this respect Bonhoeffer and Köster were in agreement. For Köster, the term church (*Kirche*) was descriptive of religious institution whilst the German word *Gemeinde* (community) focused on those who had voluntarily come to join God's new community.

In the German language, the term *Gemeinde* is difficult to pin down simply because it is used in all sorts of contexts. It is used to describe a local political group of people and a certain geographical area. It is also used to signify a collective group or person (*Kollektivperson*), as the people who happen to live in a specific geographical location very similar to the English word "parish." The new English edition of Bonhoeffer's works translates *Gemeinde* as church-community. Consequently, in English the ambivalence of the word *Gemeinde* is somewhat reduced. Readers are encouraged to equate church-community with a community of disciples. This is a clarity lacking in the original German.[64]

In *Sanctorum Communio*, Bonhoeffer began by looking first of all at the basic building blocks of any social community. To him this was expressed and rooted in the concept of the person.[65] Bonhoeffer argues that the prerequisite of a Christian concept of personhood is relationship. "The individual exists only in relation to an other."[66] Individuality or personhood is dependent on the other—the "I" only knows itself through the complex process of relating to a "You." Thus, it was persons engaged in relationships

---

62. Peter Berger, "Sociology and Ecclesiology," in Marty et al., *Place of Bonhoeffer*, 53–79: "One looks in vain through the pages of Sanctorum Communio for any utilization of empirical data concerning the relationship of religion and society.—What Bonhoeffer does, in fact, is to cap a certain philosophical approach with a theological extension. . . . As it is, the dogmatic parts of Bonhoeffer's investigation at this point of the argument, as at others, smacks a little of theological imperialism. That is, elements are taken out of other disciplines and pressed willy-nilly into a theological frame of reference" (59–60).

63. Bethge, *Dietrich Bonhoeffer*, 58–59.

64. Bonhoeffer, *Sanctorum*, 14–19. See Matters of Translation.

65. Ibid., 34: "Every concept of community is essentially related to a concept of person. It is impossible to say what constitutes community without asking what constitutes a person."

66. Ibid., 51.

The Church

which were seen by him as the basic building blocks of human communities. Next Bonhoeffer developed this theme further by extending the social I-You dimension into the I-Thou relation, the relationship with God. These were, in his view, not two separate layers of relating—one at a horizontal the other at a vertical level—they were interwoven.[67] Being human was therefore essentially a social and relational existence. Individuality was a social process and was not to be achieved, as German idealism had attempted, by the isolation of the subject from all other individuals.

Bonhoeffer linked the phenomena of isolation and self-centeredness theologically to the fall. "This [the fall] gave rise to the break in immediate community with God, and likewise in human community."[68] Sin introduced the reality of selfish demands and "voluntary isolation"[69] rather than relationships which were part of the original state characterized by openness, giving and love. Sin affected and distorted all social relations and can therefore be theologically expressed as original sin. Bonhoeffer argued that the term Adam referred to the collective person, the entire human race.

> The structure of humanity-in-Adam is unique because it is both composed of many isolated individuals and yet is one, as the humanity that has sinned as a whole. It is "Adam," a collective person, who can only be superseded by the collective person "Christ existing as church-community." Sin is the sign of belonging to the old humanity, to the first Adam; consciousness of guilt reveals to individuals their connection with all sinners. When individuals recognize that they belong to Adam's humanity, they join the peccatorum communio [community of sinners]. "The humanity of sin" is one, *though consisting of nothing but individuals. It is a collective person, yet infinitely fragmented. It is Adam, since all individuals are themselves and Adam. This duality is its essence, and it is superseded [aufgehoben] only through the unity of the new humanity in Christ.*[70]

Although sin strikes at the heart of human relationships, restoration through a new Christ community was God's gracious offer and act. Sin established a community of sinners characterized by individual isolation and a being-against-each-other. The characteristics of the church-community were modeled on the vicarious Christ, thus its members were to be

---

67. Ibid., 54–55.
68. Ibid., 107.
69. Ibid., 108.
70. Ibid., 121.

"with-each-other and for-each-other."[71] Bonhoeffer used the term vicarious not just doctrinally, to speak of the vicarious death Christ suffered on the cross. He used it also ethically, referring to an attitude of service, a being-for-each-other mindset that was to be characteristic of the members of the new humanity in Christ. Although members of the new Christ community had "died to sin,"[72] the reality of sin remained . The fact that God created a new community did not yet supersede the reality of the old order of sin at this point in time.[73] Neither did Bonhoeffer assume that the members of the *sanctorum communio* are automatically transformed into saints. God's new community had to live and exist in the context of an intrinsic tension. Its members were at the same time saints and sinners and as a communal body it had to exist at a time when God's kingdom had already come, while at the same time it had not yet fully arrived.

Bonhoeffer made clear that the historical and the present church were of a complex nature. It existed as a *sanctorum communio* but also as *peccatorum communio*. He addressed this issue somewhat by making a distinction between the essential and the empirical church. Through the word of the crucified and risen Lord, the essential church became an actualized reality. It was sustained by the Spirit who called individuals into a community of believers. He describes these people as "loving persons who, touched by God's Spirit, radiate love and grace."[74]

So far there would have been a lot of common ground and little disagreement between the Baptist Köster and the Lutheran Bonhoeffer. However, once the discussion moved to distinguishing between essential and empirical church, the potential for disagreement increased. Bonhoeffer conceded that even though Christ existed as a church community here and now, the empirical realities of that church were far more complex. To him the empirical church was "the organized 'institution' of salvation."[75] It was a legal body that administered the liturgical rite and often had some political influence within the wider society and the state. The empirical church, as a historical reality, was the product and outcome of the work of Christ within a particular region, culture and people. Set within Bonhoeffer's German context, it existed as the church-of-the-people. Nevertheless, the crucial

---

71. Ibid., 178.

72. Rom 6:2.

73. Bonhoeffer, *Sanctorum*, 124: "The reality of sin and the communio peccatorum remain even in God's church-community; Adam has really been replaced by Christ only eschatologically."

74. Ibid., 175.

75. Ibid., 208.

question was "how can a church, which as a human community is by its very nature a community of wills, be a church for all people at the same time?"[76]

Threefold Layers of Bonhoeffer's Ecclesiology

Baptismal Community (*Taufgemeinde*)

Bonhoeffer's ecclesiology accepted the church-of-the-people model as a given structure and valued it as the historical work of Christ. However, he then proceeded to distinguish within the wider body of the church-of-the-people three different layers of community. These layers can be likened to three concentric circles, of which the largest, outer ring represented all those that had been welcomed into the church by baptism. Bonhoeffer called this the Baptismal Community (*Taufgemeinde*). In baptism, God's gracious offer of salvation was extended and the call to discipleship was issued. Bonhoeffer recognized that acceptance of this offer was not fully realized at the point of baptism but had to be personally actualized. It was therefore the duty of a church that practiced infant baptism to nurture and instruct its baptized members into the faith that was potentially theirs already. Such nurturing ministry could only be provided by a caring and committed core community and Bonheoffer conceded that where this was no longer a reality, infant baptism was no longer possible. "Infant baptism is no longer meaningful wherever the church can no longer envision 'carrying' the child."[77] As a Lutheran, Bonhoeffer embraced and defended infant baptism and viewed it as a sacramental act that incorporated the child into the faith community, for "the faith of the child is that of the whole church-community."[78] But he was also conscious of the fact that a church that had ceased to have a meaningful connection between the people had ceased to be the church-of-the-people. Once that was the case, a different model of church was required. The church had to become a missionary church (*Missionskirche*). A logical implication would be, although Bonhoeffer does not state it explicitly in *Sanctorum Communio* that believer's baptism would then become the appropriate baptismal practice.

---

76. Ibid., 219.
77. Ibid., 241.
78. Ibid.

Dietrich Bonhoeffer and Arnold Köster

A Baptist's Concern

As a Baptist, Köster had a different view of baptism. However, since he lived in a society where infant baptism was widely practiced, he made careful distinctions. During a baptismal service in 1940 he said:

> There are many people amongst the church and various church fellowships, who have had a clear conversion experience with Jesus Christ. They believe that they have received the Holy Spirit and we cannot deny it. Through their personal encounter with Jesus they fulfill retrospectively what happened at their infant baptism. Such fulfillment is wonderfully protestant. However this is not a baptism that conforms to what the first Christians practiced! Who knows when we will have a similar ur-Christian context again? Maybe in a few decades? At such a time it will not be possible to maintain the practice of infant baptism.[79]

Köster was willing to respect the value of infant baptism of those who had come to a personal faith. Yet, at the same time he found it impossible to include the large swathe of baptized people into the realm of the church simply because they had been baptized as infants. To Köster, the baptismal community represented an inner and not an outer layer of the church-community.

In 1942 Bonhoeffer was asked by the Confessing Church leadership to address this issue when one of their ministers, A. Hitzer, had published a pamphlet[80] that criticized the practice of infant baptism. In his book *Discipleship* Bonhoeffer had accepted that "Cheap grace is . . . baptism without the discipline of community."[81] Yet, for him the implication was for the church to nurture all its baptized members and care for them responsibly. As far as it can be known, this remained his conviction.

---

79. Köster, 1 January 1940, *Ansprache*: "Es gibt viele Menschen aus der Kirche und den Kirchengemeinschaften, die eine klare Begegnung mit dem Jesus Christus gehabt haben und an ihn glauben, und auf Grund ihres Glaubens an das Evangelium den heiligen Geist empfangen haben; das können wir ihnen doch nicht absprechen! Von dieser Begegnung mit dem Evangelium her erfüllen sie dann rückwirkend ihre Kindertaufe mit einem wunderbaren, mit einem evangelischen Sinn. Taufe—im Sinn der urchristlichen Gemeinde—ist das aber nicht! Wer weiß aber, wie bald—vielleicht in ein paar Jahrzehnten?—eine urchristliche Situation wieder aufbrechen wird? Da wird die Kindertaufe in der Kirche vielleicht nicht mehr aufrechterhalten werden können."

80. Bethge, *Dietrich Bonhoeffer*, 611–12; Bonhoeffer, *Conspiracy*, 551–72.

81. Bonhoeffer, *Discipleship*, 44.

Word Community (*Predigtgemeinde*)

For Bonhoeffer, the word "community" constituted the second layer of his ecclesiological structure. It consisted of all those who gathered to hear God's word. Members of this group needed to be able to understand and to choose. They had to be capable of receiving and rejecting the call of God's word. "The church addressed by preaching is thus personalist in nature; it comprises members who submit to the sovereign claim of the word and also those who reject it." At this point individuals are addressed and are required to make a decision, for "the word is received only by personal appropriation."[82] At this junction Bonhoeffer stressed that those who were addressed by preaching were never just an audience or a faceless mass but were a community, where each individual member was free to exercise his or her own will. Word community was where God's word was preached, was heard and was received. The word would then draw and shape out of the wider church-of-the-people a community that freely gathered. Yet, since the heard word had to be either accepted or rejected, the listening community was at the same time both, "a church-of-the-people and a voluntary church."[83]

To Köster, the word community would have represented the outmost layer of the church. To him it was the place where God, through God's word and Spirit addressed all and everyone and would call out of it his own discipleship community.

Lord's Supper Community (*Abendmahlsgemeinde*)

The innermost layer of Bonhoeffer's ecclesiology was represented by all those who gathered round the "sacrament of the Lord's Supper." Bonhoeffer assumed that those who came to participate in the sacrament were "serious about submitting their will to God's rule in the Realm of Christ."[84]

With regard to the Lord's Supper he was most emphatic about the personal appropriation of each participant. It was firstly expressed by the individual and physical reception of the gifts of bread and wine. Yet beyond this, the gathered community could also be assured of Christ's presence in each participant and was thus renewed and empowered to love one another. It would appear that for Bonhoeffer, the Lord's Supper community represented the most central expression of church, yet he resisted nevertheless, equating the *Abendmahlsgemeinde* with the pure *sanctorium communio*. He

---

82. Bonhoeffer, *Sanctorum*, 239.
83. Ibid., 247.
84. Ibid., 242.

insisted that *sanctorium communion* existed only in the Holy Spirit through whom it became the actualized essential church community. The Spirit was always free to be at work wherever it pleased him and was therefore free to build God's church wherever he chose. Thus Bonhoeffer resisted from defining and localizing God's true church, for God's church was only to be found wherever God himself was found.

The strength of Bonhoeffer's argument was that it resisted defining and localizing the church-community to one specific group or manifestation. No group owned or acted as guardians of the Holy Spirit. For Bonhoeffer the true church was potentially present at every layer of church and was wherever it was being actualized by God's spirit. When questioned as to the whereabouts of God's church, Bonhoeffer challenged the enquirer to search for God's presence, rather than point out any particular social group or institution. Part of his ecclesiological structure was the abiding challenge of discerning where God's spirit was at work.

However, since the Spirit was potentially at work at every layer of church, how could the work of the Spirit be distinguished from human or even demonic aspirations and hopes? How could the church, when so broadly and openly defined, discern between heresy and truth? When applying this question to the historical context of the Third Reich, who was to say that Emanuel Hirsch's conclusion, that God's spirit was at work through the political currents of the time in order to revitalize the church of Germany, was wrong? Was it really beyond the Spirit to work through the people who were, after all, also members of the church-of-the-people?

A Baptist's Concern

The Baptist ecclesiological model, embraced by Köster, was far more willing to state where God's church was and where it was not. Köster affirmed that the participants of the word community (*Predigtgemeinde*) represented the potential members of God's church community. All of the people who had gathered and by their own volition accepted or rejected God's word, were therefore potential disciples of Jesus. Yet to Köster this membership, once God's word was accepted, also had to be publically affirmed and witnessed in and through believer's baptism. Every baptized believer was called to follow Jesus and as a gathered community of disciples, the church-community had to discern the mind of Christ. The basic assumption of this ecclesiological model was that a discipleship community that listened to God's word, yielded to the Holy Spirit and practiced a life of obedience was also equipped and able to distinguish between truth and heresy. This makes the Baptist model more straightforward. However, history does not allow the assumption that Baptist communities were therefore immune to deception, lies and false ideologies. Many of Köster's Täufer-Bote articles were addressed to the wider Baptist community and often expressed his concern that many fellow Baptists appeared to follow blindly the new political leader rather than their Lord Jesus Christ.

The Crisis Context

Both the Baptist and the Lutheran models of ecclesiology underwent a severe time of stress during the Third Reich period. It was not possible to have an ecclesiology that was purely theological and theoretical. In as much as the Son of God took on flesh and lived at a particular moment in time and space, every church-community also had to exist likewise as an incarnated body of believers. As such it had to endure, suffer and enjoy the constraints and possibilities of its own time and space. An adequate definition of church could not only consist of what the church was; it had also to define what it was not. This became especially urgent with regard to the relationship between the church and the state.

For the Lutheran Bonhoeffer, this meant that he both honored the church-of-the-people model, while lamenting the fact that within that model it had become widespread practice to dispense grace cheaply, with the consequence that it had become utterly devalued. Bonhoeffer's understanding of the church-community developed and deepened throughout his turbulent biographical journey. During the brief years of teaching and mentoring a small community of theology students at Finkenwalde, church-community was much more intensively practiced and lived. As a group they shared a life together that was marked by intentional discipleship and mutual commitment. During the hard years of imprisonment, Bonhoeffer began to view the traditional Lutheran model of church with increasing pessimism. "Our church has been fighting during these years only for its self-preservation, as if that were an end in itself. It has become incapable of bringing the word of reconciliation and redemption to humankind and to the world."[85]

The Baptist model of church also faced a similar crisis. Köster's own critical stance with regard to the political developments was not embraced by many other Baptist church communities. His personal charisma and leadership gifts enabled him to steer a difficult path for his church fellowship. The

85. Bonhoeffer, *Letters*, 389 (Thoughts on the Day of the Baptism of Dietrich Wilhelm Rüdiger Bethge, May 1944).

independence of the local church from the wider body of a Baptist Union enabled Köster to remain true to his convictions. The weakness of that—or was it also a strength?—was that as a local church community it was able to live in relative isolation. It could remain largely unnoticed and as such sought to live the life of faith in a kind of underground fashion.

Both Köster and Bonhoeffer were wise enough to adapt their various expressions of protest. During the early years of the 1930s Bonhoeffer and Köster published a number of critical articles. Once the Nazi regime had taken control and open protest became too dangerous, Bonhoeffer removed himself for certain periods from Germany. Similarly Köster also adopted a quieter approach and limited his ministry to the Vienna region. The historical situation required of them a change of tactics. Their task was to prepare a community of resisters rather than risk being permanently silenced by the authorities.

Bonhoeffer's Ecclesiological Eschatology

Eschatology was a dominant feature of Köster's ecclesiology. How does this compare to Bonhoeffer's eschatology and what would he have made of Köster's?

In *Ethics* Bonhoeffer developed a distinctive eschatology in the chapter "Ultimate and Penultimate Things."[86] His starting point was the event of justification by grace alone, which embraces the totality of human life. God's ultimate word of grace brought freedom and released the sinner to live a life that was shaped by the final and ultimate reality. "The dark tunnel of human life, which was barred within and without and was disappearing even more deeply into an abyss from which there is no exit, is powerfully torn open; the word of God bursts in. In this saving light, people recognize God and their neighbors for the first time. The labyrinth of their previous lives collapses. They become free for God and for one another."[87]

In Bonhoeffer's opinion God gave all in the doctrine of justification by grace. At the point of justification, God spoke his ultimate word, a word that could not be altered or changed, for it was God's final eternal verdict. Yet this ultimate word was spoken into lives that still had to journey towards the eternal. It was this fact that created the tension between the ultimate and the penultimate. For even though the ultimate superseded all that was penultimate, it nevertheless continued to exist. Bonhoeffer then drew attention to the pastoral context of being confronted by someone who was grieving

86. Bonhoeffer, *Ethics*, 146–70.
87. Ibid., 146.

the recent death of a loved one. In this context, the penultimate response of silent empathy was more appropriate than the claim of the ultimate truth that death had been vanquished. Yet, since this pastoral context forced one to exist within the constrictions of the penultimate context, the question remained as to how the ultimate was to supersede all and how it was to relate to the penultimate?

Bonhoeffer explored this question and suggested that over time two extreme solutions had been implemented by various groups. Each of these solutions attempted to resolve the tension that exists between the ultimate and the penultimate. Interestingly for this discussion, from a Christian viewpoint each of these two solutions leans towards a different kind of ecclesiology. Bonhoeffer called the first "radical Christianity" and the second he called a "compromised Christianity."[88] Each solution embraced either the ultimate or the penultimate at the expense of the other. Towards the end of the chapter, Bonhoeffer identified Western Christianity with the compromised solution.[89]

Practitioners of the compromise solution involve themselves utterly in penultimate matters. They seek to manage the world, human affairs and life by utilizing all the resources that are available now. What exists now is considered absolute, while ultimate claims are perceived as a threat to life and the orders of life as they are. Such extreme views are typically held by secular atheistic ideology. A compromised church would emphasize and value penultimate things but would also tentatively acknowledge the ultimate. However, its practical concerns, energy and policies would be absorbed by penultimate concerns. The ultimate might still have a peripheral function yet it exercised no real influence and would remain eclipsed.

Compromised Christianity

Identifying the entire church-of-the-people as a compromised church would be a gross oversimplification. Nevertheless, the very fact that such a church was intrinsically open to the world and society meant that dominant cultural assumptions and values would work themselves into the life of the church. To Bonhoeffer, Western Christianity was characterized by

---

88. Ibid., 153n30. These terms are found in *Ethics*, working note no. 61. In the edited main body of the text, the sentence reads: "The relationship between the penultimate and the ultimate in Christian life can be resolved in two extreme ways, one 'radical' and the other as compromise, noting right away that compromise is also an extreme solution."

89. Ibid., 169.

the fact that "the ultimate has been increasingly questioned over the past two hundred years."[90] This comment reflects the fact that the intellectual climate and the sentiments of the wider population had become hostile towards ultimate claims. The place of the church-of-the-people was to function as a part of the general structure of society. Its role was to provide education for the young, care for the poor, the sick and to uphold Christian culture (*Kulturprotestantismus*). In the process it had also become a church where cheap grace was dispensed indiscriminately and where a "Christian should go along with the world and not venture (like the sixteenth-century enthusiasts) to live a different life under grace from that under sin."[91] The distinction between costly and cheap grace undergirds Bonhoeffer's book, *Discipleship*. It was an attempt to revitalize a compromised church towards a more radical commitment of discipleship, without moving it to the opposite extreme edge of a radical Christianity. Bonhoeffer was both a critic and supporter of the established church. He made clear that he perceived the church to be in "essence a voluntary church"[92] but maintained nevertheless a distinction between a free church (*Freikirche*), often referred to as a sect amongst Germans, and a voluntary church (*Freiwilligkeitskirche*). His theological and prophetic effort was to awaken the vast number of potential members of the church-of-the-people to actualize voluntarily their belonging to the *sanctorum communio*.

Both Bonhoeffer and Köster would have found a lot of common ground. To both, compromised Christianity represented a serious threat to the church-community. To a large extent, each one of them directed criticism regarding this danger to their own respective church context. Historically the Baptist ecclesiology was more connected to radical Christianity; yet, in practice the policies of the German *Baptistenbund* were much more concerned with penultimate survival strategies rather than taking a stand for the ultimate. Köster seemed to have had a much greater affinity with Lutheran and Reformed theologians, whose critical stance eventually became expressed in Barmen. However, Köster was also aware of many liberal theologians and voices whom he judged as being in the business of watering down God's word and doubting even the possibility of an ultimate word of God. To Bonhoeffer, every baptized person was a potential member of the church. To Köster, these potential members would have represented at best a missionary challenge and at its worst they were a disgrace to the church of Christ. For the Baptist Köster, the life of faith and discipleship required an

---

90. Ibid., 168.
91. Bonhoeffer, *Discipleship*, 44.
92. Bonhoeffer, *Sanctorum*, 269n429.

The Church

intentional commitment to a church-community. The Lutheran Bonhoeffer considered the church-of-the-people as historically God-wrought and given reality. As such he judged it "more enduring and stable than a voluntary association."[93] One of the dangers of such a firmly rooted historical stability was an instinctive tendency towards conservatism. Its strength was that during difficult historical periods, the survival chances of such a church were greater. He expressed his convictions forcefully by stating: "It is divine grace that we have a church deeply rooted in our nation's history; the power of the church's historical nature makes God's will for us relatively independent of the momentary situation in which we happen to find ourselves. "[94]

Bonhoeffer wrote this in 1927. During the following years of conflict and crisis this view became increasingly difficult to maintain. In a world that had "come of age"[95] and where the default position of the people was no longer passive potential membership but doubt and secular convictions, the old church-of-the-people paradigm became increasingly flawed.

Radical Christianity

The radical solution disregarded all that was penultimate and sought to establish the ultimate. It adopted an all-or-nothing approach where the end became absolute. Bonhoeffer believed that such a radical view inevitably led to a disregard of the world and its creation orders. After all, was this world not going to pass away? In Christian radicalism little energy was wasted attempting to improve the world. The created world was despised and the "open church of Jesus Christ, which serves the world to the end, becomes a kind of supposed ur-Christian ideal church-community that in turn mistakenly confuses the realization of a Christian idea with the reality of the living Christ."[96]

It is quite difficult to know which group Bonhoeffer identified with the radical solution.[97] He does not explicitly refer to the sixteenth century enthusiasts in his chapter. But he does use the term enthusiasts (*Schwärmer*)

---

93. Ibid., 269–70.
94. Ibid., 270n429 cont'd.
95. Bonhoeffer, *Letters*, 426–28.
96. Bonhoeffer, *Ethics*, 156.

97. Bonhoeffer, *Sanctorum*, 222. Here Bonhoeffer lists groups that have attempted to purify the church: "Perfectionist sects in the ancient church, continuing with Anabaptists, Pietism, the Enlightenment, and Kant's secularized concept of the Kingdom of God; . . . Count Saint Simon's social expectations of the Kingdom of God, Tolstoy . . . religious-socialist Youth Movement."

in other places.⁹⁸ The term was often used by theologians of the established church traditions in a derogative fashion usually identifying with it the violent and radical Anabaptist group of Münster. The violent uprising at Münster was certainly fuelled by intense expectations regarding the ultimate end of time. It was also characterized by cruel policies that had little regard for life or any penultimate compromise solutions. However, Bonhoeffer was also acquainted with more recent movements of the radical church tradition such as the twentieth century Baptists who he had met in Germany, America and England.

Rainer Ebeling provides a thorough historical investigation of the encounters Bonhoeffer had throughout his life with Christians committed to a Free Church ecclesiology. He argues that many of these meetings were both significant and fruitful to Bonhoeffer as he developed his own ecclesiology, whether it was the incidental participation of a baptismal service at a small Baptist church in Rome or the experiences of joining the services of the Abyssinian Baptist church at Harlem, New York.⁹⁹ Even within Germany, Ebeling argues, it was highly likely that Bonhoeffer read and engaged with some of the publications of Free Church theologians, one of whom was Johannes Schneider, who had studied theology in Berlin at the same time as Bonhoeffer (1923–1927). They completed their studies in the same year and on one occasion were asked to give a lecture each attending a conference organized by the DCSV.¹⁰⁰ Schneider worked extensively on a Free Church ecclesiology and on the Sermon on the Mount.

Ebeling also draws attention to the fact that Bonhoeffer, during his pastorate in London, had a meeting with Hardy Arnold¹⁰¹ who was the son of the founder of the Rhönbruderhofs Eberhard Arnold.¹⁰² As a community of Christians the Bruderhof sought to live a life of radical discipleship modeled on the Sermon of the Mount. Bonhoeffer had, at that time, a keen interest in these issues since he was preparing himself for his role as director of the Finkenwalde seminary. The common factors were the Sermon of the Mount, issues regarding pacifism and the practical challenges and implications of leading a small community of Christians committed to a life of discipleship. Hardy Arnold mentioned his discussions with Bonhoeffer to a friend, "The basis of this yet-to-be-founded order is the Sermon on the Mount. Through religious exercises and serious study, and through the

---

98. Bonhoeffer, *Berlin*, 376–78, 386, 400, 410, 505. Bonhoeffer, *Sanctorum*, 250.
99. Ebeling, *Dietrich Bonhoeffers Ringen*, 121.
100. Ibid., 225. Deutsche Christliche Studentenvereinigung (DCSV) 1897–1938.
101. Bonhoeffer, *London*, 158–66.
102. Ebeling, *Dietrich Bonhoeffers Ringen*, 278–331.

attempt to begin to follow Jesus' words as a rule, the hope is to come nearer to the essential core of the truth of Christ, by being open right from the start about not yet knowing the will of God for our time."[103]

Bonhoeffer's ecumenical and international experiences certainly introduced him to church traditions which were quite different to the German church-of-the-people model. There is evidence that he both valued and criticized these traditions.[104] Bonhoeffer's rich and varied experiences make it unlikely that the term radical automatically referred to the dark shadows of violent sixteenth century enthusiasts. In fact, the description radical and compromise could also have addressed certain types of ideologies. However if Bonhoeffer had gone to Vienna and found himself listening to one of Köster's sermons, would he have placed him at the radical end of the spectrum? And if he had, how far to the extreme radical end would he have judged Köster to be?

Clearly, Köster's preaching had a very strong end-time perspective and he did not attempt to provide constructive suggestions to his listeners concerning the wellbeing of this world. His preferred focus was the deconstruction of false ideologies and a thorough exposure of futile penultimate efforts. In his *Ethics* Bonhoeffer wrote, "When evil becomes powerful in the world, it simultaneously injects the Christian with the poison of radicalism."[105] Would Bonhoeffer have leveled this accusation against Köster?

Before an answer to this question is attempted, one would have to discern which standpoint Bonhoeffer himself would have chosen. After all, the distinction that exists between the ultimate and the penultimate ought to be a creative one.

Resolving the Tension: Living in Christ

For Bonhoeffer both solutions contained truths but were at the same time not the truth. The only place where it was possible to hold both truths together was in Christ. Those who had received the ultimate word of justification by grace had also heard of God's ultimate word becoming flesh. The ultimate took on a penultimate form, yet this also meant that all that was penultimate was also sanctified by the presence of the ultimate within it.

Bonhoeffer's focus was existential. To him holding on to both truths meant living with the actualized Christ now. The challenge was to become all that Christ was now and to live in the reality of the ultimate, yet to

---

103. Bonhoeffer, *London*, 162.
104. Ebeling, *Dietrich Bonhoeffers Ringen*, 332–43.
105. Bonhoeffer, *Ethics*, 155.

discover at the same time Christ in the other person and become Christ to the other in service and love. This brought Bonhoeffer's argument back to his starting point. Justification by grace was ultimate truth but it also had to be received, lived and offered to the neighbor and to the world. Would the Baptist Köster agree?

The theological truth of justification by faith and the need for personal actualization of Christ was certainly of foundational importance in Köster's theology and preaching. What Köster would note, with a critical eye, was that for Bonhoeffer there was little more to eschatology than this. It was primarily the existential actualization of the ultimate in the midst of the penultimate. As such, the ultimate may or may not alter the limitations of an individual's penultimate experience of pain and suffering. Yet, it would bring purpose and direction to the choices and decisions that had to be made within the restraints that were imposed by the penultimate context. The ethical choice was now to prepare the way and to make room for the ultimate truth here and now. The concern and focus was not just what could be done now, but what could be done in the light of the approaching ultimate. The penultimate was therefore neither despised nor was the ultimate compromised. Both were held in a creative tension and both had a formative impact on the lives of those, who were justified by grace. Bonhoeffer collapsed eschatology into the actualizing task of living in Christ and living in the reality of the ultimate whilst the penultimate forces of time and space were enjoyed, endured and were reshaped with the aim of preparing the way. Bonhoeffer's emphasis was therefore existential actualization. Where Köster would have differed was in his emphasis that the fellowship of believers was on an actual historical journey towards the ultimate goal. His pastoral responsibility was to guide, preserve and purify the church community and to lead the church, like a bride, towards the waiting and coming bridegroom.

The Journey of the Church-Community

Bonhoeffer was clearly aware of historical realities and acknowledged that God was at work in these. However, he resisted following Hegel, or on a popular level Spengler, who used historical analysis in order to discern recurring patterns and cycles. Köster's approach was different, simply because his perception of history did not allow him to focus on the existential actualization. He attempted to view and interpret history by adopting a biblical perspective. His overarching premise was the sovereignty of God who ruled in and above the chaos of history. This God remained in control even when rebellious and destructive human schemes were busily at work. The essential manifestation of sin was the illusion of human beings that it was possible to become "like God" (Gen 3). Thus typical of the fallen human endeavor was to claim supreme rule and to become the creators of their own destinies.[106] The result was a confusing interaction of human sin, God's steadfast purposes and his judgments. Whilst it might not be possible to unravel all of history Köster still viewed it as a unified whole. This world, and God's church-community within it, was and is on a chronological journey towards the final day. Seeking to understand and interpret the twists and turns of history through the close study of God's word was therefore for Köster a necessary and legitimate exercise. Köster's strong belief in Christ's Lordship compelled him to ponder and to detect human hubris, God's forbearance, permissive will and judgment. On 23 April 1939 (the Sunday when Hitler's birthday was to be remembered by the German people) Köster preached: "As we think of the leader of the German people, we have to realize that his growing power and charisma are not caused by his political genius; rather it is entrusted power, so that he might be a useful tool to God, serving and achieving God's will in world history."[107]

Less ambiguously he preached on 25 February 1943, "The war is God's permission, but not God's work! The work of destruction is always the devil's work."[108] Upholding the sovereignty of God over all of history forced Köster to affirm that the Jews were God's chosen people but it also led him to interpret the persecution of the Jews as God's permitted judgment.[109] In this respect Köster emulated and adopted the style of the Old Testament prophets who had also spoken God's word and reason into the national catastrophes of God's people.

---

106. Graf-Stuhlhofer, *Öffentliche Kritik*, 69: "Sünde ist der Frevel, unser Frevel an der Königsherrschaft des lebendigen Gottes, ist unsere Auflehnung, Empörung. Wir haben uns hineinverloren in den Empörtaumel des Vaters aller Lüge, machen seine Revolution mit, glauben seiner Weltreichsbegeisterung und seiner Verkündigung von der Menschenvergottung und der Vermenschlichung Gottes. Das ist Sünde: die Entthronung Gottes und die Inthronisierung des Menschen."

107. Ibid., 203: "Wenn wir an den Führer des Deutschen Volkes denken, so müssen auch wir hier erkennen, daß alle Macht, die an ihn heranwächst, nicht aus seiner genialen politischen Haltung entspringt; sie ist ihm zugeführt, daß er sie ausübe; freie Bahn ist ihm geschenkt, um in der Weltgeschichte als Werkzeug Gottes zu dienen, [um] das auszuführen, was Gott will."

108. Ibid.

109. Ibid., 237: "Das Geschick Israels ist das Richten Gottes! Gott geht den Weg mit seinem Volk zu Ende, jetzt im Gericht. Das ist der Erlösungsweg Gottes. So ist der Weg Gottes mit Israel, so ist der Weg Gottes mit allen Völkern der Erde."

Dietrich Bonhoeffer and Arnold Köster

Eschatological Existence

The existence of the church-community was for Bonhoeffer and Köster an eschatological reality that had to be lived and embodied within the historical context of the present. Bonhoeffer's final chapter in *Sanctorum Communio* has the title, "Church and Eschatology."[110] In it he wrote: "Christian eschatology is essentially eschatology of the church-community." Bonhoeffer was concerned to show that the fulfillment of Gods' ultimate goals was relevant for the whole collective community of which the individual was a part. This communal approach corresponded with the basic premise of his thesis which was Christ existing as church-community; "Only all members together can possess Christ entirely, and yet every person possesses him entirely too."[111] Thus, as the individual was joined to the *sanctorium communio*, Christ was possessed entirely, provided the individual was part of the whole. Christ reality, which was also an ultimate eschatological reality, was therefore actualized by being and acting. It was a real indisputable truth but it also had to be enacted and actualized in the historical complexities of life.

Bonhoeffer urged his readers to find Christ in the other and to make the ultimate the paradigm for present day penultimate choices. The thrust of his argument fell on the immediate situation in which life could be shaped according to ultimate values and truths. In spite of Bonhoeffer's typical communal emphasis his approach could nevertheless be compared to a spotlight. In his eschatology he did not attempt to weigh the complex and intricate workings of God's will past, present and future. His concern was the call God placed on every believer to actualize God's reality and to become "aware of God's will to rule and implement it within the realm of the church-community."[112]

Köster and Bonhoeffer appeared to have used remarkably similar language. When asked regarding Köster's eschatology his son-in-law recalled that: "It seems that he hoped and trusted that the church of Jesus Christ would live through the time only and continually in the act of the concretization of God's word (*Ereignis werden des Wort Gottes*). The church lives in the end-times. She lives and embodies God's word, which, through the Spirit, becomes her life-giving and life-sustaining experience."[113]

Both Bonhoeffer and Köster described the existence of the church-community as eschatological, but each gave these words a different

---

110. Bonhoeffer, *Sanctorum*, 283–89.
111. Ibid., 199.
112. Ibid., 199.
113. Interview with Mr. Fuchs.

emphasis. For Bonhoeffer it represented a theological and existential truth from which followed a clear ethical imperative of preparing the way. For Köster it meant similar things but it also demanded a chronological assessment. His was not a spotlight but a floodlight approach. He scanned past, present and future and concluded: the end is near.[114] To his own son-in-law, who as a young man was deeply troubled about the fact that a whole nation had been so easily seduced by the Nazi ideology, Köster's clear and critical analysis was profoundly helpful. Yet, as he continued to reflect on Köster's eschatological focus, Mr Fuchs also noted an intrinsic tension. The following comments were made during an interview conducted in 2009. Here one has to remember that these thoughts were expressed almost fifty years after Köster's death. But they are nevertheless an interesting perspective and viewpoint of someone who heard and knew Köster personally.

> As a practical consequence it [Köster's end-time focus] was a great help for me. I also felt challenged by his message. It was as though he would grab you and point you, and the whole church, towards the ultimate goal. To Köster, the church of Jesus Christ had an eschatological existence. But—and this was an issue I myself began to work on—I cannot take someone who lives within time to the eschatological crisis point and leave them there. How is it applied? Can I live my faith expectantly? But then the question is, how can this waiting, eschatological church live and exist alongside the church that lives in the now time? At that point, I fear, I didn't fully understand Köster. It felt like being led to the ultimate point in time, yet, somehow I found that I wasn't quite able to translate how I could take the next practical steps within the present context and the challenges that I had to face in the now.[115]

Köster's biblical analysis brought a sense of clarity and prompted listeners to critically reevaluate state propaganda. Also at an important pastoral and practical level, Köster's end-time emphasis brought to the attention of his listeners the real possibility of suffering, persecution and martyrdom. In March 1945 when Köster had reckoned yet again with serious consequences, he said that "if he had to suffer he would want it to be for the sake of the gospel."[116] He had faced numerous Gestapo interrogations yet was never arrested or imprisoned. He had urged the members of his congregation to

---

114. Graf-Stuhlhofer, *Öffentliche Kritik*, 261–63.
115. See appendix 1, "Interviews," 245.
116. Graf-Stuhlhofer, *Öffentliche Kritik*, 257.

Dietrich Bonhoeffer and Arnold Köster

"be as shrewd as snakes and as innocent as doves,"[117] a strategy he himself employed when he was questioned by the Nazi authorities. His criticism was at times vocal and direct and at other times subtle and careful. He had to live in the tension of having to act shrewdly whilst remaining innocent.

Eschatological Ecclesiology and Resistance

Franz Graf-Stuhlhofer argued that Köster's approach and ministry was a form of passive resistance. One could add that it was an ecclesiological and not a political resistance. Köster resisted the interference of the state in matters of faith and church-community. He considered God's people as claimed by God. Yes, the church had to submit to those to whom authority had been entrusted, yet this did not negate the fact that within the boundaries of the church-community, disciples had to follow their Lord rather than any *Führer*.

In an interview with Karl Federmann, church member and close friend of Köster, he recalled that, "Köster also baptized Jews who had become Christians. He said that no one can forbid him to baptize a Jew who had a genuine conversion. That was in some sense risky—but it was also apolitical."[118]

Köster sought to guide and to care for God's church-community. He made it clear that disciples were called to follow Christ, and to remain obedient even to the point of death. As an eschatological community, the church journeyed through a bewildering season but had to remain steadfast, pure and true for the end was rapidly approaching. Consistent with his firm belief in God's sovereignty, Köster was convinced that all historical processes, however chaotic they seemed, were still firmly in God's hand. Attempts at taking matters into one's hand for the purpose of political change were futile efforts akin to putting a spoke into the wheel.

In contrast to Köster's tightly defined ecclesiology, Bonhoeffer's understanding of the sanctorum communion was more open and more complex. Within the model of the church-of-the-people, defining who was in and who was out was not easily established. In *Discipleship* Bonhoeffer demonstrated that he had also heard Jesus' radical and uncompromising call. At the Finkenwalde Seminary, the emphasis, expressed in his book *Life Together*, was to be an intentional church-community. Unlike Köster, who was able to remain in post as a minister of a Baptist church, Bonhoeffer was unable to continue the work at Finkenwalde[119] and was forbidden by the state authorities to publish or to preach.

117. Matt 10:16.
118. Interview with Karl Federmann.
119. The seminary was closed in September 1937 by the Gestapo.

The Church

At this junction Bonhoeffer became increasingly involved in the resistance. Bethge helpfully distinguished five different stages of resistance. First, simple passive resistance, the second type he defined as having an ideological attitude that resisted yet did not seek to establish a different political future. Köster could be counted as a resister of the first and second type. The third type Bethge defined as becoming accessories to the facts of preparation for a revolt. Resisters of the fourth type engaged in the active preparation for the post-revolt period and finally the fifth type involved active conspiracy.[120] Faced with an aggressive regime, the probable price of any type of resistance—when found out—was martyrdom. As events turned out, Bonhoeffer was one of four ordained church leaders[121] who had become actively involved in the conspiracy.

Resisters of the first and second type could usually remain true and upright. Yet if one was to go further, a double life of deceit and lies became inevitable. At the final stage it would even involve active participation in murder. These steps involved overstepping a definite boundary and according to Bethge, "After he had become connected with that 'conspiracy,' Bonhoeffer assumed that his Church would no longer be able to use him, once the facts came to light."[122] Bonhoeffer was conscious of the fact that his involvement with the resistance could not be sanctioned by a church-community bound to God's word. Was he then in any sense a martyr of the Christian church? Such a claim was more easily attributed to resisters of the first and second type.

Bethge argued that Bonhoeffer faced a "Boundary Situation"[123] and it was this that led Bonhoeffer to abandon all outward and inward security.

Bonhoeffer said in a sermon as early as 1932, without knowing how prophetic it was, that times would come again when martyrdom would be called for, "but this blood . . . will not be so innocent and clear as that of the first who testified. On our blood a great guilt would lie: that of the useless servant who is cast out into the outer darkness."[124]

Were Bonhoeffer and all the other conspirators cast out into outer darkness? Were they acting utterly outside the Christian church? Köster, it appears, would have possibly argued to that effect. More recently, the baptist theologian and pacifist McClendon argued that blame was not to be laid on

---

120. Bethge, *Dietrich Bonhoeffer*, 697.

121. Ibid.: "Of the church officials on the Protestant side, only four took that final step—Bonhoeffer and his friend Perels, and Gerstenmaier and his friend Schönfeld."

122. Ibid., 699.

123. Ibid., 696.

124. Ibid., 700.

the individual who dared to act, but on the collective failure of the German churches. "Put in the briefest terms, the thesis is that they [the conspirators] had no effective communal moral structure in the church that was adequate to the crucial need of church and German people (to say nothing of the need of Jewish people; to say nothing of the world's people). No structures, no practices, no skills of political life existed that were capable of resisting, christianly resisting, the totalitarianism of the times."[125]

However, even if there was an absence of structures that would have made it possible to engage in a nonviolent practice of "christianly resisting," were the existing ecclesiological structures of no consequence? In Köster's case the separatist approach of a clearly defined church-community resulted in a level of passive and apolitical resistance. This resistance included a willingness to pay the ultimate price for one's allegiance to Jesus Christ.

Yet, did Bonhoeffer leave the realm of the church-of-the-people as he met with people whose primary concern had become a political agenda of change? Most, if not all, were at the very least potential members of the church by virtue of their infant baptism. They might have been unable or unaccustomed to listen regularly to the word or come to the Lord's table but they were nevertheless part of the church-of-the-people; the church where God's spirit moved, called and created his *sanctorum communio* which was always also a *peccatorum communio*. Their blood may not have been innocent and clear but due to the very openness of Bonhoeffer's ecclesiology it seems hardly permissible to cast them into the outer darkness.

---

125. McClendon, *Ethics*, 211.

7

Salvation

Introduction

THE POLITICAL AGENDA OF the Nazi regime sought to claim all of life and in so doing, its program offered nothing less than its version of salvation. No longer was *'das Heil'* the exclusive topic of evangelists, preachers and theologians. No longer was it discussed at the fringes of evangelistic rallies and tent missions, where preachers sought to save souls from eternal damnation. Hitler, as the Führer, had become the savior of the people and of the German nation. The humiliation of the German nation, the hardship and the chaos of the Weimar Republic, had become a thing of the past. The Nazi party with its daring policies and its socialist concern was offering a way out and promised *'Heil'* and salvation. How many understood that this offer had strings attached? The gift of salvation came wrapped in an ideology of racism, nationalism and the assumption that everything was humanly possible to those who dared to obey unreservedly. The architects of the Nazi political propaganda machine skillfully gleaned from various ideologies and philosophers what was needed in order to paint a glorious vision of a new people and future.

Bonhoeffer and Köster wrestled with the doctrine of salvation not because it was within their theological remit but because they believed that God's salvation offer radically challenged and exposed all other idols and ideologies claiming to offer life and wholeness to be false, empty and ultimately destructive.

During the early part of 1943 Köster gave a series of seven consecutive Thursday evening lectures in the Mollardgasse. The title and theme was "The Question Regarding Humanity" (*Die Frage nach dem Menschen*).

Dietrich Bonhoeffer and Arnold Köster

The biblical starting point of these lectures was the first chapters of the book of Genesis. Köster's aim was to explore the purpose and tragic failings of humanity and, by implication, of every human being. His intention was to provide a biblical perspective to evaluate modern alternative perspectives. Bonhoeffer explored a similar topic and the Genesis texts in his lectures on *Creation and Fall*. A closer reading of the two sets of lectures provides a useful focus and enables us to compare and contrast Köster's and Bonhoeffer's theology of salvation.

When Bonhoeffer gave his inaugural lecture as *Privatdozent* for systematic theology in 1930 his title was *The Anthropological Question in Contemporary Philosophy and Theology*.[1] Köster chose a remarkably similar title for his lecture series a decade later.

In spite of the parallels, there are also significant differences that have to be kept in mind. For instance, Köster was acutely aware that some of his listeners potentially regarded the Bible as both antiquated and devoid of any intrinsic authority. Köster frequently made critical comments regarding current alternative theories throughout these lectures. He was keen to challenge and include listeners that had a critical and somewhat agnostic mindset. In contrast, the tone of Bonhoeffer's lectures was quite different. His audience was a group of theological students. Bonhoeffer was therefore able to focus much more on the exegesis of the text and to develop and engage with theological issues more freely.

Lecture 1—Humanity;
Creature and Image of God (Gen 1:26–28; 2:7)

The title of Köster's first lecture was, *Humanity; Creature and Image of God*.[2] Köster's starting point was that an encounter with Jesus as savior demanded a preliminary self-discovery. The search for Jesus was preceded by the human search for meaning and purpose. He likened this to the prodigal son's experience of coming to himself.[3] "We explore the question of being human because only when we consider the purpose and function of human existence, will we encounter the living God and gain a clear understanding of

---

1. Bonhoeffer, *Barcelona*, 389–408, 31 July 1930, Bonhoeffer's inaugural lecture at Berlin, "Die Frage nach dem Menschen in der gegenwärtigen Philosophie und Theologie."

2. Köster, 11 February 1943, 1: "Der Mensch—Kreatur und Ebenbild Gottes."

3. Köster seems to have used the Elberfelder Bible translation of Luke 15:17a. Elberfelder 1905: "Als er aber zu sich selbst kam." RSV: "But when he came to himself."

Salvation

who Jesus Christ was and is. . . . To encounter God demands, as it was with the prodigal son, "a coming to himself."[4] (Luke 15:17 RSV)

The introduction and main argument of the lecture made it clear that this was an attempt to discover what God had revealed in his word. Köster's aim was to provide a biblical perspective over against other viewpoints which are briefly mentioned. Representatives of the so called scientific perspectives were the ideas and theories of Darwin, Nietzsche, Marx and Freud. Each of these four voices, Köster acknowledged, had their own distinctive message.[5] However, they had become merged together and were now joint contributors to the somewhat muddled secular worldview of his time.

To Köster, these alternative constructs remained distinctly deficient, because they were unable to provide satisfactory answers to the basic human quest of finding meaning and purpose in life. The claims of Scripture constituted the main thrust of the lectures, yet they were repeatedly brought into a conversation with alternative theories that had become the common intellectual currency of the time. Listeners were thus drawn into a critical appraisal of powerful ideas and ideologies which, according to Köster, must be challenged; otherwise humanity was in danger of dream-walking into false offers of *"Heil"* (wholeness and salvation).

The biblical focus of the first lecture was Genesis 1:26 and 2:7. Köster argued that the origin and goal of humanity was reflected by the biblical story which showed that humans were created by God and made in the image of God. They had been given a dual citizenship, one that linked them to earth; the other linked them to heaven. Since they were taken from earth they were related to the earth and needed to honor and respect earth rather than cause its devastation.[6] As God's creatures they had been endowed with the gift of consciousness. Humans were self-aware, able to perceive, reflect and judge—but above all their existence was relational. Their relational nature and existence became Köster's main argument. Humans, made in the image of God, were relationally orientated towards God and utterly dependent on

---

4. Ibid., 1: "Wir fragen nach dem Menschen, weil es allein in der Besinnung auf den Sinn und den Zweck der Menschenexistenz es für uns Menschen kommen kann zu einer Begegnung mit dem lebendingen Gott, und zur klaren Erkenntnis Jesu Christi."

5. Ibid., 2. In the case of Darwin it was the evolutionary race theory commonly accepted and aspired to in the Nazi attempts to create a pure and noble race. Nietzsche's emphasis was raw human power that needed to be totally lived. Marx focused on the human as a collective being while for Freud human existence was primarily tied to sexual satisfaction.

6. Ibid., 6: "Aus der Erde für die Erde! Nietzsche hat da ganz recht gesagt: 'Brüder, bleibt mir der Erde treu!' weil er bei den Christen so viel Untreue der Erde gegenüber fand! Wir sind von der Erde und für die Erde,—darum stehen wir erschüttert still vor der Verwüstung der Erde."

God.⁷ To Köster this truth remained a deeply ingrained feature of every human person. Consequently everyone who had not yet found or responded to the divine Thou would remain forever dissatisfied and unfulfilled. "God has called the human being. For humans there is only one kind of possible existence, to live out of, in and for God's love. Mankind must respond to the God who speaks."⁸

For Köster the "I—Thou relationship"⁹ between the human creature and the divine creator was the defining and normative characteristic of humanity. However, he also made clear that this undeniable truth, still discernible in mankind's deep longings for love, meaning and purpose, was not a currently experienced reality. There was, Köster argued, a fundamental rift between revealed truth and the experienced reality, "between us humans and God."¹⁰ How God's word described the beginning was therefore in acute tension with present day experience.

Features of Lecture 1

Köster's exposition of the Genesis text roughly followed the expositions of other commentators. He did not assume that his listeners received the biblical text as unquestioning authority. This compelled him to address the issue of truth and authority. He saw Scripture as a witness to the truth, and argued that it was an illusionary notion to suppose that access to objective truth was at all possible. For Köster the witness character of Scripture pointed towards the necessity and reality of experienced subjective truth. "Truth is only accessible to a subjective thinker, there is no objective truth. You have to risk the experiment of faith, just as I have risked it, only then are you able to participate in the conversation."¹¹

---

7. Ibid., 5: "Gott 'schuf' den Menschen, d.h.: der Mensch hat seine Existenz in einer völligen Abhängigkeit von Gott." Ibid., 7: "Für die wahre Menschenexistenz gibt es nur eine Ausrichtung, der Mensch hat ursprünglich nur eine Ausrichtung gehabt, das ist der lebendige Gott selbst."

8. Ibid., 7: "Gott hat den Menschen gerufen. Für den Menschen gibt es nur eine Möglichkeit der Existenz, dass er heraus aus der Liebe Gottes, in der Liebe und für die Liebe Gottes existiere. Der Mensch soll dem redenden Gott die Antwort geben!"

9. Ibid.: "Professor K. Heim sagt: 'Das letzte Geheimnis des Menschen ist seine 'Du-Beziehung' zu Gott. Er war für diese Beziehung geschaffen vom Urbeginn und er wird dieses; 'Du' ewig suchen und haben wollen."

10. Ibid., 9.

11. Ibid., 3: "Nur der subjektive Denker hat die Wahrheit, es gibt keine objektive Wahrheit! Ich muss etwas erlebt haben als Wahrheit. Du musst das Experiment des Glaubens wagen, wie ich es gewagt habe, dann erst kannst du mitreden."

Salvation

Köster did not defend the Bible as objective truth[12] but argued that truth demanded a subjective existential engagement. He resisted discrediting the biblical text as mere myth but neither did he argue that the text represented objective historical facts. His preferred model was to invite the listeners to risk faith. Clearly, Kierkegaard's leap of faith analogy had influenced Köster's thinking and language. The themes of humanity's relational nature and its normative God orientation became the foundational argument upon which Köster built his theology of salvation.

LINKS TO CREATION AND FALL

Since Köster's focus was more general and thematic (the human question) his approach was less expositional and much more selective. In contrast, Bonhoeffer's exposition of the first two chapters of Genesis, covered in one lecture by Köster, took Bonhoeffer nine lectures.[13] Bonhoeffer's aim was to offer a theological exposition[14] where the book of the church was read "word for word [*buchstabieren*] like a child."[15] Unlike historical critical commentaries, whose approach was to judge, dissect and categorize the text in a so called scientific fashion, Bonhoeffer sought to hear the text as God's word. No doubt Köster would have approved of Bonhoeffer's methodology. For both, hearing the text involved making connections to the philosophical ideas that were the common currency of their time. Bonhoeffer mentioned Darwin[16] and Hegel[17] and engaged with ideas and phrases of Friedrich Nietzsche.[18]

The relational nature of humanity made in the image of God constitutes the most significant overlap. However, each emphasized different nuances as they explored what being "made in the image of God" meant. Both noted that humans were taken from earth and were thus bound to earth. Köster rejected the notion that salvation was primarily concerned with the soul rather than the body. "The well meaning teaching of justification by

---

12. Ibid., 4: "Hinter uns steht nicht: 'Du musst der Bibel glauben!' Sondern wir leben aus der Überzeugung, es ist kein anderer da gewesen, der uns in die Erkenntnis des prophetischen und des apostolischen Wortes so geführt hat, wie Jesus von Nazareth, dem wir geglaubt, und durch den Glauben, erkannt haben!"
13. Bonhoeffer, *Creation*, 102n21.
14. Ibid., 22.
15. Ibid., 23n11.
16. Ibid., 62, 76.
17. Ibid., 27.
18. Ibid., 26, 76–77, 87–88, 90, 120, 123.

faith alone has led us to believe, that we are now released from our earthy existence. No! God has created us out of earth and for the earth."[19] Bonhoeffer stated, "The human being whom God has created in God's image—that is in freedom—is the human being who is taken from earth." Both affirmed the bodily and material existence of humanity together with the unique gift of God's own breath or spirit. Humanity was taken from "mother earth"[20] but was also granted a living soul. Both insisted that human life was only possible through body and spirit and to ignore, reject or despise one or the other was living in an existential denial. "To live as a human being means to live as a body in the spirit."[21]

Köster spoke of this truth in terms of having been granted a dual citizenship.[22] For Bonhoeffer, the concept of duality and choice were primarily a manifestation of sin and the fallen condition. Life before the fall was characterized by unity and freedom rather than duality. He illustrated this through his extensive discussion on freedom.[23] For Köster, freedom was chiefly expressed by the notion of freedom of choice. Köster argued: "The fact that we are living souls means that we have received spirit from the eternal spirit, but nevertheless we are also granted independent freedom. We are beings, which can respond independently towards heaven and earth. We are neither enslaved by heaven nor earth. We are able to judge and decide."[24]

To Bonhoeffer freedom was a different notion altogether. In his view it was not something an individual had or could claim as an attribute or a quality. Freedom was only accessible and real in relation to another person. "Freedom is just not something I have at my command like an attribute of

---

19. Köster, 11 February 1943, 6: "Die schöne Lehre von der Rechtfertigung allein aus dem Glauben hat uns so geführt, daß wir uns nicht mehr als Erdwesen betrachtet haben,—nein! Gott hat uns geschaffen aus der Erde, für die Erde!"

20. Köster, 11 February 1943, 6: "Wir sind Geschöpfe der Mutter Erde [We are creatures of mother earth]." Bonhoeffer, *Creation*, 76: "Humankind is derived from a piece of earth. . . . The 'earth is its mother.'"

21. Bonhoeffer, *Creation*, 78. Köster, 11 February 1943, 6: "Wir können den Sinn unseres Lebens nicht verstehen, wenn wir nicht das verstehen, daß wir Bürger zweier Welten sind!"

22. Brunner, *Mensch*, 99. It seems that Köster followed Brunner who also referred to humanity made in the image of God as, "Der Bürger zweier Welten."

23. Bonhoeffer, *Creation*, 62–67.

24. Köster, 11 February 1943, 6: "Wir sind eine lebendige Seele heißt, wir haben Geist vom ewigen Geist, aber wir stehen auch dem ewigen Geist gegenüber in selbständigen Freiheit. Wir sind Wesen, die sich der Erde und dem Himmel gegenüber selbständig verhalten können, wir werden weder von der Erde, noch von dem Himmel verknechtet."

my own; it is simply something that comes to happen, that takes place, that happens to me through the other."²⁵

Thus freedom was not found in the act of choosing but was part of the relational existence between creator and creature. The creature's freedom was expressed in worship of the creator who had freely chosen to involve himself in creation.²⁶ In the act of creation, God the creator, especially in the creation of humankind, had made himself free for the other, for humanity. This led Bonhoeffer to interpret the essence of the *imago Dei* as a relational dimension, as "being-free-for-the-other"²⁷ rather than an ontological quality or attribute. Therefore, human beings were created male and female (Gen 1:27); their relationship as creatures was to be analogous to the relationship between creator and creature. In their being-free-for-the-other they mirrored (imaged or reflected) what God had freely granted as a gracious gift. Bonhoeffer spoke of a duality, "the duality of man and woman,"²⁸ yet to him this duality was not defined by freedom of choice. Humankind endowed with God's image could only live freely within the given relationships. God's likeness had therefore to be understood as an *"analogia relationis."*

Karl Barth adopted in 1942 Bonhoeffer's notion of analogy of relationship as the key insight on the topic of the *imago Dei*.²⁹ Köster knew and valued many of Karl Barth's writings but could not have had access in February 1943 to what Barth was teaching on creation during the summer semester of 1942. What was available to him was Emil Brunner's *Der Mensch im Widerspruch*.³⁰ Following Brunner, Köster interpreted the *imago Dei* as a relational existence that was characterized by a longing for the I-Thou relationship. Humans were endowed with a God-orientation (*Ausrichtung*) and were only able to be fully human as they lived in a relational union with God. As God's creatures made in his image, they were able to respond to the love and call of their creator.³¹ Thus, Köster's main focus of the image of God was their ability to choose freely and respond to God's gracious and loving offer of life.³²

25. Bonhoeffer, *Creation*, 63.

26. Ibid., 63: "God's self enters into God's creation."

27. Ibid.: "Being free means 'being-free-for-the-other,' because I am bound to the other. Only by being in relation with the other am I free."

28. Ibid., 66.

29. Ibid., 65n22, 162. Barth, *Church Dogmatics*, 194–96.

30. Brunner, *Mensch*. Köster's copy is extensively marked throughout.

31. Köster, 11 February 1943, 7.

32. Brunner, *Mensch*, 88. Underlined in Köster's copy: "Das Gepräge des Menschen aber kommt nur zustande durch Selbstbestimmung auf Grund der göttlichen Bestimmung, als Antwort auf Anruf, durch Entscheidung."

Dietrich Bonhoeffer and Arnold Köster

Lecture 2—Sinful and Lost Humanity (Gen 3:1–6)

The discrepancy between revealed truth and experienced reality was the topic of Köster's second lecture, *Sinful and Lost Humanity*.[33] In spite of the fact that modern men and women rejected being labeled either as sinners or as being lost, they are, nevertheless haunted by a sense of restlessness. Regardless of all human attempts at controlling their own lives and fate, Köster argued, they remained troubled by a sense of "not being able to be what they were meant to be."[34]

Köster applied the Genesis text (Gen 3:1–6) to this phenomenon and used it to draw a map of the tragic journey. Humans, originally set within God's creation order—a life in Eden, had fallen from harmony into disharmony and strife. Köster's definition of sin emphasized the broken relationship between creator and creature rather than the broken command. Sin was not so much doing wrong or acting immorally but the futile attempt at living a life that was unrelated to God. To Köster, sin was an ontological distortion, in which "mankind wrongly assumed that living without a relational dependency on God was a possibility."[35] It simply was not an option.

Köster developed this point by exploring the concept and characteristics of relationships. First, he noted that being made in God's image had a word quality. Humans were shaped by and were enabled to respond to God's word. The God-shaped life was not dependent on material things alone but on every word that came from the mouth of God. Köster likened this to a parent, who by speaking to an infant would draw out the gift of language in the child. This 'being spoken to' was for him clear evidence that love was the motive of this relationship. True love imparted and enabled the beloved to willingly and freely respond. Love therefore demanded that mankind, called and addressed by God, responded freely and of their own volition.[36]

The account of Adam who was given a helper prompted Köster to relate the image of a loving relationship between man and woman beyond the Genesis text to the apostle Paul's teaching in Ephesians 5 where it was applied to Christ's relationship with his church. "A woman is therefore not just a helper to man doing the cooking and washing, but we should begin to

---

33. Köster, 18 February 1943 (11 pages): "Der Mensch—Sünder und Verlorener."

34. Köster, 18 February 1943, 1: "Die Menschen sind immer wieder in dieser Spannung, daß das Leben, das wir leben nicht das Leben ist, das wir im letzten Grunde ahnen und wollen." Although Köster does not reference this particular insight to Emil Brunner, his language is very close to Brunner's: "Der Mensch im Widerspruch."

35. Ibid., 8: "Der Mensch hat sich falsch verstanden als Sein, das ohne Gott existieren könnte, er hat sich falsch entschieden, und seitdem ist alles Fehlentscheidung."

36. Ibid., 6: "Es gibt keine Liebe, die man erzwingen kann!"

understand through earth's deepest and profoundest relationship what God had in mind by enabling humans to relate with him."[37]

Life in Eden was characterized by a relationship between God and mankind. The calling of humanity was to become God's representatives on earth and to order God's creation according to his will. Köster believed that this was not just a static but a progressive vision of life which included the development towards full human potential as God's final aim and purpose.

But Eden was invaded by the cunning snake. Köster did not attempt to explain the origin of evil but saw the snake as a vessel or medium used by the evil one. Satan was portrayed as using a creature for the purpose of establishing a communication bridge between mankind and himself. To Köster Satan was a real and powerful reality. Scripture, he argued might not answer all our questions but it states clearly: "There is an intelligent evil power that is beyond human power. Its intention is to destroy all of God's works. Its declared aim is to draw humanity out of their loving relationship with God and to seduce us into a life where God is utterly excluded."[38]

Köster wasted no time either questioning or explaining the historical accuracies of the Genesis account but sought instead to apply the lessons of the text to the reality and choices he and his listeners faced. Exploring the nature of temptation and sin he drew attention to the fact that the act of sin was motivated by a fascination with the visible. This in turn triggered an "inspiration from below"[39] which he described as blind enthusiasm and mass hysteria. These were labels that had become a common feature of Nazi supporters and propaganda. He then listed three symptoms of sin; shame, angst and guilt, but kept reminding his audience that the essence of sin was the inner denial and refusal of being utterly dependent on God. Thus, the fall was not a single act of immorality committed by Adam and Eve but the futile attempt to live life apart from God. Life contaminated by sin turned humans, who were made in God's image, into lost sinners. Consequently, all of life was affected by God's curse. Spiritual death was followed by a physical and ultimately eternal death. Paradise was lost and could not be regained or retaken by human effort or endeavor. Sin distorted and profoundly affected

---

37. Ibid., 5: "Die Frau ist nicht nur die Gehilfin, die uns Männern das Essen bereitet und die Wäsche wäscht, sondern wir sollen durch diese tiefste und letzte Gemeinschaft die es gibt auf Erden die Gemeinschaft mit Gott begreifen und verstehen."

38. Ibid., 7: "Die 'Schrift' sagt uns nur, daß das Böse da ist! Da sind Grenzen, die wir nicht überschreiten können! Aber auf jeden Fall ist gesagt, hier ist eine Macht auf Erden, eine geistige Macht, eine Intelligenz, eine übermenschliche und untermenschliche Macht, die unbedingt das Verderben aller Werke Gottes will, die will, daß wir Menschen aus der Liebesgemeinschaft Gott gegenüber herauskommen, und daß wir unser Leben Gott gegenüber versagen."

39. Ibid., 9: "Enthusiasmus, Begeisterung, Hingerissen sein ist Inspiration von unten!"

the relational capacity of every human being, who was now tragically torn between self-worship and self-abasement.

Features of Lecture 2

Köster's method was to briefly sketch the biblical story and then add color to it, by relating it to the ideas and issues people had to face in the 1940s. For instance, doubting God's word featured both in the Genesis text and in Köster's analysis of history. Referring to Emil Brunner he made the point that the eighteenth century was a period characterized by doubting God's word. Apathy became dominant in the ninetieth century which in turn evolved into the twentieth century's open antagonism to religion. Interestingly, Köster referred to these issues in a passing sort of way. He took his listeners on a journey, pointing out crossroads and interesting avenues but he did not explore these in detail. Mostly these pointers concerned philosophers or ideologies but occasionally Köster also mentioned other commentators. For instance, he briefly referred to Jakob Kroeker's interpretation of Genesis which proposed that before the creation of mankind a universal catastrophe had occurred. Köster only touched on it in three sentences and in such a manner that the listeners were given an interpretative possibility rather than a tightly-knit argument.

Köster highlighted for the listeners a number of different layers of truths but managed at the same time to remain focused on his main theme. Building upon the first lecture, his main theme was that humanity, made in God's image, was tragically distorted by sin but not without hope.

LINKS TO CREATION AND FALL

Again, Bonhoeffer was able to engage with the text much more extensively. With regard to sin and the fall he spoke of a chain of events[40] that began with God's prohibition and finally culminated in the serpent's question. The tree of life and the tree of the knowledge between good and evil were for Bonhoeffer representatives and images of the struggle that raged in the text. The tree of life—placed at the center of the garden—represented a centered life. It spoke of a life in which the life-giving God was at the center. "Adam's life comes from the center which is not Adam but God; it revolves around this center constantly, without ever trying to take possession of this center

---

40. Bonhoeffer, *Creation*, 112.

of existence."[41] For Bonhoeffer it was a life where God was at the center and humans—orientated towards God—lived obediently and in unity with their creator. Bonhoeffer contrasted the centered life with a life where humans, by claiming the center, made themselves the center.

A life from the center was a life "beyond good and evil"; the center claiming life was a divided, a torn (*ein zwiespältiges*) life. It introduced a radical rift or split. It brought about a life where humans found themselves lost in the middle.

Bonhoeffer used terms like center and middle to express two distinct and opposite lives. It might be useful to apply Bonhoeffer's concepts of center and middle to Jeremiah's image of the potter and the clay.[42] A piece of clay flung onto the wheel and skillfully centered by the potter illustrates well the centered life of the *imago Dei*. The potter's hands are round it, support it and shape it. As the clay yields to the hands of the potter, it rests, although in an active sense, at the center. However, if the clay were to resist the touch of the potter by claiming to be the center itself, it would veer off the center. Flung off the wheel, the circular motion would change into a linear one. Humanity, with its claim to be the center has found itself stuck in the middle. To those living in the middle it has become impossible to know or even think about beginning and end.[43] The resources for living a center-claiming life are reduced to what is central, the individual selves. Such a life is, in Luther's phrase, curved in upon itself. Thus every human being becomes an ego-focused circle (*Ring*) dominated by struggle (*ringen*).[44]

Good and evil, in Hebrew *tob* and *ra*, were for Bonhoeffer important expressions of this inner split (*Zwiespalt*). They were opposites but as a pair they were nevertheless one. Following Hans Schmidt he interpreted good as pleasurable (*lustvoll*) and evil as painful (*leidvoll*) and argued that one does not exist without the other.[45] Good was only attained in as much as evil was overcome and vice versa. Thus, every good or pleasure also contained a kernel or residue of evil or pain. Was not the good pleasure of a refresh-

---

41. Ibid., 84.

42. Jer 18:1–6. In Jeremiah the potter-clay image was a warning against Israel and emphasized the sovereignty of God.

43. Bonhoeffer, *Creation*, 28: "Humankind no longer lives in the beginning; instead it has lost the beginning. Now it finds itself in the middle, knowing neither the end nor the beginning, and yet knowing that it is in the middle."

44. Ibid., 90. In his discussion on pleasure Bonhoeffer seems to refer to Nietzsche who wrote in Zarathustra "what does pleasure not desire! It is thirstier, heartier, hungrier, more terrible, more secretive than all woe; it wants itself, it bites into itself, the ring's will wrestles in it [des Ringes Wille ringt in ihr]."

45. Ibid., 88–93.

ing drink borne out of the painful experience of intense thirst? Thus, even though good and evil were opposites they were nevertheless unbreakably tied together. Hegel, in his discussion on "the Story of the Fall"[46] also argued that good, by its very definition, exists only in contrast with evil. However, for Hegel the eating of the fruit meant "that humanity has elevated itself to the knowledge of good and evil."[47] This step to cognition or consciousness was for Hegel intrinsically tied to a split and contradictory existence marked by judging, dividing and self-distinguishing yet, "In the same way as this cleavage is the source of evil, it is also the midpoint of the conversion that consciousness contains within itself whereby this cleavage is sublated."[48]

Hegel argued "that knowledge of good and evil belongs to the divinity of humanity."[49] The cleavage of good and evil established human consciousness and was therefore a necessary step for becoming truly human. Bonhoeffer argued against this notion and located the God-given life outside choice. For Bonhoeffer the cleavage between good and evil remained wholly within the realm of a center-claiming life. The final outcome of such a life was death rather than the overcoming of it.[50] "Humankind now lives only out of its own resources, by its knowledge of good and evil, and thus is dead."[51] Bonhoeffer developed and applied this even further in his later work *Ethics*.[52]

What Bonhoeffer's interpretation added to the discussion was its careful evaluation of human choice and responsiveness. Köster and Bonhoeffer agreed that the nature of sin was the human rejection of the divine human relationship. That a creature made in the image of God, could claim life without God was an utterly foolish assumption. Where they differed was in their emphasis on human choice. For Köster, Genesis 3 spoke of a wrong choice and related the devastating consequences of that fatal choice. Bonhoeffer also interpreted the act represented by the taking of the fruit, as "something inconceivable."[53] Köster argued that "mankind wrongly assumed that living without a relational dependency on God was a possibil-

---

46. Hegel, *Lectures*, 442–52.
47. Ibid., 443.
48. Ibid., 444.
49. Ibid.
50. Ibid., 44. In contrast Hegel argued, "The fact of the matter is that humanity is immortal only through cognitive knowledge, for only in the activity of thinking is its soul pure and free rather than mortal and animal-like. Cognition and thought are the root of human life, of human immortality as a totality within itself."
51. Bonhoeffer, *Creation*, 91.
52. Bonhoeffer, *Ethics*, 47–75; 301–38.
53. Bonhoeffer, *Creation*, 119.

ity." He added "he decided wrongly, and since then everything is the wrong choice [*Fehlentscheidung*]."⁵⁴ Following Brunner, Köster argued that the heart of humanity made in God's image was the ability to respond to its loving creator and to freely choose God. The fall, viewed as a wrong choice, implied that fallen humanity might be able to choose rightly again. Thus, the argument was prepared that the gospel's challenge was the demand for another choice. Bonhoeffer however, neither stressed nor explored the human choosing. In fact for him, it was tied to sin rather than to the *imago Dei*.

Lecture 3—Humanity, under God's Patience and Promise (Gen 8:20–22)

In his third lecture Köster balanced the grim reality of a life under God's curse with God's patience and promise.⁵⁵ Using the Genesis text, Köster focused on what he referred to as four major epochs or historical turning points. Each of these revealed how God responded to the rapid escalation of sin and its consequences. To Köster, these epochs represented patterns and laws of life that were still powerfully at work in the lives of individuals and nations.⁵⁶

Adam typified the first epoch. Adam's choice was to live a life without God. He desired a godless autonomy of self. The consequences of this choice were death and the total destruction of life. But God remained nevertheless patient in his dealings with mankind and repeatedly averted humanity's total annihilation. God continued his search for Adam and kept on speaking to every human being. Often the voice of God was heard in judgment, yet even this was powerful evidence of the fact that humanity had not been utterly abandoned and left to Satan's destructive schemes.⁵⁷ Adam's sin triggered the ever-unfolding history of sin, whose effect and development spread comprehensively into each successive generation and individual. Thus, in Adam all had sinned, but in Adam all were also given the promise of a seed through which salvation was to come.

---

54. Köster, 18 February 1943, 8: "Der Mensch hat sich falsch verstanden als Sein, das ohne Gott existieren könnte, er hat sich falsch entschieden, und seitdem ist alles Fehlentscheidung."

55. Köster, 25 February 1943, 1: "Der Mensch unter Gottes Geduld und Verheißung."

56. Köster, 25 February 1943, 1: "Also, darum geht es, daß wir auf die göttlichen Lebensprinzipien und Lebensgesetze stoßen, die er hineingelegt hat in jedes Menschenleben, in jede Menschengeschichte, und die durch jede Menschgeschichte und Geschichtsepoche hindurch läuft."

57. Ibid., 10: "Gottes Gericht in dieser Welt ist nicht anderes als das Eindämmen unseres Verlorenseins, weil sonst die Herrschaft Satans unabwendbar bleiben müsste."

Cain represented the second epoch. Köster compared Cain with the desire, known and shared by every sinner, to flee from the presence of God. "We feel cast out, and God's presence becomes unbearable."[58] The trajectory of Cain's isolation led to energetic efforts and a city and culture building mindset (Gen 4:17f). Köster drew parallels to modern attempts at building a culture that was devoid of God's Spirit and manifested itself in the total secularization of life. Yet, even in the midst of Cain's world, God still acted patiently and provided a threefold promise. Cain's mark granted protection, God's name was still known and finally God's community, most clearly visible in the life of Enoch, embodied the future promise of salvation. Köster interpreted the ancient text creatively and applied it freely to the world of 1943. Cain's mark became the symbol of the cross and the God community became the church which made known God's name and remained the sign and symbol of God's approaching redemption.

The story of Noah and the flood represented the third epoch or post-Eden pattern of life. To Köster it signified the complete carnal obsession of humanity characterized by a total preoccupation with the visible and tangible world. It was a world marked by "eating and drinking" (Matt 24:38) and a constant demand for freedom. Köster used the ancient story as a foil against which the present world could be critically evaluated: a world where wars are fought for the purpose of securing resources, supplies and wealth and where eternal and spiritual matters had become eclipsed. To him such a world was utterly bereft of God and signaled Satan's potential final victory. However, God's judgment—the flood—prevented the total loss of humanity and prepared the elect for a new epoch and world.[59] When Köster claimed "we are Noah's world"[60] he wanted it to be heard as a promise and as a warning. It was a reminder of the promises Noah's children received but was also a reminder of the possibility of catastrophic judgment. God's promises to Noah's world were: the seasons which reminded humanity of God's patience; human dignity as image bearer of God (Gen 9:6); proper government and the rainbow. Proper government seemed to be the most daring interpretative leap but it revealed that Köster's overall concern was to understand current events through a creative use of Scripture. It also provided Köster with an opportunity to voice a critical and no doubt risky assessment of the government of his time.

---

58. Ibid., 6: "Wir fühlen uns vertrieben von dem Angesicht Gottes weg, seine Gegenwart ist uns untragbar."

59. Ibid., 8: "Gott schlägt durch sein Untergangsgericht die Gefahr eines völligen Verlorenseins nieder und bereitet dem erwählten Überrest eine neue Zeit."

60. Ibid.

Part of God's patient provision is good government (*der Ordnungsstaat*), which is entrusted with the sword to suppress evil. That is what God meant with good government. I believe that a state loses its legitimacy when a government proclaims that it intends to regain the lost Paradise for its people. Such an endeavor represents an overstepping of a God ordained limit and God will respond appropriately. Many states and governments have ceased to be, because they had presumed on such a foolish course. We do not need to organize a revolution—God himself will act swiftly and will not suffer fools.[61]

The final and fourth epoch was Babel. Köster drew a parallel between the tower of Babel and modern society so eager to plan, organize and rally collective human potential. Babel stood for the desire to achieve human unity without God. Köster argued, just as we are Adam's, Cain's and Noah's world we are also Babel's world. Nevertheless, God's patience and promise were also set within the world of Babel and manifested itself in Abraham and his descendents. Within the unfolding story of sin, God had persistently placed his own salvation story—a story that was intrinsically tied to the story of the Jews, whom God had chosen and through whom he was preparing to accomplish his salvation purposes.[62]

Features of Lecture 3

As he had done in the two previous lectures, Köster continued to explore the Genesis texts in a creative manner. Like many preachers before and after him he sought to discern through the ancient stories patterns that were applicable to the general human condition. In his introduction to the lecture, Köster justified his use of the texts and argued that the Old Testament frequently revealed divine principles of life which remained powerfully at

---

61. Ibid., 9: "Das dritte Zeichen, daß Gott geduldig ist mit dem Menschen und seiner Sündengeschichte und uns aufspart auf seine kommende Erlösung ist der Ordnungsstaat, der das Schwert führt, um das Böse nieder zu halten. Das ist der Staat, wie Gott ihn meinte. Für mich ist das nicht mehr ein Ordnungsstaat, wenn er die Parole ausgibt, daß er mit uns vorstößt in das verlorene Paradies! Das ist eine Grenzüberschreitung. Wenn ein Staat die ihm von Gott gesetzte Grenze überschreitet, erlaubt sich Gott, ihn beim Wickel zu nehmen. Viele Staaten sind deshalb nicht mehr, weil sie das taten. Wir brauchen keine Revolution machen,—Gott selbst wird da schon zugreifen, wenn der Staat sich Gott gegenüber benimmt wie ein Lümmel."

62. Ibid., 10: "Das Weltheil ist immer im Kommen gewesen bei den Juden. Die Juden sind die Welt-Landstrasse Gottes, auf der er geschritten ist mit seiner Erlösung durch die Zeiten."

work throughout human history and in all of human life.[63] This provided him with a biblical and theological framework where the heart of the human condition was defined as a relational capacity between divine creator and human creature. Viewed from this perspective, normality was defined as being created by and sustained through a loving relationship. The rupture of that relationship was triggered by evil but was at the same time the choice and desire of humanity. The consequences were dire and were still apparent in mankind's abiding desire for autonomy. The effects of sin were contagious and devastating, yet as sin's story drew all of creation into its deadly power, God's salvation story was set persistently within it. Köster's explicit insistence that God's promise was entrusted to the Jews was historically significant.[64]

Links to Creation and Fall

Köster's thematic approach enabled him to paint on a larger canvass than Bonhoeffer who stayed within the chapters Genesis 1 to 4. Nevertheless, Bonhoeffer in his exposition arrived at similar conclusions. Their arguments pointed in the same direction but they chose to travel different routes to reach these conclusions. Both agreed that the fall had catastrophic consequences. "Disobedience fails to describe the situation adequately. It is rebellion, the creature's stepping outside of the creature's only possible attitude, the creature's becoming creator, the destruction of creatureliness, a defection, a falling away [*stürzen*] from being safely held as a creature. As such a defection it is a continual fall, a plunging down into a bottomless abyss, a state of being let go, a process of moving further and further away, falling deeper and deeper."[65]

To Köster the word autonomy describes best the hopeless striving of humankind. Bonhoeffer built his argument on the split-apart condition [*Entzweiung*] that had now become characteristic of fallen humanity. Both refused to speculate regarding the origin of evil. To Bonhoeffer it was an inappropriate theological question[66] and for Köster it was a given fact. "Satan

---

63. Ibid., 1: "Also, darum geht es, daß wir auf die göttlichen Lebensprinzipien und Lebensgesetze stoßen, die er hingelegt hat in jedes Menschenleben, in jede Menschengeschichte, und die durch jede Menschengeschichte und Geschichtsepoche hindurchläuft."

64. Ibid., 10: "Warum Gott sie in die jüdischen Hände gelegt hat, wissen wir nicht, wenn er sie in die arischen Hände gelegt hätte,—wir wären vielleicht schon längst nicht mehr; wir wären vielleicht schon verendet."

65. Bonhoeffer, *Creation*, 120.

66. Ibid.: "The question why there is evil is not a theological question, for it

is a reality for God and the Bible. Regarding Satan's origin the Bible does not give an answer."[67] However, unlike Bonhoeffer, Köster was much more willing to allow for the continuous influence of Satan's schemes and purposes. Satan's aim, the total domination of God's works was however, constantly frustrated by God who continued to set boundaries and persisted through the patient outworking of his promises in spite of the fall.

Bonhoeffer's focus was on how the fall had affected the existential human condition. He traced the devastation of the fall by exploring the relational dimension between creator and creature, creature and creature and finally creature and creation. Köster chose to demonstrate the effects of sin through his brief analysis of cultures and epochs which ultimately were driven by the relational dysfunction of people but these were not his focus.

For Bonhoeffer, the fall caused the breaking apart of life. What was one and unified became fragmented and torn apart. At the creaturely level, sexuality, the relationship between Adam and Eve, man and woman, became the first victim. Bonhoeffer related this to his earlier description of a life from the center in contrast to the center-claiming life. Characteristic to a life from the center was the recognition that the center also represented a boundary. To Adam, Eve was the limit of his "bodily form."[68] She had been taken from him but had also become the other person whom Adam was able to love in the act of being-free-for-the-other. Their relationship was analogous to how humans created as *imago Dei* were relating to their God. It was a free yielding to the other, which on the creaturely level, was expressed by their becoming "one flesh." However, yielding to their desire of each one being center to themselves their relational union broke apart. Claiming to be God themselves, their creator—who had originally been the center of their lives—became a threat. On the human level their self-centered existence forced them to view the other not as one for whom one was free but as one who had become a rival. "One person sees the other in terms of their being against each other, each sees the other as divided from himself or herself. The limit is no longer grace that holds the human being in unity of creaturely, free love; instead the limit is now the mark of dividedness. Man and woman are divided from each other."[69]

Consequently, the being-free-for-the-other changed into claiming the other for oneself. Within this self-centered existence, humanity remained

---

presupposes that it is possible to go back behind the existence that is laid upon us as sinners."

67. Köster, 25 February 1943: "Der Satan ist eine Wirklichkeit für Gott und die Bibel. Woher er gekommen ist, darauf gibt uns die Bibel keine Antwort."

68. Bonhoeffer, *Creation*, 122.

69. Ibid.

painfully aware of the lost unity. At the most distorted level an individual wills to restore unity by force and the use of coercive power, effectively aggravating the rift. Adam and Eve, who had once seen each other as united now viewed each from their new self-centered perspectives as divided. This, argued Bonhoeffer, motivated them to engage in cover-up strategies. Unable to bear their nakedness they devised means of protecting their self-centered selves. Shame, argued Bonhoeffer, was a direct result of the fall and continued to be a powerful reminder of the creaturely limit to every new generation. Their grotesque desire to have no limits and to be like God left them exposed and in constant need of a "veil"[70] or "mask."[71] Next to shame, their conscience became the other creaturely characteristic of a fallen and divided humanity. To Bonhoeffer, the conscience was not God's voice or some fragmented vestige of it placed within the human being, but it was their own voice that sought to defend themselves against God. "Conscience chases humankind away from God into its secure hiding place. Here, far away from God [*in der Gottesferne*], humankind itself plays the role of being judge and in this way seeks to evade God's judgment."[72]

Humanity in its flight found itself set between "curse and promise."[73] Next to the inner contradictions of shame and conscience, the text spoke of a fourfold curse; "Enmity with the serpent, the pain of childbirth, the toil of work, and death."[74] This fallen world was not left without God's word, even though it was an utterance of judgment. Like Köster, Bonhoeffer also spoke of the persistent word of God which even as a curse remained God's word. This meant that the cursed ground was not wholly God-forsaken but was upheld and preserved by God himself through the orders of preservation.[75]

Sin had effected the deconstruction of life, but it was unable to erase humanity's longing for union and wholeness. Shame and conscience as internal witnesses kept reminding humanity of a different kind of existence—an undivided world in which life was neither grasped nor claimed but received in the act of freely being there for the other, for God. The struggle of life in which God's word was still active as a promise left humanity with hope even in the face of death.

---

70. Ibid., 126: "The whole created world is now covered in a veil, it is silent and lacking explanation, opaque and enigmatic."
71. Bonhoeffer, *Ethics*, 304.
72. Bonhoeffer, *Creation*, 128.
73. Ibid., 131–36.
74. Ibid., 132.
75. Ibid., 135.

Salvation

Lecture 4—Jesus Christ, Fate of the World

The scriptural basis of Köster's lectures four to seven was the New Testament. In *Creation and Fall* Bonhoeffer repeatedly linked the Old Testament passage to Christ and the church. The following section seeks to provide an outline of how Köster shaped his arguments in these remaining lectures. Links to Bonhoeffer's writings will be explored after the fourth lecture and lectures five to seven.

In his fourth lecture, *Jesus Christ—Fate of the World*,[76] Köster sought to set Jesus at the center of time and humanity. Understanding the significance of Jesus Christ required a biblical rather than a materialistic or idealistic worldview. Köster's main concern was to draw attention to the person of Jesus Christ. He gave equal space to Jesus' humanity and divinity and these considerations led him to conclude that "Jesus of Nazareth alone is capable of restoring this world into God's love."[77] To Köster this was a total and an exclusive claim which challenged and negated the validity of all other salvation claims and constructs. Jesus represented the fulfillment of the Old Testament promises and Köster insisted was a "full-blooded Jew." His person and work thus imposed a stark choice on every human being. The choice was to believe and entrust one's life into the hands of the God ordained savior. Köster argued that the restoration to normality, to life as it was originally intended by God, was only accessible and possible through risky faith. "A normal human existence is only achievable through faith in Jesus Christ, because only in Jesus can we find the God who still speaks to us."[78]

Features of Lecture 4

The fourth lecture represented a tipping point. Jesus as center of history and time held the promise of life in the balance. Köster argued that the reality of human experience was a painful sense of contradiction. As Brunner did before him he referred to humanity as the *Mensch im Widerspruch*. This

---

76. Köster, 4 March 1943 (pages 1 and 7 are missing). Köster appears to mention the title of this lecture again in the seventh lecture. See Köster, 25 March 1943, 4: "Das vierte Stadium nenne ich die Wende des Schicksals. Jesus von Nazareth ist das Schicksal der Welt, und er ist die Wende unseres Schicksals."

77. Köster, 4 March 1943, 5: "Jesus von Nazareth erhebt den Anspruch, daß er allein imstande ist, die ganze Welt wieder hineinzustellen in die Liebe Gottes." And: "Jesus ein Vollblutjude."

78. Ibid., 9: "Ein Mensch kann nicht normal existieren, es sei den, er existiere im Glauben an Jesus Christus, weil nur dort Gott zu finden ist und weil wir nur dort den redenden Gott haben."

contradiction included God, self and others and was a powerful indicator of the fact that humans were restless and stuck in a miserable and unhappy condition.[79] Restoration from this human dilemma was Köster's dominant salvation theme. The God given-remedy was the work and person of Jesus Christ. In the following three lectures the restoration theme was further developed by focusing on six key theological concepts. Humanity, reconciled and redeemed (lecture five), chosen and called (lecture six), sanctified and glorified (lecture 7).

Links to Creation and Fall

Bonhoeffer shared Köster's Christ centered approach. Already in his introduction he made clear that the whole of Scripture speaks of Christ. "The story of creation must be read in a way that begins with Christ and only then moves on toward him as its goal; indeed one can read it as a book that moves toward Christ only when one knows that Christ is the beginning, the new, the end of the whole world."[80]

In his exposition of the text Bonhoeffer repeatedly built bridges to Christ. Humanity's thinking about the beginning as a creation out of nothing required the interpretive key of the death and resurrection of Christ.[81] Within the dark deep of Genesis 1:2 the darkness of Christ's passion resonated.[82] Adam's fall and history was characterized by a divided and torn apart existence but in Christ a new center and a new existence was made possible.[83] In Christ a second beginning was granted[84] while at the same time creation, under God's curse, was upheld and sustained by God's orders of preservation. Yet the sole purpose of this endeavor was "to preserve us for Christ."[85] Humanity stuck in the middle, unable to conceive of its beginning and end, discovered that in "the midst of the world, on the accursed ground itself, life is raised anew."[86] In the middle [*Mitte*] of life the mediator [*Mittler*] Christ has by his willing death on the tree ("what a strange tree of

---

79. Ibid., 3: "Das ist des Menschen Wirklichkeit: er ist Mensch im Widerspruch!"
80. Bonhoeffer, *Creation*, 22.
81. Ibid., 35.
82. Ibid., 37.
83. Ibid., 92.
84. Ibid., 136, 138.
85. Ibid., 140.
86. Ibid., 146.

Salvation

life, this trunk on which the very God had suffered and died"),[87] offered to humanity new life and resurrection.

Bonhoeffer's exposition of the creation and fall story was thoroughly Christological. His attempt was to provide a theological exposition of the Genesis text which was in itself a protest against the devaluation of the Old Testament commonly held by scholars in the 1920s and 1930s. Often these views were fuelled by anti-Jewish sentiments but even renowned scholars gave their support. Bonhoeffer's own teacher Adolf von Harnack was of this opinion that "it is not possible to perceive from the Old Testament what is Christian."[88] *Creation and Fall* was a scholarly and thorough critique of such a view.

Lecture 5—Humanity, Reconciled and Redeemed (Col 1:12–23)

In Lectures five to seven, Köster's scriptural focus shifted from the Old to the New Testament. Direct comparisons to Creation and Fall are therefore not possible. It seems best briefly to summarize Köster's remaining lectures and to conclude comparing his arguments to Bonhoeffer's thoughts in a separate subsequent section.

In *Humanity; Reconciled and Redeemed*[89] Köster began by reminding his listeners of the destructive power of sin. Applying Paul's argument from the epistle to the Romans chapters 1 and 2, Köster pointed out that society was still ignoring God and that humanity was still idolizing its own ideas and thoughts. Both individuals and humanity as a whole were at enmity with God and deserved his just wrath and judgment. There was no way out, for all human solutions fell short, thus sin's power remained unbroken. But God, even though humanity deserved his rejection, sent Jesus who became God's utter and total "yes."[90] God's wrath was set aside in Christ. "At Golgotha the second Adam, suffered our judgment and condemnation. Our God forsakenness!"[91] The enormous cost of salvation was reflected in the brutal reality of the cross. Jesus Christ's death and resurrection redeemed and reconciled a fallen and alienated humanity with a just and loving God.

In the lecture Köster challenged his listeners to have faith and to believe. He argued that understanding followed believing and not vice versa.

87. Ibid., 146.
88. Ibid., 157.
89. Köster, 11 March 1943, 1: "Der Mensch—versöhnt und erlöst!"
90. Ibid., 6: "Jesus ist das bedingungslose 'Ja' Gottes zur sündigen Welt!"
91. Ibid., 6: "Jetzt erleidet dieser zweite Adam of Golgatha unser aller Urteil, unser aller Verurteilung! Unser aller Gottesferne!"

Thus he advocated a "faith seeking understanding" against a rejection of faith on the ground of reason. Personal choice and faith were important aspects for Köster. After all, if the heart of the human existence "was being created out of love, in love and for love,"[92] the restoration of the I-Thou relationship must also be at the heart of God's salvation gift. Köster resisted certain pietistic tendencies which had reduced faith to a predominately private and personal matter for the individual soul.[93] He argued that just as the effects of sin were universal so are the effects of reconciliation. The break with God was traceable throughout human history and was still causing chaos and mayhem on the battlefields. Healing the destructive power of sin through faith in Christ had the potential and promise of achieving world redemption.[94] A church that dared to proclaim a gospel that was able to transform the world also had to reckon with the opposition of the world whose sin-tainted inclination was to construct futile alternative salvation systems based on human efforts and striving.

Features of Lecture 5

Köster argued that humanity's enmity with God could also be discerned in the writings of philosophers and poets. His two examples were Kant's verdict that "within humans resides something that is radically evil" and Schiller's play. "The Robbers."[95] Köster kept building bridges to the ideas prevalent at his time rather than just arguing from Scripture alone. Sometimes the direction of his argument began with the world and moved to the Bible; at other times he explored patterns of Scripture first and then applied these to the world. For instance two misguided responses to the cross outlined by Paul were attitudes represented by the Jews and the Greeks. The Jewish attitude was the illusion that obedience to the law can be achieved by human effort. Köster paralleled it provocatively to the Aryan mentality and the Greek to Rousseau who had argued that humanity was intrinsically good and therefore needed neither reconciliation nor salvation.

---

92. Köster, 11 April 1943, 2: "Der Mensch ist aus und in und für die Liebe geschaffen!"

93. Ibid., 8: "Jesu Sendung in die Welt hinein ist durch lange Zeit von der Christenheit beschränkt worden auf den kleinen Lebensbezirk unserer Seele, und das Evangelium ist verkürzt worden auf die Versöhnung allein."

94. Ibid., 9: "Nur auf dem Boden der Versöhnung gibt es die neue Lebensgestaltung, die 'Menschenbruderschaft gibt es nur auf dem Boden der Gotteskindschaft.'"

95. Ibid., 2.

Salvation

Lecture 6—Humanity, Chosen and Called (Eph 1:1–14)

In the sixth lecture, *Humanity; Chosen and Called*[96] Köster explored the miracle and mystery of faith. He sought to strike a balance between the demand for a personal subjective choice and faith-decision with the truth that all human choosing was utterly dependent on having been chosen and called by God. He criticized the notion that, "sometimes we appear to believe that God's ability to reconcile and redeem was utterly dependent on our believing."[97] Köster argued that personal believing was dependent on God's own prior objective salvation act. All personal and subjective responses were based on what God had done in and through Jesus Christ. The subjective salvation event always followed God's prior objective faith event.[98] To the unbeliever such a distinction made little sense but to the believer it became a profound and wonderful mystery.

For Köster the purpose of God's calling was defined by Romans 8:29: "For those God foreknew he also predestined to be conformed to the likeness of his Son." This enabled Köster to return to the restoration theme, for what had been distorted, perverted and almost destroyed was to be restored into the likeness of his Son. God called believers to become like Jesus, in life, death and as a new creation. Such a high calling was truly staggering and prompted in believers a worshipful response and a profound concern toward those who were not chosen. Köster confessed that he was unable to fully grasp this profound mystery. "Who can understand it? Those who do may do so, I cannot. It is a mystery and God's own secret and we should honor God's hidden paths. God has not chosen all even though he has reconciled and redeemed all. The mysterious calling of the few unfolds within the all encompassing context of reconciliation and redemption. God only chooses some."[99]

Köster did not ignore unsettling questions regarding God's apparent arbitrariness, but rather than attempt complicated explanations he steered his listeners towards a sense of wonder and worship. Each believer had been God's thought and choice since the beginning of the world. Yet,

---

96. Köster, 18 March 1943 (10 pages, page 6 missing): "Der Mensch—erwählt und berufen."

97. Ibid., 2: "Das will doch bedacht sein! Wir tun so wichtig mit unserer Frömmigkeit, daß wir fast glauben, Gott kann ohne uns nicht versöhnen und erlösen!"

98. Ibid., 2–3: "Objektive Heilsgeschehen . . . subjektive Heilsgeschehen."

99. Ibid., 5: "Wer kann das begreifen? Wer es begreifen kann, der begreife es, ich begreife es nicht! Das ist Gottes Geheimnis, und wir wollen Gottes verborgene Pfade ehren! Gott hat nicht alle erwählt! Gott hat alle versöhnt und alle erlöst. Aber auf dem Boden der Versöhnung und Erlösung geht auf einmal das Geheimnis der Erwählung der wenigen Menschen vor sich. Gott trifft eine Auswahl aus den vielen Menschen."

God's purpose reached even beyond this for his call was to make them into his representatives on earth. They were to become kings and priests who brought God's liberating rule to earth. The scope of God's salvation purpose was universal and not confined to a narrow circle of believers. Jesus' followers were sent and commissioned to bring God's word and call to a world that was still alienated from God's rule. God's eternal choice and powerful call were to be articulated through the feeble witness of the faithful. Yet, Köster insisted, as God's word was proclaimed it created its own space, was aided by God's Spirit and led people to Jesus Christ. Such proclamation had to be done faithfully and patiently rather than in a coercive manner.[100] The church might be weak and its members might be feeble—after all they remained mere justified sinners[101]—yet, God's call and salvation purposes were proclaimed and embodied through them.

In the final section Köster reminded his listeners that God's call was still active and was heard wherever the gospel message was proclaimed. He expressed this by stating: "Through the act of preaching, God's choice and calling becomes real and through the act of listening, saving faith becomes possible."[102] Köster's emphasis was to see salvation as a participatory act rather than a solitary event. To him the mystery of redemption was primarily experienced by a living encounter with the proclaimed word. He argued that few people came to faith through reading God's word by themselves but through someone witnessing and proclaiming God's word to them. Köster finished by reminding the saved that they had been chosen "out of many for the many."[103] Their calling was to be certain of God's choice and to participate in God's salvation story as they themselves became his voice and a living manifestation of his grace.

Features of Lecture 6

A key distinction for Köster was the objective and subjective salvation event. The objective salvation event was prior and entirely dependent on God but

---

100. Ibid., 8: "Wir Prediger aber haben viel zu viel erwartet. Wir sind gewesen wie die kleinen Kinder, die heute Bohnen pflanzen und morgen schon nachsehen, ob schon etwas gewachsen ist! Wachstümlich geht es auch auf dem Boden des Glaubens . . . Wir sollten ihn aber nicht mit Keulenschlägen schlagen, um ihn zu etwas zu machen, was natürlicherweise wachsen soll!"

101. Ibid., 8. Köster refers here to Luther's phrase, *simul iustus et peccator*.

102. Ibid., 9: "Die Herauswahl geschieht, indem Gott durch die Predigt seines Wortes, durch das Hören dieser Predigt den Glauben, der errettet, ermöglicht."

103. Köster 18 March 1943, 9: "Dann bist du einer der Auserwählten aus den Vielen für die Vielen."

it also corresponded with the human subjective experience of being saved. He argued that it was impossible to separate "what God works in me and what is my doing."[104] His inclination was to stress God's act, assuming that when due respect to the objective salvation event was given, the subjective experience was to follow.

To Köster, faith was of a thoroughly corporate nature. His emphasis was the calling of the individual into a community. Conversion was thus not just an event where the individual sinner turned to God, but was a shared journey where God's word was proclaimed in the context of a believing community.

Lecture 7—Humanity, Sanctified and Glorified (Heb 10:4–10, Rom 8:28–30, 1 Cor 1:26–30)

In the last lecture of the series, *Humanity, Sanctified and Glorified*,[105] Köster recapitulated some of the main themes of the series and related these to some contemporary voices and trends. The aim of these seven lectures was to provide a biblical overview regarding the question concerning humanity. The term biblical indicated that it was quite distinct from other ideas and concepts. Biblical insight was radically different to scientific discoveries or results; it was rather God's abiding conversation with mankind. An attempt to read the Bible with a scientific methodology was ignoring that the Bible was "God's word spoken to humanity about humanity."[106] For Köster, God's word represented an invitation to respond. To an unbeliever the journey to faith involved a conversion experience. Few people, he argued, have a dramatic Paul of Tarsus type of conversion. More commonly it was a gradual process. Ultimately conversion remained the work of the Holy Spirit. "It is impossible to force people into conversion during an eight day evangelistic rally. The Spirit of God works when and where he wants."[107]

Köster reminded his listeners that other alternative views were often opposed to the biblical view. Thus, to embrace what God's word revealed

---

104. Ibid., 3: "Man kann das nicht so säuberlich auseinander schneiden, das was Gott in mir wirkt und mein Tun."

105. Köster, 15 March 1943 (10 pages): "Der Mensch—geheiligt und verherrlicht."

106. Ibid., 1: "Die Bibel ist kein Buch für naturwissenschaftliche Entdeckungen und Ergebnisse, sonder es ist das Wort Gottes zu den Menschen und über den Menschen! Wer die Bibel nicht so liest, liest sie falsch!"

107. Ibid., 2: "Man kann die Menschen nicht in einer 8 tägigen 'Evangelisation' vergewaltigen, der Geist Gottes kommt wann, und wo er will bei einem Menschen."

was, by implication, an act of defiance against certain philosophers[108] and political leaders.

For Köster, the final truth and aim of humanity was that any person who in faith had turned to Christ had embarked on a process of sanctification. Faith was listening to God, rather than intellectual understanding. Faith was also trusting that God was at work in the lives of his followers as he was transforming them into the likeness of the son. The sanctification of every believer was wholly dependent on God rather than human efforts. To Köster, reconciliation and sanctification were intractably bound and were not two different sequential realities. "Luther taught justification by faith . . . yet, what followed was a holiness movement whose claim was 'Luther has taught us justification but now we need to live a holy life. We need to build on top of the justification by faith a justification of life.' This led to a terrible legalism."[109]

Köster insisted on the primacy of faith rather than works. It mattered little whether the believer subjectively felt sanctified; what mattered was the reality that through faith, access to God's gracious work of Jesus Christ had been granted. Through faith in the cross and resurrection of Jesus, the believer was redeemed and had received a new sanctified quality of life. The only appropriate human response was to give praise and to become thankful.

> Are you wondering, am I a sanctified child of God?
> Ask yourself, am I giving thanks to him?
> Are you wondering, am I a justified child of God?
> Ask yourself, am I giving thanks to him?[110]

Köster's little self-test formula welded sanctification and justification together into one reality. It is significant that in this context he also felt compelled to state, that "ceasing to give thanks makes it impossible for God to give."[111] One is tempted to ask, whether giving thanks was a necessary

---

108. Ibid., 2–3. He briefly mentioned Goethe, Schopenhauer, Kant, Rosenberg and Nietzsche.

109. Ibid., 5: "Das ist ein Gedanke, den Luther leider nicht ganz deutlich for Augen hatte, obwohl er von seinem Verständnis der Rechtfertigung allein aus dem Glauben hätte darauf stossen müssen. Es kam darum die 'Heiligungsbewegung' hinterher, die sagte: 'Luther hat uns gerecht gesprochen, nun kommt es darauf an, daß wir auch heilig leben, und auf der Glaubensgerechtigkeit eine Lebensgerechtigkeit aufbauen.' Und da war auf einmal eine furchtbare Gesetzlichkeit da!"

110. Ibid., 5: "Bist du ein Heiliger Gottes? Frage dich, ob du ihm dankst? Bist du ein Gerechter Gottes? Frage dich ob du ihm dankst!"

111. Ibid., 5: "Danken, das ist das Geheimnis der Heiligen Gottes! Wer dankt Gott für seine Gaben, daß wir nach jeder Saat, wieder eine Ernte haben dürfen? Wenn man

human work that was required of the faithful? Köster would have rejected the term work and would have argued that gratitude was a natural response. Köster adopted a typical Lutheran emphasis of faith alone and the believer's utter dependency on God's gracious initiative. Nevertheless, the paradox between justification and sanctification was not completely resolved. On the one hand everything depended on divine initiative and on God's objective salvation act. Yet, on the other hand the individual person still had to believe, often requiring a leap of faith, and consequently had to live a life that was characterized by thankfulness. Equally, the glorification of every believer was also characterized by a similar paradoxical tension. For the reality of being glorified, hidden now but becoming apparent upon Christ's return, was a truth and certainty that had to be rediscovered in and through God's word by faith. Thus, listening to the proclaimed word of God made a believer "wonderfully blissful."[112] The necessary habit upon which the subjective experience of salvation, certainty, peace and joy was dependent upon was being attentive to God's word.

Köster finished the series by challenging all those who were asking themselves, "what shall we do?"[113] to believe and, according to the manner of the early church, be baptized. Drawing on Emil Brunner's book "Truth as Encounter" he argued that believer's baptism was the time honored place where the divine human encounter was initiated and affirmed. In baptism the believer began to live in the reality of the salvation that had been freely granted by God's grace.[114] In baptism the individual believer joined the fellowship of the saved whom Köster likened to the few who had entered Noah's ark.[115]

Gott nicht dankt, kann Gott eines Tages auch nicht mehr weiter geben, dann gibt er auch nicht!

112. Ibid., 8: "So wunderbar selig!"

113. Ibid., 9, quoting Acts 2:37.

114. Ibid., 9: "Ich las kürzlich noch bei Emil Brunner 'Wahrheit als Begegnung,' da schildert er, daß es Glauben nur gibt in der Begegnung des Menschen mit den lebendigen Gott. Die Taufe ist in der urchristlichen Gemeinde die Aufnahme der personalen Korrespondenz des Gläubigen mit Gott. In der Taufe nimmt der Gläubige Verkehr mit Gott auf. Darum werde ich immer Prediger einer Täufergemeinde sein, wenn ich dem Baptismus auch oft sehr gram sein muß um seiner Haltung in heutiger Zeit willen!"

115. Ibid., 10: "Wenn wir in der Arche Noah sind, weil wir in die Wunden Jesu glaubend eingegangen sind, haben wir nichts anderes zu tun als diesen Athanasiusdienst, daß wir in die leichtfertige Welt diese rettende Störungssendung hineinrufen!"

Dietrich Bonhoeffer and Arnold Köster

Features of Lecture 7

Köster had repeatedly reminded his listeners that the gospel claims were universal. Followers of Jesus were both kings and priests, called to represent God himself. Their message was world redemption which was God's unique gift rather than human achievement. Nevertheless, the final image of this lecture was of a city consumed by lust. The object of its lusting was represented by a beautiful female dancer, her skin covered by a thin layer of gold. Beautiful to behold but it was to disguise the fact that she was carrier of a deadly contagious disease. Köster likened God's people to the few whose task was to broadcast a disturbing message of impending judgment and to draw people into the safety of God's ark.

Links to Bonhoeffer's Writings

In the final three lectures Köster chose to follow well established patterns of soteriology. Bonhoeffer's own contributions to that topic were quite unique and distinctive. Even though Bonhoeffer chose to develop his arguments quite differently there were nevertheless significant overlaps between the two. To both, a process of restoration had been made possible in Christ. Bonhoeffer demonstrated in his theological exposition that the creation story was not about scientific information or mythology but was a pointer towards the possibility of salvation. What Christ offered was nothing less than a new creation. Köster explored this through the concepts of humans becoming reconciled, redeemed, chosen and called. Bonhoeffer preferred to explore the creation topic. He did this by connecting and applying the concepts he had developed in his theological exposition of *Creation and Fall* to the topic of salvation that had become possible in and through Jesus Christ.

Bonhoeffer had described the essence of the *imago Dei* as relational, as a being-free-for-the-other. In his lectures on Christology he connected this insight to Christ. Claiming that it was impossible for a stuck-in-the-middle humanity to understand beginning and end he stated at the beginning of his Christology lectures "To speak of Christ is to be silent, before the inexpressible."[116] Thus ultimately Christ's work and person also remained a mystery unless Christ was first encountered as the one who was *pro me*. Fallen humanity was reduced to living from its own resources and was therefore unable to reach beyond itself. It had to be reached first by Jesus Christ. "His being-Christ is his being-for-me.... The very core of his person

---

116. Bonhoeffer, *Berlin*, 300.

Salvation

is *pro-me*."[117] In Christ, God freely chose again to be for humanity. Just as in creation "God's self enters into creation,"[118] he entered the realm of fallen human existence, although in a veiled and hidden form, in the "likeness of flesh."[119] In Christ, who was wholly God and wholly human, a torn and disunited world is redeemed and becomes a new creation. In Christ, God was present again and remained present beyond the incarnation event which was limited to space and time. The presence of God in the world continued in the "form of Word, sacrament and church-community."[120]

To fallen humanity, salvation was the new creation and the restoration of the *imago Dei* in Christ. To Bonhoeffer, salvation was of a relational nature, for it was the restoration of the *analogia relationis*. The restoration began with the I-Thou relationship but also had a wider significance. For a person's access and introduction to the *pro me* Christ was dependent on Christ's presence in word, sacrament and church-community. Salvation had therefore next to the divine human relation also a human to human and human to creation dimension. The restoration of the subjective *me* was its release into being-free-for-others.

> Not all the individuals, but the church-community as a whole is in Christ, is the "body of Christ," it is "*Christ existing as church-community.*" It bears the sins by receiving forgiveness through the word and seeing its sins wiped out on the cross, it indeed lives *by the word* alone, but in doing so it has the Spirit. . . . And knows itself reconciled and justified in the cross of Jesus. It has itself died and risen in Christ, and is now the *nova creatura* [new creation] in Christ.[121]

Bonhoeffer had written the above quote in his earlier work Sanctorum Communio, but continued to explore, apply and develop this theme in *Creation and Fall*, his *Christology* and *Ethics*.

In relation to Köster's lecture on humanity sanctified and glorified, Bonhoeffer also applied the topics he had developed in *Creation and Fall*. In the *Ethics* Bonhoeffer explored and applied the tension that existed between the paradox of justification by faith alone and sanctification through the ethical application of a life lived from the center. His chapter *God's love and the Disintegration of the World*[122] was an extensive

117. Ibid., 314.
118. Bonhoeffer, *Creation*, 63.
119. Bonhoeffer, *Berlin*, 313.
120. Ibid., 314.
121. Bonhoeffer, *Creation*, 190.
122. Bonhoeffer, *Ethics*, 299–338.

discussion on this topic. In it Bonhoeffer repeated much of what he had said in *Creation and Fall* concerning the nature of sin which he had defined as split-apart existence. He then proceeded to explore how a renewed Christian life overcame this profound disunion and estrangement (*Entzweiung*). For Bonhoeffer, the task of ethical reflection, or to use Köster's term, sanctification, lay not in the ability to distinguish between good and evil but in superseding it. To Bonhoeffer salvation and a sanctified life was a simple life, a life beyond the knowledge of good and evil. Bonhoeffer persistently related the concept of good and evil to the tragic dilemma of the fallen condition which had its origin in the gaining the knowledge of good and evil. He argued that the real choice was either to be known and chosen by God or to grasp that knowledge. Such grasping usually masked itself through a pious demeanor, yet nevertheless desired to assume the role of a judge and to become like God. Bonhoeffer illustrated this by pointing to the Pharisees who epitomized the state of disunity of fallen humanity. "Pharisees are those human beings, admirable to the highest degree, who subject their entire lives to the knowledge of good and evil and who judge themselves as sternly as their neighbors—and all to the glory of God, whom they humbly thank for this knowledge."[123]

Their passion and commitment was always to distinguish between what was good and evil. They sought to achieve this by way of weighing every possible life situation in order to arrive at an informed decision. Their motivation was to live holy lives, yet since they relied on the knowledge of good and evil they remained tied to the very essence of the fall.[124] Christ lived and represented a total contrast to the Pharisees. Jesus simply sought the will of God. "He lives and acts not out of knowledge of good and evil, but out of the will of God."[125] Being a follower of Jesus, Bonhoeffer then argued, meant being transformed into the very same Christ-like life pattern. "Jesus demands that knowledge of good and evil be overcome, he demands unity with God."[126] Bonhoeffer illustrated this by Christ's "do not judge" (Matt 7:1) commandment, which was, "a stab in the heart of those who know good and evil."[127] For Bonhoeffer the test of a Christian judgment, which in some cases may even include suspending fellowship, was the reconciliatory nature of it. Its concern was not to create further disunity but to extend the

---

123. Ibid., 310.

124. Ibid., 314: "In this sense the doing of the Pharisee, which means the person who implement the knowledge of good and evil to the very last detail, is pretence and hypocrisy; this arises out of a disunited existence, rather than from intentional malice."

125. Ibid., 313.

126. Ibid., 314.

127. Ibid., 313.

work of reconciliation. The focus was therefore to know Christ rather than the knowledge of good and evil. Such a life faced the constant difficulty of being in itself "incapable of overcoming [*aufheben*] and conquering the knowledge."[128] Therefore the only way forward was: "the new life that is in Jesus alone. It is the liberating call to a single-mindedness [*Einfalt*], to turn around; it is the call that, by itself, overcomes the old knowledge resulting from the fall and instead instills the new knowledge of Jesus, that knowledge which consists entirely in doing the will of God."[129]

Bonhoeffer acknowledged that the life in Jesus, although referred to as a life of simplicity, was in its day to day application quite complex. God's will, often deeply hidden, cannot be reduced to fixed rules nor should it be automatically equated with the voice of the heart. It was "always new and different in each life circumstance."[130] Bonhoeffer argued that a disciple's life was a gradual and continual process in which a believer was changed, formed and renewed into the image of Christ. This sanctifying process was not mechanical but relational and had to take place again and again.

For Bonhoeffer and Köster the Christian life was not defined by a driven and unholy activism but by being found and loved by Christ. For Bonhoeffer, "to love God means simply to allow God to elect and conceive us in Christ." Speculations regarding election and predestination were tied to a life of disunity rather than unity with God.[131] It was fallen humanity's attempt to know rather than to be known and loved. To be known and loved by God was a pure gift. It was the discovery of Christ *pro me* that created for disunited humans the possibility of loving God and living a renewed life of unity. "To love God is merely the other side of being loved by God."[132]

---

128. Ibid., 318.

129. Ibid.

130. Ibid., 321.

131. Ibid., 301–2: "Instead of gladly accepting the choice and election of God, they want to choose on their own and thus be the origin of election. So, in some sense, they carry the secret of predestination within themselves. Instead of only knowing themselves in the reality of being elected and loved by God, they now must know themselves in the possibility of choosing, of being the origin of good and evil."

132. Ibid., 337.

8

Conclusion

Introduction

THIS THESIS HAS ENDEAVORED to listen to two distinct Christian voices in the midst of Germany's Third Reich turmoil. The voice of Dietrich Bonhoeffer continues to be heard by many within and without the Christian churches. His writings and life story have attracted and inspired subsequent generations and he is widely regarded as the foremost Christian witness of that period. Compared to Bonhoeffer, the voice of Köster is barely audible and is only remembered by a few. The writings of Bonhoeffer are varied and allow readers to engage with the academic, teacher, catechist, preacher, friend, lover, novelist and poet. Köster's thoughts and messages have been preserved exclusively as the voice of a preacher and columnist. Thus, the range of Köster's voice is much narrower and reveals little of personal struggles and doubts. Compared to the extensive amplification of Bonhoeffer's thoughts and writings, it is but a still small voice. Nevertheless, it is the voice of a courageous witness at a time when many other Baptists were muzzled by fear and blinkered by a narrow vision of salvation.

Listening to two voices is not quite the same as recording a conversation. Had the Lutheran and the Baptist met what would they have discussed? Would they have discovered in the other's point of view mutual agreement and a shared concern? How would they have challenged each other's points of view? Would they have been able to resolve their differences? Beyond these historical puzzles, a more pertinent question for today's followers of Christ is to ask how the lives and writings of Bonhoeffer and Köster help and challenge the present church-community.

Conclusion

Salvation—Pious Stories of Conversion

Eberhard Bethge remembers that "Bonhoeffer always greatly disliked stories of conversions told by pietists for purpose of edification."¹ What caused this dislike? Did the thinker and theologian object to a simplistic reading and interpretation of the Bible? Bonhoeffer's twin sister, Sabine Leibholz, recalled that one of their shared childhood experiences was their mother reading Bible stories to them.² She also mentioned the arrival of their nanny, Fräulein Horn, from the pietistic Herrnhut Community. She became an integral part of the household where her faith and Christian songs were remembered by the children. Bonhoeffer mentioned her, affectionately calling her Hörnchen, in a letter he sent to his parents in 1944.³ During his lifetime, Bonhoeffer's view of Scripture had undergone a profound change. He himself referred to a time prior to giving his lectures on *Creation and Fall* when he began to see the Bible in a new way. "I came to the Bible for the first time."⁴ He linked this new way of reading the Bible to the discipline of asking questions, and hearing it as God's spoken word. In essence, it was having a dialogue with Scripture as opposed to a scientific approach of dissection. It was a way, of letting Scripture speak the truth to the reader rather than judicially discerning some truths within it—in as far as they corresponded and acceptable to the current body of knowledge. "The word of God [is] neither fiction nor fairy tale nor myth: on the contrary one must read it word for word [*buchstabieren*] like a child and learn to rethink completely what the historical critical commentaries teach us."⁵

Clearly, in Bonhoeffer's mind, these stories of conversion were different to the childlike reading of the Bible. What seems more likely is that he was uneasy with a forced "decisionism"⁶ often associated with Baptist preachers. Interestingly even Köster recalled how a preacher "literally took hold of every member of the congregation and challenged them individually by asking, 'have you repented?'" He preferred it when preachers "had the courage to expect the Holy Spirit to work and simply speak in a sober matter-of-fact manner."⁷ It appears that Bonhoeffer and Köster shared a

1. Bethge, *Dietrich Bonhoeffer*, 156.
2. Leibholz, *Dietrich Bonhoeffer*, 320.
3. Bonhoeffer, *Letters*, 316.
4. Bonhoeffer, *Creation*, 153.
5. Ibid., 23n11.
6. McClendon, *Ethics*, 208.
7. Köster, 18 Juni 1944, 11: "Ich denke an einen Prediger in Köngsberg, der jeden Menschen in der Versammlung ganz buchstäblich beim Knopfloch nahm und fragte: 'Bist du bekehrt?' . . . Das ist furchtbar! Wenn ein Prediger kommt, der den Mut hat mit

certain dislike of emotionally charged conversion stories, yet how did they relate God's gift of salvation to the human need of having to make a choice?

The German church faced, beside the political and economic crisis, a crisis of faith. Most of the people preserved an outward allegiance to the church, but were inwardly in doubt and disillusioned with organized religion. The need to reconnect the increasingly secular population with the Christian message was widely acknowledged. Even amongst members of the Confessing Church Bonhoeffer discerned a willingness to stand up "for the 'cause' of the church, and so on, but little personal faith in Christ."[8]

Bonhoeffer's context was the academic world where theologians sought to legitimize the Christian faith and the Bible through rational and scientific research. Köster's hinterland was the revivalist tradition with an evangelistic outlook. Even the German Christians sought to revitalize the appeal of the church and argued that their nationalistic political vision was effectively engaging with the masses and "proclaiming the Gospel."[9]

In 1943 Köster gave a lecture on Kierkegaard whose overriding concern was "to show Christendom how it was possible to become a Christian within Christendom."[10] Köster argued that Kierkegaard's thoughts and influence were ubiquitous. "In these present days every thoughtful person, psychologists, anthropologists, theologians of Catholic, Protestant and Separatist persuasion, everyone involved in humanities . . . all are influenced by Kierkegaard."[11]

Kierkegaard's concern was the nominal and hollow Christendom of his days. Religion was reduced to providing appropriate rituals at births, marriages and burials. Being a respectable citizen and being a Christian had become synonymous. Sadly, what was true in Kierkegaard's time was also true, Köster claimed "to ninety percent today."[12]

Köster distilled from a number of Kierkegaard's writings[13] four overlapping stages of life; the aesthetical, ethical, religious and the Christian-

---

dem Wirken des Geistes zu rechnen und nur die 'Sache' redet,—dann atmet man auf."

8. Bonhoeffer, *Letters*, 500.

9. Schlingensiepen, *Dietrich Bonhoeffer*, 171.

10. Köster, 13 May 1943: "Stationen auf dem Lebensweg."

11. Ibid., 2: "Dass ich Sören Kierkegaard heute heranziehe, tue ich aus dem bestimmten Grund, weil in unseren Tagen alles, was irgendwie denkt, die Psychologen oder die Anthropologen, die Theologen der katholischen wie der protestantischen und der freikirchlichen Kirche, oder irgend ein Mensch auf dem Boden der Geisteswissenschaften, wer immer die Frage nach dem Menschen bewegt, kommt heute her von Kierkegaard, das ist etwas sehr Eigenartiges."

12. Ibid., 9.

13. Ibid., 4. Entweder—Oder, Der Begriff der Angst, Die Reinheit des Herzens, Die

Conclusion

believing stage. The ultimate goal of every faith journey was an existential encounter with the living God and the challenge "to leap head over heel into faith and into following Jesus."[14] Thus, Köster argued, discipleship and the "willingness to lose life in order to gain it"[15] was how Kierkegaard sought to restore and revitalize Christendom.

In *Discipleship* Bonhoeffer's verdict of nominal Christianity and those who maintained organized religion, was that costly grace had been distorted into cheap grace.[16] His own conviction was that, "*only the believers obey, and only the obedient believe.*"[17] For Bonhoeffer, the Christian life expressed itself through discipleship which required "taking certain steps. The first step, which responds to the call, separates the followers from their previous existence."[18] Clearly Köster had much in common with the Bonhoeffer of *Discipleship*. They were united in their focus on a volitional commitment of following Jesus. However, how did they integrate this concern into their understanding of salvation?

The shared premise of Bonhoeffer's *Creation and Fall* and Köster's lectures on *The Question Regarding Humanity* was that God's word was living and powerfully addressed the human situation and dilemma. For the Baptist Köster, this biblical view was an integral part of his own tradition. Luther's *sola scriptura* had been weakened within the academic circles in which Bonhoeffer worked and was nurtured. Yet Karl Barth's focus on revelation was welcomed by both Bonhoeffer and Köster. Bonhoeffer's theological exposition of the Old Testament text of Genesis was a significant contribution to this new way of a scholarly engagement with Scripture. Köster, who was critical of liberal and academic theology, would have embraced and welcomed much of Bonhoeffer's contribution.

For Köster, salvation was both comprehensive and complex. He used the Old Testament stories as creative diagnostic tools for a deeper biblical understanding of the human dilemma. He assumed that most people's souls were restless and painfully aware that their lives fell drastically short of the "ought" their consciences demanded.

Since God was involved in the affairs of the world, the task was to discover what God was doing and to distinguish God's work from the destructive

---

Krankheit zum Tode, Der Angriff auf die Christenheit, Furcht und Zittern, Stadien auf dem Lebensweg, Das Walten der Liebe.

14. Ibid., 9.

15. Ibid., 10: "Der Repräsentant des virten Stadiums ist der Märtyrer, der, um der Nachfolge Jesu willen bereit ist, das Leben zu verlieren, um es zu gewinnen."

16. Bonhoeffer, *Discipleship*, 43–56.

17. Ibid., 63.

18. Ibid., 61–62.

schemes of Satan's work. The pivotal point of God's salvation purposes was Jesus Christ. Thus all human self-understanding was intrinsically linked to understanding the person and work of Jesus Christ. In Christ, restoration of what had been remained the answer to the human quest—being and living as the image of God—had again become a possibility. Köster rejected attempts to make salvation a mere personal and private matter of an individual's soul. Salvation had universal implications and was therefore relevant to every aspect of life. Köster's main focus was the restoration of what was at the heart of human existence—the relational dimension of the I and Thou.

Bonhoeffer's theological exposition supported the bulk of Köster's conclusions. However, he chose to structure his own material differently. It seems likely that Köster would have wanted Bonhoeffer to lay greater emphasis on the necessary human choice for God. He might have considered Bonhoeffer's existential analysis profound, but lacking in emphasis on the human responsibility to make an existential decision. Brunner's interpretation of the *imago Dei*, as the ability to respond to God, was much closer to how Köster shaped his arguments. However, one has to bear in mind that their target audiences influenced their distinctive manner of interpretations. As an academic *Privatdozent*, Bonhoeffer was addressing students in 1932–33. Köster gave his lectures to an audience of ordinary people, whose lives, in 1943, were rocked and threatened by an escalating and increasingly uncertain war. Life and death decisions were forced upon the listeners and their families by the world.

Bonhoeffer would have appreciated a great deal of what Köster had to say in his lectures. Clearly, Köster sought to interpret Scripture theologically by engaging firstly with God's word and secondly with the philosophers of the time. Yet, comparing their different arguments and concerns, one is tempted to conjecture that Bonhoeffer would have been wary of Köster's tendency of drawing sharp distinctions. Köster retained an element of decisionism. To him there was a choice to be made between God and Satan, between the church and the world and ultimately between good and evil. Bonhoeffer would probably have feared that such attempts came perilously close to the fatal assumption that a Christian knowledge of good and evil was possible. His own answer in *Ethics* was to seek union in Christ rather than disunion, dichotomy and *Entzweiung*.

Köster's implicit assumption was that salvation and union in Christ were found in the church-community which in turn was separated from a god-forsaken world. His comfort and firm belief was that the present chaos was passing and that God was in control. Köster highlighted the reality of God's judgment but also spoke of God's patience and promises. Ultimately God's will and reign was to prevail over Satan and every kind of human rebellion. The church was set within this multilayered world and was—as God's ark—a place of salvation at a time of intense turmoil. Within it Christians were saved and preserved for God's future reign.

Köster emphasized personal salvation and challenged his listeners to risk a leap of faith. The task of being church was to gather the saved and to proclaim the gospel message to the unsaved. The need for a decisive element of Christian following was also argued by Bonhoeffer in his *Discipleship*. However, gradually Bonhoeffer's focus became a corporate and world transforming salvation. His application included the individual (Christ *pro me*) who was at the same time sent to the other. The task of the church community was to live and represent God's kingdom, new creation and ultimate reality. The church-community's calling was therefore of a world-transforming nature.

It is significant that Köster, in spite of his close affiliation to Kierkegaard's call for a radical Christian discipleship, also proposed a revision of Kierkegaard. In his 1943 lecture he argued that radical following represented an impossible demand and added to the four stages a fifth one; "new creation." Against Kierkegaard Köster argued: "What makes us Christians is not following Jesus, but being redeemed through Jesus Christ."[19] Thus, in the matter of salvation, the Baptist's decision focus was kept in check by the emphasis on God's free gift of grace. Both Bonhoeffer and Köster refused to resolve the Pauline tension between "work out your own salvation with fear and trembling" and the "God who is at work in you, enabling you both to will and to work" (Phil 2:12–13 NRSV).

The Church—Baptism and Deep Faith

On 24 March 1944 Bonhoeffer wrote to his friend Eberhard Bethge, "The New Testament has no rule about infant baptism. It is a gift of grace, bestowed on the church to be received and used in deep faith, and therefore it can also be a striking witness to faith for the congregation."[20]

The Baptist Köster would have found it impossible to agree with such a statement. His ecclesiology was shaped by believer's baptism and he called infant baptism "a forgery of Christendom and a terrible swindle against those falsely certified as Christians."[21] It would have been difficult

19. Köster, 13 May 1943: "Stadium der Neuschöpfung . . . was uns zu Christen macht, ist nicht Nachfolge Jesu, sondern Erlösung durch Jesus Christus."

20. Bonhoeffer, *Letters*, 329.

21. Täufer-Bote, 1932, No 5, 4: "Die Kindertaufe ist eben doch die Falschmützerei im Christentum und ein furchtbarer Betrug an denen, die man dadurch zu Christen stempelt."

for Köster to understand how Bonhoeffer was able to condemn "baptism without the discipline of community"[22] and at the same time justify infant baptism "because it is indeed baptism."[23]

Each sought to address the misuse of infant baptism. Bonhoeffer even argued that, "a misuse of infant baptism . . . will therefore necessarily lead the church-community to an appropriate limitation of its practice and to a new appreciation of adult baptism."[24] He was fully aware of the dangers but was nevertheless unable to reject the practice outright. To Bonhoeffer infant baptism remained a gift of grace and, providing it was used in deep faith, it was baptism indeed. In concord with Luther he stressed the priority of God's choice rather than human decision.[25] In contrast the Baptist focus was that a believer's baptism was a public witness to the fact that God established his church through a responsive community of followers. "We [the congregation] do not have the right or the ability to measure the height, depth or width of every decision. It is a personal matter only known by God. What is most important is that every human being arrives sooner or later at this decisive point. Baptism for the early Christians was a decision before God . . . our baptism is a decision for God."[26]

Such a decision cannot be expected of "an infant eight days old"[27] nor could it be made in isolation by believing adults. Ultimately, Köster reminded the congregation, no human decision could be made without God's prior calling. Yet, as God's gospel call was heard and received, believers were led to repentance and to submitting themselves to God. "Baptism is a decision of the heart; it is a life turning decision! . . . Baptism is a faith decision that risks taking God's proclaimed word seriously. It risks considering God's gospel word of greater value than everything else on earth."[28]

22. Bonhoeffer, *Discipleship*, 44.

23. Ibid., 211.

24. Bonhoeffer, *Conspiracy*, 567.

25. Ibid., 559: "Faith is . . . not conscious comprehending, responding, deciding [Sichentscheiden], but the pure reception of salvation." Ibid., 570: "'Decision for Christ'—itself an [un]biblical term—is the activist perversion of the passive character of faith."

26. Köster, 2 May 1943, 1–2: "Wir haben nicht das Recht, auch nicht das Vermögen, auch nicht den Maßstab, die Höhe und die Tiefe und die Breite einer jeden Entscheidung zu messen. Das ist das ganz Persönliche des Menschen vor Gott. Aber die Hauptsache ist, dass es einmal in dem Leben des Menschen zu dieser Entscheidung vor Gott kommt. Und im Urchristentum war die Taufe die Entscheidung vor Gott . . . unsere Taufe ist Entscheidung für Gott."

27. Ibid., 2.

28. Ibid., 4: "Taufe ist Herzensentscheidung, ist Lebensentscheidung! Hier fällt eine Entscheidung in diesem Augenblicken vor Gott am Evangelium von Jesus Christus, die Entscheidung der Buße, dass wir garnichts haben, dass Gott alles hat und alles ist in

Conclusion

Köster held God's gracious gospel call in tension with the human obligation to freely decide and respond to God's free and costly call. In baptism believers received forgiveness of sins and were granted the gift of the Holy Spirit.[29]

For Köster baptism represented the visible joining together of God's call, human response and the equipping and commissioning of the baptized as followers of Christ. The church-community was defined and shaped by this event. To Bonhoeffer, church-community, although theologically defined by baptism, lacked this definable lucidity. If one were to apply Avery Dulles' six models of the church,[30] Bonhoeffer's understanding of church would come close to the "Mystical Communion"[31] model; while Köster's would correspond with the "Community of Disciples"[32] model of church. In 1944 infant baptism evoked in Bonhoeffer the need for deep faith. What Bonhoeffer separated, God's gracious call and the reciprocal human response, Köster merged into one.

What makes Bonhoeffer's stance confusing was that he argued for a radical break with the world in *Discipleship*. "Those who are baptized no longer belong to the world, no longer serve the world, and are no longer subject to it. They belong to Christ alone, and relate to the world only through Christ. The break with the world is absolute. It requires and causes our death. In baptism we die together with our old world."[33]

How the church community as the body of Christ was to maintain a break with the world became the focus for Arnold Köster's ministry. Bonhoeffer located this separation theologically in baptism but relocated an individual's personal decision into Jesus' call to discipleship. "Whether disciples want to or not, they have to make a decision; each has to decide alone. Each is called alone. Each must follow alone. . . . Christ has untied the person's immediate connections with the world and bound the person immediately to

---

Christus Jesu. So ist Taufe eine Entscheidung des Glaubens, das Wagnis, Gott ernst zu nehmen im Predigtwort. Es ist das Wagnis, Gottes Wort im Evangelium mehr gelten zu lassen als sonst irgend etwas auf Erden."

29. Täufer-Bote, 1932, No 5, 3.

30. Dulles, *Models*. In the first edition (1974) of his book Avery Dulles worked with five different but complementary models. The church as (1) Institution, (2) Mystical Communion, (3) Sacrament, (4) Herald, (5) Servant. A new chapter was added in the second edition of his book (1987). The church as (6) Community of Disciples.

31. Ibid., 39–54: "Dietrich Bonhoeffer developed the notion of the Church as an interpersonal community." (See page 40).

32. Ibid., 195–217.

33. Bonhoeffer, *Discipleship*, 208.

himself. . . . He stands not only between me and God, he also stands between me and the world, between me and other people and things."[34]

For Bonhoeffer, the practice of infant baptism required a church-community in which "the act of salvation already accomplished once and for all will be repeatedly remembered in faith."[35] Since Christ was present in the church-community, each would, it was hoped—in due course—freely respond to God's call. However, the reality of the German church-of-the-people was that a large proportion of the baptized were firmly tied to the world, other people and things. For Bonhoeffer, the painful tension between the ideal and the actual reality of church was much greater than for Köster.

Bonhoeffer's experiences of church were diverse. He served local congregations, lectured at the university, worked as a chaplain to students, was ecumenically involved, had experiences overseas and served as a director of a theological seminary. Köster's focus was primarily the local church-community in Vienna. He maintained regular connections to other local churches and the *Baptisten Bund* in Germany, but his ecclesiology was primarily shaped by the pastoral needs and challenges of a local church-community.

His efforts were to preserve, guide and care for a community, which in baptism had resolved to follow Jesus. He was fully aware of the fact that God's sovereign purposes were not exhausted with the salvation of the individual sinner but reached beyond to world-renewing cosmic intentions. The church's life and purpose were set into this eschatological context. Its role and calling was to journey through this world and in the midst of it, bear witness to God's constant redeeming activities in a world disfigured by a spirit of rebellion and revolt. He understood the power and danger of ideological worldviews and was convinced that the church-community needed to rediscover and to hold fast to its own Christian worldview shaped by God's word and its experience of baptism.

Believer's baptism was the central focus in Köster's ecclesiology. For Bonhoeffer, set within the church-of-the-people context, baptism had a profound theological significance but was ultimately peripheral. It became the hazy church boundary within which Christ continued to call and establish his community of followers. Conscious of the enormous challenges the German church faced, Bonhoeffer hoped in 1935 that "a new kind of monasticism . . . with . . . a life of uncompromising discipleship"[36] would bring about the restoration of the church. Bonhoeffer gathered people who

---

34. Ibid., 92–94.
35. Ibid., 212.
36. Bonhoeffer, *London*, 285. Schlingensiepen, *Dietrich Bonhoeffer*, 175.

voluntarily agreed to share "a daily order of prayer, brotherly exhortation, free personal confession, common theological work and a very simple communal life."[37] This radical monastic-type community and vision came closest to Köster's understanding of church. However, in 1944 Bonhoeffer had moved away from this vision of uncompromising discipleship. "I thought I myself could learn to have faith by trying to live something like a saintly life. I suppose I wrote *Discipleship* at the end of this path. Today I clearly see the dangers of that book, though I still stand by it. Later on I discovered . . . that one only learns to have faith by living in the full this-worldliness of life."[38]

Contrary to the "full this-worldliness of life," Köster strove to relate to the church-community God's vision of the end and the restoration of all things. He related this vision to the immediate challenges of their fragile human existence. Whether it was doubt, fear, suffering or the threat of death, each in turn was set into the context of an eschatological perspective. The church was not called to bring about the end through its own effort but to trust God. Yet, just as Jesus had overcome evil through his own suffering, the church was also called to suffer.[39] The suffering of the church was a witness to the cross of Christ and had a priestly and substitutionary significance.[40] The church was not released from the world but was subjected to the groaning of this present creation. As the followers of Christ journeyed through the world they were messengers of God's gospel and their calling was to be a prophetic community. "One should not come to the cross and say: With the cross Christ has forgiven you your sins. People cannot hear that today. However, when I begin to explain that we ourselves are simply unable to renew this world and when I then point out that God's reconciliation is the precondition for the renewal of the world, then people begin to listen, for that is the urgent question of our time."[41]

37. Bethge, *Dietrich Bonhoeffer*, 385.

38. Bonhoeffer, *Letters*, 486.

39. Köster, 17 January 1943, 2 Cor, 67: "Nur wer das Kreuz des Christus versteht, wird herausgenommen aus allem Egoismus seines Lebens, und hineingestellt in die Liebe zu den Menschen."

40. Täufer-Bote, 1932, No 5, 2: "Wundert es uns, wenn der Geist auf Erden immer leidender Geist ist? Wundert es uns, dass wir als seine Zeugen immer unsere Leiden und Verfolgungen finden? Wundert uns die Kreuzesnachfolge der ewigen Lieben? Dienst an der Welt von Gott her ist immer Leiden um dieser Welt willen. Dazu ist uns der Geist gegeben."

41. Köster, 5 April 1943: "Man soll nicht mit dem Kreuz kommen und sagen: Mit dem Kreuz hat der Christus dir deine Sünden vergeben. Dafür haben die Menschen heute kein Ohr. Wenn ich aber anfange und die ganze Problematik anfasse, daß wir es nicht schaffen, die Welt neu zu gestalten, wenn ich sage, daß mit der Gottesversöhnung die Voraussetzung für die Weltneugestaltung da ist, dann haben wir wieder Leute, die

Dietrich Bonhoeffer and Arnold Köster

The World—Seize the Wheel

During the period of the Third Reich Christian witness was forged in the furnace of crisis. The world of politics and the world of faith, which had previously been assigned to separate spheres, were forced together by the claims and demands of a totalitarian regime. How was the Christian church-community to act responsibly? Was it sufficient to proclaim a prophetic message? Had the time come not just to protest and to "bind up the wounds of the victims beneath the wheel but to seize the wheel itself?"[42] Bonhoeffer had raised this prospect in 1933 in his essay, *The Church and the Jewish Question*.[43] In it Bonhoeffer distinguished the true church of Christ from a "church that is regarded essentially as a cultural function of the state." Bonhoeffer argued, at that time, that a possible concrete opportunity for the church who dared to seize the wheel would be a collective boycott of funeral services. His suggestion was not well received. However, Bethge judged the potential effectiveness of such a daring public stance as "not illusory."[44] The scale and impact of such an interdict would have affected countless people and would have raised national and international concerns. Such a policy was only possible for a church-of-the-people which had a recognized cultural function. Had Baptist pastors pursued a similar collective strategy it would have remained unnoticed and illusory.

A decade later Bonhoeffer used a similar phrase in a private conversation.

> During one of their walks round the prison yard in Tegel Dietrich Bonhoeffer was asked by a fellow-prisoner how as a Christian and a theologian he could take it upon himself to participate in the active resistance against Hitler. In the brief time given him under the eyes of the warders, he answered with a story: If he, as a pastor, saw a drunken driver racing at high speed down the Kurfürstendamm, he did not consider it his only or his main duty to bury the victims of the madman, or to comfort his relatives; it was more important to wrench the wheel out of the hands of the drunkard.[45]

Bonhoeffer's sense of responsibility led him to endorse the attempt of wrenching the wheel out of the hands of a madman. His steps into the resistance were not taken lightly nor did he ever claim that involvement

---

zuhören, weil das die große Frage unserer Tage ist!"

42. Bonhoeffer, *Berlin*, 365.
43. Ibid., 361–70.
44. Bethge, *Dietrich Bonhoeffer*, 224, 658.
45. Zimmermann and Smith, *I Knew Dietrich Bonhoeffer*, 82.

in the conspiracy could be done with a good conscience. Bonhoeffer was aware that these were steps that took him outside and beyond the ethical boundaries of the church and assumed that "his Church would no longer be able to use him, once the facts came to light."[46] It is true that few dared to take this radical step but it is also true that very few were able to take it. Bonhoeffer's involvement in the plot was made possible through his family connection which gave him an insight into the internal and ruthless workings of the Nazi government. Bethge also drew attention to the fact that in 1940 Bonhoeffer, unlike most of his colleagues, was not tied to a parish. "Perhaps his life would have taken a different course if Bonhoeffer had been a pastor of a parish in that year."[47]

Köster was in local ministry and was geographically removed from Berlin where the grinding wheels of the Nazi government were situated. In their theological reflections, Bonhoeffer and Köster wrestled with Scripture and with Luther's two kingdom teaching. The unique nature of the church as a called-out (*ek-klesia*) entity was contrary to a totalitarian vision that viewed all of life as political. The authors of the Bible distinguished God's kingdom from the world. Yet, as these concepts were applied, the New Testament authors also took into account that the world represented a fluid and shifting context. The biblical spectrum included God-ordained authority (Rom 13:1) and an authority dominated by the antichrist and the beast of Revelation 13. Followers of Christ were always faced with shifting contexts, and had therefore perpetually to discern, apply and redefine the nature of the world's authority (*Obrigkeit*). Karl Barth wrote in 1939: "Thus there is clearly no cause for the Church to act as though it lived, in relation to the State, in a night in which all cats are grey. It is much more a question of continual decision, and therefore of distinctions between one State and another, between the State of yesterday and the State of to-day."[48]

Luther's concept of the two separate realms was shared by Lutheran, Reformed and Baptist theologians. However the application of these presuppositions was much debated and differently interpreted. Confessional Lutherans sought to remain faithful to Luther's strict duality. Their focus was to define and maintain the separate roles and responsibilities of church and state. The critical overlap between the two realms was the individual believer who inwardly—in a personal union (*Personalunion*)—was always both a person of the world (*Weltmensch*) and a person of Christ (*Christenmensch*). This view acknowledged that government had the potential to do

---

46. Bethge, *Dietrich Bonhoeffer*, 699.
47. Ibid., 696–97.
48. Barth, *Church and State*, 31–32.

good but was equally capable of distorting and exploiting this God-given mandate. By holding the two realms in perpetual tension, the possibility of doing good was tempered with skepticism. The order of government was at best preservative rather than a final remedy for a world distorted by sin.

The German Christians defined state authority much more positively as God-ordained order. The office of state authority was theologically invested with divine authority ordained to vanquish the forces of chaos and bring about a new order. The reformed wing of the German church-of-the-people was either caught up by the radical political movement or sought, along with Karl Barth, to distance itself. What motivated assent and dissent was that one group perceived the emerging nationalistic movement as divinely approved, while the other rejected it.

Bonhoeffer sought to move beyond the separation of realms and risked a radical this-worldliness of life. The trajectory of his journey was determined by a unique set of tragic circumstances and opportunities. He energetically participated in the church struggle, using lawful means, and subsequently chose to participate in an unlawful conspiracy. Reflecting on his experiences he came to conclude that: "The boundaries between resistance and submission can't be determined as a matter of principle, but both must be there and both must be seized resolutely. Faith demands this flexible and alive way of acting."[49]

Arnold Köster was a resolute critic of worldly hubris and power, but never had the opportunity to get involved in a plot. His theological understanding of the complex relation between church and world was not only informed by Luther but also by the Anabaptists. Contrary to Luther, sixteenth century Anabaptists rejected the Christendom worldview. To Anabaptists the presence of the church in society had to be real and concrete rather than a mysterious invisible church. Church-community was defined as discipleship community. Nevertheless, Anabaptists had to live their lives in the world. Authority structures had to be acknowledged and taxes had to be paid. Life on earth was grounded in a world where believers rubbed shoulders with non-believers, neighbors, citizens and rulers. Their challenge was to find ways of managing these interconnected areas of life. Some groups embraced pacifism, others proposed more moderate solutions. However, the basic distinction between the magisterial reformers and these radicals was that to them the kingdom of God was much more rigorously separated from the affairs of the world. The world was still seen to be God's world; however, since believers considered themselves separate, the realm of the world became the domain of the unbelievers. It became a realm in which the

---

49. Bonhoeffer, *Letters*, 304.

Conclusion

radical application of gospel life was deemed impossible. It was perceived as a realm which, due to the nature of sin, was ambivalent, confusing and often hostile to God's people.

It was clear to Köster that to the church, the world represented an enormous challenge but also a divine calling. Commenting on Revelation 17 he said in 1943, "our obligation to pray for the state authority (*Obrigkeit*) takes the church of Jesus Christ into a desperate need and dilemma."[50]

Köster's response to the political crisis was to protect the church-community from an invasion of an illusionary worldly hope. He sought to isolate worldly solutions from the promised kingdom of God and insisted that the world with its systems and methods was unable to achieve salvation *(Heil)*. Rather, it was the church's task to offer salvation to the world—a salvation that had to be realized by membership to an alternative and countercultural community. Köster acknowledged on the one hand that God was at work in the world and that believers were part of this world, but also insisted that there was a radical difference between the kingdom of God and *Weltstaat*. Being mindful of that difference made it impossible and foolish to engage naively with the world. His political theology, restrained and shaped by crisis, was one that primarily understood the church's task to remain separated from the world while offering to the world a prophetic message and the possibility of an alternative vision and community.

In 1943 Köster also used the phrase "to seize the wheel"[51] in a sermon. However, he applied it to the presumptuous and pointless efforts of "the great ones in this world" who sought to seize the wheel of fate. The rise of

---

50. Köster, 16 September 1943, 4: "Dass da gerade die Gemeinde Jesu Christi in tausenfältige Not gerät mit ihrem Auftrag, für die Obrigkeit zu beten, das begreifen wir von hier aus sehr deutlich. Aber das ist das Bild, das Johannes uns zu geben hatte! Der Weltstaat in der Stadt des Antichristus, der ganz das Tier aus dem Abgrund geworden ist und in das Verderben geht, der seine Macht nicht mehr begrenzen lässt, und darum nicht mehr segensvoll sein kann durch die Macht des lebendigen Gottes."

51. Köster, 5 April 1943. Köster gave a lecture at an Allianz gathering entitled, "Das christliche Weltbild." During that lecture Köster uses a phrase also used by Bonhoeffer, although in a different context: "Ich habe vorher das 'mechanistische Weltbild' genannt. Da haben die Menschen die Vorstellung, daß die ganze Natur eine große Maschine ist. Die Welt ist wie ein mechanischer Apparat, der weiterläuft, es geht immer weiter, auch wenn einmal Zwischenfälle kommen, wie z.B. Elementarereignisse, Naturkatastrophen, oder Elementarereignisse auf den Schlachtfeldern, die eine Störung bringen. Aber schließlich renkt sich alles wieder ein. Wir empfinden alle, wie sehr solch eine Weltanschauung den Menschen beeinflußt. Man sagt: 'Das Rad ist ein wenig in Unordnung greaten,' und da sind vielleicht Große in der Welt, die sagen: 'Wir könne diesem Rad in die Speichen fahren und alles wieder in Ordnung bringen.' Aber wir entdecken, daß ganze Zeiten gerädert werden durch diesen Versuch, samt den Großen, die den Versuch wagten!"

the mighty, however real, was ultimately vain. But how should the church-community respond to the world caught up in rebellion and destruction?

Separation or keeping the world at a critical distance was for Köster only one part of the answer. His resistance was characterized by submission, service, substitutionary suffering and maintaining a subversive presence. Köster's submission to worldly authority was shaped and constrained by his eschatological vision. It enabled him to judge the efforts and promises of worldly leaders against God's ultimate purposes. Existing in this world, the church-community's calling was to journey faithfully towards the end. Consequently, to followers of Jesus this meant not only "participating in seeing the glory of Christ [now] . . . but also taking part in the suffering of Christ in the world."[52] For Köster, the church's service to the world consisted of proclaiming and living this subversive message.

Finally . . .

Köster and Bonhoeffer faced boundary situations. They had to test, explore, and, it can be argued, even go beyond the boundaries and limits set by God's word and commandments. Like every human being they were defined by the boundaries within which they could act, choose and believe. The Lutheran Bonhoeffer and the Baptist Köster were shaped by their personalities, upbringing, education, Christian experiences, commitments, and roles. These limits defined their unique realm of influence. Each sought to follow Jesus within the scope of their own lives. Yet, each also explored the boundaries of their faith.

In spite of their differences they shared the desire to follow Christ. In their theological application, Bonhoeffer was the original and Köster the pragmatic thinker. Their unique characteristics and charisma influenced their style and their methodology of constructing their arguments. Inhabiting their historical contexts they sought to commit every part of their existence to Jesus Christ. Set within the rise and fall of the Third Reich they were forced to go to the limit and, in the case of Bonhoeffer, even go beyond it. Their walk and commitment were visionary and courageous but also plagued with doubts and fears. Their choices were different to the choices the church of Jesus Christ has to make today.

---

52. Köster, 13 August 1944, 46: "Diese Gegenwart ist ein sein in den Leiden des Christus in dieser Welt. Wer an Christus glaubt wie Paulus, wer zum Dienst für den Christus bestellt ist—und das ist nicht nur Paulus—dann hat dieser Mensch nicht nur Anteil am Schauen in die Herrlichkeit des Christus, dass er ihn anbeten kann in Geist und in der Wahrheit, sondern er hat Anteil an dem Leiden des Christus in dieser Welt."

Conclusion

Clearly, the task of "preparing the way"[53] continues to be the calling of every subsequent generation of Jesus' followers. Walking the way in the confusing fog of concrete historical challenges means to hear and retain the double message of: "You must persevere, and by God's grace, you will."[54] The inner strength of Bonhoeffer's and Köster's following was their confidence in the sufficiency of God's grace, their commitment to God's word and his church-community.

Bonhoeffer and Köster traced their steps with a mixture of conviction and uncertainty. In 1940 Köster described the challenge of following as walking in darkness needing light for the path. "It is the light of God's word which enables us to recognize the way. It does not illuminate the whole stretch of the journey, but acts like a flash of lightening, helping us to keep on track. We still have to do the walking for it is not possible to know every letter [step] in advance."[55]

This indicates that the actual application of following often felt like groping in the dark; however the focus of their faith was the one whom they sought to follow, Jesus Christ. Bonhoeffer's poem "Who am I?" balances the prolonged and painful experience of uncertainty in the last line with, "Whoever I am, thou knowest me; O God, I am thine!"[56]

Their theology and their understanding of the world was christocentric. Köster expressed this in radical, down-to-earth terms, "Either Christ is the center of our thinking or he means nothing to us."[57] Bonhoeffer expressed it metaphysically, "All concepts of reality that ignore Jesus Christ are abstractions."[58] They used different words and addressed different audiences; however, their shared passion was to make the one they followed, Jesus Christ, central to their existence.

Clearly, tensions exist between the ways in which Bonhoeffer and Köster chose to respond to the challenges imposed upon them by the Third Reich. In some ways their lives represent extreme boundaries of Christian discipleship. It is possible to judge Bonhoeffer's involvement in a murderous

---

53. Bonhoeffer, *Ethics*, 161.

54. McClendon, *Doctrine*, 142.

55. Köster, 21 April 1940: "Wenn wir Jesus-Nachfolger sein wollen, dann brauchen wir Licht für unseren Weg. Im Lichte des Wortes können wir unsere Wegstrecke sehen, um recht zu gehen. Es beleuchtet oft nicht den ganzen, weiten Weg, aber es gleitet wie ein Blitzstrahl über den Weg, dass wir die rechte Richtung einhalten; gehen müssen wir selbst, wir können nicht [zuvor] Buchstaben für Buchstaben einsehen!"

56. Bonhoeffer, *Ethics*, 459–60.

57. Köster, 20 August 1944, 52: "Entweder ist der Christus das Zentrum unseres Denkens, oder er bedeutet uns überhaupt nichts!"

58. Bonhoeffer, *Ethics*, 54.

plot as a tragic this-worldly distortion of Christian discipleship. Equally is it possible to dismiss Köster's eschatological emphasis as pious escapism. However, a closer engagement with their work has shown that such verdicts are gross oversimplifications. It is much more profitable to see them as representing the creative tension that maps out, for the present church-community, the scope of its own following. They are like opposite barriers, which have been erected at a dangerous point of the road. As barriers they give direction and orientation, yet ultimately their intention and purpose are to keep travelers safely on course and closest to Jesus Christ.

Appendix 1

A Fictional Encounter

WHY WAS THE OUTSPOKEN critic Arnold Köster never arrested by the Nazis? When older members of the Baptist church in Vienna are asked this question they respond by telling the tale that an arrest warrant was issued by the Berlin authorities. However, the postbag containing the warrant was destroyed en route from Berlin to Vienna when the train suffered a direct hit during an aerial bombardment. During the final chaotic months and weeks of the Third Reich the matter was forgotten and the arrest warrant never reissued.

This concluding section imagines that Arnold Köster was arrested and subsequently transported to Berlin. It imagines that he was then incarcerated at Tegel prison where he shared, for a brief time, a cell with Dietrich Bonhoeffer. Their conversation would have been cautious and polite. It would have taken some time before each could be sure that the other was genuine. Once this was established they would have been able to discuss their shared concerns and hopes. Faced with uncertainty and possible execution their conversation would have been frank and to the point. Neither would have sought to score points against the other's church tradition. They would have found themselves imprisoned as followers of Christ, each at the mercy of a desperate and hostile regime. As ministers of the church their interest in the wellbeing and future of Christ's church would have been a shared concern and topic.

The following dialogue between the two is fictional but is also rooted and guided by this thesis' research and the comparison between the Lutheran and Baptist follower of Christ.

Bonhoeffer: "May I ask what occasioned your arrest?"

Köster: *"Well, some would say I was asking for it."*

A Fictional Encounter

Bonhoeffer: "Asking for it? What do you mean?"

Köster: "I have tested and explored the limits of protest for many years. I have consistently warned my members, and anyone else who cared to listen, against a blind enthusiasm for this regime. I labored hard to teach and preach a biblical world which de-masks the present day ideology as man-made hubris and antichristian. Forgive my bluntness, but if I have to die I prefer to die with a good conscience rather than deluded and accommodating. More importantly, I believe it is a Christian's duty to follow Christ and him alone for he is our ultimate leader (Führer)."

Bonhoeffer: "I am surprised. I was under the impression that the leaders of the Baptist churches had embarked on a policy designed to pacify the government, in order to secure their survival and to be granted permission to conduct tent missions and evangelism. Their chosen focus seemed to be rescuing souls from eternal damnation. I always felt that winning souls for eternity without rooting salvation into the complex realities of everyday life was a way to create a disjointed Christian existence. Faith is reduced to a pious but private section of life rather than claiming the whole of a believer's life."

Köster: "Your criticism saddens me. Yes, it is true many Baptists have adopted ways and methods which have brought little honor to the gospel of our Lord Jesus Christ, but there are always exceptions. I myself have consistently sought to expose state propaganda through the witness of Scripture. My aim was to direct the eyes of the faithful towards Christ rather than any pretentious messianic claims and promises. Promises which, I recollect, many Lutheran pastors also supported, at least in the initial euphoria."

Bonhoeffer: "True enough. So what was it that made you resist? What made you act differently?"

Köster: "My resistance is a long and a weary one. Right now, I am frightened and worried about my wife, children, friends and my congregation. Viewed from a purely rational point of view this world has become a dark and godforsaken place. I fear that God's judgment is upon our nation and people. Nevertheless, I do believe that this present darkness will pass. We might rage against God with tanks and armies but in the end human striving will cease and will have to submit to the sovereign one, the Lord of lords."

Bonhoeffer: "I also believe that Germany's guilt deserves God's judgment. Yet, being a German and being a disciple of Christ makes this cup of God's wrath doubly bitter. I resist, reject and detest much that is done by Germans and in the name of the German people and nation. But I am at the same time implicated by virtue of my origin and citizenship. As a

A Fictional Encounter

Christian I can take refuge in Christ, yet simple acts of obedience and Christian liberty are constrained and often interpreted as acts of treason against the German people."

Köster: "Paul's word of having to 'submit to governing authorities' has become a pressing challenge for our generation. However, our submission does not absolve government from its responsibility. God will punish perpetrators of injustice even though you and I might not live long enough to see it happening. I also believe that God will bring down any government that persistently acts maliciously rather than committing itself to the tasks of restraining evil and establishing justice. God will act, he will not suffer fools for long. Our calling and task as disciples of Jesus is to remain faithful and to have the courage to suffer willingly and vicariously in the face of evil."

Bonhoeffer: "Vicarious representation has occupied my own thinking a great deal. I find it particularly challenging to know how *remaining faithful* has to be applied at this time. In Scripture Jesus is portrayed as one who 'was led like a lamb to the slaughter'. This is a powerful image of passive endurance, but his death is also referred to as 'the victory that has overcome the world' (1 John 5:4). Victory implies resolve and determination and the defeat of the world. Suppose a madman careers his car into a crowd of innocent people what would remaining faithful demand? Would it be sufficient to raise the alarm and to shout warnings? Would it be required of us to bind up the wounded? Or does vicarious action oblige us to grab the steering wheel even if it means knocking out the mad driver? Clearly, the church requires discernment for it must respond appropriately. I had hoped that the combined protest of the various Christian churches would have modified, tempered, and possibly even prevented some of the madness that is upon us now. The dark clouds of war have rendered all public protest impossible. Yet, could it be that where the church has failed to speak and act collectively, individuals might still have to take it upon themselves to risk active vicarious resistance?"

Köster: "It depends what you mean with active vicarious resistance. Christians must resist the devil and I have come to the desperate conclusion that our national leaders have created a system driven by madness and the demonic. However, apart from being unable to justify any form of violent resistance on the basis of the Sermon on the Mount, I cannot see how I or any of my church members would have had a concrete opportunity to engage in political resistance. As a servant of God and his Word I considered it my duty to preach prophetically and to expose the twisted ideologies of the world as man-made hubris and lies. We, as a church community in Vienna have—using your example—done much shouting. We have also sought to aid the wounded and persecuted but grabbing the wheel has never even been possible. This regime will face God's ultimate judgment and as things stand it is more likely to be brought about by a crushing defeat rather than a revolution. I am convinced that God will act and bring about change. The church has been entrusted with the gospel and must proclaim it to the world. It cannot become an instrument for violence but must seek to change the world by the power of God's word, which is its only legitimate weapon."

Bonhoeffer: "The weapon of the church and the weapons of this world are indeed very different. Yet, however we differentiate between the two, many of your church members and my former students are obliged right now by the world to wield its weapons against their Christian brothers and sisters of other nations. We speak of civic duty and we bow to the inevitable. Does this not show that every theological dichotomy that claims to clearly divide between world and church, good and evil does more harm than good?"

Köster: "I agree, simplistic solutions cannot sustain the church community. But, must we not also listen to the Scriptures which speak of light and darkness, life and death, salvation and condemnation, of the Christ and the Antichrist?"

Bonhoeffer: "My concern is not these distinctions, but the claim that it is possible to know the difference. It fosters the illusion that once one has chosen the good, one is safe. I believe that such a mindset inevitably leads towards the slippery slope of self-justification. Have not Lutherans and Baptists retreated into the supposed safe realm of the church while leaving the world to get on with its own affairs? As it turned out there are no safe places, after all here we are in prison. Yet, even prison is not outside God's reach and presence and neither is this dark and chaotic world. God has claimed this world in the incarnation of Jesus and he still loves it and desires to save it. To Christian's the only legitimate safe place is Jesus Christ. He is our savior, which means that neither our salvation nor our discipleship is based on knowing the difference between good and evil but in being known by him."

Köster: "Grace and grace alone is the only basis of my salvation. Therein, I take great comfort and I do not claim any merit. I know that God's grace preceded, carried and prepared my faith. Justification by faith alone is my constant support as I seek to follow Christ day after day. Christ is my savior and my Lord. But as followers we are equipped by his Spirit and his word. We are in sore need of both, yet, as we apply ourselves to God's word he does shed light into our darkness, illuminates, corrects and guides our thinking. We are enabled to gain a different perspective and worldview, we are given discernment and through this process we can dare to make distinctions. Moralistic claims and self-justification are a terrible distortion and abuse, yet, as we look to Christ we are also guided in our walk. I am very reluctant to tell other Christians what they should or should not do. My goal has always been to enlarge Jesus Christ in the minds and hearts of my brothers and sisters and to trust that through the agency of the Spirit he will transform minds and hearts himself."

Bonhoeffer: "It seems that we are not very far apart from each other. May I ask you how God's word and Spirit have shaped your own worldview? I ask this, please forgive, as a Lutheran who, as you know often bundle Baptists into the category of enthusiasts (*Schwärmer*). Which in the present context I take to refer to people who, in an effort to become perfect, withdraw from active engagement with the world and its demands as much as possible. They endure the present but their hope is focused on an eschatological future where God, having executed judgment will establish his eternal reign."

Köster: "Your description does fit some church communities I have encountered. Of course I might respond with a similar caricature of cultured Protestantism (Kulturprotestantismus): people for whom being religious has become a way of living a respectable life rather than a relational commitment to Jesus Christ. But let us not waste time arguing over stereotypes. In answer to your question I would say that my worldview was and is shaped by Christ, by his incarnation, life, death, resurrection and ascension. Above all, I am greatly encouraged by Christ's cosmic claim and lordship, outlined dramatically by Paul's letter to the Colossians. Christ's claim clearly exposes the numerous claims of all other man-made ideology and –isms as empty and false. One of the tragic consequences of sin is humanity's abiding futile but determined search for salvation apart from and outside God. The Antichrist with his many new and varied disguises always has and always will promise salvation (Heil). Yet, salvation is found in no-one else but Jesus Christ. I do not need to preach to you; after all, we do read the same Bible. However, one thing I openly confess, and in this we might differ, my worldview is profoundly shaped by eschatology. Look around, we find ourselves in the midst of a terrible storm and approaching chaos. I cannot but place all my hope in the God who reigns and is coming soon. God's justice has not yet been revealed, for we and this time is still distorted by human sin, disobedience and Satan's schemes. But the Lord of lords is on his way, the church must stand firm and offer, like a lighthouse, direction and salvation to all and everyone."

Bonhoeffer: "I appreciate your frankness and would also say that my faith and worldview is profoundly shaped by eschatology. Our difference might be that I argue that Christ's ultimate coming does more than just give us hope for the future and the ability to endure the present. Clearly, Cultured Protestantism with its focus on the present has lost sight of the end. However, some Christian churches, like the Baptists are so focused on the approaching end-times that they seem to have given up on the present. I believe that the ultimate, the establishment of God's final justice and reign, must shape and transform the present, our penultimate existence. There is a difference between knowing that the Lord is on his way and to actively prepare the way for his coming. Sitting at the train station we can either passively wait for the arrival of the next expected train but after realizing the inadequacy or lack of tracks we might have to take action and start working on the tracks."

Köster: "You make it sound as though the return of the Lord is dependent on human efforts and ingenuity. Are we not surrounded by ideologies which argue that collective man-made efforts can build a better future? I suspect your version might be in danger of merely adding a Christian garb to present day ideologies. Waiting and keeping our lights burning, just as the virgins did in Matthew 25 seems to me what is required of the church. The bridegroom will come at the appointed hour, we, his church, must be ready."

Bonhoeffer: "Yet, what does being ready mean? I believe readiness is best expressed in the activity of preparing the way. As our attitudes, choices, values and decisions are informed and shaped by the ultimate we will find that our penultimate existence is transformed. This transformation is based on man-made effort but as the coming one intrudes our penultimate existence we will perceive the world differently. Our being in Christ will reshape and introduce God's grace, justice and love into the reality of this world. I believe that eschatology is therefore intimately tied to ethics and to how we live and act as followers of Jesus."

Köster: "I am intrigued but also skeptical. It might be true that in some cases eschatology fosters an attitude of disengagement and passivity, but it can equally sharpen the proclamation of God's word and evangelism. On a pastoral and practical level, resting in the sure knowledge of God's approaching future is both liberating and a healthy antidote against legalistic distortions of the gospel. We are not the sole makers of our own destiny. Ultimately we are in God's hand and utterly depend on his grace and promise. I do not advocate a resigned and passive faith but to me the active nature of faith is much more rooted in baptism than in eschatology. Lutherans are keen to emphasize that baptism, especially infant baptism, is a powerful expression of received grace. Baptists would add that it is also the celebration and calling of the believer into service and discipleship. Baptism marks the beginning of an active journey that finds embodiment and expression within the community of believers and in the world into which all the baptized are being sent by the Holy Spirit. As the community of disciples gathers around the word and the Lord's Supper it is continually equipped and directed towards mission and service."

A Fictional Encounter

Bonhoeffer: "I am a Lutheran and have been deeply concerned about a dangerous cheapening of grace, often represented by the careless practice of infant baptism. Nevertheless, I remain committed to the positive possibilities of this open invitation of grace infant baptism represents; as long as genuine faith and commitment is expressed on behalf of the infant by parents or godparents. Thus far it is an integral part of our German heritage which, I admit is increasingly a relic of the past. The historic heritage of our Christendom structures is disintegrating. We are, I fear, approaching a religionless age, a society no longer shaped by Christian concepts and values. What kind of adaptations will the church of Christ have to make in order to remain faithful to its calling and commission?"

Köster: "Christendom's impact on our culture has been very profound and is certainly much deeper than the more recent rationalism or the prevalent nihilism of our days. Both the Catholic and Protestant church have been guardians of the Christendom heritage for many centuries. In contrast the old Anabaptists and the present day Free-Churches are somewhat removed from it. It requires determination and in some cases a fair amount of suffering for a discipleship community to exist outside the traditional church patterns. This counter cultural characteristic has forced and encouraged believers of my tradition towards a practical discipleship focused expression of faith. Predictions are notoriously difficult but my gut feeling is that with the decline of traditional Christianity, the church of God will survive in intentional discipleship communities."

Bonhoeffer: "You may well be right. However, one of the dangers of such communities will be that in their conscious effort to separate themselves from the world, their outlook will become provincial and exclusive. How can these church communities maintain God's mission focus? Will they still seek and discover Christ in the other? Even when this other is not part of the intimate and well defined circle of the church community? How will they remember that God so loved the world that he sent his one and only son? How will they remember that the prime purpose of the Church is to bring and offer salvation to the world?"

Köster: "Separatism for its own sake is clearly contrary to the life and ethos of the New Testament churches. God's church is always a sent community. Having said this, I would also argue that when a Christian community is placed in a sustained hostile context it might have to adopt a passive and secret underground mode of existence. Jesus himself taught us to be 'as shrewd as snakes and as innocent as doves'. (Matthew 10:16) I see a similar tension in the book of Daniel. During the early chapters the protagonists engage with and openly confront the political elite. However, in the latter half of the book their role becomes much more subdued and passive. They were given insights and were sustained by visions, which in turn enabled them to endure turbulent times. The church must learn to differentiate and judge circumstances wisely. God protected Daniel's friends when they were thrown into the fiery furnace. Yet, this was and is not always the case; many have been martyred for their faith ever since. It might be our path, I don't know. Others might preserve the faith and the faithful as they disengage themselves from wickedness and the demands of a godless state or system. This is in itself a form of resistance through which a holding environment is created where prayer, reorientation on God's word and critical reflection are made possible. In due course the church will then be equipped to proclaim the gospel in a timely and appropriate manner."

Bonhoeffer: "What about the training and financial support of clergy, administration of funds and properties? What about liturgy and education? Listen! I can hear the guards approaching . . ."

Appendix 2

Interviews

Introduction

In August 2009 I conducted three separate interviews. In the first interview Herr Richard Matschinger (Matschinger R.) and Frau Erika Altmann (EM), members of the Baptist Church Vienna-Mollardgasse 35, responded to the questions. On the following day two more interviews took place, one with Herr Fuchs in Ternitz and the other with Herr Karl Federmann in Schrems. All three interviews were structured around 18 core questions or topics. Occasionally some extra questions were interjected either by me (Paul Spanring) or Franz Graf-Stuhlhofer.

The following topical summary of these interviews is my translation of the German. A CD containing the recordings has been attached to my thesis, Spanring Paul, "Following Jesus: Two distinct Christian voices in the midst of Germany's Third Reich turmoil." PhD diss., Bristol University 2009.

Background Information

Interview with Richard Matschinger and Erika Altmann in the courtyard of the Baptist Church Vienna-Mollardgasse 35. The interview took place after the Sunday service on 2 August 2009.

Interviews

Erika Altman (born: 1930)

Erika Altmann's parents worked in Romania before and during WWI. Her father was an electrical engineer. He worked in Moldavia before the First World War and then moved to Romania to work at a car manufacturing plant. During the WWI he was drafted into the army and became a POW in Italy. After WWI the family attended a German-speaking Baptist church in Bucharest.

During the war years of WWII the family decided to move back to Germany. Her father found work at Daimler Benz but later moved to Vienna and attended the Baptist Church Vienna-Mollardgasse 35. Erika Altmann was at that time a young teenager.

Richard Matschinger (born: 1925)

Son-in-law of Arnold Köster. His parents (mother came from an old German Protestant family, father was Catholic but converted to Protestantism) met before WWI in Hungary but moved to Vienna after the war. Richard Matschinger was born in 1925 in Vienna, Nussdorf. His father joined the police force but died in 1935.

Richard Matschinger was 14 years old when WWII began. When he was 19 years old he was drafted into the army and joined the so-called Arbeitsdienst. He was stationed in France, mostly in the south of France, and was part of an Anti-Aircraft-Battery Unit.

During his childhood and teenager years he was encouraged by his mother to attend the children's and youth services of the Lutheran church. During the war years his mother (and sister) joined the Baptist congregation and were baptized in the Mollardgasse.

Matschinger R., "As a young soldier I received the typescript sermons of Köster which were my first contact to the Baptist church ... During the war I attended only one service but after the war I joined my mother and sister and became a regular member. I was baptized in 1947 together with 28 other candidates. Many people desired baptism at that time. Possibly because of the uncertainty of that time, many people had either just returned from the POW camps or were refugees. I then got to know Köster's family and eventually married one of his daughters ..."

Herbert Fuchs (born: 1928)

Interview with Herbert Fuchs, took place on the 03.08.2009 in his home in Ternitz. He was also a former son-in-law of Arnold Köster. Sadly, his wife

Ursula died early. When Köster died in 1960, Herbert Fuchs inherited a substantial part of Köster's library. The collection consisted of theological journals, books and commentaries. He has not only kept these books but also read them extensively himself. Herbert Fuchs was seemingly the only one from the Köster family who, at that point in time, expressed interest in theological literature.

At the beginning of the interview Mr Fuchs showed us the first volume of Barth's Dogmatic which Köster had marked extensively. He also noted that Köster was an avid reader of Jakob Kroeker's books. In contrast to Karl Barth, Kroeker's style is pietistic and he produced many devotional expositions of scripture. To Herbert Fuchs it is puzzling that Köster seemed to have read Kroeker much more after the war years, during the latter part of his life and ministry.

Fuchs had little personal contact with Köster during the years of WWII. He was the son of an evangelistic travelling preacher (*Reisemissionar*) who was based in Ternitz. (Ternitz is south of Vienna, the distance between Ternitz and Vienna-Mollardgasse 35 is 70 km) Fuchs attended the small Baptist church in Ternitz. Their family home was often frequented by visiting preachers. As a young man he observed that these other Baptist preachers and brothers never seemed to mention Köster.

Fuchs recalls: "My contact with Köster was thus not via the church. It came about when I had a severe personal crisis [around 1945–1946]. It was my older sister who advised me to go and attend the services in the Mollardgasse. I then—maybe 3 to 4 times in a year—travelled up to Vienna and attended these services. Whenever I went I was always touched and encouraged—even though Köster didn't try to impress me as a listener."

"My crisis was the whole issue of guilt and a sense of utter disillusionment with what had happened. Then all of a sudden this clear word. I was struggling with the question: How was it possible that the Austrian people lost their humanity and willingly joined the Hitler movement? Of course there were historical factors . . . but I was especially concerned that for the other members of the Baptist church in Ternitz this question of guilt was never an issue. They just carried on, as though nothing had happened. They clung to their pietistic interpretations of the Bible . . . I didn't discern that anyone was at all concerned. As a young person I became disillusioned. But as I heard Köster preach I discovered that through a faithful reading of scripture and through insight in God's revelation, the deception had been discerned."

"Somehow the brothers in Ternitz did not manage to address let alone solve the guilt question. Nor were they able to bring a critical and prophetic message warning the members of the church-fellowship against the Nazi enthusiasm during the pre-war years."

Interviews

Karl Federmann (born: 1921)

Interview with Federmann took place on the 3rd August 2009 in his home in Schrems. (Schrems is north-west of Vienna, the distance between Vienna and Schrems is 158 km)

Federmann K., "I was 17 years old when Hitler came and 7 years older when he was gone again. National Socialism's seduction was incredibly powerful."

Federmann is the son of a judge who had a keen interest in philosophy. His mother had a basic traditional understanding of the Christian faith. Their son was educated in a Gymnasium (Grammar School). At the outbreak of WWII, Federmann was old enough to be drafted into the Wehrmacht. During the last year of the war he was wounded and lost a leg. He became a Christian through Köster's ministry and an active member of the Baptist Church Vienna-Mollardgasse 35 during the post-war years. He was a deacon during the lifetime of Köster and also became the *Gemeindevorsteher* of the church. Together with Gertrud Hoffmann Federmann published a collection of Köster's sermons and lectures in 1965 (Lampenlicht am dunklen Ort). Federmann left the Baptist Church Vienna-Mollardgasse 35 in 1977.

INTERVIEW QUESTIONS AND RESPONSES

What were the prominent themes of Köster's preaching for you?

Matschinger R., "For me it was his teaching on justification by faith. That was a fundamental theme for Köster . . . and he continually explored it in great depth . . ."

Altmann E., "Yes, I also grew up with this focus and was baptized when I was 16 years old . . . for me it began by attending Sunday school (first in Bucharest and then here in Vienna) but later I joined the main services. Then, all of a sudden, I was really gripped by the sermons and found them very interesting."

Was his focus on justification by faith influenced by Luther?

Matschinger R., "It was based on Paul rather than Luther . . ."

Altmann E., "Luther merely confirmed what the apostle Paul taught . . ."

Matschinger R., "One can also note this emphasis on how often Köster preached on and through certain sections of the New Testament i.e. Romans, Acts and John . . . Another feature was that Köster didn't like huge evangelistic gatherings. He preferred to meet people in their homes. A feature of his ministry was the home bible study groups (*Hausgemeinden*). These gatherings often occurred on two or three evenings during a normal week. That was on top of the gatherings that were conducted at the Mollardgasse, which happened either on a Wednesday or Thursday in the so called small hall. The attendance of these mid-week meetings often was between 70 to 100 people. The main hall was used for the Sunday services with around 400 worshippers attending during the war years . . ."

Fuchs H., "He preached Jesus to the church . . . and he strove to bring the members of the congregation into a deeper understanding of God's glory through the revelation of Jesus Christ. That was his explicit focus. This Christological focus was informed by the teaching of the apostle Paul."

"His style was not rhetorical in the sense that he sought to impress the congregation. Rather, when he preached, it was as though he, as a person, took a back-seat in order to make room for God's word. He did not preach himself—he sought to bring God's authoritative word. Unlike some other preachers his style was not aimed at whipping up emotions—he was utterly unconcerned - he simply was alone with his Lord (during the act of preaching) and delivered God's word expecting that God's Spirit would confirm what he preached in the hearts of the listeners."

Was his preaching ministry "different" and if so—what made it different?

Matschinger R., "I couldn't really compare . . . every preacher has his own unique style . . . for me Köster always had the ability to speak topically (*zur Sache*). That is why he had his difficulties with the Gestapo during the war. He was frequently interrogated by them . . ."

Altmann E., "I remember that on one occasion after a Sunday afternoon service he mentioned to us that he had to go to the Gestapo on Wednesday . . . and he told the congregation, 'Brothers and sisters I am scared . . . ' we had never heard him admit that before. But there was also a man attending the service from the Ukraine . . . he spoke very little German . . . but this man wrote on a torn bus ticket (*auf einem halben Fahrschein*) the text 'when they bring you before judges fear not, the Spirit will speak for you.' Leaving the service he gave the note to Köster. A few weeks later he told my parents that he was really afraid, but when he received that note fear left him. When he was then interrogated he was shouted at but managed to stay calm. The session took over two hours but as he left the official even bowed before Köster. And he then told my parents this was not because of his own personal authority but it was because of God's Word and power."

Interviews

Fuchs H., "He was different to others because his focus was the exegetical exposition of God's word. That is how I experienced him. He opened up God's word in a living and relevant way."

Federmann K., "His persistent and deliberate focus. He understood himself to be a servant of the word of God. His Lord instructed him and gave direction. Thus, as servants we are influenced from "outside" (*außengesteuert*) by him. It is not what I do but what the Lord does in me or tells me to do."

If you had to use a metaphor in order to describe what the Mollardgasse was for you which image would you use? Would you say that image has changed . . . i.e., in the pre-war, war and post-war period?

Matschinger R., "I felt 'at home.' We were an interesting group of people and as young people we did many things together. The church-fellowship became a home."

Altmann E., "For me too, it was a home and I always knew where I belonged. It became a place where I was rooted and where one could always come back to in order to rediscover one's rootedness in the faith. And all those who opposed it or made fun of it, became unimportant. My experiences and friendships were rooted within the fellowship."

Fuchs H., "Set within the context of my own personal crisis (and questions) Köster and the Mollardgasse became a place that gave me clarity—clarity in my thinking and in my faith. I did not support the political opposition—after all their concern was a mere struggle for power. I wanted to know whether anyone from within the faith had heard the Good Shepherd's voice. I wanted to know where his sheep are. Then I discovered that there was one who had heard the Lord's voice and had proclaimed it—to me this became a liberating experience . . . All of a sudden I discovered that there was a light in the darkness."

What was the main task of the church during the crisis period of the 1930s until 1945 and what was the main task of the church during the post-war rebuilding period?

Matschinger R., "I believe he spoke less of the task of the church and more of the task of each and every believer. After all, every believer is joined as a member to the head of the church, Jesus Christ. He spoke very positively of the church and emphasized that each individual member was equipped with gifts and was to exercise these in obedience to the head of the church. To be a member was to become part of one body."

Gifts are also a responsibility, represent a calling . . . were the members of the fellowship encouraged to exercise their gifts within or outside the church? How were they expressed in everyday life?

Matschinger R., "His focus was to help us recognize our gifts but he never tried to define in detail how these were to be exercised nor did he put pressure on the congregation. For instance, I was a trained accountant and in due course I became the treasurer of the church. I just naturally offered my services and assumed these responsibilities . . ."

Fuchs H., "His concern was to keep the church of Jesus Christ free and pure from demonical influences. Köster had no direct missionary disposition. I must explain—he was not against mission, but his method of mission was to simply bear witness to Jesus. He did this not forgetting the Zeitgeist, indeed he critically engaged with it, but his primary focus was always confessing Christ in the everyday events of life."

Federmann K., "The task of the church is to listen, to keep and to resist—but to resist without the use of force. I can tell you a concrete instance. Some of the church services were attended by spies or informers. They were taking notes and reported back to the Nazi authorities. After one service, one of these informers approached Köster and said: 'Politically, we cannot touch you yet, with regard to your worldview you are our greatest enemy.' Therein was a difference between Köster and Bonhoeffer, Bonhoeffer acted politically. Köster had to go many times to the Gestapo—he didn't tell me the details of these interrogations—but he told us that one of his interrogators approached him after the war requesting that he would issue a Persil-certificate[1] for him. On that occasion he said to Köster, 'Every time you came into my office an inner voice told me to watch out and to be careful.'"

Was the so called church struggle of the Confessing Church (i.e. Barmen) ever a topic within the church-community?

Matschinger R., "I believe there was little of that in Austria. Köster did join the Evangelical *Allianz* soon after his arrival here in Vienna. Through these contacts he knew the Lutheran bishop and superintendent, also the Methodists."

Altmann E., "I also developed many good friendships with other Christian churches. . . ."

Fuchs H., "He has—at least in his preaching—never assumed the role of a direct opponent. To him the Nazi movement was God's way of executing

---

1. Letters testifying to the occupying forces that the person in question was not involved with the Nazis.

Interviews

judgment over the people. He understood his role and responsibility to be that of protecting the church from the Nazi spirit (ideology). His eschatological focus provided him with an alternative viewpoint."

Federmann K., "The confessing church did not exist in Austria. There were only very few who practiced resistance in that form. I knew one person quite well. He was a Lutheran pastor (originally from Baden-Württemberg) His name was Jakob Ernst Koch and he was a minister in the Ramsau. But his church members were very pro-Nazi and they subsequently removed him. They didn't want his preaching, so he took up a post at another church. He was also a regular visitor of the Evangelical *Allianz* meetings."

"Most of the Austrian Lutheran churches were pro-Hitler, some more some less. One outright Nazi supporter was the Lutheran theologian Professor Enz. However, he had a real conversion experience after the war. He talked extensively with Köster, expressing his own sense of despair about the delusion that had taken hold of him."

What relations and links existed to the American support churches? What effects did these outside contacts produce?

Matschinger R., "These were German speaking Baptist churches in North America... I believe most of the contacts were established through Füllbrand, who was the mission inspector for the *Donaulandmission* (missionary work of the eastern regions, Romania etc.). Füllbrand had originally come from Russia and was supported by these American churches. Since he lived in Vienna, the church here (Mollardgasse) was also noted and supported by these American Baptists. They were also instrumental in providing funds which made it possible to build the church building here in the Mollardgasse in 1921 and (at a later date) in Ternitz. At that time, the church-fellowship was devoid of legal representation. Thus, in order to sign contracts a trust was established (*Hilfsverein der Baptisten*). That trust still exists today."

"During the war years the church-fellowship Mollardgasse received no American support but it resumed again after the war."

Did these international contacts make people perceive things differently to the Nazi propaganda?

Matschinger R., "There were some loose contacts, some infrequent visits... But I personally (again I must remind you that I wasn't here during the war) don't remember that it was much of an influence.

How did Köster's focus on the imminent return of Christ and his consistent criticism of the Nazi ideology affect the day-to-day life of the church members? Did

Interviews

he offer any concrete perspectives and possibilities to the congregation in order to help them live in accordance with a biblical worldview?

Matschinger R., "Yes, his sermons were very much characterized by the end-time theme . . . Jesus Christ yesterday, today and forever . . ."

Such preaching can make one either passive, i.e. waiting till it happens—or active, i.e. getting ready for it. How were you affected by this recurring end-time theme?

Matschinger R., "Responses can be quite different . . . I believe that one can be quite future focused but at the same time one can also be mindful of the present, of the need to live and act now. In a way the end-time focus forced the issue of faith alone upon the minds of the listening congregation."

Fuchs H., "As a practical consequence it was a great help for me. Yet, I also felt challenged by his message. It was as though he would grab you and point you, and the whole church, towards the ultimate goal. To Köster the church of Jesus Christ had an eschatological existence. But—and this was an issue I myself began to work on—I cannot take someone who lives within time to the eschatological crisis point and leave them there. How is it applied? I can live my faith expectantly, but then the question is, how can this waiting, eschatological church live and exist alongside the church that lives in the now time. At that point, I fear, I didn't fully understand Köster. It felt like being lead to the ultimate point in time, yet, somehow I found that I wasn't quite able to translate how I can take the next practical steps within the present context and the challenges that I had to face in the now."

"It seems that he hoped and trusted that the church of Jesus Christ would live through the time only and continually in the act of the concretization of God's word (*Ereignis werden des Wort Gottes*). The church lives in the end-times. She lives and embodies God's word which through the Spirit becomes her life-giving and life-sustaining experience."

Federmann K., "When Köster returned from WWI he was sent to the Baptist seminary by his church. During his final year he had to submit a dissertation. It was entitled *the Antichrist*. This became the main thrust of his ministry. At that time there were many political movements and parties in Germany. Communists and socialists on the one hand, monarchists and conservatives on the other. But also nationalistic parties which eventually resulted in the rise of National Socialism. He felt called into a kind of resistance—so he had told me—which consisted of opposing antichristian human solutions. His only weapon in this struggle was the word of God. The antichrist is a person who assumes the role of the messiah. The messiah is the one who is ordained by God to rule and govern the world."

Interviews

"Köster was convinced that the only effective opposition against National Socialism was a focus on the parusia, the expected imminent return of Christ. He constantly talked about the imminent return of Christ - indeed it remained an abiding characteristic of his ministry. The apostles expected his return . . . why, so Köster argued, should we not even more expect the arrival of the returning Lord? Yet, at the same time, as we are told in the parable of the returning Lord, no one can know the exact time of the Lord's return."

"The practical consequence was the ministry of the word (*die Predigt*). The biblical and prophetical proclamation of God's word was his weapon against National Socialism. That was his focus and it kept the church fellowship together throughout these turbulent times. In fact, he was also heard by others. Especially through the joint meetings of the Evangelical *Allianz* his message was heard and appreciated by many other Christians."

"His ministry encouraged the members of the congregation to live expectantly, to wait for the Lord's return. Köster formulated it thus: Faith and doing (*Glaube und Tun*)—but doing consists already in the act of preserving (*festhalten*) what was heard. We, the Christian church, do not start movements that change the world. But when we have listened to God's word through the Holy Spirit we become receptive . . . He constantly reminded the church to listen. He often said, 'I also have simply received God's word—it is not my word—but God's Spirit has entrusted me with this message. We simply have to take it in and keep it.' Of course the heard word demands obedience. For that reasons we find many concrete instructions in the New Testament."

In regard to the Jewish issue what practical acts and choices were possible and pursued at a personal level and as a church community?

Matschinger R., "There were a number of Jewish brothers and sisters who attended our services, something that was forbidden. Upon entering the church building they discreetly had to cover the Star of David. Yet Köster often preached that the people of Israel have their own unique place in God's salvation plan (*Heilsgeschichte*). Jews were able to come, were received, some even were hidden by families who were members of the church . . ."

Altmann E., "Yes, some were hidden over many years and occasionally we heard that in some instances they had been found and were moved to concentration camps. Köster always, at the end of a service, greeted everyone individually. However, since it was forbidden to have any contacts with Jews, the arrangement was that they said their good-bye separately in the vestry. There they were safe and out of sight from harmful informers. In that way they were also able to bring their own worries and concerns to Köster."

Matschinger R., "Köster was able to write many letters of recommendation for Jews who managed to emigrate either to Switzerland or America before the outbreak of the war."

Fuchs H., "For Köster, God's sovereignty remained a constant. But within that over-arching structure he and the church were called to act responsibly and in freedom. He helped many Jews—I know this specifically from Miss Hoffmann. One of the things Köster said was: 'In my church there is no racism. We are brothers and sisters of one Lord and there is no Jew or Gentile.' He fiercely defended this viewpoint. I only vaguely know that many Jews [Jewish Christians?] approached him and that Köster somehow provided assistance and help."

Federmann K., "Regarding the Jews, Köster preached clearly but not politically. He never said, 'What are the Nazis doing? Why are they mistreating the Jews?' But he did preach that the people of Israel are the chosen people of God. Whoever touches these people touches God's apple of the eye (Zech 2:8). He also baptized Jews who had become Christians. He said that no one can forbid him to baptize a Jew who had a genuine conversion. That was in some sense risky—but it was also apolitical."

Were there concrete acts of help?

Federmann K., "I don't know of any concrete acts of assistance. But there were some 600 people in the church fellowship and there must have been people who needed help. The policy of the church-fellowship was to give help in a discreet manner . . . whenever people needed help whether it was food or money the church (especially during the post-war years) provided it discreetly.

How did the church practically respond to the issue of growing Nazi and SS sympathies? Responding to enthusiastic Nazis who considered themselves Christians . . . Responding to Nazis after the war . . . Dealing with people when some of the congregation wore the party symbol whilst others had to wear the Star of David . . .

Matschinger R., "Yes, there were some who actually wore the party emblem, but this was a difficult issue—since I was not personally here during that time I can only relate what others have told me. But sometimes it was very tense. Some were forced to wear the Star of David while others wore the party emblem. It has to be remembered that some people were somewhat forced to join the party, due to the nature of their profession or employment."

Interviews

Yet, it was possible for these people to attend the services and to listen to a preacher who spoke in a rather direct way against the whole system?

Altmann E., "Some people found it quite annoying that Köster persistently criticized the Nazi ideology. I know of one lady, she also came from Bucharest and married an Austrian, she often expressed irritation to my parents as they walked home after the services."

Regarding after the war . . .

Matschinger R., "Politics as a topic was not mentioned in church. For Köster it was important that people participated in the life of the church and in the home groups. Many early Nazi supporters later realized how wrong they were. Again, one has to remember, that there was also a lot of very clever deceit. For instance, we didn't know for a long time about the true nature of the concentration camps nor were we aware that people with special needs were simply removed."

Fuchs H., "Yes, there were some. Köster did not yield to these people and he wasn't afraid to speak out. He knew very well who these Nazi supporters were. Some tried to harm him—but I cannot say more to that. But he did tell me that he demanded from these brothers, once the Nazi regime had collapsed, that they would publically express their repentance before the church. He tried to make clear that this is the church of Jesus Christ, that forgiveness is possible and that these people can remain in the church. But they should openly declare that they had been wrong and that their own nationalistic sentiments had led them astray. However, he told me in a personal conversation, he was saddened and depressed about the unwillingness of many to conform to his demands. They considered such a public act to be beneath their dignity. To him the minimal requirement was a pastoral conversation—a kind of private confession—but ultimately he wanted to set repentance in the context of the church community. Some did conform but not everyone. However, I myself was never part of a service where such an act of public repentance was performed."

Fuchs H., "Personally, I would have liked that the leaders of the Baptist churches in Austria (others I didn't know) be much more honest and contrite. But people seemed to prefer to simply move on and to live a pious lie. To me this dilemma represented a total chasm (despair), a crisis of faith . . ."

At least this seems to indicate that for Köster justification by faith alone was not a convenient blanket that guaranteed forgiveness. He felt that real repentance is part of it and is costly . . .

Fuchs H., "Yes, to him the church belonged to the Lord and he considered it as his responsibility to lead the church (The Lord's bride) towards the Lord, protecting it and keeping it pure. Thus, for him it was abhorrent to discern any dirt and sin within the church. Yet, at the same time he also had to deal with people who were morally reprehensible. These people were able to approach him and confess their sins."

"I remember when I was courting his daughter, she introduced me to her father and I told him the truth (regarding my hopeless prospects). He listened, took me to one side and asked me, 'Do you love the Lord Jesus?' That was his overriding concern - this simple pietistic question. I responded, 'Yes, but I'm just beginning.' He said, 'Good. But I have one more question, do you love Ursula?' 'But, of course!' I replied. He then gave his assent. He did not concern himself with finances and prospects."

"I got married to Ursula in 1958—Köster died in 1960 and his wife (widow) first lived in Vienna with her youngest daughter. However, eventually we took her into our home here in Ternitz. She stayed with us until she died."

Federmann K., "I believe that nobody could really be an enthusiastic supporter of the Nazis. There were no party members—for these people must have lived a double life. No, I believe that it was impossible. In the church such a person heard about the imminent return of the Lord and passages from the book Daniel, but from the party he heard that it was their own efforts that were to bring about the promised glorious kingdom (1000 years). I believe that it would have caused a massive internal conflict in these people."

How was it possible to apply what Köster preached in one's practical everyday living? Facing the issue of 'guilt'—during and after the war . . . When the government acted in an unchristian manner—how could one live and act? How was it possible to help each other?

Matschinger R., "In some ways these became two separate worlds"

Altmann E., "For instance, I had a friend in school and we realized very soon that one had to give appropriate answers. Answers that said one thing but often, and we understood that, meant the very opposite. Often insiders knew what one really meant (intonation, slight irony)."

Was it then important to remain inwardly distant?

Altmann E., "Even though we sometimes had to say lies, it didn't matter because we knew what was true."

Matschinger R., "Here I have to note, that it was never forbidden to talk about Christ. Apparently, it was planned but it never came to it. We were always allowed to preach and it was this freedom that Köster had claimed for himself and his ministry. Thus, during the interrogations session he could argue that he was merely preaching what is written in the Bible."

Altmann E., "Even Hitler often quoted the Bible . . ."

Yet, how was it possible to be—as a Christian - inwardly opposed (distanced) to the regime but at the same time utterly involved and woven into it as a citizen? How could one live with this tension and with that guilt?

Matschinger R., "These kind of considerations were too far-fetched . . . one didn't think about it. One was utterly disempowered against those who were in power and it would have been futile trying to oppose them. I believe that we didn't live a lie. For instance I was never questioned whether I am for or against Hitler. I was for Christ, and in some sense one was able to make these personal decisions. After all we were still able to go to church."

"Was this emphasis on justification by faith alone one way of coping with these really difficult moral dilemmas?"

Matschinger R., "Yes, absolutely, because the whole goal was a different one. Yes, one was faced with an overwhelming power, but power always comes to an end sooner or later. The real 1000 year Reich will come but was not yet."

Federmann K., "Yes, there were many young people in the Church who had been involved in the war as soldiers (*Wehrmacht*). No one was part of the SS—to my knowledge. But regarding the whole question of guilt, Köster said that there is no such thing as a collective guilt. One cannot say that everyone who had to live through that period, without radically opposing the system, was automatically guilty. Köster tried to remain apolitical. When there were elections and all sorts of voting going on he never sought to steer the congregation one way or another. He merely said 'be wise and without falsehood but keep your eyes open and use your spiritual mind.'"

Köster was in some ways an authoritarian leader of the church. What were his reasons and justification? How did that work out in regard to: State, Other Christian communities, Baptist Union, Internal criticism within the fellowship?

Matschinger R., "Yes, it is true he had an authoritarian leadership style and possibly for good reasons. The positive outcome was that he kept the Church community together. He knew everyone *[All three to four hundred?]* Yes, all of them. He had baptized most of the members and knew them well through the home-group network. With regard to state he was willing to submit to the authorities. After all, God may permit someone to be in authority even though that person is not liked by the church."

Altmann E., "Yes, he kept good relationships to other churches, for instance the Lutheran and the Methodist churches, but also with members of the *Altkatholischen Kirche* . . ."

Matschinger R., *[Regarding the German Baptist Union]* "He maintained good contacts to the seminary where he had trained and especially to Lukey. Paul Schmidt, the General Secretary of the German Baptist Union, was someone who had to cooperate somewhat with the state in order to secure the survival of the Baptist churches. I believe that he became after the war a scapegoat for others. In some ways, he had to organize and voice certain issues diplomatically in order to pacify the regime."

Fuchs H., "I only encountered Köster during annual meetings. I felt that in spite of his charisma and authority he remained a remarkably humble person. However, when he happened to disagree theologically with someone, he was always ready to argue his case. During his time there was no one who was in any sense intellectually his equal."

"Regarding the Baptist Union . . . In spite of certain tensions he remained a friend to many in the union. Regarding the *Allianz* . . . It seems to me that when there were disagreements, he argued his case rather than attack the person who had a different opinion."

"Regarding the Oxford Group . . . This was contrary to his understanding of the gospel of grace. To him the true concern was not to better mankind (moral re-armament) but to bring about a new birth. He advocated the totality of grace. He rejected the self-improvement tendency of that movement. He understood his pastoral task to be preaching Jesus. Doubtless he also advised people but the main focus remained a Christ-centered proclamation. His ethic was therefore not so much defined by what can be done, but by a determined look towards Jesus."

Federmann K., "Köster was in a leading position in the Evangelical *Allianz*, was well respected and gave direction to the movement. He gave direction through his own preaching but he was also influential in the planning process of the joint programs and in the selection of the various guest speakers. He had a personal charisma and authority."

Did Köster alter his critical stance towards state and politics in the post-war years? Did the strict division between church and world become somewhat less during the period of rebuilding?

Interviews

Matschinger R., "I believe that he did not change much. He had his eschatological viewpoint and remained focused on the life of the church."

Did the political nature of his preaching change?

Matschinger R., "In some ways it wasn't necessary anymore. Yet, he remained relevant and in his sermons always sought to build bridges to current events. Looking back to 1938, Köster viewed the *Anschluss* as God's will—after all it happened, and was therefore part of God's permissive will. For him Austria becoming part of Germany was a natural course of events. Indeed, on a personal level he was close to the German Baptist Union."

Fuchs H., "He had his difficulties with the American Baptists and their emphasis on evangelism. He felt that their motivation was based on human effort, on what can be done and achieved. To them it was important to be busy and active. Köster rejected this kind of activism but other Baptists in Austria welcomed it. These people really meant well. They planned their activities, made their calculations (i.e. when we convert such a number of people, then . . .) but Köster rejected these human strategies. He himself was well able to talk with people evangelistically, but he felt uncomfortable with this 'doing' aspect. God gives, we are not meant to do his work—we are merely called to recognize and tune into what God himself is doing."

State and the various models of government . . . is every state bad?

Fuchs H., "No, I think that would go too far. Köster understood government as a God-given order, although it is only an order of judgment. What Köster rejected was that any government, which inevitably has to carve out its own ideology, attempted to take over or sought to interfere with the church of God. He resisted any such attempts."

Is his position close to Luther's Two Kingdom teaching?

Fuchs H., "He simply risked leading the church, adopting an eschatological attitude, in the given time. It was a risk but it was this kind of attitude that he embodied and lived."

Federmann K., "Köster always spoke of the church-fellowship (*Gemeinde*) rather than church (*Kirche*). For him the church-fellowship was the body of believers that was instituted by God. This meant that nobody could be part of this body unless they were lead by the Spirit and exercised personal faith. The public declaration of being joined to this body is baptism. The state is also a body (*Körperschaft*) and fulfils its own function and purpose. These two cannot be mixed together. It follows that a church-fellowship that seeks public recognition acts against the Spirit and the scriptures."

Interviews

"Köster argued for a strict separation of state and church. He said that as citizens of the state each was obliged to dutifully fulfill the various obligations that government imposed. Yet, within the life of the church God speaks and rules through his word. Whoever speaks against God's word is in danger but he who keeps the Word will be kept."

"I don't know how a Christian would have had to act when ordered to murder people, to commit a criminal act. I can only say that I was kept from committing terrible acts. I was drafted into the army in February 1941 and remained there until I was wounded in 1945. I was twice in Russia and then on the Balkan, but I can say that have never consciously took aim or shot at another human being."

Regarding post-war period . . .

Federmann K., "The book *Lampenlicht am dunklen Ort* contains a reprint of one Köster's sermons where he exposed the *Hackenkreuz* as a pagan symbol. However, he also spoke after the war in similar terms of the Pentagram. The Pentagram was used by the Soviets and the Americans as their national symbol. In pagan mythology the Pentagram was an important symbol. In German mythology it was called the *Drudenfuß*. A *Drud* was a witch, thus it represented a demonic symbol. I don't quite know why both powers chose it as their symbol. Köster argued that even though the Austrians were enthusiastic regarding the Americans and wary regarding the Russians, ultimately both were the same."

"Set in the context of the life of the church—after the war there were many American evangelists who assumed that in Europe there were many pagans who needed to be evangelized. Köster helped the church to see a different way of rebuilding its life. Regarding the new movements, he reminded the church that National Socialism was based on human effort, a mad attempt to change the world. However the American approach was also based on the same motivation, they were in fact no better, no worse."

"Many members of the church reproached Köster and said, 'Are you crazy? First you condemn the Nazis and now the Americans?' But he simply replied, 'I'm part of the body of Christ. That is my place and I am not interested in programs that are based on human efforts.' He did not accept support from the Americans, even though they offered it. Neither did he accept support from the German Baptists. His help was to remind the church that they should remain who they always were; followers of Jesus Christ."

Does it mean that for Köster the disciple of Jesus has to remain apolitical?

Interviews

"Yes, apolitical but always a gospel person, a disciple who hears the word and acts accordingly. To bear witness to the truth—this had become an internal truth. He did not suggest that one had to evangelize with banners, etc. but emphasized a witness-bearing, confessing life."

What was the function and effect of providing and distributing Köster's sermons in a written format?

Matschinger R., "These sermons were used amongst the local church members but they were also sent out to others. The purpose was to help people reflect and to think deeper."

Altmann E., "Erika Hoffmann had asked Köster what she could do and he then suggested this kind of ministry to her. Over time it became a very important ministry for the church community. When people had moved away they were able to keep a meaningful link with the church. For instance, my own husband became a Christian through the regular reading of these sermon notes..."

Fuchs H., "Yes, I too received some of these sermon notes. They even made their way to Ternitz."

How and when did Köster mention the Anabaptists, i.e. Hubmayer. Did the Anabaptists influence the self understanding of the Baptists at the Mollardgasse, or was it derived from Onken and the German Baptist movement?

Matschinger R., "I didn't discover anything about that."

Fuchs H., "My subjective impression is that he was more at home with the Anabaptists, even though he knew about their weaknesses. He had some manuscripts regarding the history of the Anabaptists."

Federmann K., "He was very clear in this question. He said that the Baptists—during the Reformation—clearly followed the Scriptures and in that sense went much further than the magisterial reformers. For example, the issue of baptism (Federmann makes a reference to a sermon Köster preached from the gospel of John). Köster said, 'I don't want to make you into Baptists, but I want you to have personal relationship with Jesus.' He was not advocating one denomination. His desire was that people experience Jesus. The German Baptists were thoroughly entangled with Hitler. The General Secretary was a member of the Nazi party. But Köster was strictly against that and he said that he had more and more contacts to Lutherans and Catholics."

Köster had studied reformed Theologians like Barth and Brunner, but also Lutherans like Schlatter. Was this recognizable for the listening congregation?

Matschinger R., "I believe that he engaged with many different voices and theologians—he never attempted to give the impression that he knew everything. He was quite critical of philosophers; I still recall a comment of his: *'Hütet Euch von den scheinbar scheinenden Beweisen.'* Beware of the seeming obvious proofs."

Fuchs H., "It was only noticeable in his Christ-centered preaching ministry."

"I found his relationship with Schlatter surprising. He said during his time at the seminary that he had studied Schlatter while his close friend Lukey had studied Kant. He had good relations and friendships to Protestant Lutheran theologians. For instance Professor Enz often preached in the Mollardgasse."

Köster read a lot of reformed theologians. Yet, part of reformed theology is that the state is also transformed by the gospel not just the church. Did Köster agree . . . ?

Federmann K., "Köster had never really taken that on board. And there is an interesting distinction between Bonhoeffer and Köster. I would say that in some sense Bonhoeffer propagated a Christianity in which being a Christian consisted of a sincere humanitarianism (*Mitmenschlichkeit*). This was firmly rejected by Köster. Of course, there is a social component in the gospel, the Good Samaritan, the Sermon on the Mount, but it is not the center of the gospel. The center is Jesus Christ himself. He is savior and he is Lord of the world."

"The needs of the world cannot be solved by us (the church) not hunger, war, pain or death. Köster always listed these factors. People want relief, they want help. But Köster always rejected claims that the gospel could provide such relief. Indeed, were not prophets of the Old Testament pushed to the margin of society? They did not offer solutions to humanitarian crisis. Also, how did Jesus die on the cross? What did he actually 'do' on the cross? Jesus simply stayed on the cross and endured the humiliations, died and was brought back to life on the third day by God. That is also the way for his church-fellowship. Her calling was not to change the world but to bear witness to Christ. She simply had to bear witness whatever the response. When the people accept that witness—great! When people reject her witness and persecute the church—the church has then to endure it . . . the church should not seek acceptance, argue for tolerance or use political tactics in order to gain respite or recognition - methods the Catholic Church has employed for centuries. Not even Luther had social betterment and transformation on his agenda. Yes, he willingly used the authority of the local dukes but he used them for the purpose of proclaiming the gospel."

What was the unique blessing of Köster's preaching ministry? From what did it protect you? In what were you challenged?

Fuchs H., "I felt a new freedom. I felt that there was a real presence of the Holy Spirit, who cleansed everyone but rejected no one, but was at the same time a lofty Holy Spirit. And in the midst of my own crisis listening to Köster I felt again accepted by God. I took comfort in the message that the sinner who repents was accepted."

"Listening to Köster I felt I was exposed to a message that brought light and freedom. He preached the word of God and it reached me and shaped my experiences."

"The challenge; he never taught a directive ethic (ethic as a law). His challenge and expectation was that through the proclamation of the crucified Jesus the listeners were released to live out the gospel truth."

What were the strengths and weaknesses of Köster's preaching?

Federmann K., "I am still a follower of Köster – his weakness . . . well; one could say that he was somewhat intolerant. Preachers whom he considered were deviating from the biblical message he would not permit to preach. I noticed that especially in the post-war years. For instance he rejected the American influence and thus was not able to forge friendships with these people."

"A kind of weakness was to some extent his authority. But it was also a strength, because he led the fellowship in such a way that they remained one. There were no great debates or splits. I remember how two sisters had a serious dispute but Köster managed to reconcile the two. And they remained part of the church."

What were the abiding strengths?

Federmann K., "I became a Christian through the ministry of Köster. Beyond that . . . I gained through him and my membership with the church a new worldview. I received a liberal education, my father was a judge but his real interest was philosophy. He read Goethe, Hegel and Tolstoy and was very musical. I was able to attend a grammar school for my education. My mother had a basic simple faith. I myself did what was expected of me. As a teenager I got confirmed, but my own thinking was all over the place (*unkontrolliertes Denken*). Through the ministry of Köster, my whole thinking was anchored to God's word."

Exposing worldviews that sought to glorify human endeavor was one of the key concerns of Köster's preaching. How did the listeners connect to the highly philosophical struggles? Were there opportunities to discuss and explore these themes further?

Matschinger R., "I don't think that many listeners really understood the detailed philosophical debates Köster sometimes referred to. Yet, if someone felt that there was need for further discussion that was made possible in the various home groups. During these informal sessions it was possible to ask questions and to engage further."

Fuchs H., "Philosophy only remained at the edge of his preaching ministry. Yes, he would indicate what were the issues and questions but then moved on to God's word. Listeners only understood partly the philosophical contexts that were addressed in his sermons."

At one point (in 1943) Köster criticizes the edifying preaching style. Did he have anyone in particular in mind?

Fuchs H., "I believe he talked about the Zeitgeist and sought to reveal what were the roots and origins of that spirit. The accusations of only engaging in edifying sermonizing applied to the whole of the Baptist movement. He wanted to urge them on to engage in the spiritual warfare that was being waged. His stance caused concern to many and he had certain encounters in Germany where others openly rejected his critical stance. In a sense, his point of view was very close to the confessing Church. I don't know why it never came to a closer association or any concrete contacts. Maybe he considered them too political—I just don't know."

Federmann K., "I would say that this comment needs to be balanced with other comments. His preaching ministry was also comforting, edifying. He did not attempt to whip up emotions. He wouldn't make people fanatical. But when people came to him with their troubles and concerns, for instance when people heard about the loss of loved ones, he brought comfort to these people."

"The other important factor is that one also has to remember that Köster underwent a certain theological development. There was one phase in his life where he was strongly influenced by Karl Barth's theology. But during the latter phase of his life his focus became Adolf Schlatter. Barth argued strongly against a simplistic edification, having come from a liberal background."

When Karl Barth. . . . When Schlatter?

Federmann K., "In 1943 it was definitely Barth, also during the first post-war years. But then maybe from 1950 onwards it was predominately Schlatter.

Interviews

Köster appreciated Schlatter's exact and close reading of the biblical text. That became more and more important for him."

"Personally I have difficulties with Schlatter. He wrote a book (*Kennen Sie Jesus*) where he expressed pro-Nazi sentiments. He wrote (Federmann quotes from memory), 'Faith produces change . . . through faith a quarrelling married couple can change and become reconciled again. Since this is true at the personal level it must also be possible within the political realm. Since we have put our trust in Adolf Hitler, change has happened.' When I read that, and I only read it recently, I broke with Schlatter."

Follow up phone conversation with Mr. Federmann K., 08.08.2009 [He offered a clarification regarding the relationship between church and state.]

Federmann K., "Since the church-fellowship was not able to own properties (*keine Rechtsperson*) a trust was established. The financial support came from the German Baptist Churches in America, Forest Park. Every church member of the Baptist Church Vienna-Mollardgasse 35 was also a member of this trust. Once a year the trust members were obliged to hold a meeting during which the financial reports were given and matters could be discussed. Usually this annual meeting happened straight after a mid-week Bible study evening at the Mollardgasse and only lasted about 20 minutes. In that way Köster and the church fellowship followed to the letter of the law. Yet, theologically Köster repeatedly said: the church-fellowship is not a trust (*die Gemeinde ist kein Verein*)."

"Also, a certain Lutheran Superintendent Traar said to Köster after the war: 'You were the only one who did not yield to the political pressure of the Nazi regime.'"

Appendix 3

Arnold Köster Source Material

THE FOLLOWING COPIES OF Köster's sermons and lectures were made available to me by the Baptist Church Vienna-Mollardgasse 35. The vast majority of the material is readable. However, not all sermons and papers are complete. Occasionally a few pages are missing or have become, due to the copying process, illegible.

1938–39, 1 Pet, 22 pages.

March 1939, *Der Christ und die Zeit*, Ps 111.

1 April 1939, First Sunday after Easter, Luke 24:13, Matt 26:59–68, 28:16–20, 3 pages.

20 April 1939, *Israel ist ein Typus für die Gemeinde Jesu Christi*, Gen 32:21ff.

23 April 1939, Isa 44:24–28, 45:1–25, 4 pages.

27 August 1939, *Gott spricht, bevor ein Gericht hereinbricht*, Amos 3, 2 pages.

27 August 1939, 4 *Gebetszüge*, Dan 9, 2 pages.

3 September 1939, *Elias am Horeb*, 1 Kgs 19:9–13, 2 pages.

8 October 1939, *Wie wurde der Glaube der ersten Jünger und was war der Inhalt des Glaubens der ersten Jünger?* John 1:19—12:11, 2 pages.

21 April 1940, *Welche Haltung haben wir als gläubige Christen irdischen Größen gegenüber einzunehmen?* Luke 7:1–10, 2 pages.

1 May 1940, Ps 91, 2 pages.

19 May 1940, *Die Könige der Erde lehnen sich auf . . .* , Ps 2, 4 pages.

26 May 1940, *Es sinnen die Übertreter auf gottloses Treiben . . . Herr, deine Güte reicht, so weit der Himmel ist*, Ps 36, 2 pages.

Arnold Köster Source Material

9 August 1940, *Saget Johannes wieder, was ihr sehet und höret!* Matt 11:2-6, 2 pages.

18 August 1940, *Meine Seele ist still zu Gott der mir hilft!* Ps 62, 3 pages.

1 September 1940, Isaiah, 18 pages.

15 September 1940, *Der Leidcharakter dieser Weltzeit wird aufgehoben werden!* Rev 21:1-6, 3 pages.

22 September 1940, *Ein Gebet Moses, des Mannes Gottes,* Ps 90, 3 pages.

29 September 1940, *Wesen und Wirklichkeit der Existenz des Menschen,* Gen 2:5-17, 3:17.19, 4 pages.

6 October 1940, *Das Buch von dem Ursprung Jesu Christi...,* Matt 1:1-17, 3 pages.

6 October 1940, *Der Mensch lebt nicht vom Brot allein, sondern von jedem Wort, das durch den Mund Gottes ergeht!* Matt 4:1-4; Rom 7:22—28:1-4, 2 pages.

13 October 1940, *Wer unter dem Schirm des Höchsten sitzt,* Ps 91, 1 page.

17 October 1940, *Gebete,* 1 page.

20 October 1940, *Die prophetische Situation der Gemeinde,* Isa 6, p4.

27 October 1940, *Siehe, ich habe eine geöffnete Tür vor dir angebracht,* Rev 3:7-13, 4 pages.

1 December 1940, *Ansprache vor der Taufe,* Ps 24:3f ; Acts 10, 4 pages.

22 December 1940, *Die herzliche Barmherzigkeit unseres Gottes,* Luke 1:57-80, 4 pages.

29 December 1940, *Ewig wird der Herr thronen!* Ps 68, 4 pages.

29 December 1940, *Befiehl dem Herrn deine Wege!* Ps 37:5, 3 pages.

1 January 1941, *Sehet zu, dass euch niemand beraube durch die Philosophie und lose Verführung,* Col 2-3:4, John 11:38-45, 4 pages.

5 January 1941, Rom 9:6-29, 4 pages.

12 January 1941, Rom 9:14-23, 4 pages.

19 January 1941, *Israel, das Geheimnis der Geschichte,* Rom 9:18-29, 5 pages.

26 January 1941, Rom 9:30—10:1-21, 6 pages.

2 February 1941, Rom 11, 5 pages.

9 February 1941, Rom 12, 6 pages.

16 February 1941, Rom 12:9-21, 2 pages.

16 February 1941, *Wir setzen unser Ziel nicht in das, was gesehn wird, sondern in das, was nicht gesehen wird!* 2 Cor 4:1—5:10, 5 pages.

23 February 1941, *Aber am letzten Tag des Festes, der am herrlichsten war, trat Jesus auf...*, John 7:37–39, 5 pages.

11 March 1941, *Die Freiheit vom Verdammungsurteil (Reihe: Die Freiheit der Kinder Gottes)*, Rom 7:21—28:4, 8 pages.

16 March 1941, *Heldengedenktag*, Rom 5:6–8, 4 pages.

16 March 1941, *Wie ist uns die Bibel Gottes Wort? (Vortragsreihe: Ist das Wort der Bibel glaubwürdig?)*, Ps 19, 8 pages.

20 March 1941, *Wie ist die Bibel entstanden? (Vortragsreihe: Ist das Wort der Bibel glaubwürdig?)*, 2 Tim 3:14–17, 7 pages.

23 March 1941, *Wie lese ich die Bibel recht? (Vortragsreihe: Ist das Wort der Bibel glaubwürdig?)*, Ps 119:73–107, 6 pages.

27 March 1941, *Die Botschaft der Bibel! (Vortragsreihe: Ist das Wort der Bibel glaubwürdig?)*, 2 Pet 1:10–21 u. 2:1–2, 10 pages.

6 April 1941, *Palmsonntag*, John 12:9–38, 5 pages.

6 April 1941, *Das Königtum Jesu*, Zech 9:9–10, 4 pages.

7 April 1941, *Einführung in die Offenbarung des Johannes*, 6 pages.

13 April 1941, *Fleisch und Blut können die Herrschaft Gottes nicht erlangen*, 1 Cor 15:1–28, 3 pages.

20 April 1941, *Jesus und die ungelösten Fragen in unserem Leben*, Luke 24:13–35, 4 pages.

27 April 1941, *Der Welt überwindende Glaube!* Ps 97, 1 John 5:4, 6 pages.

4 May 1941, *Die nachösterliche Frage Jesu an seine Jünger*, Luke 24:26, 4 pages.

8 May 1941, *Der Prophet Obadja*, Obad, 6 pages.

11 May 1941, *Die Freiheit der Kinder Gottes: Die Freiheit vom Verdammungsurteil*, Rom 7:21—28:4, 8 pages.

18 May 1941, Rom 15:1–13, 6 pages.

18 May 1941, *Die Freiheit der Kinder Gottes: Die Freiheit vom Gesetz der Sünde und des Todes*, Ps 51, 8 pages.

22 May 1941, *Martha-Christentum und Maria-Christentum*, Luke 10:38–42, 5 pages.

25 May 1941, *Die Freiheit der Kinder Gottes: Die Freiheit von den Dingen*, Ps 73, 7 pages.

1 June 1941, *Ansprache vor der Taufe (Pfingstsonntag)*, Acts 2:1–42; 10:44–48, 6 pages.

8 June 1941, *Heilsgewißheit und ihre Gefährdung*, Rom 5:1–11, 5 pages.

9 June 1941, *Der Antichrist,* Rev 13, 11 pages.

12 June 1941, Song of Songs, 8 pages.

15 June 1941, *Was ist Beten?* Ps 90, 4 pages.

15 June 1941, *Die Merkmale der Messianität Jesu,* Matt 16:13-20; 26:57-66, 11 pages.

19 June 1941, *Die Opferung Isaaks,* Gen 22:1-19, 6 pages.

29 June 1941, *Elia, der Prophet des lebendigen Gottes. Oder Von Weg und Schicksal der Kirchen in der Weltzeit,* 1 Kgs 19:1-18, 2 Kgs 2:1-15, 9 pages.

6 July 1941, *Taufgottesdienst,* Acts 8:26-40, 4 pages.

10 July 1941, *Jesus und Pilatus oder Die Begegnung zwischen Weltstaat und Gottesreich,* John 18:33-40, 6 pages.

20 July 1941, *Kreuzesnachfolge,* Phil 3:17-21, 7 pages.

18 September 1941, *Hermagedon* (Armagedon), Rev 16, 3 pages.

1 October 1941, *Warum immer wieder das prophetische Wort?* 3 pages.

16 October 1941, *Volk ohne Gott,* 7 pages.

7 November 1941, *Das Christuszeugnis im Alten Testament,* Gen 4:25—25:32, 33 pages.

16 November 1941, *Das Bekenntnis zur Gottheit Jesu,* Mark 9:1-29, 5 pages.

7 December 1941, *(Vor dem Abendmahl) Du bereitest mir einen Tisch im Angesicht meiner Feinde,* Ps 23, 5 pages.

21 December 1941, *Wir gehören zu denen, die sein Erscheinen lieb haben!* Matt 11:1-30; 2 Tim 4:8, 6 pages.

24 December 1941, *Die große Freude,* Luke 1:1-4; 2:1-21, 4 pages.

25 December 1941, *Das Christfest der Einsamen,* Luke 2:21-40, 4 pages.

25 December 1941, *Und das Wort wurde Fleisch und zeltete unter uns...,* John 14-16, 4 pages.

1 January 1943, *Ihr sollt sitzen am Tisch des Herrn und nicht am Tische der Dämonen,* 1 Cor 10:15-22; 11:23-26, 6 pages.

10 January 1943, 1 Cor 16, 6 pages.

14 January 1943, *Christentum oder Christus oder „Ich habe kein Christentum, sonderen einen lebendigen Christus",* 1 Cor, 11 pages.

17 January 1943, *Von Gottes Führung und Bewahrung,* Ps 2, Matt 2:13-23, 4 pages.

17 January 1943, 2 Cor (Series last date 6 June 1943), 120 pages.

Arnold Köster Source Material

24 January 1943, *Gefährdungen des Glaubens und ihre Überwindung*, John 11:1–45, 7 pages.

28 January 1943, *Die Gottesbotschaft des Buches Hiobs (Eine Antwort auf die Frage nach dem Rätsel des Leides)*, Job 1:20–22; 2:7–10; 38:1—42:6, 11 pages.

31 January 1943, Ps 46, 5 pages.

4 February 1943, *Die Gemeinde Gottes in den Krisen der Zeiten*, Isa 8:5; 9:6, Eph 2:20, 6 pages.

7 February 1943, *Mein Volk kennt seinen Gott nicht mehr! (Stalingradpredigt)*, Jer 8, 6 pages.

11 February 1943, *Der Mensch - Kreatur und Ebenbild Gottes*, Gen 1:26–28, 2:7, 9 pages.

14 February 1943, *Selig sind, die da hungern nach der Gerechtigkeit*, Matt 5:6; Ps 32, 5 pages.

18 February 1943, *Der Mensch - Sünder und Verlorener*, Gen 3:1–6, 11 pages.

21 February 1943, *Kein Unglück fürchten!* Ps 23, 4 pages.

25 February 1943, *Der Mensch unter Gottes Geduld und Verheißung*, Gen 8:20–22, 11 pages.

4 March 1943, *Jesus von Nazareth, Menschensohn und Gottessohn*, Mark 10:45, 10 pages.

7 March 1943, *Der Geist Gottes gibt Klarheit, der Teufel verblendet*, 2 Cor 3:7—4:6, 2 pages.

7 March 1943, *Am Tische Jesu, Wir, die Zöllner und die Sünder*, Luke 15:1–7, 4 pages.

11 March 1943, *Der Mensch - versöhnt und erlöst*, Col 1:12–23, 12 pages.

18 March 1943, *Der Mensch - erwählt und berufen*, Eph 1:1–14, 10 pages.

21 March 1943, *Die Stunde der Christenheit heute*, 1 Sam 3, 9 pages.

25 March 1943, *Der Mensch - geheiligt und verherrlicht*, Heb 10:4–10, Rom 8:28–30, 1Cor 1:26–30, 10 pages.

1 April 1943, *Weissagung und Erfüllung*, John 1:43–51, 8 pages.

8 April 1943, *Die Botschaft des Propheten Micha*, Mic 1:1–3; 5:1–4; 7:18–20, 11 pages.

15 April 1943, *Babel - das Reich Nimrods*, Gen 10:6–12, 11 pages.

18 April 1943, *Jesus der König (Palmsonntag)*, Luke 19:29–44, 7 pages.

22 April 1943, *Drei Stadien auf dem Glaubensweg*, John 12:20–33, 4 pages.

23 April 1943, *Die sieben Worte Jesu am Kreuz*, Matt 27:11–54, 5 pages.

Arnold Köster Source Material

25 April 1943, *Welche Machtwirkungen gehen von dem Auferstandenen in die Welt hinein, jetzt und hier?* 1 Cor 15:12-28, 4 pages.

25 April 1943, *Erwiesen als Sohn Gottes*, Heb.

29 April 1943, *Ein seelsorgliches Gespräch über das Gebet*, John 4:19-26, 10 pages.

2 May 1943, *Was ist der biblische Sinn der Taufe?* 4 pages.

2 May 1943, *Was bedeutet die Begegnung mit der Auferstehungsbotschaft?* Luke 24, 4 pages.

6 May 1943, *Der ungeborgene Mensch (Ein seelsorgliches Gespräch)*, Ps 90:12; 42:1-3; Luke 15:24, 10 pages.

09 May 1943, Ps 104, 7 pages.

13 May 1943, *Stadien auf dem Lebenswege (Kierkegaard)*, 13 pages.

16 May 1943, *Ist einer Mutter Herz auch groß - Gottes Herz ist größer,* Isa 49, 5 pages.

27 May 1943, *Wie wahr ist doch Gottes Wort*, Dan 9, 7 pages.

6 June 1943, *Darum, sorget nicht (Seelsorgliches Gespräch)*, Matt 6:19-34, 8 pages.

10 June 1943, *Das Denken unserer Zeit vor der Gottesfrage (Seelorgliches Gespräch)*, Col 2:1-10; 2 Cor 4:3-6, 12 pages.

13 June 1943, *Der Geist Gottes schwebte brütend über dem Chaos (Pfingstsonntag)*, Ezek 37; Gen 1:1-3, 6 pages.

17 June 1943, *Das Lukasevangelium, Lukas der Arzt*, Luke, 15 pages.

27 June 1943, *Unsere Augen sehen nach Dir*, 2 Chr 20, 6 pages.

4 July 1943, *Der Jesus des apostolischen Glaubens*, Phil 2:1-11, 6 pages.

4 July 1943, *Wir, die Geladenen am Tische Jesu (Abendmahl)*, Luke 14:1-24, 4 pages.

11 July 1943, *Sie sollen erkennen, dass ich der Herr bin*, Ezek 29:1-16, 7 pages.

18 July 1943, *Gott hat mich unbeschreiblich lieb!* Rom 8:28-39, 7 pages.

18 July 1943, *Das Geheimnis Israels*, Rom 11:25-36, 7 pages.

1 August 1943, *Glaubst du von ganzem Herzen? So mag es wohl sein! (Taufe)*, Acts 8:26-39, 5 pages.

1 August 1943, *Was die Gemeinde Jesu Christi in dieser gegenwärtigen Weltzeit ist, und was sie tun soll,* 1 Tim 3:15—14:1, 7 pages.

12 August 1943, *Ich lasse dich nicht . . .*, Gen 32:22-32, 7 pages.

15 August 1943, *Und nun spricht der Herr*, Isa 43:1-5, 5 pages.

2 September 1943, *Die von den Hecken und Zäunen* . . . , Luke 14:22–23, 6 pages.

2 September 1943, *Die Stunde der Christenheit heute!* 2 Pet 3:1–13, 10 pages.

5 September 1943, *Drei grosse, klare Gemeindeaussagen über Jesus von Nazareth*, Eph 1:22–23, 5 pages.

16 September 1943, *Die Stadt des Antichristus (Beitrag zum Thema „Die Stunde der Christenheit heute",* Rev 17:1—18:24, 11 pages.

23 September 1943, *Die gebrechlichen Einrichtungen der Welt (Seelsorgerliches Gespräch)*, Ecclesiastes 1; Rev 21, 12 pages.

26 September 1943, *Die Machttaten des Christus*, Matt 9:26–31, 5 pages.

3 October 1943, *Selig sind die Toten*, Rev 14:13, 6 pages.

7 October 1943, *Die Bestimmung des Menschen*, Ps 119:89–96, 10 pages.

13 October 1943, *Die Stadt Gottes*, Rev 19–22, 11 pages.

31 October 1943, *Der Sinn des Sterbens*, Ps 90, 1 Cor 15:52–57, 11 pages.

7 November 1943, *Verklärte Leiblichkeit*, 1 Cor 15:35–49, 8 pages.

21 November 1943, *Und Gott gedachte an Abraham*, Gen 15–29, 5 pages.

28 November 1943, *Der Knecht Gottes (Adventspredigt)*, Isa 42:1–8, 8 pages.

5 December 1943, *Ich aber harre des Herrn*, Ps 52:10–11, 5 pages.

5 December 1943, *Also hat Gott die Welt geliebt (Taufe)*, John 3:16; Isa 40, 6 pages.

12 December 1943, *Zeiten der Erquickung vom Angesicht des Herrn*, Acts 3:19–20, 7 pages.

19 December 1943, *Fürchte dich nicht*, Luke 1:28–38, 5 pages.

25 December 1943, *Kommt und seht* . . . , Isa 9:1–6, 5 pages.

26 December 1943, *Weihnachtsgeschichte, Weihnachtsoffenbarung, Weihnachtsglaube*, Luke 2:1–20, 4 pages.

31 December 1943, *Seid getrost, ich bins, fürchtet euch nicht*, Mark 6:45–52, 6 pages.

1943–44, *Bergpredigt*, Sermon on the Mount, 72 pages.

2 January 1944, *Bleibendes*, 1 Cor 13, 4 pages.

2 January 1944, *Das Gottesgeheimnis der Weltgeschichte*, Rom 11:32–36, 7 pages.

11 June 1944, Col, 120 pages.

22 October 1944, *Das Geheimnis Europas*, Dan 2:44–45, 8 pages.

Arnold Köster Source Material

22 October 1944, *Der Jakobskampf,* Gen 32; 33:1–11, 7 pages.

3 January 1945, *Wir wissen aber . . . ,* Rom 8:28–39, 7 pages.

3 January 1945, *Es werden alle Völker kommen und zu deinen Füßen anbeten . . . ,* Matt 2:1–12, 4 pages.

4 January 1945, *Fasset eure Seelen mit Geduld,* Luke 21:19, 8 pages.

18 January 1945, *Dennoch soll die Stadt Gottes fein listig bleiben . . . ,* Ps 46, 6 pages.

21 January 1945, *Der Weg Kains oder Von Geschichte und Wesen der Weltkultur,* Gen 4:1–16, 10 pages.

25 January 1945, *Was betrübst du dich meine Seele, und bist so unruhig in mir? Harre auf Gott!* Ps 42:6, 6 pages.

25 January 1945, *Die Stunde der Versuchung,* 6 pages.

11 February 1945, *Deshalb umgürtet die Hüften eures Geistes!* 1 Pet 1:13, 3 pages.

18 February 1945, *Sprich zu meiner Seele: Ich bin deine Hilfe,* Ps 35:3b, 5 pages.

25 February 1945, *Lebendiges Wasser,* John 4:10–14, 5 pages.

1 March 1945, *Vom Guten Sterben (Seelsorgerliches Gespräch mit christusgläubigen Menschen der notvollen Gegenwart),* 2 Cor 5:1–10, 4 pages.

4 March 1945, *Jesus macht die Freude voll,* John 2:1–11, 6 pages.

9 March 1945, *Wie kommen wir auch in der gegenwärtigen Zeit als christusgläubige Menschen zu der Freude?* Phil 1, 8 pages.

18 March 1945, *Das Ziel ist nahe!* 1 Pet 4:7–8, 8 pages.

18 March 1945, *Jesus macht seine Liebe voll,* John 13, 7 pages.

1 April 1945, *Ich lebe, und ihr sollt auch leben (Ostersonntag),* John 14:19, 4 pages.

29 April 1945, *Was will Gott?* Ps 129; Matt 6:8–15, 6 pages.

13 May 1945, *Die Ethik des Auferstehung (Seite 95–102),* Col 2:20—23:5a, 8 pages.

17 May 1945, *Die Verfehlung der Gegenwart,* Heb 13:5–6; Acts 4:12; 2 Cor 5:20; Luke 12:32, 7 pages.

27 May 1945, *Die Ethik des Gewissens oder die Ethik der Gnade,* Rom 3:19–31, 15 pages.

18 June 1945, *Der alte und der neue Mensch,* Col 3:9–11, 8 pages.

11 July 1945, *Gelobt sei der Herr täglich,* Ps 68:20–21, 4 pages.

1 August 1945, *Das Hohe Lied, Die Gemeinde der Sehnsucht,* Song of Songs, 21 pages.

9 August 1945, *Die Welt im Zeichen des Pentagramms (Ein seelsorgerliches Gespräch)*, Rev 13:10–18; 7:1–4, 9 pages.

15 August 1945, *Die Sprache des Glaubens*, Ps 130, 6 pages.

16 September 1945, *Gerechtigkeit Gottes*, Gen 15:1–6, 8 pages.

1945, *Der Gottesinn der Weltgerichte* (Date illegible), 7 pages.

30 September 1945, *Gott und die Seinen in ihrem Alter*, Isa 46:3–4.

21 October 1945, *Wie war das möglich?* 9 pages.

18 November 1945, *Wir dürfen sagen . . .*, Heb 13:5–6, 5 pages.

1 December 1945, *Gemeinde im Advent Gottes*, Matt 2:6, Isa 40, 4 pages.

25 December 1945, *Gott sei Dank für sein unaussprechliche Gnade*, 2 Cor 2:15; Luke 2:1–20, 7 pages.

1946, Revelation, 147 pages.

16 October 1947, *Die Botschaft des Proheten Daniel*, Dan, 78 pages.

1938–1947 Allianz, Allianzprotokoll, (43,000 words). Typescript of Minutes held by F. Graf-Stohlhofer, Vienna-Mollardgasse 35.

1930–1942 Täufer-Bote. Copies of the Täufer-Bote are kept at the *Zentrales Oncken-Archiv des Bundes Evangelisch-Freikirchlicher Gemeinden.*

Bibliography

Akin, Daniel L. "An Expositional Analysis of the Schleitheim Confession." *Criswell Theological Review* 2 (1988) 345–70.
Althaus, Paul. *The Ethics of Martin Luther*. Philadelphia: Fortress, 1972.
———. *Grundriss der Dogmatik*. Erlangen, Germany: Universitätsbuchhandlung Merkel, 1933.
———. "Kirche und Staat nach Lutherischer Lehre." *Theologia militans* 4 (1935) 1–31.
———. *Um die Wahrheit des Evangeliums*. Stuttgart: Calwer, 1962.
Ballor, Jordan J. "The Aryan Clause, the Confessing Church, and the Ecumenical Movement: Barth and Bonhoeffer on Natural Theology, 1933–1935." *Scottish Journal of Theology* 59 (2006) 263–80.
Barth, Karl. *Christengemeinde und Bürgergemeinde*. Theologische Studien 20. Munich: Kaiser, 1946.
———. *Church and State*. London: SCM, 1939.
———. "The Church between East and West." *Cross Currents* 2 (1951) 64–77.
———. *Church Dogmatics*. Vol. 3, *The Doctrine of Creation*. Part 1, *The Work of Creation*. Edinburgh: T. & T. Clark, 1958.
———. "Die Kirche Jesu Christi." *Theologische Existenz Heute* 5 (1933) 1–24.
———. *The German Church Conflict*. Ecumenical Studies in History 1, edited by Allchin et al. London: Lutterworth, 1965.
———. "Theologische Existenz Heute." *Zwischen den Zeiten*, Beiheft Nr. 2 (1933).
Barnett, Victoria. *For the Soul of the People*. New York: Oxford University Press, 1992.
———. "Transcending Barmen: Confessing in Word and Deed." *Christian Century* 111 (1994) 495–98.
Bauman, Clarence. "Theology of 'The Two Kingdoms': A Comparison of Luther and the Anabaptists." *Mennonite Quarterly Review* 38 (1964) 37–49.
Bax, Douglas S. "The Barmen Theological Declaration: Its Historical Background." *Journal of Theology for Southern Africa* 47 (1984) 12–20.
Bergsten, Torsten. *Balthasar Hubmaier: Anabaptist Theologian and Martyr*. Valley Forge, PA: Judson, 1978.
Bernanos, Georges. *Tagebuch eines Landpfarrers*. Frankfurt: Fischer Verlag, 1986.
Bender, Harold S. *The Anabaptist Vision*. Scottdale, PA: Herald, 1944.
Best, Ernest. *Disciples and Discipleship*. Edinburgh: T. & T. Clark, 1986.
Bethge, Eberhard. *Dietrich Bonhoeffer*. London: Collins, 1970.
Bekenntnisschriften der evangelisch-lutherischen Kirche. Göttingen, Germany: Vandenhoeck & Ruprecht, 1956.

Bibliography

Biddle, Mark E. "Obadiah - Jonah - Micah in Canonical Context: The Nature of Prophetic Literature and Hermeneutics." *Interpretation* 61 (2007) 154-66.

Bloedhorn, Klaus, Jr. *Untertan der Obrigkeit?* Witten-Stockum: Verlag am Steinberg, 1982.

Bonhoeffer, Dietrich. *Barcelona, Berlin, New York: 1928-1931.* Translated by Douglas W. Stott. Edited by Clifford Green. DBWE 10. Minneapolis: Fortress, 2008.

———. *Berlin: 1932-1933.* Translated by Isabel Best et al. Edited by Larry L. Rasmussen. DBWE 12. Minneapolis: Fortress, 2009.

———. *Creation and Fall.* Translated by Douglas Stephen Bax. Edited by John W. de Gruchy. DBWE 3. Minneapolis: Fortress, 1997.

———. *Conspiracy and Imprisonment, 1940-1945.* Translated by Lisa E. Dahill. Edited by Mark Brocker. DBWE 16. Minneapolis: Fortress, 2006.

———. *The Cost of Discipleship.* London: SCM, 2003.

———. *Discipleship.* Translated by Barbara Green and Reinhard Krauss. Edited by Geoffrey B. Kelly and John D. Godsey. DBWE 4. Minneapolis: Fortress, 2001.

———. *Ethik.* Munich: Chr. Kaiser Verlag, 1953.

———. *Ethics.* Translated by Reinhard Krauss et al. Edited by Clifford Green. DBWE 6. Minneapolis: Fortress, 2005.

———. *Gesammelte Schriften, IV.* Edited by Eberhard Bethge. Munich: Chr. Kaiser Verlag, 1961.

———. *Letters and Papers from Prison.* Translated by Isabel Best et al. Edited by John W. de Gruchy. DBWE 8. Minneapolis: Fortress, 2010.

———. *Life Together and Prayerbook of the Bible.* Translated by James H. Burtness and Daniel W. Bloesch. Edited by Geffrey B. Kelly. DBWE 1. Minneapolis: Fortress, 1996.

———. *London, 1933-1935.* Translated by Isabel Best. Edited by Keith W. Clements. DBWE 13. Minneapolis: Fortress, 2007.

———. *Nachfolge.* Munich: Chr. Kaiser Verlag, 1985.

———. *No Rusty Swords.* Vol. 1 of the collected works of Dietrich Bonhoeffer. Edited by Edwin H. Robertson. London: Collins, 1965.

———. *Sanctorum Communio.* Translated by Reinhard Kraus and Nancey Lukens. Edited by Clifford Green. DBWE 1. Minneapolis: Fortress, 1998.

———. *Temptation.* London: SCM, 1961.

———. *The Way to Freedom.* Vol. 2 of the collected works of Dietrich Bonhoeffer. Edited by Edwin H. Robertson. London: Collins, 1966.

———. "Zur Frage nach der Kirchengemeinschaft." *Evangelische Theologie*, Heft 6 (June 1936) 214-33.

Bornkamm, Günther, et al. *Tradition and Interpretation in Matthew.* London: SCM, 1982.

Bosch, David J. *Transforming Mission.* New York: Orbis, 2001.

Braaten, Carl E. "The Doctrine of the Two Kingdoms Re-Examined." *Currents in Theology and Mission* 15 (1988) 497-504.

Brunner, Emil. *Der Mensch im Widerspruch.* Berlin: Furche Verlag, 1937.

Brunner, Emil, and Karl Barth. *Natural Theology: Comprising "Nature and Grace" and "No."* London: Centenary, 1946.

Burleigh, Michael. *The Third Reich.* London: Pan, 2000.

Bibliography

Burkholder, Lawrence J. "The Anabaptist Vision of Discipleship." In *The Recovery of the Anabaptist Vision*, edited by Guy F. Hershberger, 135–51. Scottdale, PA: Herald, 1957.

Cahill, Lisa S. "The Ethical Implications of the Sermon on the Mount." *Interpretation* 41 (1987) 144–56.

———. *Love Your Enemies*. Minneapolis: Fortress, 1994.

Chatfield, Graeme R. "Balthasar Hubmaier and the Clarity of Scripture." PhD diss., University of Bristol, 1993.

Clements, Keith W. "The Freedom of the Church: Bonhoeffer and the Free Church Tradition." In *Bonhoeffer's Ethics: Old Europe and New Frontiers*, edited by Guy Carter et al., 155–72. Kampen: Kok Pharos, 1988.

———. "The Mutual Contributions of Church History and Systematic Theology: The Holocaust and Dietrich Bonhoeffer as a Case Study." *Pacifica* 20 (2007) 162–84.

———. *What Freedom? The Persistent Challenge of Dietrich Bonhoeffer*. Bristol: Bristol Baptist College, 1990.

Cochrane, Arthur C. *The Church's Confession under Hitler*. Pittsburgh: Pickwick, 1976.

Colwell, John E. *Promise and Presence: An Exploration of Sacramental Theology*. Milton Keynes, UK: Paternoster, 2005.

———. "A Radical Church? A Reappraisal of Anabaptist Ecclesiology." *Tyndale Bulletin* 38 (1987) 119–41.

Conway, John S. *The Nazi Persecution of the Churches, 1933–1945*. Vancouver, BC: Regent College Publishing, 1968.

Couenhoven, Jesse. "Law and Gospel, of the Law of the Gospel? Karl Barth's Political Theology Compared with Luther and Calvin." *Journal of Religious Ethics* 30 2 (2002) 181–205.

Court, Gillian. *Heart of Flesh*. London: Churches Together in Britain and Ireland, 2007.

De Gruchy, John W. "Freedom of the Church and the Liberation of Society." In *Bonhoeffer's Ethic: Old Europe and New Frontiers*, edited by Guy Carter et al., 174–89. Kampen: Kok Pharos, 1988.

———. "The Reception of Bonhoeffer's Theology." In *The Cambridge Companion to Dietrich Bonhoeffer*, edited by De Gruchy, 93–112. Cambridge: Cambridge University Press, 1999.

Diener, Michael. *Kurshalten in stürmischer Zeit*. Giessen, Germany: TVG Brunnen Verlag, 1998.

Duchrow, Ulrich, et al. *Umdeutung der Zweireichelehre Luthers im 19. Jahrundert*. Gütersloh, Germany: Gütersloher, 1975.

Dulles, Avery. *Models of the Church*. Expanded ed. New York: Doubleday, 2002.

Dumas, André. *Dietrich Bonhoeffer: Theologian of Reality*. London: SCM, 1971.

Ebeling, Rainer. *Dietrich Bonhoeffers Ringen um die Kirche*. Giessen, Germany: Brunnen-Vlg TVG, 1996.

Eck, Otto. *Urgemeinde und Imperium*. Gütersloh, Germany: Bertelsmann, 1940.

Ericksen, Robert P. *Theologians under Hitler*. New Haven: Yale University Press, 1985.

Feil, Ernst. *The Theology of Dietrich Bonhoeffer*. Translated by H. Martin Rumscheidt. Philadelphia: Fortress, 1985.

Fiddes, Paul S. *Tracks and Traces: Baptist Identity in Church and Theology*. Carlisle, UK: Paternoster, 2003.

Friedmann, Robert. *The Theology of Anabaptism*. Scottdale, PA: Herald, 1975.

Goldingay, John. *Old Testament Theology*. Vol. 1. Downers Grove: IVP, 2003.

Bibliography

Graf-Stuhlhofer, Franz. "Die Faszination des Themas 'Endzeit' für Bibelleser im 20. Jahrhundert." *Freikirchenforschung* (2001) 156–77.

———. "Das Kriegs-Ende in Wien im Spiegel der Predigten eines NS-kritischen Baptistenpastors." *Österreich in Geschichte und Literatur* (1996) 113–28.

———. "Nationalsozialismus als Konkurrenz zum christlichen Glauben." *Evangelischer Presseverband Österreich* (1996) 137–83.

———. Öffentliche Kritik am Nationalsozialismus *im Großdeutschen Reich*. Neukirchen-Vluyn, Germany: Neukirchener, 2001.

———. "Predigten während Stalingrad." *ZFG Zeitschrift für Geschichtswissenschaft* 48 (2000) 1078–97.

———. "Täuferkirchen in der Ostmark." *Österreich in Geschichte und Literatur* 44 (2000) 73–93.

———. "Von den 'Grenzen des Möglichen' im Dritten Reich." *Geschichte und Gegenwart* 18 (1999) 13–35.

Green, Clifford. "Human Sociality and Christian Community." In *The Cambridge Companion to Dietrich Bonhoeffer*, edited by John W. De Grunchy, 113–33. Cambridge: Cambridge University Press, 1999.

Green, Lowell C. *Lutherans Against Hitler*. St. Louis: Concordia, 2007.

Guelich, Robert A. "Interpreting the Sermon on the Mount." *Interpretation* (1987) 117–30.

Hauerwas, Stanley. *Performing the Faith*. London: SPCK, 2004.

———. *Sanctify Them in the Truth*. Edinburgh: T. & T. Clark, 1998.

Hauerwas, Stanley, and William H. Willimon. *Resident Aliens*. Nashville: Abingdon, 1989.

Hegel, Georg W. F. *Lectures on the Philosophy of Religion*. 1 volume ed. Berkeley: University of California Press, 1988.

Hershberger, Guy F. *The Recovery of the Anabaptist Vision*. Scottdale, PA: Herald, 1957.

Hirsch, Emanuel. *Die gegenwärtige geistige Lage*. Göttingen, Germany: Vandenhoeck & Ruprecht, 1934.

Holl, Karl. *Die Bedeutung der großen Kriege*. Tübingen, Germany: Mohr Paul Siebeck, 1917.

———. *Gesammelte Aufsätze zur Kirchengeschichte*. (Band I) Tübingen, Germany: Mohr Paul Siebeck, 1927.

Honecker, Martin. *Kirche als Gestalt und Ereignis*. Munich: Chr. Kaiser Verlag, 1963.

Hopewell, James F. *Congregation: Stories and Structures*. London: SCM, 1988.

Horsch, John. "Menno Simons' Attitude toward the Anabaptists of Muenster." *Mennonite Quarterly Review* 10 (1936) 55–72.

———. "The Rise and Fall of the Anabaptists of Muenster (Concluded)." *Mennonite Quarterly Review* 9 (1935) 129–43.

Jüngel, Eberhard. *Das Evangelium von der Rechtfertigung des Gottlosen als Zentrum des christlichen Glaubens*. Tübingen, Germany: Mohr Siebeck, 1999.

Käsemann, Ernst. *Commentary on Romans*. Translated by Geoffrey W. Bromiley. London: SCM, 1973.

Kelly, Geffrey B., and Burton F. Nelson. *The Cost of Moral Leadership*. Grand Rapids: Eerdmans, 2003.

Kierkegaard, Sören. *Philosophische Broken*. Translated by Emanuel Hirsch et al. Gütersloh, Germany: Gütersloher, 1985.

Bibliography

Kingsbury, Jack D. "The Place, Structure and Meaning of the Sermon on the Mount within Matthew." *Interpretation* 41 (1987) 131–43.
Kittel, Gerhard, and Gerhard Friedrich, editors. *Theological Dictionary of the New Testament*. 10 vols. Translated by Geoffrey W. Bromiley. Grand Rapids: Eerdmans, 1964–76.
Klaassen, Walter, et al. *Anabaptism in Outline*. Waterloo, ON: Herald, 1981.
Klepper, Jochen. *Unter dem Schatten deiner Flügel*. Stuttgart: Deutsche Verlags-Anstalt, 1956.
Köster, Arnold. *Ist die gegenwärtige Weltkatastrophe Krise oder Untergang?* Vienna: Verlag Ruferstimmen, 1932.
———. *Lampenlicht am Dunklen Ort*. Zusammengestellt von Karl Federman. Vienna: Sensen-Verlag, 1965.
———. "Sermons and Papers." Collection of sermons and lectures between 1938 and 1947. Transcripts held in Vienna by Franz Graf-Stuhlhofer. Made available to the author by the Baptist Church Vienna-Mollardgasse 35. See appendix 3.
Lane, Anthony N. S. *Justification by Faith in Catholic-Protestant Dialogue: An Evangelical Assessment*. London: T. & T. Clark, 2002.
Leibholz-Bonhoeffer, Sabine. "Dietrich Bonhoeffer: A Glimpse into Our Childhood." *Union Seminary Quarterly Review* 20 (1965) 319–31.
Liechty, Daniel. "Andreas Fischer: A Brief Biographical Sketch." *Mennonite Quarterly Review* 58 (1984) 125–32.
Lilje, Hanns. *Das letzte Buch der Bibel*. Hamburg: Furche Verlag, 1961.
Lischer, Richard. "The Sermon on the Mount as Radical Pastoral Care." *Interpretation* 41 (1987) 157–69.
Loewenich, Walther von. *Martin Luther, Der Mann und das Werk*. Munich: List Verlag, 1982.
Longenecker, Richard N., editor. *Patterns of Discipleship*. Grand Rapids: Eerdmans, 1996.
Luther, Martin. *The Bondage of the Will*. Old Tappan, NJ: Revell Company, 1957.
———. *Career of the Reformer*. Vol. 31, bk. 1, of *Luther's Works*. Philadelphia: Fortress, 1957.
———. *Christian in Society*. Vol. 45, bk. 2, of *Luther's Works*. Philadelphia: Fortress, 1962.
———. *Commentary on Romans*. Translated by Theodore J. Mueller. Grand Rapids: Kregel, 1954.
———. *Lectures on Romans*. Saint Louis: Concordia, 1972.
Marsden, John. "Paul Tillich and the Theology of German Religious Socialism." *Political Theology* 10 (2009) 31–48.
Marty, Martin E., et al., editors. *The Place of Bonhoeffer*. London: SCM, 1963.
Matheson, Peter, et al. *The Third Reich and the Christian Churches*. Edinburgh: T. & T. Clark, 1981.
May, Georg. *Kirchenkampf oder Katholikenverfolgung*. Stein am Rhein: Christiana-Verlag, 1991.
McClendon, James W., Jr. *Biography as Theology*. Nashville: Abingdon, 1974.
———. *Doctrine*. Vol. 2 of *Systematic Theology*. Nashville: Abingdon, 1994.
———. *Ethics*. Vol. 1 of *Systematic Theology*. Nashville: Abingdon, 2002.
———. *Witness*. Vol. 3 of *Systematic Theology*. Nashville: Abingdon, 2000.

Bibliography

McGrath, Alister. E. *Iustitia Dei: A History of the Christian Doctrine of Justification*. 2nd ed. Cambridge University Press, 2002.

———. *Luther's Theology of the Cross*. Grand Rapids: Baker, 1994

———. *Reformation Thought: An Introduction*. 2nd ed. Oxford: Blackwell, 1993.

Moltmann, Jürgen. *On Human Dignity*. Edingburgh: SCM, 1984.

———. *Theologie der Hoffnung*. Munich: Kaiser, 1964.

———. *Theology of Hope*. Edingburgh: SCM, 1970.

Müller, Christine-Ruth. *Bekenntnis und Bekennen, Dietrich Bonhoeffer in Bethel (1933) Ein lutherischer Versuch*. Munich: Chr. Kaiser, 1989.

Murray, Stuart. *Biblical Interpretation in the Anabaptist Tradition*. Kitchener, ON: Pandora, 2000.

Nessan, Craig L. "Reappropriating Luther's Two Kingdoms." *Lutheran Quarterly* 19 (2005) 302–11.

Nestingen, James A. "The Two Kingdoms Distinction: An Analysis with Suggestion." *Word & World* 19 (1999) 268–75.

Nygren, Anders B. "Luther's Doctrine of the Two Kingdoms." *Ecumenical Review* 1 (1949) 301–10.

Oberman, Heiko A. *Luther: Man between God and Devil*. New Haven: Yale University Press, 1989.

Packull, Werner O. *Hutterite Beginnings: Communitarian Experiments during the Reformation*. Baltimore: Johns Hopkins University Press, 1995.

Pangritz, Andreas. "Politischer Gottesdienst: Zur theologischen Begründung des Widerstands bei Karl Barth." *Communio Viatorum* 39 (1997) 215–47.

Plant, Stephen. *Bonhoeffer*. London: Continuum, 2004.

Potter, Andy. "Swiss Anabaptism and the Sword." Originally published in *Anabaptism Today* 19 (1998). Online: http://www.anabaptistnetwork.com/node/158.

Pugh, Jeffrey C. *Religionless Christianity: Dietrich Bonhoeffer in Troubled Times*. London: T. & T. Clark, 2008.

Reimer, A. James. *The Emanuel Hirsch and Paul Tillich Debate*. Lewiston, NY: Edwin Mellen, 1989.

Rengsdorf, K. H. "Mathetes." In *Theological Dictionary of the New Testament*, edited by Gerhard Kittel and Gerhard Friedrich, translated by Geoffrey W. Bromiley, 4:415–61. Grand Rapids: Eerdmans, 1989.

Rieger, Joerg. *Christ & Empire*. Minneapolis: Augsburg Fortress, 2007.

Roon, Ger van. *Widerstand im Dritten Reich*. Munich: C. H. Beck, 1979.

Schaff, Philip, editor. *Nicene and Post-Nicene Fathers: St Augustine's City of God*. Grand Rapids: Eerdmans, 1988.

Scharf, Kurt. *Widerstehen und Versöhnen*. Stuttgart: Radius, 1988.

Schlatter, Adolf. *Romans: The Righteousness of God*. Translated by Siegfried Schatzmann. Peabody, MA: Hendrickson, 1995.

Schlingensiepen, Ferdinand. *Dietrich Bonhoeffer, 1906–1945: Martyr, Thinker, Man of Resistance*. Translated by Isabel Best. London: T. & T. Clark, 2010.

Scholder, Kaus. *A Requiem for Hitler*. London: SCM, 1989.

Snyder, Arnold C. *Anabaptist History and Theology: An Introduction*. Kitchener, ON: Pandora, 1995.

———. "The Birth and Evolution of Swiss Anabaptism, 1520–1530." *Mennonite Quarterly Review* 80 (2006) 501–645.

———. *Following in the Footsteps of Christ*. London: Darton, Longman and Todd, 2004.

Bibliography

Spener, Philipp J. *Pia Desideria*. Leipzig: 1841.
Spengler, Oswald. *The Decline of the West*. English abr. ed. London: Unwin, 1961.
Spoerri, Theophil. *Die Götter des Abendlandes*. Berlin: Furche, 1932.
Stayer, James M. *Anabaptists and the Sword*. Lawrence, KA: Coronado, 1972.
Stroup, John. "Political Theology and Secularization Theory in Germany, 1918–1929: Emanuel Hirsch as a Phenomenon of His Time." *Harvard Theological Review* 80 (1987) 321–68.
Strübind, Andrea. *Die unfreie Freikirche*. Giessen, Germany: TVG Brockhaus/Oncken, 1995.
Thielicke, Helmut. *Der Evangelische Glaube*. Band 1–3. Tübingen, Germany: Mohr, 1973.
———. *Geschichte und Existenz*. Gütersloh, Germany: Bertelsmann, 1935.
———. *Modern Faith and Thought*. Translated by Geoffrey W. Bromiley. Grand Rapids: Eerdmans, 1990.
———. *Theologische Ethik*. Band 2, teil 1. Tübingen, Germany: J.CB. Mohr, 1986.
———. *Theologische Ethik*. Band 2, teil 2. Tübingen, Germany: J.CB. Mohr, 1987.
Thompson, W. D. J. Cargill. *The Political Thought of Martin Luther*. Totowa, NJ: Barnes & Noble, 1984.
Tillich, Paul. *On the Boundary*. London: Collins, 1967.
———. *The Theology of Paul Tillich*. Edited by Charles W. Kegley and Robert W. Bretall. New York: Macmillan, 1952.
Vedder, Henry C. *A Short History of the Baptists*. London: Kingsgate, 1897.
Villa-Vicencio, Charles. "The Protestant Quest for a Political Theology: Augsburg, Barmen and Ottawa." *Journal of Theology for Southern Africa* 47 (1984) 47–58.
Vogel, Heinrich. "Und führe uns nicht in Versuchung!" *Theologische Existenz Heute*, Heft 62 (1939) 1–62.
Weber, Max. "Politik als Beruf." Vortrag, October 1919. No pages. Online: http://www.textlog.de/weber_politik_beruf.html.
Westin, Gunnar, and Torsten Bergsten. *Balthasar Hubmaier Schriften*. Gütersloh, Germany: Gütersloher, 1962.
Willmer, Haddon. "Costly Discipleship." In *The Cambridge Companion to Dietrich Bonhoeffer*, edited by John W. De Gruchy, 173–89. Cambridge: Cambridge University Press, 1999.
Wingren, Gustaf. "The Doctrine of Creation: Not an Appendix but the First Article." *Word & World* 4 (1984) 353–71.
Winter, Bruce W. *After Paul Left Corinth*. Grand Rapids: Eerdmans, 2001.
Wolkan, Rudolf. *Die Hutterer, Österreichische Wiedertäufer und Kommunisten in Amerika*. Vienna: Wiener Bibliophilen-Gesellschaft, 1918.
Wright, Nigel. G. *Disavowing Constantine: Mission, Church and the Social Order in the Theologies of John Howard Yoder and Jürgen Moltmann*. Carlisle, UK: Paternoster, 2000.
———. *Free Church, Free State*. Milton Keynes, UK: Paternoster, 2005.
———. *Power and Discipleship: Towards a Baptist Theology of the State*. Oxford: Whitley, 1996.
Wright, Nicholas Thomas. *The Climax of the Covenant*. Edinburgh: T. & T. Clark, 1991.
———. *The New Testament and the People of God*. London: SPCK, 1992.
Wright, Jonathan R.C. *"Above Parties": The Political Attitudes of the German Protestant Leadership, 1918–1933*. London: Oxford University Press, 1974.

Bibliography

Wüstenberg, Ralf K. *A Theology of Life*. Grand Rapids: Eerdmans, 1998.
Yoder, John Howard. *The Politics of Jesus*. Grand Rapids: Eerdmans 1972.
Yoder, John Howard. *The Royal Priesthood*. Edited with an introduction by Michael G. Cartwright. Grand Rapids: Eerdmans, 1994.
Zabel, J. A. *Nazism and the Pastors*. Missoula, MT: Scholars, 1976.
Zimmermann, Wolf-Dieter, and Ronald Gregor Smith, editors. *I Knew Dietrich Bonhoeffer*. Translated by Käthe Gregor Smith. London: Fontana, 1973.
Zimmermann, Sandra. *Zwischen Selbsterhaltung und Anpassung*. May 2011. Online: http://www.bruederbewegung.de/pdf/zimmermann.pdf.

www.ingramcontent.com/pod-product-compliance
Lightning Source LLC
Chambersburg PA
CBHW070237230426
43664CB00014B/2335